D0176209

I Can't Get Over It

— A Handbook for —

Trauma Survivors

SECOND EDITION

APHRODITE MATSAKIS, Ph.D.

specialist in

POST–TRAUMATIC STRESS DISORDER

New Harbinger Publications, Inc.

Publisher's Note

This publication is designed to provide accurate and authoritative information in regard to the subject matter covered. It is sold with the understanding that the publisher is not engaged in rendering psychological, financial, legal, or other professional services. If expert assistance or counseling is needed, the services of a competent professional should be sought.

Distributed in Canada by Raincoast Books

Copyright © 1996 Aphrodite Mataskis
New Harbinger Publications, Inc.
674 Shattuck Avenue
Oakland, CA 94609

Cover design by SHELBY DESIGNS AND ILLUSTRATES

Library of Congress Catalog Card Number: 96-67946

ISBN-10 1-57224-058-X
ISBN-13 978-1-57224-058-2

Printed in the United States of America

New Harbinger Publications' website address: www.newharbinger.com

10   09   08

30   29   28   27   26   25   24   23   22   21

"Suffering is the sole origin of consciousness," wrote Fyodor Dostoyevsky in *Notes from the Underground*. This book is dedicated to all who have suffered as the result of human cruelty, human error, or tragic events beyond their control.

There is more than anger, there is more than sadness, more than terror. There is hope.

—Laura Davis and Ellen Bass,
The Courage to Heal

Contents

Acknowledgments

I would like to acknowledge both Leslie Tilley, for her excellent organizational suggestions and other editorial revisions, and the staff at New Harbinger Publications, for their support during the writing of this book. I would also like to thank my daughters, Theodora and Magdalena, for their patience with me as I undertook this project.

Most of all, however, I would like to thank the trauma survivors who trusted me enough to share their stories and their struggles as they attempted to bind their wounds and reclaim their lives. The massive emotional, and often financial and physical, losses some of these individuals sustained as a result of their traumas were often unbelievable. The fact that they nevertheless desired to overcome their pasts and lead productive, loving lives filled me with respect and humility, and inspired me to write this book in hopes that it would help, to whatever extent possible, to alleviate some of the pain and help open the doors to hope and renewed faith in life.

Introduction

Red and blue lights were flashing all around me, but this time they weren't on a police car or ambulance—they were on a dance floor. I wasn't being rushed to an emergency room; I hadn't been beaten. Instead I was dancing with a kind, gentle man who I liked and who cares for me. Suddenly I realized that this was the first time I'd remembered the abuse since yesterday.

What a miracle! After so many years of hurting, I had gone through an entire day without the pain, and without doing anything to blot out the pain either. I didn't even have to try to feel good—it just happened.

I was so glad then that I hadn't killed myself all the times I thought about it. I felt so strong to have survived all that I did and still be able to enjoy myself and care about people.

I wasn't sure it could ever happen, but I guess I am finally starting to heal.

—Claire,
a domestic violence survivor

Claire had been severely beaten by her former husband for most of their marriage. After she left him, she, like many trauma survivors, used alcohol and other substances to blot out her memories of the abuse. She pretended to herself and others that the beatings had never happened. When she did admit they had happened, she dismissed them as unimportant.

Then one day something, a love scene in a movie, shattered her denial. She remembered the early days of her marriage, before the abuse began, and then she remembered the beatings, and all the pain and humiliation. She began to have difficulty sleeping and to suffer from depression, anxiety attacks, and low self-esteem.

All of these problems are symptoms of post-traumatic stress disorder or PTSD, a psychological syndrome that can develop in perfectly normal people who have undergone life-threatening or otherwise overwhelmingly stressful experiences.

Claire decided to consult a therapist to try to get some relief from her symptoms and the memories that plagued her. Her therapist made it clear from the beginning that Claire was not mentally ill—instead she had been wounded by life and needed to heal those wounds.

The therapist warned, however, that the healing process would be neither painless nor quick. Claire would need to stop running from the past, and she would have to face at least some of her memories and feelings directly. In return, if she saw the healing process through, Claire would not only regain some of her former sense of well-being and wholeness, but would gain additional strength, or empowerment, from having survived her experiences. And so she has.

PTSD—A Normal Reaction to an Abnormal Amount of Stress

If you suspect that you suffer from PTSD, do not be alarmed. PTSD is an entirely normal reaction to an abnormal amount of stress. Having PTSD does not mean you are mentally ill, nor does it mean that you are weak or somehow deficient. Think of it this way: no matter how strong your leg bones, if enough force is applied, they will break. Given the proper care, they can also heal. And so can you.

In some cases, however, a leg may be so damaged that it can never return to its former state. Your losses may be similarly enormous. But even in this most sad situation, with support, you can find ways of coping with your permanent loss and discover new talents to develop and new reasons for living.

Although we use separate words for them, the mind, emotions, and body are part of one whole. When trauma occurs, it affects the whole being—not just the mind or emotions, but the physical, biological "parts" of the human being as well. Increasing evidence indicates that many of the emotionally distressing symptoms of PTSD have a biological basis (*New York Times* 12 June 1990; van der Kolk 1988b), as further explained in Chapter 2. In short, the symptoms of PTSD are not "in someone's head" or a play for attention. Rather they are the aftereffects of an event or series of events severe enough to profoundly alter a person's thinking, feelings, and physical reactions.

These events need not have gone on for years, months, or even hours. A single life-or-death incident lasting as little as a few seconds can be enough to traumatize you. In those few moments, your emotions, identity, and sense of the world as an orderly, secure place can be severely shaken or shattered. The rupture can be so profound that, try as you might, you just "can't get over it."

Many of the emotional and cognitive (thinking) changes that trauma survivors experience are appropriate to the situation of the trauma. Often these changes hold survival value; they may even have saved lives during the traumatic episode. Afterwards, however, these survival mechanisms are no longer useful, and can be harmful—or at least prevent the survivor from leading a fulfilling life. For example, a woman who learned as a child to bury her emotions to protect herself from an abusive parent, might find in the present that being out of touch with her emotions deprives her of the comfort of friendship or the experience of falling in love.

The Healing Process

If you have been traumatized, some of your trauma-related thoughts, feelings, and ways of coping may always stay with you. Healing does not mean forgetting or minimizing your losses. But with outside help and effort on your part, you can learn to manage many of your detrimental trauma-related beliefs and behaviors. They won't melt away overnight or disappear painlessly or without a trace, but they need not continue to rule your life.

As you begin the healing process, however, it may seem like it gets worse before it gets better. When you first begin this book, you may feel relieved as you discover that you are not alone, that countless others suffer from PTSD. You may feel elated to learn that you are not crazy, that PTSD is a normal reaction to being victimized, abused, or put in a life-threatening situation with few means of escape.

But as feelings and memories you have suppressed rise to the surface, you may feel panicky or overwhelmed. Some survivors report feeling as if they are choking, drowning, or "falling apart." In their book, *Courage to Heal*, Ellen Bass and Laura Davis (1988) aptly call this initial stage of healing the emergency stage.

During the emergency stage, denial of the traumatic event lifts, and you begin to look at the reality of the event and its negative consequences. Many survivors compare this stage of healing to a natural catastrophe. For example, some sexually abused women describe the emergency stage as feeling like being caught in a tornado, avalanche, or earthquake (Bass and Davis 1988).

(If you do not feel emotions like these in reading this book, it may be that you do not need healing, or that you have already recovered from your traumatic experience. Alternatively, you may still be in a state of denial or emotional numbing as a result of the trauma.)

During the emergency stage, you will probably experience an increase, rather than a decrease, in your PTSD symptoms. This will not last forever. However, because symptoms tend to emerge or intensify during the emergency stage, it is critical that you have the support of a qualified therapist, a support group, supportive family and friends, or all three. (Appendix A offers guidelines and assistance for finding therapists and support groups.)

Not only during the emergency stage, but throughout the healing process, you will need to talk to others about the trauma and your reactions to it. Allow yourself to focus on, even to be obsessed with, the traumatic event for a while. Such focus and attention is a necessary part of healing and, like the emergency stage, will not last forever.

Taking as good care of yourself as possible throughout the healing process (and afterward) is vital. This includes proper nutrition, exercise, and rest, as well as trying to accept whatever stage of the process you are in and however you are feeling at the time. You may want to decrease some of your outside obligations and try to reduce external stresses in your life in order to focus on healing. The more time and energy you can devote to healing, the more quickly and thoroughly you will be able to heal.

In addition, if in the traumatic situation you experienced extreme temperatures; lack of adequate nutrition, water, or medical care; poor living conditions; sleep deprivation; or an injury to the head or other part of the body, you need to consult a medical doctor to have any resulting health problems treated.

Know that remembering the trauma and reexperiencing the emotions attached to it will not bring the event back to life. As painful as remembering is, it is not the same as reliving the experience in actuality. You may, however, feel threatened when thinking about the event. This is not a "crazy" reaction—it is perfectly normal given what you have experienced. (Keep in mind, though, that you may not need to relive the entire trauma, or even most of it, to make gains in the healing process.)

If you start to feel extremely afraid or anxious, you will need to take steps to calm yourself. You may also need to seek help from others. The following section describes warning signs and what to do about them.

Cautions

You need to monitor your reactions to the healing process, preferably with the help of a mental health professional. If during the emergency stage or at other times during healing process, you experience any of the following reactions, seek professional help immediately and do *not* continue to read this book without first consulting your physician or counselor.

- Hyperventilation, uncontrollable shaking, or irregular heartbeat
- Feelings that you are losing touch with reality, even temporarily, for instance, having hallucinations or extreme flashbacks of the event
- Feeling disoriented, "spaced out," unreal, or as if you might be losing control
- Extreme nausea, diarrhea, hemorrhaging, or other physical problems, including intense, new, or unexplainable pains or an increase in symptoms of a preexisting medical problem, for example blood sugar problems if you are diabetic
- Self-mutilation or the desire to self-mutilate
- Self-destructive behavior such as alcohol or drug abuse, self-induced vomiting, or overspending
- Suicidal or homicidal thoughts
- Memory problems

Also call for help if you are having so much emotional pain, anxiety, or anger that you fear you are going to die. Mild anxiety is to be expected, but extreme anxiety or despair needs professional attention as soon as possible.

If you are unable to contact a mental health professional and are truly frightened, go to the emergency room of a local hospital. Meanwhile, do the following:

- Stop reading this book (or doing whatever healing work you are engaged in) and focus on something else.
- Touch a physical object.
- Talk to someone right away.
- Avoid isolating yourself or taking alcohol, drugs, or other mood-altering substances.
- If you are angry, try expressing it in a safe way, by talking to a trusted friend, punching a pillow, or tearing up a telephone directory, for example.
- Do something pleasurable and relaxing: take a hot bath, go for a long walk, listen to favorite music, pet the cat.

Even if you feel certain you do not need professional help, if you experience any of the reactions listed above, take a break from reading this book and follow one of the suggestions.

Keep in mind that having a strong reaction to thinking about the trauma or otherwise working on healing does not make you a "failure."

Developing symptoms as a result of reading this book or being in therapy does not reflect an inability to heal or a hidden unwillingness to heal.

Instead, your reactions probably reflect the degree of traumatization you endured, which was not under your control. Your reactions have nothing to do with strength of character. If you need to stop at any time and take a breather, whether for a day or a few weeks, you can always come back later and examine the past. Remember that it is not necessary for you to remember all or even most of the past in order to function or for healing to begin.

You should also be aware, however, that there are those who have been so severely traumatized that they may be better off leaving the past unexamined. The memories of torture victims, prisoners of war, and concentration camp survivors may be better left buried. If you fall into one of these categories, or find that the reactions listed above occur so frequently and intensely that the "healing" process is making your life unlivable, you should concentrate your efforts on finding relief from your symptoms, rather than remembering and coping with the trauma itself. The following section describes this book chapter by chapter, with descriptions of where to find information on coping with the various symptoms of PTSD.

How to Use This Book

This book will not attempt to delude you into thinking that you can overcome your traumatic experiences and their negative effects by completing a few written exercises. Nor will this book at any point trivialize your pain by giving you platitudes such as "If life gives you lemons, make lemonade." There is no magic formula that will undo all your pain and losses.

What this book does attempt to do is to explain what PTSD is and what causes it. It also presents some techniques for coping with the symptoms and side effects of PTSD and trauma, and it places trauma and PTSD in a larger sociological context. The healing process is presented step by step, with journal-writing exercises to help you gradually uncover the trauma itself, subsequent events that have contributed to the development of your symptoms, and the thoughts and feelings you have that stem from your experiences.

The book is divided into four parts, each of which consists of several chapters, along with introductory text that describes the chapters that follow and offers guidelines for reading those chapters and completing the exercises.

The first part, "Understanding PTSD," encompasses the first five chapters. Chapter 1, "What Is PTSD? Do I Have It?," describes the diagnosis and symptoms of PTSD and offers a series of questionnaires to help you determine if you in fact suffer from PTSD. If you have already been diagnosed by a professional as having PTSD, read this chapter anyway to gain some general information on the syndrome, determine the severity of your PTSD, and put down in writing which symptoms most trouble you.

Chapter 2, "The Biochemistry of PTSD," deals with the problems that most commonly accompany PTSD: depression, substance abuse, and compulsive behavior. Questionnaires are included to help you determine whether you suffer from either depression or a substance abuse problem. Chapter 2 also describes the physical effects of trauma on the human body, including the central nervous system, which will help you understand many of the symptoms of PTSD.

Chapter 3, "Feelings, Thoughts, and Traumatic Events," discusses the devastating feelings of self-blame, survivor guilt, and low self-esteem that commonly accompany PTSD. Also discussed is the crucial importance of getting in touch with your feelings and the link between what you feel and what you think. Exercises are presented to assist in all of these tasks.

Chapter 4, "The Three Levels of Victimization," deals with the ways trauma can affect your view of the world and yourself. Of primary importance here is the often negative influence of the larger world on the trauma survivor's feelings and attitudes. Almost inevitably, others' blaming attitudes, insensitivity, even cruelty, greatly exacerbate the pain of the original trauma, making the survivor's recovery that much harder.

Chapter 5, "Why Am I Acting This Way?—Triggers," discusses the events that can spark PTSD symptoms, such as flashbacks or anxiety attacks. It also offers exercises for identifying these "triggers," which vary from person to person, and suggestions for heading off such episodes and for coping with them when they, inevitably, occur.

Part II, "The Healing Process," begins with Chapter 6, "Stage 1: Remembering the Trauma." Here you will work on reconstructing the traumatic event you experienced and reframing it in terms of what you have learned about trauma in general and your experience in particular.

In Chapter 7, "Stage 2: Feeling the Feelings," you will continue the work you began in Chapter 3 of acknowledging and learning to live with the emotions engendered by your experiences. Chapters 8 and 9 further build on this work to deal with the two most powerful emotions connected with trauma: anger and grief. Chapter 8, "Living with Anger," helps you identify the sources of your anger and learn to manage it so that you, not your anger, control your life. Chapter 9, "Understanding Grief and Sorrow," deals with the experience of loss, which is integral to traumatic experiences. Even if the full extent of your losses is not clear to you now, Chapter 9 will help you identify, acknowledge, and heal from those losses—without necessarily forgetting them.

Chapter 10, "Stage 3: Attaining Empowerment," concludes Part II. This chapter sums up the progress you have made in healing, and offers suggestions and strategies for continuing that growth.

Part III, "Specific Traumas," is quite different from the other two parts. Each chapter in this section deals with a different type of trauma. The topics covered are crimes committed by strangers (Chapter 11); rape and sexual assault (Chapter 12); domestic violence, including sexual abuse (Chapter 13); the suicide of a close friend or family member (Chapter 14); natural catastrophe (Chapter 15); vehicular accidents (Chapter 16); and war and combat (Chapter 17).

The purpose of these chapters is to help you put your experiences in a larger historical, social, and political perspective, not in order to downplay what you've been through, but to reveal how your reactions are normal and typical of other people who have lived through similar events.

You may read the chapter or chapters in this section that apply to you at any time—you need not wait until you have worked through all of Chapters 1 through 10. You may even want to read your chapter early on in the healing process and then read it again after you have worked through Chapter 10.

Similarly, the exercises in Chapters 11 through 17 might be useful more than once. They are tailored to the experiences and feelings of those who have survived the type of trauma covered in each chapter. These exercises may be completed before, after, or at the same time as the other exercises in the book.

Finally, at the end of the book, in Part IV are two appendixes. Appendix A, "Getting Help—Survivor Groups and Therapy Programs," offers guidelines and resources for finding and selecting therapists, treatment programs, and support groups. Appendix B, "Resources," is just what the title implies: a list of names, addresses, and phone numbers of organizations and publications that can help you get assistance, learn, and heal. The listings are arranged alphabetically by topic; a list of topics appears at the beginning of the appendix.

Questionnaires and Exercises— Keeping a Journal

Each of the chapters in this book includes either questionnaires or written exercises. The more honest and complete you are in completing this work, the more you will learn about yourself and the more you can help yourself change in the ways you want to.

Working through this book is a *process:* you will reread, reevaluate, and expand on your work as you go along. For that reason, you need to keep a journal that contains of all the writing you do in completing the exercises in this book. You may already keep a personal diary, or you may decide to begin one after you have begun to heal, but right now you need to make a separate "healing journal" for the work you do in this book.

I recommend that you buy a three-ring binder, some dividers, and some looseleaf paper. Since you will be asked, as you work through the book, to go back, reread, and add to the writing you have done for previous exercises, using a looseleaf notebook will enable you to add sheets as necessary. You will also be asked to write on a number of specific topics, including the traumatic event, your feelings toward yourself, and your triggers. The dividers will make each topic distinct and easy to find later on.

A Final Note

As you work through this book, you need to keep several things in mind. Despite recent interest in the effects of trauma on human beings, our knowledge of the full range of human reactions to overwhelming stress is limited. Just as trauma survivors sometimes choose to deny that the trauma occurred, so does society sometimes choose to deny the fact of unjustifiable human suffering. As a result, professional interest in the area of traumatology has been relatively sparse compared to research and study of other problems.

Nevertheless, ample evidence exists showing that healing is possible. Remember, however, that this book is only a beginning guide to recovery. No self-help book, regardless of its quality, is a substitute for individual counseling or other forms of in-depth help. You will probably need the assistance of caring friends, other survivors, and qualified professionals in understanding and meeting the challenges the trauma has thrust upon you. Establishing and maintaining contact with a social support system is critical. Any investment of time or money you make now in your recovery will be returned many times later on.

The pace at which you heal will be your own, determined by the natural healing powers within you. The purpose of this book is merely to stimulate and support the healing power you already possess.

The promise of healing is not that all your scars will be erased or that you will never hurt again. Rather, its promise is that the energy you now spend suppressing the past, running from it, or hiding it from yourself and others, can be yours to invest in the present—in your goals, relationships, spiritual growth, and creativity.

Finally, as you tackle the challenge of understanding the trauma and discovering your inner self, remember to congratulate yourself for having, in the words of Ellen Bass and Laura Davis (1988), the "courage to heal."

Part I

Understanding PTSD

The five chapters that follow offer an in-depth description of post- traumatic stress disorder and the problems often associated with untreated PTSD: clinical depression and addictions such as alcoholism, drug abuse, eating disorders, and compulsive gambling. Untreated PTSD, coupled with continuing life stresses or subsequent traumas, can so deplete the body's neurological and biochemical reserves that a clinical depression results. Substance abuse and compulsive behavior, though ultimately self-destructive, can be forms of self-medication for the symptoms of PTSD: the substance or activity brings a temporary relief.

How to Use These Chapters

Chapter 1, "What Is PTSD? Do I Have It?" and Chapter 2, "The Biochemistry of PTSD," are designed, respectively, to help you determine whether you suffer from PTSD and whether you have a clinical depression or engage in some addictive behavior as a result of the PTSD. Although it may be painful and difficult for you even to contemplate having any of these problems, unless you are aware of a problem, you cannot hope to correct or alleviate it.

After completing Chapter 1, you will have determined whether you have PTSD, and if so, whether you have full-blown or partial PTSD or a few PTSD symptoms. You will also have a sense of the degree to which your PTSD has impaired your ability to work and relate to others. After completing the questionnaires in Chapter 2, you will know whether you suffer from a clinical depression, one of the various addictions, or both. If you do, medical attention and specialized help will be needed.

If you discover that you suffer from one or more of the problems described in these chapters, do not disparage yourself; you are more than your problem. You, as a human being, are more than just a PTSD case, an alcoholic, or a compulsive eater. These are but parts of yourself. But left unattended these problems can consume more of your life than you want to give them. One reason for reading this book is to understand your conflicts and pain surrounding the trauma, and to prevent the symptoms you so despise from dominating your personality.

Healing from PTSD, which is the subject of Part II of this book, requires that you be aware of the nature of PTSD, clinical depression, and addiction. It also requires that you be familiar with your emotions. In Chapter 3, "Feelings, Thoughts, and Traumatic Events," you will learn what feelings are and what they are not, how feelings are different from thoughts, and how thoughts can influence feelings. You will be helped in learning to identify feelings and to distinguish one feeling from another, so that when the suppressed feelings underlying PTSD and its frequent companions, depression and addiction, begin to emerge, you will not feel as overwhelmed and confused.

Chapter 4, "The Three Levels of Victimization," takes a broader look at trauma in terms of the levels of victimization: the trauma itself, the reactions of others to the trauma, and the internalization of a "victim mentality" in the trauma survivor. The concept of "secondary wounding," the tendency of individuals and societal institutions to be nonsupportive (if not antagonistic) toward trauma survivors, is defined and explained. You will be asked to remember some of your secondary wounding experiences and record their impact on you. You will also be asked to examine how the trauma and the secondary wounding experiences that followed the traumatic event continue to influence the way you see yourself, others, and life in general.

In Chapter 5, "Why Am I Acting This Way?—Triggers," you will be shown how your trauma and secondary wounding experiences may be continuing to influence the way you react to "triggers"—those individuals, places, or life situations that are reminiscent of your traumatic experiences. Triggers can cause extreme reactions: numbing, rage, panic or anxiety reactions, addiction, nightmares, and other psychological reactions and symptoms of PTSD.

Coping with triggers is one of the most troublesome aspects of being a trauma survivor. Chapter 5 tries to help you overcome any self-disparagement that stems from having triggers. It will explain the biological and psychological "whys" of triggers, help you identify your personal triggers, and offer you a variety of methods by which you can reduce the impact of triggers on your life.

At all times, remember to read only as much at a time as you can manage without intense anxiety or discomfort. Refer back to the "Cautions" section in the introduction to this book. Should you develop one of the reactions listed in that section, stop immediately and follow the directions given there.

1

What Is PTSD?
Do I Have It?

You know you have PTSD when it's a gorgeous day outside and you feel nothing but anger and more anger, pain, and despair. You know there are tears behind the anger, but you just can't get to them. Like there's this rock in your heart weighing you down, killing you, but you can't move it.

It takes everything you've got to act civilized and not "go off" on people. So you hide a lot, pretend a lot. Even if you use drugs or alcohol or food to cool out, you still hide a lot, and you still hurt.

—Lisa, an incest survivor

Lisa is a trauma survivor, one of the many people in this country who currently suffer from a problem called post-traumatic stress disorder or PTSD. PTSD symptoms are estimated to affect, at the very minimum, some 8 to 9 percent of our population (Wolfe 1989, Greene 1994). Recent studies (Greene 1994, Figley 1995) show that PTSD develops, on average, in 25 percent of those exposed to a traumatic stressor:

- In 2 percent of those exposed to an accident of any kind
- In 25 to 33 percent of those exposed to a community disaster
- In 25 percent of those who experienced traumatic bereavement
- In 30 percent of Vietnam veterans
- In 65 percent of those experiencing nonsexual assault
- In 84 percent of battered women in shelters
- In 35 to 92 percent of those who were raped

With the escalation of crime in our country and the continued prevalence of domestic violence, war, natural disasters, and vehicular, technological, and occupational accidents, the number of people suffering from PTSD can only be expected to increase.

PTSD: A New Name for an Old Problem

Under different names, post-traumatic stress disorder has been documented by doctors, historians, and poets as far back as the days of the ancient Greeks. For example, the historian Herodotus wrote that during the battle of Marathon in 490 B.C. an Athenian soldier who had suffered no wounds became permanently blind after witnessing the death of the soldier standing next to him. In the 17th century, Samuel Pepys wrote of the panic and distress of those who survived the great fire of London in 1666: "A most horrid, malicious, blood fire . . . So great was our fear . . . it was enough to put us out of our wits." For weeks after the fire, Pepys, like many other survivors of the fire, suffered from insomnia, anger, and depression, all common symptoms of PTSD (Bentley 1991).

In the 19th century, the French neurologist Jean-Martin Charcot diagnosed women who reported having been sexually abused as children and battered wives as suffering from hysteria. Freud and his followers perpetuated this view into the 20th century. In reality, however, the symptoms of these women were those of PTSD. Earlier, during the middle ages, abused girls and women with severe PTSD symptoms were often assumed to be witches or possessed by demons, and were subsequently put away, burned at the stake, or hung (Herman 1992).

The Uniqueness of the PTSD Diagnosis

At some time in your life you have probably cut your finger with a knife. If the blade was dull, you may have suffered only a little nick. If the blade was sharp, you may have bled all over. If the blade was very sharp and the force behind it was great enough, you might even have lost part of your finger.

The extent of your injury depended more on the sharpness of the blade and the power behind it than on the toughness of your skin. Given enough force, even extremely tough skin would not protect you from the knife, and anyone else in the same situation would also be injured, even if he or she had the toughest skin in the world.

The same holds true on a psychological level. There are events in life that would make almost anyone "bleed all over." It is such events that make people susceptible to developing PTSD.

In the past, many medical and mental health professionals believed that people suffered from depression, anxiety, and certain other symptoms primarily because of internal psychological conflicts and problems, rather than in response to external events. In the case of nontraumatized persons, this belief is not necessarily false. It is, however, incomplete, in that it fails to take into account the effect of social and economic pressures, as well as other outside stresses, on the individual.

In the case of trauma survivors, trauma alone, regardless of any previous psychological problems, can lead to the development of a variety of symptoms. These symptoms are reactions to a single, overwhelming external event, or series of such events, far more than they are to any internal psychological problem.

Ample research shows that, given sufficient stress, other factors, such as an individual's previous mental stability and psychological state, are irrelevant in predicting the development of PTSD (Adler 1990). During World War II, for example, some soldiers with sterling records of mental health and family stability developed PTSD. In contrast, other soldiers who had preexisting social or psychological problems, did not develop PTSD. The critical variable in the development of PTSD was the degree of exposure to combat—the amount of stress to which the soldier had been exposed (Frye and Stockton 1982, Matsakis 1988).

Similarly, a large-scale study of crime victims found that a victim's race, sex, educational status, or income level did not predict whether he or she would develop PTSD. Neither did a history of previous psychiatric illness—for example, panic disorder, agoraphobia, or depression—predict PTSD. The determining factor was instead the stressfulness of the crime. PTSD rates were lower among individuals who had been the victim of a relatively low-stress crime, such as a burglary that occurred when no one was home.

In contrast, PTSD rates were higher among individuals who had endured high-stress crimes: those in which the individual or others were injured, a weapon was involved, or there otherwise was or appeared to be a threat to life (Chambless et al. 1990).

Over and over it has been found that the development of PTSD symptoms, and the severity of those symptoms, has more to do with the intensity and duration of the stressful event than any preexisting personality pattern.

In the *Diagnostic and Statistical Manual of Mental Disorders (DSM-IV)*, the official handbook of psychiatric problems, the listing for post-traumatic stress disorder is the only diagnosis that places the origin of the symptoms on external events rather than on the individual personality. The PTSD diagnosis is also the only one that recognizes that, subject to enough stress, any human being has the potential for developing PTSD or PTSD symptoms.

What this means to you is that, although your pretrauma personality, belief system, and values certainly affected your reaction to and interpretation of the traumatic event, you did not develop PTSD because of some inherent inferiority or weakness in your personality. Trauma changes personalities, not the other way around.

The DSM-IV *Criteria for*
Post-Traumatic Stress Disorder

According to the official definition of PTSD in *DSM-IV*, to qualify as having PTSD you must meet the following criteria:

- Criterion A: You have been exposed to a traumatic event involving actual or threatened death or injury, during which you respond with panic, horror, and feelings of helplessness.

- Criterion B: You reexperience the trauma in the form of dreams, flashbacks, intrusive memories, or unrest at being in situations that remind you of the original trauma.

- Criterion C: You show evidence of avoidance behavior—a numbing of emotions and reduced interest in others and the outside world.

- Criterion D: You experience physiological hyperarousal, as evidenced by insomnia, agitation, irritability, or outbursts of rage.

- Criterion E: The symptoms in Criteria B, C, and D persist for at least one month.

- Criterion F: The symptoms have significantly affected your social or vocational abilities or other important areas of your life.

PTSD can be either acute or delayed-onset. Acute PTSD occurs within six months after a traumatic event. In delayed-onset PTSD, the symptoms occur anytime later than six months after the traumatic event. This can be 1 year, 20 years, or even 40 years after the traumatic event. For example, previously asymptomatic 60-year-old people can develop PTSD in response to having been sexually or physically abused as children.

Criterion A: A Traumatic Event

In life, we all face crises, large and small, ranging from the loss of a wallet to the death of a loved one. Yet these events, although stressful and often called traumatic, are not considered true trauma. *Trauma*, in the technical sense of the word, refers to situations in which you are rendered powerless and great danger is involved. Trauma in this sense refers to events involving death and injury or the possibility of death and injury. These events must be unusual and out of the ordinary, not events that are part of the normal course of life. They are events that evoke a state of extreme horror, helplessness, and fear, events of such intensity and magnitude that they would overtax any human being's ability to cope.

For example, although the loss of a job or a parent may change your life forever, these events are not considered traumas because they are expected life losses. However, if instead of losing one family member, you lost several family members or friends in an accident or natural disaster, you would be considered a trauma survivor. Such simultaneous multiple losses are clearly out of the ordinary and overwhelming.

In general, the word *trauma* is reserved for natural catastrophes (hurricanes, floods, fires, earthquakes, and so on) and man-made catastrophes (war, concentration camp experiences, physical assault, sexual assault, and other forms of victimization involving a threat to life and limb).

Victims of vehicular accidents and crimes other than those listed can also develop PTSD, as can individuals injured on the job, if they sustain severe injuries. Depending on the situation, witnessing death or injury or its aftermath can also lead to PTSD, as can the loss of a child.

You are in a traumatic situation when you either know or believe that you may be injured or killed or that others about you may be. For example, if a mugger says he will shoot you, you have every reason to believe you are in danger; such a situation would definitely be classified as a trauma. If the mugger says nothing but you sense from the look on his face or certain gestures that he is capable of murder—or for any other reason you believe you may die or be seriously injured during the mugging—you are also being traumatized.

PTSD can also develop in persons who witness trauma on a daily basis or are subject to nearly constant and unabated stress as part of their job. This statement holds true even for individuals who are carefully screened for mental health problems prior to admission to their field. For example, PTSD has been found among rescue workers, firefighters, health care professionals, and police officers, as well as in nurses and doctors who served in Vietnam and other wars.

Trauma Means Wounding

Perhaps you have heard a doctor talk about head trauma, bone trauma, or trauma to some other part of the body. On a physical level, trauma has two meanings. The first is that some part or particular organ of the body has been suddenly damaged by a force so great that the body's natural protections (the skin, skull, and so on) were unable to prevent injury. The second meaning refers to injuries in which the body's natural healing abilities are inadequate to mend the wound without medical assistance.

Just as the body can be traumatized, so can the psyche. On the psychological and mental levels, trauma refers to the wounding of your emotions, your spirit, your will to live, your beliefs about yourself and the world, your dignity, and your sense of security. The assault on your psyche is so great that your normal ways of thinking and feeling and the usual ways you have handled stress in the past are now inadequate.

Being traumatized is not like being offended or rejected in a work or a love relationship. Such events can injure your emotions, your pride, and perhaps your sense of fairness, but they are not of the order of magnitude of trauma. During trauma, you touch your own death or the deaths of others. At the same time, you feel, or are, helpless to prevent death or injury.

As human beings, we must all confront the fact of our mortality. We and our loved ones will die some day, no matter who we are or what we do. Usually this awareness becomes most powerful in our middle or later years, when we see parents and their contemporaries dying or when we ourselves acquire an illness. However, if you have survived a rape, aggravated assault, flood, or war, or if you are a rescue worker or a nurse in an emergency room in an area with a high rate of violent crime, you will confront the existential reality of death sooner, and more vividly, than most.

Depersonalization and Trauma

During trauma you are subject to a process called *depersonalization*. Depersonalization refers to the stripping away of your personhood—your individuality and your humanity. The sense of being depersonalized or dehumanized is especially strong when the injuries sustained or the wounding and death witnessed seem senseless or preventable.

At the moment of attack, whether the assailant is a mugger, rapist, enemy soldier, or a hurricane, you do not feel like a valuable person with the right to safety, happiness, and health. At that moment, you feel more like a thing, a vulnerable object subject to the will of a power or force greater than yourself (Haley 1984).

When the assailant is a natural force, such as a tornado, the catastrophe can be explained away as an accident of fate (provided human error was not involved). However, when the assailant is another person, your trust in other human beings and in society in general can be severely shaken or shattered entirely.

Questionnaire for Criterion A

This questionnaire and those that follow will help you determine whether you suffer from PTSD. They are based on the official definition of PTSD in *DSM-IV*, the handbook used by all mental health professionals. As you do these questionnaires, be sure to record your responses in your journal, as described in the introduction to this book. If you skipped over the introduction, go back and read it now, paying particular attention to the "Cautions" section and the one entitled "How to Use This Book."

Using this questionnaire, describe in your journal the traumatic event or events that happened to you and your feelings during and after the event. Be as specific and detailed as you can. This process may bring up memories you would rather forget. It may also give rise to pain, anger, sadness, or remorse. However, your purpose in reading this book is to better understand what happened and how what happened has affected your life. Through this understanding, you will be able to exert greater control over your present and future life experiences.

As you read this questionnaire and those that follow, keep in mind the recommendations listed in the "Cautions" section of the introduction. If at any point you begin to hyperventilate or gag, feel faint or dizzy, or begin to experience hallucinations, flashbacks, or out-of-body experiences, stop immediately, and follow the instructions in that section.

According to *DSM-IV*, you must have experienced a traumatic event or series of events in order to qualify as having PTSD. In your life you may have experienced several frightening, sad, or unhappy events, and many major losses. However, only certain events can be categorized as traumatic. By answering the following questions in detail, you can determine whether or not you have been traumatized.

1. Have you ever been in a natural catastrophe, such as an earthquake, fire, flood, hurricane, tornado, volcano, landslide, or a dangerous dust storm or windstorm? Have you experienced a community or work-related disaster, such as an explosion or chemical spill?

2. Have you ever lived in a refugee or concentration camp or been tortured?

3. Were you ever sexually or physically assaulted, either by a stranger, a group of strangers, a family member, or anyone else?

    Sexual assault includes fondling and molestation; oral, anal, or vaginal sex; or any other forced sexual activity. Physical assault includes any form of physical contact intended to intimidate or cause pain. Being hit, slapped, thrown down stairs, beaten with fists or a weapon—stick, belt, billy club, gun—or being threatened or attacked with a weapon, are all considered forms of assault.

4. As a child, were you physically maltreated with excessive beatings or spankings? Were a parent's or caretaker's disciplinary measures sadistic?

    For example, were you ever forced to eat worms or insects, to stand nude in the cold or in front of others, or to injure a pet, sibling, or another person? Were you ever confined in a cage, a closet, or tied up? Were you deprived of adequate nutrition and medical care you needed?

5. Have you ever witnessed the death, torture, rape, or beating of another person as part of war or crime? Have you ever seen someone die or be badly injured in a car, airplane, or other such accident?

6. Has anyone in your family or a close friend been murdered or committed suicide?

7. As a child, did you ever witness the beating, rape, murder, torture, or suicide of a parent, caretaker, or friend?

8. Have you ever been in a war, either as a combatant, a medic, a prisoner of war, or a member of a support team or grave registration unit? Were you ever, in any way, exposed to combat, enemy or friendly fire, or atrocities?

9. Have you ever been kidnapped, abducted, raped, burglarized, robbed, or mugged?

10. Were you ever injured in a burglary, robbery, mugging, or other criminal episode, or in a car, boat, bicycle, airplane, or other vehicular accident?

11. Have you ever been involved in a situation in which you felt that you or a member of your family would be harmed or killed? Even if your life or the lives of your family members were not directly threatened, did you distinctly fear that you or they were in serious danger?

    It does not matter if, in retrospect, you realize your fears were unfounded. Neither does it matter if, later on, you decided you were "overreacting" or "foolish" for your fears. The critical issue is whether at the time of the trauma, you perceived the situation as life threatening to yourself or others.

12. Were you ever a member of a medical team, a firefighting team, a police force, a rescue squad, or a rescue operation that involved at least one of the following conditions?

    • Danger to your safety and life

    • Witnessing death and injury

    • Making life-and-death decisions

    • High-stress working conditions—long hours, unsafe conditions

If the answer to any one of these questions is yes, then you have experienced a traumatic event. However, to meet the first *DSM-IV* criterion for PTSD, you must also have responded to the traumatic event with either fear, helplessness, or horror.

Even if you meet Criterion A, you do no necessarily have PTSD, but it does place you at risk for suffering from or developing either partial or full-blown PTSD or some PTSD symptoms. To have PTSD, you also must meet five other criteria: You must reexperience the trauma, show evidence of numbing or other avoidance behavior, exhibit signs of hyperarousal, have all of these symptoms for at least one month, and have experienced difficulties at work, or home, or in other important areas of your life as a result of these symptoms.

Criterion B: Reexperiencing the Trauma

The fundamental dynamic underlying PTSD is a cycle of reexperiencing the trauma, followed by avoidance or repression of the traumatic memories and a numbing of emotions. This cycle of intrusive recall, followed by avoidance and numbing, has a strong biological component, which you will read about in Chapter 2.

During the recall stage of the PTSD cycle, your memories and the emotions associated with them will emerge, in conscious or unconscious awareness, over and over again in a variety of forms. You may have intrusive thoughts or images, dreams and nightmares, even flashbacks about the event. You may suddenly find yourself thinking or feeling as if you were back in the original trauma situation, or you may experience physical pain or medical problems for no apparent reason. All these phenomena are part of the process of reexperiencing the trauma.

According to Freud, reexperiencing the trauma, including repeating it in present-day life, are ways of dissipating the intense psychic energy generated by the trauma and of trying to gain mastery over it. It is as if you were watching a movie that ended sadly. You replay the movie, hoping that perhaps this time the ending will be a happy one. It isn't, of course, but you keep watching the movie again and again anyway. The unresolved trauma can absorb so much psychic energy in some trauma survivors that they have less psychic energy to devote to work, friends, and family, and most importantly to themselves, in the present.

Dreams, Nightmares, and Insomnia

You may have dreams or nightmares about the traumatic event. During these dreams you may shake, shout, and thrash about. You may or may not remember the dream upon awakening. However, the feelings of terror and fear you experience in the dream may persist for quite some time.

Some dreams or nightmares may be almost exact replays of the traumatic event, or they may be very similar. Other dreams, however, may simply incorporate the feelings you had during the trauma—helplessness, fear, anger, and grief.

Partially as a result of these dreams, falling asleep and staying asleep may be major problems for you. Or it may be that at night, without the distraction of the activities of the day, thoughts of the traumatic event begin to surface. You might start thinking about the event itself or about other events involving losses and threats to safety, or you might experience vague anxiety, nameless fears, or a generalized irritability. Alternatively, sleep problems may indicate that you are suffering from a biochemical depression, as well as PTSD. Chapter 2 will help you determine this. Alcohol and drug use can also affect sleep patterns. Insomnia is also associated with hyperarousal—another symptom of PTSD (see Criterion D, below).

Flashbacks

A flashback is a sudden, vivid recollection of the traumatic event accompanied by a strong emotion. During a flashback you do not black out or lose consciousness, but you do, temporarily, leave the present and find yourself back in the original traumatic situation. You may see the scene of the trauma, smell it, and hear its sounds. You may or may not lose your awareness of present reality. You may find yourself acting as if you were actually in the original traumatic situation, or you may not. You may alternate between the current reality and experiencing the past. A flashback can last anywhere from a few seconds to several hours.

In an auditory flashback, you hear sounds associated with the trauma. Such sounds include human voices, such as screaming or sobbing, or other sounds, such as banging or explosions. Auditory flashbacks differ from the voices associated with schizophrenia and other psychoses in that the sounds are almost direct replicas of those heard during the traumatic event.

For example, when Mr. Gregg walks by ditches, sometimes he hears the screams and sobs of the soldiers he saw die in ditches during World War II. These are considered auditory flashbacks. Sometimes flashbacks include only one of the senses, sometimes more. For example, some flashbacks are only visual; others are visual and auditory.

You don't have to be a combat veteran to have flashbacks. Flashbacks have been documented among survivors of Nazi concentration camps, crime victims, victims of occupational and technological disasters, and rape and incest survivors (*DSM-IV*, Carmen 1989, Bard and Sangrey 1986, Herman 1989, T. Williams 1987a). Flashbacks tend to occur among persons who have had to endure situations where there was an "intense, chronic, or pervasive loss of security" and lack of safety (Blank 1985).

You may be reluctant to acknowledge or tell anyone that you are having a flashback for fear of sounding "crazy." Flashbacks are not a sign that you are losing your mind, but rather that some traumatic material is breaking forth into your consciousness. The more you deal with the trauma on a conscious level—by talking about it, writing about it, or otherwise getting it out into the open—the less need there will be for it to appear in flashbacks or nightmares.

Other Forms of Reexperiencing the Trauma

Somatic flashbacks are an additional form of reexperiencing the trauma. During somatic flashbacks, a physical pain or medical condition emerges as a means of expressing the feelings and bodily states associated with trauma.

For example, Lewis usually develops a short-lived medical condition around the anniversary of a deadly attack on his squad. Georgia lost her parents in a murder-suicide in the month of June. The first June after their deaths, she broke out in hives. The second June, she developed a urinary tract infection. The third June, she contracted bronchitis; the fourth June, severe headaches.

The hives, infections, and headaches were real and needed medical care. And while it could be argued that Georgia might have developed these conditions even if she had not been traumatized, the fact that she never had these conditions before and that they manifested themselves only in June suggests that they are trauma related.

Another form of reexperiencing the trauma, which may be a kind of unconscious flashback, consists of suddenly feeling painful or angry feelings that do not seem clearly related to any particular memory of the traumatic event. For example, you may experience irritability, panic attacks, rage reactions, or intense psychic pain, without any conscious thought of the traumatic event.

"I can understand why I sulk or explode when I hear about another cop being killed in the line of duty. But many times I get moody or angry for no reason at all," explains a police officer. What this man, and his family, may not fully appreciate is that often there is a reason for the emotional upset, even though that reason may not be obvious. The reason may lie in the intensity of his repressed feelings about the deaths or injuries of other police officers, or in the very real possibility that someday he will be injured or killed on the job.

Questionnaire for Criterion B

According to the official definition of PTSD in *DSM-IV* you must be able to answer yes to at least one of the following questions. In your journal, write about the ways you reexperience the trauma. Again, try to be as specific as possible; include information on frequency, duration, and so on. Also note the date you first began to reexperience the trauma (as closely as possible).

1. Do you, on a persistent or recurring basis, find yourself having intrusive or involuntary thoughts of the traumatic event? Do you find yourself thinking about the trauma when you don't mean to or when you are trying hard *not* to think about it? Do visions or pictures of the trauma pop into your mind?

2. Do you have dreams or nightmares about the event?

3. Do you have dreams or nightmares that are not replays of the actual event, but that take place in the location where the event occurred, contain some of the actions involved in the event, or include some of the feelings you felt during the event?

    For instance, if you were raped in a parking lot, you may dream about the parking lot without any vision of the rape. Or you may dream about being attacked in some other way or about drowning, suffocating, falling into a well, or watching your house catch on fire. These are not rape dreams, but they capture the feelings of helplessness, fear, anger, and anxiety you most likely experienced during the rape. PTSD-related dreams also include those about a life-threatening event happening to a member of your family or someone you love.

4. Do you find yourself suddenly acting or feeling as if you were back in the original trauma situation? For example, do you have flashbacks, see visions, or hear sounds of the event? Do you have waves of strong feelings about the trauma or otherwise feel as if you have just lived through the trauma again, even without having a flashback or a vision?

5. Do you have physical reactions when exposed to events that are similar to or symbolize the traumatic event?

   Such physical reactions include hyperventilation, sweating, vomiting, dizziness, muscle or stomach cramping, shaking, or physical pain not related to any medical condition. For example, someone raped in a green car might feel faint when she sees a green car. A medical staff person who served in a combat zone might start sweating when he sees pictures of wounded soldiers or articles on treating war casualties. If the traumatic event occurred in May, you might start having stomach cramps around that time of year.

6. Do you become extremely upset (angry, teary, confused, frightened, anxious, or panicky) at people, places, or events that resemble an aspect of the original trauma?

7. Do you become distressed around the anniversary date of the trauma?

How many of the above questions were you able to write about? If you had an affirmative response to at least one of these questions, then you have met the reexperiencing criterion for PTSD.

Even if you answered no to all these questions, continue on with the questionnaires in this chapter. Quite possibly you do not suffer from full-blown PTSD, but from partial PTSD, and even partial PTSD requires healing.

Criterion C: Numbing and Avoidance

Reexperiencing the trauma can be cyclical or it can be sporadic. You may be symptom free for many weeks or months, but then begin to suffer as anniversaries of events associated with the trauma approach. A personal loss or other current-life stress or change—even positive changes such as the birth of a baby or a wedding—can call up memories or flashbacks. In addition, sometimes "triggers" in the environment—people, places, and things that remind you of the trauma—can set off a memory.

Whenever or however you reexperience the trauma, it is usually pure agony. As a result, both emotionally and physically you alternate between being "hyper" (discussed later) and being "numb" or "shut down."

Emotional Shutdown or Psychic Numbing

What happens when you shut down is similar to something that happens when the human body is injured. Have you ever cut yourself and not felt the pain immediately, or been whiplashed in a car accident but not felt the soreness until several days later? The body often emits a natural anesthetic that permits us some time to take care of our wounds and do whatever is necessary to protect ourselves from further injury.

For example, due to this natural anesthetic, severely wounded soldiers have walked miles to safety. Similarly, abused women and battered children sometimes report experiencing minimal pain from their injuries during or immediately after being attacked.

In a similar way the psyche, in self-protection, can numb itself against onslaughts of unbearable emotional pain. During whatever traumatic event you endured, it was probably essential for you to put aside your feelings. Feeling those emotions at the time could have been life threatening.

For example, if a rape victim began to connect with her feelings while being assaulted, she would be less able to assess the dangerousness of her assailant or figure out how to escape or otherwise minimize the threat of injury. Similarly, in the midst of a hurricane or tornado, you would most likely be preoccupied with how to stay safe, not with your emotional reactions.

This deadening, or shutting off, of emotions is called *psychic* or *emotional numbing*. It is a central feature of PTSD and has been found among survivors of all forms of assault, survivors of natural catastrophes, survivors of the bombing of Hiroshima and the Nazi holocaust, and other war-related situations. Many researchers believe that, like the body's natural anesthetic, emotional numbing may be partially biological (van der Kolk 1990).

Avoidance and Triggers

During the times you reexperience the trauma, you may experience some of the feelings associated with the trauma that you did not feel, or felt only partially, due to the psychic numbing that attends trauma. These feelings of fear, anger, sadness, and guilt may shake you to the core. In response to the power of these feelings, you may shut down, just as you did during the traumatic event. Shutting down serves as a means of reducing the intensity of these feelings, so that the mood swings and variations in your energy levels don't make you feel "crazy" or out of control.

Otherwise, if you don't understand what is going on inside you, you might start berating yourself and want to lash out at others—or simply hide.

Having flashbacks, being hyper, and shutting down are not only personally painful but are states that can be easily misunderstood and misinterpreted by others. Hence you may find yourself, to avoid the pain, avoiding situations that you have found bring forth (or that you fear might bring forth) either hyper or numbing symptoms. As a result, you, like so many other trauma survivors, may find yourself retreating—mentally, socially, and physically.

For example, just as rape survivors may stay inside their homes at night, hurricane survivors may stay inside when only a minor thunderstorm is predicted. Flood survivors may avoid water-related activities, and car- or airplane-accident survivors may drastically limit their travel. Medics, nurses, and doctors who have worked in high-stress environments may seek work in nonmedical fields. Similarly, people who have suffered massive injuries on the job may change their line of work.

Crime victims may avoid the site of the crime or places that remind them of the crime; if the crime occurred in a restaurant, they may have great difficulty dining out for quite some time. War veterans may avoid the sound of popcorn popping because it reminds them of airplanes or helicopters. Or they might avoid plastic trash bags or fires because they are reminded of body bags or burning villages.

Every trauma survivor has his or her own set of triggers that can touch off memories of the trauma. Avoiding trigger situations makes utter sense—you are trying to prevent a resurgence of your PTSD symptoms. However, the avoidance can generate yet another set of problems, again particularly in relationships. For that reason, exercises to help you understand and manage your trigger situations and avoidance behaviors are given in Chapter 5.

Questionnaire for Criterion C

The following questions concern psychic numbing and avoidance behavior. Answer yes to the following questions only if the symptoms described presented themselves *after* the traumatic event. If any of the numbing or avoidance behaviors listed below were present prior to the traumatic event, they are not a symptom of PTSD. Describe your yes answers in detail in your journal, and note the date the symptoms began, as accurately as possible.

1. Since the traumatic event, have you ever had periods of time when you felt emotionally numb or dead inside? Have you ever had periods when you have had great difficulty feeling tender, loving feelings, or any feelings at all, except perhaps for anger, resentment, and hatred?

2. Have you tried not to talk about the event or avoided thoughts or feelings associated with it?

3. Since the traumatic event, have you felt alienated and apart from others?

4. Have you had a sense of doom or foreboding since the event? Do you feel that you will die young or never experience the rewards of living? For example, do you feel you will never have a family, a career, the love of others, financial security?

5. Have you lost interest in activities that used to involve you or give you pleasure? These might include sports, hobbies, and other recreational activities, participation in a group, activities involving socializing with others, and eating, dancing, sex, and other sensual activities.

6. Are you unable to remember certain aspects of the trauma? For example, do you have difficult remembering when it began or how long it lasted? Are there certain details or entire episodes you can't recall? Are there hours, days, weeks, months or years you can't remember at all? Do you have difficulty remembering the names, faces, or fates of any of the other people involved in the trauma?

To how many of the above questions did you answer yes? If you have answered yes to at least three of the above questions, then you have met Criterion C for PTSD. Remember, only those avoidance or numbing symptoms that appeared *after* the traumatic event count. If you had one of these symptoms prior to the traumatic event, do not include it as a yes response.

Even if you answered yes to less than three of the above questions, continue reading this chapter and completing the following questionnaires. It may well be that even if you don't suffer from full-blown PTSD, you have partial PTSD or troublesome PTSD symptoms that need attention.

Criterion D: Hyperarousal Symptoms

The fourth PTSD criterion concerns symptoms of increased physical alertness or, in psychological terms, hyperalertness or hyperarousal.

Fight-or-Flight and Freeze Reactions

Trauma involves life-threatening situations. The possibility that you might die or be injured gives rise to feelings of terror and anxiety. Or, if you are not threatened yourself, you may feel horror and grief at seeing others die or be injured. You may also be angry at the circumstances that are causing the devastation. All of these trauma-generated emotions— the fear, anxiety, and anger—are emotions that have a strong physiological component. They cause your body to react and change your body chemistry.

In a dangerous situation, your adrenal glands may begin to pump either adrenaline or noradrenalin into your system. Adrenaline places your body into a state of biological hyperalertness. Your heart rate, blood pressure, muscle tension, and blood-sugar level increase. Your pupils dilate. The blood flow to your arms and legs decreases, while the flow to your head and trunk increases so that you can think and move better and more quickly. This is called the fight-or-flight reaction.

Alternatively, if your adrenals pump noradrenaline into your system, you may have a freeze reaction, during which moving or acting is difficult, if not impossible. Some PTSD sufferers have described their freeze reaction as "moving or thinking in slow motion." Others find themselves temporarily unable to move at all. However, even if you freeze, you will most likely be experiencing some of the other symptoms of hyperarousal.

If you experience hyperarousal symptoms, you are experiencing an adrenaline surge like that you may have experienced during the trauma.

Questionnaire for Criterion D

According to *DSM-IV*, PTSD sufferers must have at least two of the following symptoms of increased arousal:

- Difficulty falling or staying asleep
- Irritability or outbursts of anger
- Difficulty concentrating
- Hypervigilance or overprotectiveness toward oneself and others
- Exaggerated startle response (jumping or otherwise overreacting to noises or the sudden appearance of a person)

Answer yes to the following questions only if you experience the symptoms relatively frequently and you came to experience these symptoms persistently *after*, not before, the traumatic event. Record and describe any yes answers in your journal along with the date you first experienced the symptom.

1. Do you have difficulty falling or staying asleep? Is your sleep fitful and disturbed in any other ways?

   Insomnia may be a particular problem for you if you were traumatized or abused while in bed, reclining, or asleep. Due to your experience, an association has been made in your mind between being asleep or lying down and being in danger. Therefore, you may feel you have to be on alert at bedtime. Insomnia tends to be a special problem for war veterans, incest survivors, crime victims, and anyone else who has been physically or sexually attacked while sleeping.

2. Do you suffer from periods of irritability that are not directly associated with any present stress or problem in your life? Do you feel tense much of the time? Does your high tension level ever lead to outbursts of anger, such as smashing plates, punching holes in the wall, throwing objects around the house, yelling at other drivers, shouting at family members, friends, or co-workers? Do you frequently have to restrain yourself from lashing out at others?

3. Do you have difficulty concentrating? Can you concentrate enough to read an entire magazine article or book, or can you read only a few paragraphs or pages at a time? Are you easily distracted when trying to complete a job or listen to someone talk?

4. Are you overprotective, or in psychological terms, hypervigilant? Are you extremely concerned with your safety and the safety of your loved ones?

   For example, when you enter a room, do you stand by the door or some other exit for a while to scan the room for potential danger? Do you examine people to see if they might be carrying a weapon or could be dangerous in some other way? Do you identify places where it would be safe to hide in case of trouble? Whether with others or alone in your home, do you situate yourself so that you can keep surveillance over your environment or make a quick escape in case of danger? Do you carry or sleep with a weapon?

   Do you try to restrict the comings and goings of people you care about for fear they will be injured? Do you have an "anxiety attack" if a family member is late coming home? Do you insist that family members and friends call you when they arrive at their destination or if they plan to be even five or ten minutes late?

   Do crowds make you anxious? Do you avoid shopping malls, parades, movie theaters, concerts, circuses, or large parties? Do you avoid situations where it is difficult to control your level of safety? Do you drive in an excessively cautious manner, even by the most conservative standards? Do you double- or triple-check seatbelts before setting out?

5. Are you easily startled? Do you jump at loud or sudden noises or at noises that resemble some aspect of the trauma?

   For example, if you are a combat veteran, do you dive to the floor if you hear an airplane overhead? Do you jump if someone touches you from behind or wakes you from your sleep? If you were a victim of a crime committed by an intruder in your home, do you startle when someone unexpectedly comes into the room?

To how many questions did you answer yes? If you have answered yes to at least two of the above questions, and the symptom did not exist before the trauma, then you have met the hyperarousal criteria for full-blown PTSD. Whether or not you have met the hyperarousal requirement, continue on to the next sections to determine the severity of your PTSD symptoms. Once this has been done, you can begin to work on managing these symptoms using the methods presented in later chapters of this book.

Criterion E: Duration

After undergoing any experience that is dangerous, frightening, or distressing, it is normal to experience shock, fear, confusion, helplessness, anxiety, and depression. PTSD, however, is something more. PTSD includes these reactions, but on a deeper, more complex, and more enduring level, as indicated by the *DSM-IV* criteria you have read about above.

According to *DSM-IV*, PTSD symptoms must persist for at least 30 days in order to be considered PTSD. This is, of course, just a rule of thumb. There isn't much difference between 30 days and 31 or 32 days. However, if the symptoms persist much longer than five or six weeks, you should seek help. The sooner you seek help, the quicker you can enter the recovery stage.

Refer back to the answers you wrote in your journal in response to the questionnaires, and note when the symptoms began.

Criterion F: Degree of Impairment

PTSD cases are not all the same. PTSD takes different forms in different people, depending on their personality, their spiritual or religious beliefs, their culture, the amount and quality of their social support system, and the meaning they and their family and community ascribe to trauma.

Criterion F addresses the degree that your PTSD symptoms affect your life. You can have PTSD without it taking over your entire life. The crucial question in assessing the severity of your PTSD is, How much does it affect my ability to work, love, and play?

The answer to this question is highly subjective. No specific guidelines to what constitutes "impairment" exist, except in the most extreme cases. Obviously, if you can no longer work because you cannot tolerate crowds or commuting, because you cannot concentrate on the task at hand due to intrusive thoughts, or because you do not have the energy to complete your duties due to depression or insomnia, then your vocational abilities have been significantly affected.

Similarly, if you are unable to maintain friendships, family relationships, or intimate involvements due to your distrust, negative mood states, cynical or critical attitudes, or other aftereffects of the trauma, your personal life has suffered a great deal due to the trauma.

Man-Made vs. Natural Catastrophes

Two other important considerations in assessing the degree to which you suffer from PTSD are whether you are a survivor of a natural or a man-made disaster and whether you are a single-trauma or a multiple-trauma survivor.

According to *DSM-IV*, survivors of man-made catastrophes suffer from longer and more intense PTSD than survivors of natural catastrophes. Because, it is argued, natural catastrophes can be explained away as acts of God or bad luck, natural-catastrophe survivors are less likely to lose their trust in other human beings and in society than are survivors of man-made catastrophes.

However, in many cases the suffering caused by natural disasters involves one or more significant human errors or betrayals, either by individuals or institutions. For example, in the case of the 1972 Buffalo Creek Flood in West Virginia, survivors did not blame excess rain or the hand of God for causing the dam to break. Instead, many held the Pittston Coal Company's failure to build an adequate slag pile responsible (Jacob 1985, Green et al. 1990).

Similarly, survivors of the massive fire at the 1977 Beverly Hills Supper Club outside of Cincinnati, Ohio, did not blame fate, but faulty wiring, for the disaster. Or, in the case of the tornadoes that hit northeastern South Carolina in 1984, Andover, Kansas, in 1991, and other recent tornadoes, the tornado-warning system failed (Jacob 1985, Madakasira and O'Brien 1987, *Washington Post*, 30 April 1991).

Natural-catastrophe survivors may also feel betrayed or let down by rescue operations and other services. For example, they may have to face long lines, delays, and considerable red tape before they receive promised compensations for their losses. And in many cases, when the compensation appears, it is not adequate to cover the losses suffered. In sum, from the survivor's point of view, there are few purely natural disasters. Consequently, natural-trauma survivors may have more in common with survivors of man-made catastrophes than is often thought.

However, survivors of natural disasters do in fact differ from other survivors, especially abuse survivors, in that they tend to be less stigmatized. Natural-catastrophe survivors are in general spared the "blame-the-victim" attitudes that frequently afflict survivors of man-made catastrophes.

For example, in many cases victims of rape, incest, and other types of abuse are blamed for either provoking the abuse or for accepting it, as if it had been their choice. Furthermore, survivors of man-made catastrophes are much more likely to be seen by others as lacking in strength, caution, intelligence, or moral integrity. The message they are given is, What happened to you is your own fault. If you had been more careful, less stupid, more righteous, it wouldn't have happened to you.

These and other nonsupportive messages are part of a process called secondary wounding, which you will read about in Chapter 4.

Single-Trauma vs. Multiple-Trauma Survivors

The extent of your PTSD will also be influenced by whether you have been exposed to one or more than one traumatic incident. Rape is traumatic; however, incest, which typically involves multiple rapes or molestations over an extended period, is more traumatic. Similarly, seeing people die in a car accident, although traumatic, is generally not as traumatic as being in combat or being a policeman in a deteriorating neighborhood and seeing death and violence day in and day out.

Several prominent researchers and therapists who have worked with trauma survivors have noticed differences between individuals subject to one-time assaults to their psyche and life and those subject to repeated threats. For example, Lenore Terr (1991), who has extensively studied PTSD in traumatized children, suggests that individuals who have endured a one-time or "Type 1" trauma suffer from different effects than those who undergo repeated or "Type 2" traumas. People who have experienced Type 2 traumas are more likely to exhibit dissociation and other forms of self-hypnosis as well as extreme mood swings. Psychologist Judith Herman (1992), who has studied abused children and incest survivors, suggests that the syndromes resulting from such abuse and other forms of severe, repeated trauma be called "complex post-traumatic stress disorder."

One of the differences between Type 1 and Type 2 survivors can be recovery time. For example, one-time rape survivors who get good help soon after the rape can recover in six months to a year. In contrast, incest survivors, depending on their age and the severity of their molestation, may require anywhere from two to three years or longer to heal.

Questionnaire for Criterion F

To determine the degree to which your PTSD has affected your life, answer the following questions in terms of your overall functioning over the last year. Although your symptoms may be more severe and troublesome around anniversaries of the trauma or during periods of external stress, answer the questions in terms of your behavior and mood for the year as a whole.

Part I: First, review the number of PTSD symptoms you recorded in your journal for each of the criteria. Make a note of your answers to the following questions:

1. Criterion A: How many traumas have you experienced?

2. Criterion B: Only one form of reexperiencing is necessary to meet the criteria for PTSD. In how many ways do you reexperience the trauma? How much is that in excess of the required number?

3. Criterion C: Two forms of numbing or avoidance behavior are necessary to meet the *DSM-IV* criteria. How many of the questions in the Criterion C questionnaire did you answer yes to? How much is that in excess of the required number?

4. Criterion D: Three hyperarousal symptoms are necessary to constitute PTSD. From how many hyperarousal symptoms do you suffer? How much is that in excess of the required number?

5. How long have you been experiencing PTSD symptoms?

6. Criterion F: In what ways have your PTSD symptoms or other reactions to the trauma affected your ability to work, relate to people, or to live your life?

Part II: Which of the following paragraphs (adapted from *DSM-IV*) best describes you now? Keep in mind the number of symptoms you have in excess of the *DSM-IV* criteria for PTSD.

1. I have few (if any) PTSD symptoms in excess of those required to meet the *DSM-IV* criteria for PTSD. My symptoms have not seriously interfered with my ability to work or study, to socialize, or to maintain healthy family and other relationships.

     Sometimes I become anxious before an exam or an evaluation at work. If I am under a great deal of stress, I may fall behind at work or school and have some trouble sleeping or concentrating. However, in general I am satisfied with life and am able to manage most situations. I have at least a few gratifying personal relationships.

2. I have just a few PTSD symptoms in excess of those required to meet the *DSM-IV* criteria for PTSD. My symptoms only moderately interfere with my social, occupational, and personal adjustments. Sometimes I have panic or anxiety attacks or periods of depression, but I get over them. I don't have a lot of friends and I wish I didn't clash so often with my co-workers and family members. However, I have been able to hold a job, stay in school, and maintain a few important relationships.

3. I have many symptoms in excess of those required to be diagnosed as having PTSD. My symptoms have severely affected either my work, my personal life, or both. I find it hard to work or concentrate and to get along with most others. I feel the traumatic event dominates my present life.

4. I am so depressed that I avoid other people, stay inside a lot, and am troubled by thoughts of suicide or homicide. Sometimes I cannot keep myself clean or take care of myself by making necessary medical or other appointments. At times I am a danger to others, as well as myself, and I have trouble in almost every area of life.

5. Prior to the traumatic event, I suffered from a mental or emotional disorder. The trauma only increased the severity of my previous problem.

6. Prior to the traumatic event, I suffered from a mental or emotional disorder that was under control and not severely affecting my life. However, the traumatic event lead to a reemergence of my previous psychological problem.

7. The traumatic event has led to the development of new mental and emotional disorders.

8. At times I hallucinate or am delusional. I have trouble thinking clearly or rationally. I make poor financial and personal decisions and feel cut off from almost everyone.

If statement 1 describes you best, you are probably suffering from a mild case of PTSD. If statement 2 describes you best, your PTSD is probably in the moderate range. However, if any of statements 3 through 8 best describe your current level of functioning, you have a severe case of PTSD.

Full-Blown vs. Partial PTSD

If you met all the above criteria, you are suffering from PTSD. If you did not meet all the above criteria, but you did meet some of them, you may have partial PTSD rather than full-blown PTSD. In general, to meet the *DSM-IV* criteria for partial PTSD, you must have met the following conditions (refer back to your journal):

- Criterion A—you have endured a trauma.

- You have experienced five or fewer of the symptoms from Criteria B, C, and D—the reexperiencing, avoidance, and hyperarousal criteria.

- Criterion E—you have experienced symptoms for at least a month.

- Criterion F—your symptoms have significantly decreased your ability to work, relate to others, or otherwise function.

If you meet all four of these conditions, then you suffer from partial PTSD and would benefit from healing.

Other Reactions to Trauma

PTSD is not the only reaction to trauma. Many people with PTSD also suffer from clinical depression, dissociation, or somatization, and some experience these disorders but not PTSD. In her book *Trauma and Recovery* (1992), Dr. Judith Herman points out that many trauma survivors do not develop the full range of PTSD symptoms. Rather, their lives become burdened with other, equally disruptive disorders.

Dr. Herman's point, and it is significant, is that there are cases where an individual's major response to a trauma is clinical depression, dissociation, or somatization—and not the DSM-IV range of PTSD symptoms. These three reactions are equally valid and understandable reactions to trauma as PTSD, and in many cases their symptoms overlap with those of PTSD.

Clinical depression is discussed in Chapter 2. Dissociation and somatization are complex phenomena whose description could encompass entire books. In addition, in recent years, both have become catch-all words, referring to various psychological phenomena.

Dissociation

For the purposes of this book, however, the word *dissociation* refers to the various ways people disconnect from traumatic experiences emotionally, mentally, or both. Dissociation is not an act of volition; people do not decide or plan to dissociate. Dissociation happens involuntarily. In many traumatic situations, "tuning out" or "spacing out," which are colloquial names for dissociation, may be the only means of escape or psychic survival.

Dr. Bessel van der Kolk (1995) identifies four kinds of dissociation, all involving some degree of emotional numbing or emotional or mental distancing from the traumatic event, including partial and total amnesia.

In the first kind of dissociation, the senses and the emotions disconnect. You may see something, but you don't react as might be expected or you don't react at all. For example, children of battered women may dissociate while their mother is being beaten. The beating is occurring within their view, but they watch television or eat dinner as if nothing extraordinary were going on. In one documented case, a seven-year-old stared at his mother blankly and asked her to bring him ketchup for his hamburger, even though his father was stabbing her in the arm.

An example of an unexpected reaction is that of Roberta, a nurse who worked in a refugee camp attending to victims of torture and mutilation. She was not sadistic by nature, yet she poked fun at the refugees, laughed at the corpses, and took pictures of the dead and wounded for her scrapbook. Similar inappropriate reactions to the dead and dying have been found among combat veterans, concentration camp survivors, and civilian survivors of war.

The second kind of dissociation is called depersonalization or derealization. Here you don't feel like a person but like a robot or thing. All the others involved in the traumatic event also seem unreal. You may be physically injured, yet you feel very little physical pain because you feel more like an object than a human being. If others around you are in emotional or physical pain, you don' react because, to you, the entire situation is not real. It is not uncommon for survivors to bite, hit, or try to injure themselves physically so they can feel "real" or "alive."

The third kind of dissociation ranges from a floating, distant feeling of detachment from events and the emotions associated with those events to total or partial amnesia surrounding those events and the associated emotions. For example, you might have no feeling during the traumatic event. Or you may see, hear, smell, or comprehend what is happening around you, but only in part. You are not in an imaginary netherworld, but your emotions and senses are distant from the events surrounding you. This kind of dissociation frequently leads to amnesia. Later on, you may not recall the trauma or may be confused or vague about the specifics of the event. Later on, you may also have no recollection of having emotions during the event.

A prime example of this form of dissociation is the statement frequently made by child abuse survivors that they remember nothing or very little about the abuse they experienced. Similarly, combat veterans often report an inability to remember what they did for periods of days, months, or even a year. They might have vague memories of a battle but not be able to remember the names of the men they fought with or how many died next to them.

In the fourth kind of dissociation, memory is compartmentalized in distinct states. The extreme form of this is multiple personality disorder, where memories of different parts of abuse are stored in different personalities within the person.

Somatization

Somatization refers to situations where physical pain or physical problems are forms of rexperiencing the trauma. As Dr. Herman (1992) stresses, somatization most often occurs in situations where expressing feelings is dangerous. For example, Judy, age 25, ceased to menstruate after her husband began physically abusing her, although he never struck her below the waist. Since Judy's physicians found her in excellent physical condition, her psychiatrist surmised that Judy's loss of menses was due to severe anxiety and repressed anger, feelings Judy could not talk about at home without risking a beating.

Carlton, age five, lived with his mother, but according to the custody arrangement, spent alternate weekends with his father. Carlton suffered from severe leg cramps every time he was scheduled to visit his father. His father was physically abusing him during visits, but Carlton was afraid to tell his mother or teacher because his father had threatened to harm them if he told. Carlton's father had also said that if the police found out about the beatings, they would put him in jail. "You don't want your daddy to go to jail, do you? Then I'd lose my job and you and mommy would be poor," the father said.

Carlton was afraid to tell the truth, but when his father came to pick him up, Carlton would say he was crippled. "I can't walk. My legs hurt too much. I can't go with you this time Daddy," Carlton would say.

Now That I Know, What Comes Next?

Congratulations. You did it. You persisted in finishing this chapter—no matter how difficult it was to look at the trauma and its negative effects. As a result, you now know if you have PTSD or only some symptoms of PTSD, and you know whether it is partial or full PTSD.

Should future life stresses or trauma increase your partial PTSD to full PTSD, or intensify the degree to which your PTSD symptoms hinder your life, you will not need to panic and conclude that you are losing your mind. Since you are now aware of the symptoms of PTSD, you can take a more objective look at yourself and say, It's PTSD, not insanity, not psychosis, not some incurable mental cancer.

The more you learn about PTSD, the more in control of your life you will feel. Even if you only have a few PTSD symptoms, you will benefit from any information you can acquire about PTSD in all its aspects, because knowledge is the best antidote to fear. If you had a serious physical illness, you would want to know the severity of your condition. This way you could better plan your treatment and self-care program. A mild case of diabetes, for example, could necessitate limited life changes and minimal medical care. In contrast, a severe case could mean extensive life changes and intense medical attention. In a parallel manner, if your PTSD is mild, you may not need long-term intensive therapy. However, if your PTSD is severe, you may need to consider options such as inpatient care, psychiatric evaluation for medication, and a combination of individual counseling and group support.

Although PTSD is commonly viewed as a psychological problem, it also has a biological or physical aspect. The following chapter presents some of the basics of the biological effects of trauma and how the impact of trauma on the central nervous system can set the stage for the development of clinical depression, a serious addiction, or other disorder. In that chapter you will be helped in identifying whether you suffer from depression, addiction, or other problems often associated with PTSD, not so that you can berate yourself, but so that you can take corrective action.

It bears repeating that PTSD is not incurable. Healing is possible. It also bears repeating that our knowledge of trauma and its effects is limited. Physicians, mental health professionals, and others concerned with trauma survivors are still learning about the various aspects of PTSD. For example, studies of the physiology of PTSD are in their infancy, as are studies of what kinds of healing techniques work best for various kinds of trauma survivors.

PTSD is complex and its expression varies considerably from one person to the next. Although you may have much in common with other trauma survivors, you are unique. As you read the following chapters, keep in mind a phrase commonly heard in 12-step meetings: "Take what you want and leave the rest."

You are the expert on your own trauma. Not every finding about PTSD will apply to you and not every suggested coping skill will be helpful to you. Only you can determine what helps and what does not. Friends and professionals can help you uncover your own truth and support you emotionally. They can also offer suggested courses of action and alternative ways of viewing the trauma. Only you, however, can decide which of these suggestions applies to you and would benefit you.

2

The Biochemistry of PTSD

Like the rest of the body, your central nervous system is vulnerable. Given enough physical or emotional stress it too can bend or even break. When you experienced your trauma, your central nervous system received a series of shocks. The greater the intensity and the longer the duration of the trauma, the greater the possibility that the delicate biochemical balances of your body might have been disrupted.

Despite an increase in research in to the biochemistry of PTSD in recent years, there is no single definitive theory as to how trauma affects the body. One theory is that trauma destabilizes the autonomic nervous system; another is that trauma changes body chemistry so that the individual is more prone to anxiety. Yet another hypothesis is that trauma disrupts certain specific biochemical balances, for example, catecholamine levels (Munroe 1995, McFarlane 1995).

No single biological explanation is satisfactory in that no one theory can explain the wide range of PTSD symptoms in trauma survivors. It is an established fact that PTSD, for some trauma survivors, has both physical and emotional effects.

However, the biochemical shifts that can occur as a result of trauma do not happen to every trauma survivor. Just because you lived through a trauma, does not necessarily mean that your biochemistry has changed.

If you are a one-time trauma survivor, many of these biological changes may not apply at all, or they may apply only under very limited circumstances. But there are no hard and fast rules. For example, children who witness the violent deaths of family members or friends can suffer from biological changes just as readily as soldiers who spent time in prisoner-of-war camps. Incest survivors, refugees, battered wives, abused children, prisoners of war, combat soldiers with extended tours of duty, and others who have endured long-term, repeated, or severe trauma are those most likely to be affected.

As you read on in this chapter, you may be able to determine whether or not your biochemistry was affected by the trauma you endured. If, in fact, your biochemistry was altered by the trauma, you will likely have experienced certain problems. These problems include difficulties in thinking clearly, in regulating your emotions, in relating to other people, and critically important, in sustaining hope for the future. Trauma-induced biological changes can also lead to or contribute to the development of clinical depression or a substance-abuse problem. These conditions are the subjects of later sections in this chapter.

Biological Changes and the Healing Process

Some trauma-induced biological changes are linked to memory tracts in the brain. Almost automatically, in the presence of people, places, objects, or situations that remind you of the traumatic event, these biochemical changes can trigger either the reexperiencing phase or the numbing-avoidance phase of PTSD. As discussed in Chapter 1, in the reexperiencing phase you can expect to have memories, dreams, or flashbacks of the trauma. In the numbing-avoidance phase you can expect to feel shut down inside and to want to withdraw from others.

Because of these biological changes, you may have periods when, against your will, you feel as if you were still living under the conditions of the original traumatic event. You may know—and perhaps your therapist, family members, and friends are telling you—that you're safe and the danger is past. Biochemically, however, your body is screaming "It's still going on. Can't you feel it?"

Even if you have tried with all your might to erase the trauma from your mind, like almost all trauma survivors you probably found yourself unable to do so. If the alterations in your biological makeup are significant enough, under certain circumstances, your body and mind may involuntarily revert to the emotional climate and mindset of the original traumatic event. And sadly, in ignorance of the biology of PTSD, you may have concluded that you were a failure for being unable to control your reactions.

If this is starting to sound terribly dire and frightening, bear in mind that even if your central nervous system has been affected, you can minimize many of the negative biological effects. You can counteract these effects by gaining some knowledge of the biology of PTSD and by working toward healing with the help of this book and your therapist. If necessary, certain medications can also help. Using all these tools, you need not be a prisoner of your past.

For example, at the very minimum you can learn to anticipate and prepare for—rather than panic in response to—some of your PTSD-related reactions. You may be unable to eliminate some of your reactions, but you can learn to manage them, instead of letting them control your actions. You may not be able to eliminate all the pain and distress that attend your PTSD reactions, but you can learn to respond increasingly in a way that best meets your goals in any specific situation.

This chapter briefly presents some of the biological aspects of PTSD, and then shows how they are related to clinical depression and substance abuse. You will be guided in determining if, in addition to (or as a result of) PTSD, you suffer from depression or a substance abuse problem. If so, you will need specialized counseling for these problems.

The Role of the Adrenals

In the last chapter, you read about the fight-or-flight and freeze reactions that human beings have in response to life-threatening situations. The source of these reactions is the adrenal glands: two diamond-shaped organs located on top of the kidneys. In response to the threat of danger, the adrenal glands secrete large doses of either adrenaline or noradrenaline. Adrenaline provides a supercharge of energy, which enables people to move with more speed and power than usual. In contrast, noradrenaline makes people freeze or go numb. This reaction is similar to the way some animals play dead when threatened.

During adrenaline surges, the heart rate increases, the pupils dilate, digestion slows down, and blood coagulates quicker, to prevent too much blood being lost. The lungs become more efficient, providing the increased oxygen necessary to fight back or run away as powerfully as possible. The increased oxygen can also vastly improve the acuteness of the senses and the mind's alertness. Sounds, smells, and other sensory data, for example, are perceived more vividly. The brain uses this sensory data to assess the situation, thus maximizing the chances for survival. Due to the increased oxygen, the brain can work more quickly and efficiently to make the best decisions possible. Consider the following example.

> On her way to the babysitter's house with her small daughter, Mary realized she had forgotten to bring diapers. So when she passed a convenience store, she decided to run in and buy some. Thinking it would only take a second, she left her baby in the car. But when she came out of the store a minute later, her car was rolling backwards down the hill, toward a busy intersection.
>
> Although Mary was 50 pounds overweight, had not exercised in years, and the glasses she needed for distance vision were in the car, the adrenaline surge she experienced enabled her to clearly see the traffic at the bottom of the hill, and she was able to run fast enough to stop the car before it rolled into the traffic. Not only that, but by herself she pushed the car back up the hill into the parking lot.
>
> Remembering the incident she said, "I didn't think—I just reacted. I felt like a wild animal being chased by tigers.

Knowing that my baby was in that car made me run faster than I've ever run in all my life. I guess it was stupid of me to shove the car all the way back up the hill. I could have really hurt myself, but I had all this energy. I was so charged up I just didn't think."

If, on the other hand, Mary's adrenals had pumped her with noradrenaline, instead of a fight-or-flight reaction, she could simply have frozen, as Sarah did.

Sarah was sitting by her living room window watching her husband show their baby daughter the roses twining on the fence, when suddenly a dog jumped over the fence and attacked the child.

Though Sarah was a pediatric nurse who had seen many injuries and illnesses, at the sight of her own child being harmed, she became immobilized, unable even to call for help. Fortunately, her husband had an adrenaline reaction that enabled him to save the child. Afterwards, however, Sarah's self-recriminations for her temporary paralysis were enormous.

Similarly, soldiers in battle, victims of rape and battering, survivors of natural catastrophes, and victims of muggings sometimes report having frozen or been unable to act. Combat medics, rescue workers, firefighters, and others on whom people depend for quick, decisive action, frequently suffer massive guilt because during a particular episode they "went limp," "couldn't think," or "couldn't do anything." The truth is, however, that these individuals, like Sarah, probably couldn't help it. They were not experiencing a failure of courage or a lack of dedication, but were most likely having an involuntary noradrenaline freeze reaction.

At first glance, an adrenaline surge may seem preferable to a noradrenaline response. However, adrenaline surges can be highly problematic, because they cannot be turned off at will.

Just as Mary used her excess adrenaline to push the car up the hill, soldiers in battle are easily tempted to discharge their excess adrenaline through abusive violence, needless killings, or other acts of destruction. And the same dynamic might apply to some police officers or others involved in security work. Although the adrenaline surge does not excuse excessive violence, even in battle, the hyperalert adrenaline surges triggered by pursuit or combat do play an undeniable role in incidents of excessive violence.

Adrenaline and Trigger Situations

The adrenaline surge is also a major contributor to the hyperalert symptoms of PTSD: the startle response, insomnia, nightmares, and so on. If you suffer from PTSD, situations that remind you of the original traumatic event can trigger an adrenaline surge. The adrenaline surge then in turn activates memories and feelings associated with the traumatic event, leading to extreme distress. You may become agitated, irritable, or even have rage reactions, increased night terrors, or flashbacks. Alternatively, you may have a numbing reaction after exposure to a person, place, or object reminiscent of the original traumatic situation. Or you may alternate between reexperiencing the trauma and shutting down.

Since both hyperalertness and numbing can be painful, you may find yourself avoiding trigger situations—those that remind you of the original traumatic event. Such avoidance behavior may limit your opportunities and options. On the other hand, staying away from or minimizing your contact with situations that trigger your PTSD symptoms makes perfect sense emotionally. In either case, there may be trigger situations you cannot or do not wish to avoid because they potentially enrich your life. The exercises on coping with triggers in Chapter 5 will provide you with suggestions and guidelines for managing your reactions and reducing your stress levels in distressing situations.

When Stress Is Prolonged

The adrenals, like the rest of the body, are not designed to handle prolonged stress. When subjected to repeated trauma or emergencies, the adrenals can be permanently damaged—leading to overfunctioning during subsequent stress, which causes the hyperarousal and numbing phases of PTSD.

Under severe stress, in addition to massive secretions of adrenaline or noradrenaline, a variety of neurotransmitters are released. Neurotransmitters are the chemical substances that enable impulses to be transmitted from one nerve cell to another (Bourne 1990). Among their many functions, neurotransmitters help regulate the intensity of emotions and moods.

If you were subjected to repeated or intense trauma or stress, certain of your neurotransmitters may have been depleted. The lack of these "buffer" neurotransmitters can lead not only to clinical depression, but to mood swings, explosive outbursts, overreactions to subsequent stress, and the startle response. Depletions of some neurotransmitters can result in overdependence on other people, feelings of I can't make it without you, or its opposite, an unrealistically independent or counterdependent stance of I don't need anyone; I can make it on my own. The learned helplessness syndrome is another possible development.

The Learned Helplessness Syndrome. In a famous series of experiments conducted by Martin Seligman (1975), animals were subjected to electric shocks from which they couldn't escape. No matter what they did, or didn't do, they couldn't stop the pain. At first the animals fought, tried to get away, and uttered cries of pain or anger. Then they sank into listlessness and despair. Later on, in a second set of experiments, the same animals were shocked again—only this time, by pressing a certain lever or completing some other simple task, they could stop the electric current. But they made no effort to do so.

The animals had learned to be helpless. Due to their previous experiences, even when a means of escape from the pain was provided, these animals were too defeated, perhaps too affected neurologically, to take the simple action that would end their suffering.

The result of these experiments was Seligman's learned helplessness theory. This theory has been applied not only to traumatized animals, but to human beings trapped in inescapable negative circumstances—individuals who have been traumatized. According to Seligman (1975), "When an organism has experienced trauma it cannot control, its motivation to respond in the face of later trauma wanes. Moreover, even if it does respond and the response succeeds in producing relief, it has trouble learning, perceiving, and believing that the response worked. Finally, its emotional balance is disturbed; depression and anxiety, measured in various ways, predominate."

Since Seligman's original studies, much more work on learned helplessness has been completed. This new research shows that animals subjected to inescapable shock have some of the same neurotransmitter depletions as animals separated from their mothers at a very young age. (Both electric shock and separation are considered traumas.) In addition, both the shocked and the separated animals have the same kinds of neurotransmitter depletions as humans who have endured prolonged stress. Both sets of animals also exhibit the hyperalert stage of PTSD, with overactivity and outbursts of anger and aggressiveness, followed by numbing or listlessness and despair and a lack of interest in food, sex, and play (van der Kolk 1988b, Rossi 1986).

A variety of trauma survivors—notably abused women and children, prisoners of war, concentration- or refugee-camp survivors, and torture survivors—have been shown to be especially vulnerable to developing learned helplessness syndrome. For example, one major reason abused persons have difficulty leaving their abusers and striking out on their own is learned helplessness. Similarly, prisoners of war and some combat veterans also struggle long after they have been released from prison camps or military duty with the passivity, anxiety, and depression that comes with having learned to be powerless.

If you have been subject to ongoing physical or sexual abuse or other forms of repeated trauma, you may be at special risk for having acquired the learned helplessness syndrome to some degree. However, learned helplessness is not irreversible. You can, with effort and support, unlearn what the trauma ingrained. One step at a time, you can learn to take more and more control over your life. And each small success will encourage you to take the next risk and the next step. Exercises in Chapter

10, on empowerment, are specifically designed to help you overcome learned helplessness and take stock of your progress.

However, if as a result of the biological aspects of PTSD you have developed a clinical depression or a major substance abuse problem, then you must first get special assistance with these problems. You will be severely impeded in achieving your goals if either of these problems is left untreated.

Depression

Depression is by far the most common psychiatric problem in our country. Many mental-health professionals estimate that one-third of adult women and one-tenth of adult men can expect to suffer from at least one bout of depression in their lifetime (Beck 1973, Rovner 1991). Unfortunately, very few of these individuals recognize the symptoms. Even if they do, they often fail to get help. Don't you be one of them. Like PTSD, depression is a highly treatable condition. There is no necessity for, or purpose in, continuing to suffer needlessly.

What Is Depression?

Everyone has "the blues" from time to time, and when it happens, we often say we're depressed. There is a difference, however, between those feelings and biochemical or clinical depression.

For example, depression is part of the grieving process. However, the depression that is part of the five stages of grief (denial, anger, bargaining, depression, and acceptance) does not constitute true clinical depression. In normal grieving, the depression tends to lessen over time— although it may take years. In clinical depression, however, the sadness tends to grow over time. Other components of clinical depression include mixed feelings towards oneself and others and/or active self-hatred and physiological problems such as sleep disturbances and fatigue. Indecision, inability to concentrate, memory problems, lowered sex drive, confusion, and crying spells are other symptoms.

In clinical depression, the negative feelings are so overwhelming that they impair your ability to function. You can't make it to work, or it is a struggle to get there. You stop going out. You avoid socializing. The smallest task seems like a monumental chore, and you can't concentrate enough to finish a newspaper article, much less a book. You have trouble meeting the most basic obligations to your family or yourself. Indecision plagues you.

The symptoms of depression are not only painful in themselves, but they create fear. When you can't concentrate on the task at hand, you start to feel insecure about yourself and begin to worry that you won't be able to meet your responsibilities or take care of yourself. The symptoms, as well as the panic they create, can chip away at your self-esteem.

The lowered self-esteem, in turn, creates additional feelings of worthlessness, because in our society self-confidence is valued. It isn't "popular" to have low self-esteem, which puts pressure on the depressed person to hide all difficulties from others. This pretending creates further stress, and only increases the depressed person's fatigue and sense of isolation from others.

Clinical depression can also impair your reality testing. For example, you become hypersensitive to the reactions of others, and consequently, your views of how they feel about you may be distorted. Or you may feel utterly hopeless about situations in which there is, in fact, considerable hope.

Causes of Clinical Depression

Not only is clinical depression widespread, but numerous studies suggest that it is on the rise among all age groups, especially young adults. Experts attribute the rise in depression, in part, to increasingly difficult economic conditions. The increased depersonalization, and the breakdown of traditional support structures during the past two decades, are also contributing to the rise in depression. Depression rates are especially high among groups who are oppressed in some manner, for example, the poor, minority groups, women, and the handicapped. Depression is also prevalent among victims of abuse, violence, or other traumas.

As a trauma survivor, you are at risk for developing a clinical depression. Or you may already have a clinical depression you are unaware of. Some studies indicate that at least 50 percent of individuals with PTSD also suffer from depression. This depression is frequently, but not necessarily, a result of the trauma. But whether the depression predates the trauma or developed afterward, the effect is the same.

There are many different explanations for what causes clinical depression, as the following sections show. No one of these theories is 100 percent accurate in all cases, but they all have some validity in some instances. Clinical depression is caused by many factors, some of which are beyond individual control. Several of these causes can be directly related to trauma.

As you read these sections, keep in mind that causes for depression may vary over time—a given depressive episode may have an entirely different cause than the one preceding or following it. And the theory that explains one person's depression will not apply to another's. Think about which of these theories apply to you—which ones make sense in terms of feelings and experiences you have had.

Biological Theory. One way of looking at depression is as the result of disturbances in the neurotransmitter system, usually caused by the depressed person having been subject to severe stress for a prolonged period of time—as you read about above. Due to the stress or trauma, the person's biochemistry becomes so strained that it cannot perform its functions as it did before the traumatic event. Breakdown of the neurotransmitter system can lead to low self-esteem, hopelessness, and other forms of negative thinking, and to difficulties with concentration, sleep, and decision making. It can also lead to irritability, anxiety, loss of the ability to experience pleasure, and hypersensitivity to the reactions of others—all of which are classic symptoms of depression.

Depression is also associated with physical illnesses, especially those of a chronic or severe nature, such as stroke, cancer, and heart disease. In addition, depression can result from severe injury and permanent disability, or from the multiple medications that might be needed due to these problems. Physical illness, disability, and medication tax the neurotransmitter system immensely. They also put a strain on other bodily functions.

Physical injury or illness also often creates other problems—financial, social, sexual, and emotional. These stresses further disturb biochemical balances and negatively affect the central nervous system.

If you were already ill or disabled when the traumatic event occurred, were suffering from malnutrition or sleep deprivation, or you were seriously injured during the trauma, you are at special risk for developing depression. The risk is especially high if a part of your body essential to your work or interests was affected. For example, a dancer who lost the use of her legs in an accident would lose not only her work but her means of creativity as well—a double blow that would almost certainly lead to depression.

Loss and Grief Theory. The dancer's depression over her loss in part fits Freud's view of depression. He believed that depression was the result of grief over the loss of a love object. However, the kind of grief he was referring to was grief that was mixed in with anger and hostility toward the loved one. Freud also felt that the loved one need not be dead. The death of the relationship with the loved one was sufficient to cause depression.

The concept of the loved one can be extended to include a cherished ideal, such as patriotism, certain spiritual values, or self-respect. Consequently, losing a long-held value or ideal or your dignity can also lead to depression. If your dignity or self-respect was assaulted not only by the trauma but subsequently by others' negative reactions to your feelings, you may be at a special risk for depression. Similarly, if your assumptions about the goodness and justice of the universe, or other values, were shattered by the trauma, your subsequent grieving may also develop into depression.

For example, in all of this century's wars, some soldiers have become disillusioned with the government or the military after observing hypocrisies, incompetence, and errors that resulted in needless deaths among their comrades. Many of these soldiers lost faith in military authority; some experienced a lessening of their patriotism as well. The resulting feeling among these men was not only anger, but grief. They had lost the very ideals that caused them to join the military in the first place.

Behavioral Theory. The behavioral view of depression states that depression is the natural result of inadequate reinforcement, rewards, or recognition. Depression can easily develop among people who are inadequately rewarded or appreciated by others in their environment. Depression also results when people are unable to adequately appreciate, reward, or lovingly care for themselves.

Some popular self-help books on "how to love yourself" espouse or imply the idea that if you only can love and accept yourself, you don't need love and acceptance from others. In my experience, people need both. They need the recognition, love, and approval of at least a few other people as well as self-love and self-appreciation. Trauma survivors are sometimes deprived of both; they lack reinforcement from others and self-reinforcement.

Vietnam veterans and many service workers are prime examples of depression caused by lack of reinforcement. In general, until recently, the Vietnam veteran was far from appreciated by our society. Instead of a welcome-home parade such as greeted the Persian Gulf veterans, the Vietnam veteran was castigated and rejected for his sacrifices. Similarly, some rescue workers work long hours for relatively low pay and receive little recognition for their many heroic efforts on behalf of others. Such situations are the breeding grounds for depression.

Were you, as a trauma survivor, denigrated or not properly acknowledged for your efforts to survive or to help others survive? Did you have to withstand long-term traumatic conditions where you received few rewards for your efforts? If so, you may be at risk for depression.

Learned Helplessness Theory. Part of learned helplessness is a belief that you cannot exert control over the important events in your life. This feeling of helpless resignation or fatalism can lead to a clinical depression. Due to direct experience with powerlessness, and because of the biochemical changes that can occur during trauma, trauma survivors are especially susceptible to learned helplessness, and consequently, to depression.

Cognitive Theory. The cognitive view of depression is similar to the learned helplessness theory. However, cognitive theory states that depression is a problem of your thoughts and beliefs, rather than your feelings. Once you think or believe you are helpless or ineffectual, then such thinking controls your behavior. Negative thinking can result in negative events, which further reinforce your negative thinking and view of life.

Cognitive theory further states that depressed people misinterpret life events, distorting their view of the world, themselves, and the future in a hopeless direction. Such distortions and misinterpretations are often directly related to trauma, which in some cases teaches survivors that they are ineffectual, incompetent, or powerless (Burns 1980).

Anger-Turned-Inward Theory. People who do not know how to express their anger, are afraid to express their anger, or feel they do not have the right to express it, often turn that anger inward on themselves— resulting in depression. Turning their anger inward is frequently a cause of depression in trauma survivors who have experienced the following:

- Situations in which expressing anger could have caused their death (as is often the case with crime victims, refugees, and other captives) or could have led to physical abuse or other forms of punishment (as happens with abused women, children, and elderly persons). Even when the abuse or captivity is over, the "habit" of suppressing anger can be difficult to unlearn.

- Situations in which there is no clearly identifiable target for the anger: there is no one person or identifiable group to express anger toward (as is the case when a large bureaucracy or institution is nonresponsive to a survivor).

For example, toward whom do Holocaust survivors, survivors of torture by totalitarian regimes, or mistreated Vietnam and Korean war and World War II veterans, direct their rage? In these cases, as one survivor stated, "Everybody was responsible, but nobody was responsible."

Similarly, at whom or what can natural-catastrophe survivors vent their anger? Yelling at nature is less than satisfying. Blaming God or other supernatural forces poses a similar problem, complicated by the fact that those who direct their anger at a spiritual being often turn to that same being for protection, direction, and love. For those people it may be easier or safer to turn their anger inward than to risk a loss of faith by blaming their god.

Other Causes. Depression can also be caused by events unrelated to trauma. These include an acute brain syndrome, some other organic mental disorder, or a psychiatric problem such as schizophrenia or paranoia.

In some cases, depression is hereditary. If you have a family history of clinical depression or manic-depressive illness, it does not automatically mean that you will develop that problem. However, the strain of the trauma can bring forth these and other latent genetic-based psychiatric disorders. Therefore, if one or more of your family members has suffered from depression, watch yourself carefully for symptoms of depression.

One final note about depression. Some depressed people tend to get "depressed about depression." They interpret their symptoms of depression as signs of personal inadequacy and failure, and feel great shame and guilt over being depressed. Their feelings are reinforced by three factors: societal attitudes that blame people for their own pain, societal ignorance about depression, and cultural norms that view any person in emotional pain as "weak" or "deficient."

These are the same attitudes that oppress people with PTSD. (You'll learn more about this in Chapter 4, on victimization.) These unsympathetic attitudes do not reflect reality; they reflect people's ignorance about mental health matters and their fears about themselves.

Questionnaire: Clinical Depression

A severe clinical depression, in which you are barely able to talk, walk, or function, is easy to identify. However, it is more difficult to tell the difference between feelings of sadness, frustration, and discouragement, which are a normal part of life, and mild or moderate clinical depression. (You may want to review the description in the section "What Is Depression?") One difference is that in clinical depression, the despondency lasts a long time or is cyclical: the depressed feelings may go away and then return later.

Some depressions are reactive, in that they arise in response to a specific set of stressful events. Others are considered chronic, in that they have lasted for over two years without a period of two months or longer of relief. Still other depressions are considered constitutional, in that they are based in hereditary or other long-term factors.

The following questions will help you determine whether you have experienced what is called a major depressive episode. They are adapted from *DSM-IV*. Jot down your answers in the margin or in your journal.

1. Have you ever suffered from a depressed mood that lasted at least two weeks?

2. Have you ever, for at least two weeks, suffered from a loss of interest in or an inability to experience pleasure?

If you answered no to both of these questions, then it is highly unlikely that you suffer from depression. However, if you answered yes to at least one of these questions, continue on.

3. Over the same two-week period, did you feel depressed most of the day, nearly every day, as noticed by yourself or by others? (Feeling depressed can also be expressed as irritability.)

4. Over the same two weeks, did you or others notice that you lost most of your previous interest or pleasure in all or almost all of your daily activities, nearly every day?

5. Over the same two-week period, did you gain or lose more than 5 percent of your body weight (when not dieting) or did you notice a major increase or decrease in your appetite?

6. Over the same two-week period, did you have insomnia or hypersomnia (sleeping a lot) nearly every day?

7. Over the same two weeks, did you feel fatigued and without energy nearly every day?

8. Over the same two-week period, did you feel hyperactive and agitated or the opposite, underactive and sluggish, nearly every day, as observed by others, not just yourself? (This question refers to physical sensations, not to emotional restlessness or sluggishness.)

9. Over the same two-week period, did you feel worthless or extremely guilty about relatively inconsequential matters nearly every day? (This does not include feeling guilty about being physically ill.)

10. Over the same two weeks, did you have trouble concentrating or thinking or suffer from indecision nearly every day?

11. Over the same two-week period, did you have recurring thoughts of death or suicide (with or without a specific plan), or did you devise a specific plan for killing yourself or attempt suicide?

If you have answered yes to at least five of these symptoms and you also meet the following two criteria, you are considered to have had a major depressive episode. First, these symptoms must have caused important problems in vocational, social, personal, and other areas of functioning. Second, none of the following conditions applies:

- An organic brain problem or other medical problem caused or maintained the symptoms.

- What you experienced was a normal reaction to the death of a loved one.

- You experienced delusions or hallucinations.

- You suffer from schizophrenia, schizophreniform disorder, delusional disorder, or psychotic disorder.

- The symptoms are the result of substance abuse or some other form of substance or medication.

If you have met the criteria for a major depressive episode, do not despair. Like PTSD, depression is a highly treatable condition. Although our knowledge of it, like our knowledge of PTSD, is still in its infancy stages, the last ten years have seen a virtual explosion of interest in and research into depression. Improved treatment methods and many forms of effective medications exist that were not available 10 to 15 years ago.

The most important step you can take is to go for help. But don't go to just any counselor or psychiatrist; find one who specializes in depression. Depression, like PTSD, will not go away by itself. It is likely to worsen over time, and you can become so depressed that you will be unable, or unwilling, to receive the help you need and deserve.

Substance Abuse

If you have PTSD, you know what it means to be hyperalert. You can't sleep. You're constantly on guard, and you never know when those memories and nightmares will be coming back to haunt you. Equally horrible is that numb feeling. You're so bored, so shut down, that you feel more like a stone than a human being.

You might have found the feelings you experience in either the hyperalert or numbing stage of PTSD so unbearable that you have tried to drown them with alcohol, stuff them down with food, stifle them with drugs, or obliterate them with compulsive gambling, sexual activity, or spending. But no matter what you do, your symptoms slip back. The fact that you have compromised yourself to the point of addiction, only to find that addiction doesn't work to take away the pain, simply increases your desperation. This desperation, in turn, may serve to escalate your dependence on the mood-altering substance or compulsive activity.

The dependence began as a means of reducing anxiety, pain, and fear—at first it provided you with comfort and relief. However, you may have found by now that instead of having less anxiety, fear, and guilt as a result of your dependence, you have more. Your body, your mind, your relationships, your finances, and worst of all, your self-esteem have probably suffered because of it.

If you have turned to a mood-altering substance (such as alcohol, drugs, or food) or to a mood-altering activity (such as compulsive gambling or sexual activity) you are not unique among trauma survivors. Researchers have found high correlations between traumatization and substance abuse or other addictions and compulsions. The populations studied thus far include war veterans, natural-catastrophe survivors, fire and technological-disaster survivors, and abused persons, including men, women, and children.

Although much more research needs to be completed in this area, studies thus far have found rates such as the following:

- Approximately 50 to 60 percent of women and 20 percent of men in chemical dependency recovery programs report having been victims of childhood sexual abuse. Approximately 69 percent of women and 80 percent of men in such programs report being victims of childhood physical abuse (Kunzman 1990b, Bigham and Resick 1990).

- Anywhere from 40 to 60 percent of women in recovery for bulimia, anorexia, and compulsive overeating report victimization experiences (Slogan and Leichner 1986; Kunzman 1990a, b; Bigham and Resick 1990; Zweben 1987).

- The trauma of war has been implicated in the relatively high rates of substance abuse among combat veterans, with anywhere from 50 to 65 percent of PTSD-afflicted Vietnam combat veterans reporting alcohol or drug abuse. High rates of alcohol abuse have also been noted among World War II and Korean War combat veterans (Jelinek and Williams 1984, Keane et al. 1983, Matsakis 1988, Lacoursiere et al. 1980).

- Severe trauma has also been documented among compulsive gamblers seeking help, among runaway and delinquent children and adolescents, and among both male and female prostitutes and actresses and models in pornographic films and magazines (Taber et al. 1987, Courtois 1988, Finkelhor 1979, Brown and Finkelhor 1986).

- Researchers have also noted increases in alcohol consumption among survivors of fires, floods, and other natural disasters.

PTSD-Related Causes of Addictions and Compulsions

Addictions and compulsions are complex phenomena. They have many possible causes, ranging from genetic and biochemical factors to social pressures to dysfunctional family backgrounds. However, in the case of trauma survivors, in many instances addictions and compulsions serve as forms of self-medication for the symptoms of PTSD. Ironically, they can serve as both stimulants for the numbing phase and sedatives for the hyperalert stage.

For example, a drink, a pill, a snack, a sexual encounter, or a shopping spree can induce some feeling during the numbing phase. Or that same drink, drug, or binge can produce a calming effect on the hyperalert symptoms.

Drugs and food can also help fight insomnia, bad dreams, and intrusive thoughts. Alcohol helps induce sleep, for example, as well as suppressing REM sleep, during which many dreams and nightmares occur. Food and drugs can quell the anxiety, anger, and other strong feelings of the hyperalert stage. (However, these same substances can lower inhibitions against expressing frustration and rage in a verbally or physically abusive manner.)

Addictions and compulsions can also be used by PTSD sufferers to handle the avoidance symptoms of PTSD, which include the tendency to isolate from others. "I couldn't handle the people at work (at parties, or at home) if I didn't drink (do drugs, binge)," some trauma survivors say. Their addiction or compulsion gives them the courage and confidence they need to feel comfortable with others; without it they might choose to be virtual hermits, limiting their contact to their immediate families and needed professionals.

A mood-altering substance or compulsive activity may partially or almost totally eliminate some of the undesirable symptoms of PTSD—for a while. But eventually it creates its own set of financial, interpersonal, and social problems. And when these problems become overwhelming, they recreate the overwhelming nature of the original traumatic event.

Addictions, Compulsions, and Depression. PTSD can also lead to substance abuse via depression. If the PTSD has contributed to the development of a biochemical depression, substance abuse or compulsive activities can medicate not only the PTSD but also the depression.

Recent research has shown a substantial correlation between alcoholism and depression, as well as between eating disorders and depression. In some studies, for example, over 80 percent of alcoholic men have been shown to suffer from biochemical depression (Anixter 1990). Experts are not clear, however, about which comes first—the alcohol abuse or the depression. On the one hand, alcohol can serve to make tolerable some of the symptoms of depression. On the other hand, prolonged alcohol use, with its debilitating effects on the body and on the individual's ability to function, can actually create a biochemical depression.

Also, some of the initial symptoms from alcohol observed in detox treatment programs are similar to depressive symptoms. Thus the only way to tell if an alcohol-addicted person also suffers from depression is for him or her to be assessed for depression two or three weeks after withdrawal from alcohol. For the nondepressed individual, the symptoms of depression may largely disappear after two or three weeks of sobriety. However, for the dually affected individual, the depressive symptoms persist for at least two weeks following withdrawal and sobriety.

In the area of eating disorders, several studies have shown that over half of bulimic and anorectic women suffer from depression or come from families with histories of depression. As with alcoholism and depression, sometimes it is not clear which came first—the eating disorder or the depression. On the one hand, the eating disorder may have begun as a means of coping with the sad, lonely, angry, hopeless, and otherwise negative feelings associated with depression. On the other hand, prolonged, extreme dieting can create biochemical depression by stressing the neurotransmitters and by depriving the body of adequate nutrients. Such dieting is common among all who suffer from eating disorders, whether anorexia, bulimia, or compulsive overeating.

For people with eating disorders, the only way to determine whether they suffer from clinical depression is to wait until they have achieved some mastery over the disorder itself. Ideally, the overeating, self-starvation, or bingeing and purging will have stopped, or at least be at a manageable level, before it is determined whether the person also suffers from depression.

Further evidence of the relationship between depression and addiction lies in recent research that shows antidepressants to be exceptionally successful in controlling binge drinking, and binge eating (Wadden et al. 1986, Liberman et al. 1986, Wurtman and Wurtman 1989, Lee et al. 1985).

Assessing for Substance Abuse

If you have PTSD and you also use a substance or some particular activity to control your symptoms, you may fall into one of the following three categories:

No prior history of compulsion or substance abuse. You never abused alcohol, drugs, food, money, and so on prior to the traumatic event. However, you did so during the traumatic event or immediately afterwards. Or perhaps you only began abusing years afterwards, when for one reason or another the trauma emerged from suppression.

Prior history of moderate use. Before the traumatic event you were a moderate or occasional drinker, drug user, or overeater. Or every now and then you spent money or gambled excessively or had sex promiscuously. However, before the trauma, although you were out of control sometimes, these behaviors did not disrupt your life in any substantial manner. For example, perhaps you drank at parties and sometimes became intoxicated, but basically alcohol was not a problem. Or maybe you tended to overeat when disturbed. At times you binged, but food was not the center of your life and you never gained more than three or four pounds even when you did indulge.

But then you increased your usage of alcohol, drugs, food, or behavior to cope with the trauma. And somewhere you crossed over the line from casual substance abuser to a true addict. Now your addiction absorbs much of your time and attention. Whereas before you could stop drinking or taking drugs, now you cannot. Whereas before you were mildly concerned about your weight and eating, now you are obsessed with them. The questionnaires that appear below will help you determine whether you have crossed the line from occasional, recreational use to a genuine dependency or addiction.

History of substance abuse or addictive or compulsive behavior. If you were already abusing alcohol, drugs, or food or being compulsive about certain activities when the traumatic event occurred, the trauma may have functioned to increase your addictive or compulsive behavior. And because the abuse or compulsion predates the trauma, your healing process will probably include many more issues than just the traumatic event.

However, you cannot ignore the traumatic event. Just because you were addicted before does not mean your addiction today has little or nothing to do with the trauma. You will need to trace the effect of the trauma on your addiction the same as someone who was not addicted prior to the trauma.

The questionnaires that follow will help you determine whether you are an occasional substance user, a substance abuser, or an addict; whether you just occasionally overeat or you have a serious eating disorder; whether you are a recreational gambler or a pathological one; and whether your spending habits or sexual activity are areas of concern.

The questionnaires are based on definitions of dependency and addiction in *DSM-IV*. Although *DSM-IV* provides definitions of alcohol and drug dependency and abuse, eating disorders, and pathological gambling, it does not define compulsive spending or compulsive sexual activity.

Many people drink or overeat when they are distressed or to express joy. Similarly, many people gamble, buy things they can't afford, or over-indulge in sex for the same reasons. These relatively normal human excesses should not automatically be considered addictions or compulsions. However, such behaviors can become addictions or compulsions when they begin to become a means of coping with or escaping from certain emotions and life challenges. How much? and How often? are important questions to ask about your particular addiction or compulsion. Yet, for compulsive spending and compulsive sexual behavior, as well as for most other addictions and compulsions, the crucial issue is not how much or how often you practice them, but *why* you practice them and what effect they have on your life.

Questionnaire: Alcohol and Drug Use

Although a distinction is often made between alcohol and other drugs that affect the mind or behavior (psychoactive drugs), in *DSM-IV*, alcohol is considered a drug and is classified as such. Thus, in the following questions the word *drug* should be understood to mean alcohol as well. To determine whether you suffer from an alcohol or drug addiction, answer the following questions in your journal or in the margin.

Part I: Dependence or Addiction

1. Have you taken the drug in larger amounts or over a longer period of time than you intended?

2. Does the drug (either taking it or withdrawing from it) interfere with fulfilling your responsibilities at work, at school, or at home, or does it make life dangerous for you? For example, is your work attendance or driving record affected?

3. Have you given up or reduced your involvement in important social, work, or recreational activities due to your drug use?

4. Do you continue to use the drug even though you know it creates serious legal, medical, family, social, or psychological problems?

5. Have you found that today you need at least 50 percent more of the drug in order to obtain the same effects as when you began using it? Do you find yourself needing more and more of the drug to produce the same effect?

The following two items may not apply to marijuana, PCP, or hallucinogens (LSD, mescaline, DMT):

6. Do you experience withdrawal symptoms within a few days or even hours after you stop or reduce your intake?

7. Do you use your drug to relieve or avoid withdrawal symptoms?

8. Do you sincerely want to stop using drugs, but find your efforts to do so unsuccessful?

9. Do you spend an inordinate amount of time finding your drug of choice, consuming it, or recovering from using it?

Part II: Withdrawal Symptoms

Withdrawal symptoms vary from drug to drug. Withdrawal symptoms for various drugs (adapted from *DSM-IV*), including alcohol, opiates and opioids, amphetamines and similar drugs, cocaine, and the various types of sedatives, are listed below.

Alcohol withdrawal. After you have stopped drinking entirely or reduced your intake of alcohol for a few days, do you experience:

- A tremor of the hands or eyelids?

- Nausea or vomiting?

- Malaise or weakness?

- Physical hyperactivity (rapid heartbeat, sweating, elevated blood pressure)?

- Anxiety, depressed mood, or irritability?

- Transient hallucinations or illusions?

- Headache, insomnia, or grand mal seizures?

If you have experienced at least two of these symptoms and, in addition, these symptoms interfere substantially with your social relationships, employment, or other important areas of your life, then you suffer from alcohol withdrawal.

Opiate and opioid withdrawal. The opiates include opium, heroin, and morphine; opiates are those drugs that act like opiates. You must meet three of the following symptoms after several minutes or days of abstinence from or a reduction of opiate and opioid use or after taking a substance that counters the effects of an opiate or opioid in order to be considered in withdrawal.

- Depressed mood

- Nausea or vomiting

- Muscle aches

- Dilated pupils, goosebumps, or sweating

- Diarrhea

- Yawning

- Fever

- Insomnia

- Runny nose or eyes

These symptoms must cause significant difficulties in your life and must not be due to any other physical or mental disorders.

Amphetamine withdrawal. If, after several days or more of no longer taking or significantly reducing your intake of amphetamines or a similar drug, you feel depressed, irritable, or anxious, and in addition you experience two of the following symptoms for at least 24 hours, you can be considered to be suffering from amphetamine withdrawal:

- Psychomotor retardation (heavy feeling in the muscles, difficulty moving)

- Increased appetite

- Vivid, unpleasant dreams

The symptoms must not be caused by some other physical or mental disorder and must cause significant problems in the major areas of your life.

Cocaine withdrawal. Symptoms of cocaine withdrawal are similar to those of amphetamine withdrawal. If after several days or more of not using cocaine or reducing your use of it, you feel depressed, irritable, or anxious, and you experience two of the following symptoms, then you can consider yourself to be suffering from cocaine withdrawal:

- Fatigue

- Insomnia or hypersomnia (sleeping a lot)

- Psychomotor agitation (physical agitation and restlessness, for example, inability to sit still, twitching of one of the muscle groups, or a general inability to relax)

These symptoms must not be caused by some other physical or mental disorder.

Hypnotic or anxiolytic withdrawal. Hypnotic drugs, or sedatives, include various sleeping pills and tranquilizers, such as Nembutal, Seconal, Compazine, Noctec, Placidyl, Equanil, and Quaalude. The anxiolytic, or anxiety-reducing, drugs include librium and valium. If, after several weeks or more of not using or significantly reducing your usage of a sedative, hypnotic, or anxiolytic drug, you experience at least two of the following symptoms, you can be considered as having withdrawal symptoms from these drugs:

- Nausea or vomiting

- Hyperactivity of the autonomic system (rapid heartbeat, sweating)
- Anxiety or irritability
- Marked shaking or tremor of the hands, tongue, and eyelids
- Marked insomnia
- Temporary visual, tactile, or auditory hallucinations
- Psychomotor agitation
- Grand mal seizures

If you have two or more of these symptoms and they have persisted for at least a month, you are considered to be addicted to or dependent on the drug. These symptoms must not be caused by some other physical or mental disorder and must cause disturbances in major areas of your life in order to be considered sedative, hypnotic, or anxiolytic withdrawal.

Part III: Alcohol and Drug Abuse

It may be that you are not yet addicted, but that you are on the road to addiction via substance abuse. The following questions will help you determine, if, in fact, you do abuse drugs.

Drug abuse is considered less serious than drug dependency or addiction, but it can lead to addiction. Answer the following questions, bearing in mind that the words *drug* and *alcohol* are used interchangeably:

1. Do you continue to use psychoactive drugs despite knowing that if you keep using you will create or worsen any existing social, occupational, psychological, or physical problems you have?

2. Do you use psychoactive drugs in circumstances that endanger your physical health or your life? For example, do you drive intoxicated or high?

If you answered yes to one of the above questions and the situation has existed for at least one month or has occurred repeatedly over a longer period of time, then you can be considered a substance abuser. See "Getting Help," at the end of this chapter.

Assessing for Eating Disorders

If food is your addiction, you might be like an alcoholic. Alcoholics often sneak drinks and have bottles hidden in the closet. Similarly, you may eat alone and have bags of cookies hidden in the closet. Drinking to ease the pain of trauma and its aftermath has caused some social drinkers to cross over the line into alcoholism. Similarly, you may have crossed the line from an occasional binge to compulsive overeating, and if you binge and purge, to the hell of bulimia.

But there are other forms of eating disorder as well. If you have an eating disorder, you likely fall into one of three categories:

- Food-restricting (anorectic)—You are obsessed with not eating and feel a revulsion toward food. You are also obsessed with your body image and weight.

- Non–food-restricting (bulimic)—You at times limit food intake, but other times you binge and then use purging, laxatives, or excessive exercise to maintain a substandard weight. You may alternate between being obsessed with eating and being obsessed with not eating.

- Compulsive overeating—You binge, eat when you aren't hungry, or find it difficult to stop eating. You may hide or lie about your eating and feel worried or guilty about eating.

Record your answers to the following questions in your journal or in the margin.

Questionnaire: Anorexia Nervosa

According to *DSM-IV*, if you answer yes to *all* of the following questions, you are considered to be suffering from anorexia nervosa.

1. Is your body weight 15 percent below that expected for your age and height?

2. Are you intensely afraid of gaining weight or becoming fat, even though you are truly underweight?

3. Do you believe you are fat or overweight even though, in reality, you are not? Do parts of your body "feel fat" to you, even though the bathroom scales, other people, or your own eyes tell you that those parts are very thin?

4. If you are a woman, have you missed at least three menstrual periods in a row?

Questionnaire: Bulimia Nervosa

If you can answer yes to *all* of the following questions, you meet the *DSM-IV* criteria for bulimia nervosa:

1. Have you binged (eaten a large amount of food in a relatively short amount of time) at least twice a week for three months?

2. To compensate for the weight you think you might have gained due to your bingeing, have you made yourself vomit, used laxatives or diuretics, dieted or fasted, or exercised strenuously at least twice a week for three months?

3. When you binge or overeat, do you feel as if your eating is out of control—that you can't stop even if you want to?

4. Are you obsessed or overly concerned with your body shape and weight?

5. Do you binge, then either vomit, exercise excessively, or use laxatives, enemas, or diuretics during times when you are not anorectic?

Questionnaire: Other Eating Disorders

If you feel your eating is erratic or otherwise abnormal, but you do not meet the criteria for anorexia nervosa or bulimia nervosa, then you may fit into *DSM-IV* category called Eating Disorder, Not Otherwise Specified. Examples of these include the following:

- Making yourself vomit in order not to gain weight, even though you are not overweight and do not binge

- Having all the aspects of anorexia nervosa but still having your monthly menstrual flow

- Having all the symptoms of bulimia nervosa except that your binges occur less than twice a week or have persisted for less than three months

- Having all the aspects of anorexia nervosa except that your weight is within a normal range

- Reacting to eating small amounts of food by exercising, vomiting, taking laxatives, or otherwise trying to lose weight

- On a frequent basis, putting large amounts of food in your mouth, chewing it, then spitting it out

Questionnaire: Compulsive Overeating

Compulsive overeating is not classified as an eating disorder in *DSM-IV*, except perhaps under Eating Disorder, Not Otherwise Specified. However, since this addictive illness affects many trauma survivors, particularly women, a checklist for compulsive overeating is provided below. Compulsive overeating is an insidious addiction because overeating is not considered illegal or immoral, as are drug and alcohol addictions. Also, being overweight or overly interested in food is not outside the norm in our society.

1. Do you often feel depressed, guilty, angry, or inadequate?

2. Are you frequently on a rigid diet?

3. Do you regularly experience stomach aches or constipation?

4. Do you eat large quantities of food in a short period of time? Are these foods usually high-calorie, simple-carbohydrate foods that can be easily ingested (cookies, chips, candy)?

5. Do you eat in secret, hide food, or lie about your eating?

6. Have you ever stolen food or money to buy food so that you could start or continue a binge?

7. Do you feel guilt and remorse about your eating behavior?

8. Do you start eating even when you are not hungry?

9. Is it hard for you to stop eating even when you want to?

10. Do you eat to escape problems, to relax, or to have fun?

11. After finishing a meal, do you worry about making it to the next meal without getting hungry in between?

12. Have others expressed concern about your obsession with food?

13. Do you worry that your eating behavior is abnormal?

14. Do you fall asleep after eating?

If you have answered yes to five questions or more you may be a compulsive overeater (Matsakis 1990).

If you meet the criteria for anorexia, bulimia, compulsive overeating, or other form of eating disorder, it is relevant to your recovery from PTSD. See "Getting Help," at the end of this chapter.

Assessing for Compulsive Behavior

Like addiction or substance abuse, a compulsion is the repetition of an unwanted, irrational act. If you are addicted to an activity, on some level you probably know that your compulsion is hurting you more than it is helping you. However, such an admission alone, even with a sincere attempt to stop "cold turkey," will probably not prevent you from engaging again in compulsive gambling, overspending, compulsive sexual behavior, or other compulsive acts, because the compulsion serves a purpose—albeit poorly.

For example, the low self-esteem that can result from trauma or a nonsupportive childhood can motivate compulsive spending. The spending may be a means of giving to yourself or of giving to others so they will love you. Similarly, compulsive sexual activity may be a means of feeling loved and accepted, since sexual intercourse is an act that generally means love and acceptance. And gambling, like overspending and compulsive sexual activity, can be used to numb feelings and awareness of painful issues, as well as to provide a temporary high. Other compulsions work in similar ways—gambling, sex, and spending are simply three of the most common compulsive behaviors.

Compulsive behavior also mimics power, control, and mastery—the very qualities that were lost in the trauma and subsequent life events. In the end, however, these feelings of love and control are too fleeting to be truly healing.

The questionnaires that follow will help you determine whether your behavior constitutes a compulsive activity. Record your answers in your journal or in the margin.

Questionnaire: Compulsive Gambling

In the *DSM-IV*, compulsive gambling is called pathological gambling; it is classified as an impulse-control disorder. You meet the criteria for classification as a pathological gambler if you can answer yes to at least five of the following questions:

1. Are you preoccupied with gambling or with obtaining money to gamble?

2. Do you need to increase the size or frequency of your bets to generate the amount of excitement you look forward to having?

3. Have you tried to control or limit your gambling but been unsuccessful?

4. Do you become anxious or irritable when you try to control or stop your gambling?

5. Is your gambling a way of reducing the stress you feel or alleviating negative mood states, such as feelings of depression or helplessness?

6. Do you return to gamble the day after you lose money?

7. Do you hide the extent of your gambling from others?

8. Have you broken the law to obtain the money to gamble?

9. Do you continue to gamble even though you know the gambling can jeopardize your job, relationships, or certain life opportunities?

10. Do you rely on others to help you with financial crises caused by your gambling? (Your gambling also must not be a result of a manic episode or a manic-depressive illness.)

Questionnaire: Other Compulsive Behaviors

There are no formal criteria for determining whether you are a compulsive spender or engage in sexual or other behaviors in a compulsive manner. However, with regards to compulsive spending or compulsive sexual activity, as well as to other addictions and compulsions, there are questions you can consider:

1. Can you stop? What happens when you do stop? Do you experience physical or psychological withdrawal symptoms? For example, do you

you experience physical symptoms such as "the shakes," drowsiness, confusion, or even panic symptoms such as gagging or dizziness? Or perhaps you experience psychological symptoms such as anxiety, sadness, depression, numbing, or irritability?

2. To what extent has your behavior affected your life? Has it adversely affected your work or school involvement, social life, sex life, family life, or physical health?

3. Are you concerned about your behavior? If so, why does it trouble you?

If you feel you have lost the power of choice over your behavior, it may well be a compulsion. Similarly, if your behavior is disrupting your life so much that you, or significant others, are concerned, you may want to discuss your concerns with a qualified therapist.

Getting Help

If you have met any of the criteria for depression, addiction, substance abuse, or compulsive behavior, you should seek help in dealing with the problem—few people are successful at doing so on their own. Furthermore, dealing just with the symptom (the depression, addiction, or compulsion) is inadequate. Only healing the pain behind the symptom has real power. Remember, aside from any hereditary or other biological factors, addictions and compulsions are basically means of coping with anger, loss, and other forms of emotional pain, and with any clinical depression that may have resulted from that pain. Until these feelings are dealt with, the behavior tends to persist.

Regardless of what program or therapist you choose to help you with your problem, be sure that the counselor has knowledge and expertise in that area. Appendix A gives general information on obtaining professional assistance. Appendix B lists organizations and written materials that offer help with specific PTSD-related problems.

3

Feelings, Thoughts, and Traumatic Events

In ancient Greek mythology, Poseidon was the god of the ocean, rivers, and lakes and of earthquakes. He was also the god of emotions and symbolized the unconscious.

In contrast to Poseidon stood his brother Zeus, the king of gods and god of the sky. Zeus valued logic, clear thinking, and rational planning. As far as Zeus was concerned, emotions, especially the turbulent emotions Poseidon represented, were a nuisance—and a threat. In Zeus's view, emotions interfered with the maintenance of an orderly universe, or at least one he could control.

Zeus lived at the top of Mount Olympus, close to the sky and as far from his disorderly brother's home at the bottom of the sea as he could get. However, when Poseidon caused the oceans to storm, rivers and lakes to flood, or the earth to tremble, Zeus and everyone else had to pay attention to Poseidon and respect his power.

The message of this myth is obvious. No matter how much you, like Zeus, would like to keep your feelings at a distance or submerged in the ocean of your unconscious, it cannot be done. If Zeus, king of the gods, could not make his brother shut up and go away, then neither can you command your emotions to remain silent.

Feelings are real and powerful things. Although you cannot see or touch them, feelings can heavily influence your behavior, your thoughts, even your spiritual life. No matter how you push down your feelings, try to make them go away, or pretend that they don't exist or are relatively unimportant, they will eventually surface and clamor for attention: Here I am. Here I am. Deal with me now! In fact, the further you push your emotions away, the more violently they are bound to erupt. One of the most important components of the healing process is to find and come to terms with your feelings. At first, as these feelings emerge, they may seem to wash away what you had considered the foundations of your life—your views of yourself and the world. Your relationships can be affected, and you may not be able to think as clearly as you used to. At times, you may even fear that you are losing yourself.

But in finding your emotions you do not lose yourself, but instead find yourself. In addition to your feelings, you also find some of the missing pieces of the trauma. These missing pieces, and the feelings related to them, need to be acknowledged and understood for you to become whole.

For a while, and perhaps for quite some time, the emotional upheavals caused by the healing process might seem to carry you further away from, rather than closer to, serenity and peace of mind. Eventually, however, your psychological earthquakes and floods will subside and you can build yourself anew.

Poseidon was the god not only of turmoil, but of infinite possibilities. When he crossed the sea in his chariot, drawn by golden-maned horses symbolizing beauty and power, the sea became smooth and calm before him.

Learning About Feelings

Your journey back to health and well-being is a journey of increasing awareness of your feelings. Indeed, the process of healing is dependent on understanding your feelings and learning to manage them in ways that do not isolate you from others or otherwise harm you.

But you cannot feel those feelings unless you first identify them. This section will help you begin to become aware of your emotional life. As you proceed in this book, as well as in other healing efforts, your awareness of your feelings will grow.

This process takes time, however; you'll need to be patient. Trees don't grow in a day. Babies don't run before they walk. You are no different. You cannot expect yourself to become a master at self-awareness without first taking a few baby steps. In fact, learning about your feelings is a lifelong journey—one that begins with learning to identify and label your feelings and to differentiate your feelings from your thoughts.

The Link Between Feeling Identification and Feeling Awareness

"Getting in touch with your feelings" is a common phrase nowadays, but what does it really mean? You might be confused about it, as was Harry, a survivor of child abuse.

> "This might sound stupid coming from a 50-year-old
> man, but I don't know what to say when you ask me about

my feelings. My mother used to beat me a lot, and she was always too drunk to take me to the doctor when I was sick. How did I feel about that? Sometimes I can't remember how I felt, or even if I felt at all. I don't even know what to call it when I do remember.

"I know when I get mad, and I know when I cry. But is keeping my mouth shut when my wife yells at me a feeling? What are the names and the words for feelings? Just what is a feeling?"

Harry's questions were not stupid at all. Very few people learn about feelings unless someone in their life took the time to teach them—which in Harry's case clearly had not happened. But such a teacher would have first identified the feeling for him by putting a name or label on it. In addition, this teacher would have distinguished different levels of the same feeling. For example, Harry used the word *anger* to describe every feeling from mild irritation to extreme annoyance to murderous rage—he had never learned how to accurately differentiate and label the various degrees of emotion.

What was worse, though, was that Harry had often been beaten for showing any feelings at all. Child abuse survivors almost always have special difficulties recognizing their feelings. In the first place, they have learned to be attuned to the feelings of their abuser, instead of their own, for purposes of survival. Secondly, trauma by its very nature, because of the powerful feelings involved, leads to numbing, suppression and various forms of dissociation—also for purposes of survival. This combination forces abuse survivors to be out of touch with their emotions.

Regardless of the kind of trauma you have survived, it is critical that you learn what a feeling is and be able to give it a name. To do that you need to have at your command a vocabulary of words to describe your various feelings. The following sections, adapted from *The Anxiety and Phobia Workbook*, by Edmund Bourne (1990), will help you label your feelings and distinguish them from thoughts. Included is a Feelings List—a list of words that label and describe emotions.

Note: If you have been in therapy or a 12-step program, some of the material in this section may already be familiar. Nonetheless, it may be helpful to review it, since later sections will build on these concepts.

What Is a Feeling?

A feeling is neither a thought nor an action. "I should have . . ." is not a feeling; it's a thought. "My friend forgot to pick me up for the party because I'm not smart enough" is also a thought. It is different from feeling inferior, rejected, angry, depressed, or disappointed because you were forgotten. Similarly, feeling angry at the friend or thinking about hitting, cursing, or stealing from that friend in revenge is not the same as actually acting on those thoughts.

Feelings vs. Thoughts. Although feelings and thoughts are not the same, they are often intimately related. Some feelings arise out of the way you perceive things and the thoughts you have as a result. For example, suppose that during an interview for a job the interviewer had a blank look on her face the entire time. You might leave the interview *thinking*, I did poorly. I'll never get the job, and consequently *feeling* incompetent, inferior, and dejected.

But suppose you then learned that an hour before your appointment, the interviewer had been told of the death of a friend. How might that information change your thinking about your performance in the interview and your subsequent feelings about yourself?

Or, to return to the previous example, if your friend failed to pick you up because she had car trouble or fell asleep after a hard day, your thoughts and feelings would probably be entirely different than if you assumed it had something to do with you personally.

Later on in this chapter, you will begin to learn to distinguish your thoughts about the specific events of your particular trauma from your feelings. As you slowly acquire a more accurate, more concrete, and more rational view of what happened during the trauma, and why those events occurred, some of the more negative feelings you have about yourself, others, and the trauma itself may change. However, certain feelings will remain.

You cannot "think away" the trauma entirely by changing the way you think. There is no magic wand that can take away all the loss and anger associated with trauma. But you can considerably reduce unnecessary and unfounded self-blame, guilt, and anger at others by learning how to distinguish your thoughts from your feelings regarding the trauma.

The Characteristics of Feelings. Unlike thoughts, feelings involve a physical reaction. Excitement can cause perspiration and an increased respiration rate, for example. Sadness can result in tears or at least a "weepy" feeling. Joy can make you laugh or smile. Physical pain can be caused by other emotions. Whatever the feeling, it is not "all in your head."

Feelings also often appear in combination—they are more often complex than simple. For instance, a parent whose child is a little late coming home from a date might be both worried and irritated. "The common expression *sorting out* [your] feelings reflects the fact that you can feel several things at once" (Bourne 1990).

For trauma survivors, anger and grief tend to go hand in hand. Often guilt is involved as well. Humiliation, which is caused all too often by the reactions of others who do not understand trauma survivors' plight, can also be a mixed feeling, involving anger, hurt, and sadness.

Feelings can also be contagious. Friends' happiness can be infectious—think about how hard it would be not to join in with a group of people who are laughing. Unfortunately, it is just as easy to "catch" emotions that are less than joyous. Childhood abuse survivors in particular are susceptible to taking on the feelings of others—having learned to do so as a survival mechanism. On the other hand, if you are in numbing due to the trauma, the emotions of others may not affect you at all.

Tuning In to Your Feelings

At any given time, you are feeling something, even when it seems otherwise. When you feel at peace with yourself, for example, you may not think you are feeling anything. But you are in fact experiencing that wonderful feeling of serenity.

Some of your feelings may be at the surface of your awareness and thus easy to identify. Others you may have to dig for. Some signs of suppressed feelings are muscle tension, physical pain with no medical cause, depression, ennui or boredom, agitation or anxiety, dizziness, and involuntary urges to overeat, overspend, abuse alcohol or drugs, or hurt yourself.

Try the following techniques to help you tune in to exactly what you are feeling right now:

1. Quiet your body—or move it. The most commonly prescribed methods for getting in touch with your feelings involve getting inside yourself, by sitting still for a few minutes, meditating, or practicing muscle relaxation (see Chapter 5). However, if you suffer from bouts of extreme physical tension and anxiety, sitting still or meditating can be agitating, rather than soothing. Therefore, you may choose to "quiet" your body by moving it through exercise, dance, or physical labor.

2. Ask yourself, What am I feeling? Don't expect to know right away; give yourself some time to discover your feelings. Also recognize, and indeed expect, that you may be feeling more than one emotion.

   Alternatively, if you are in a numb state, you may not be able to identify any feelings at all. If you are, do not be overly concerned about it. The numbing may serve a very important purpose: protecting you against feelings that are too distressing or too overwhelming for you to handle.

Bear in mind as you practice these techniques that it is very common and normal for trauma survivors to have "stuck points" in identifying their feelings. When this happens, don't berate yourself for not being able to come up with an answer. Instead congratulate yourself for trying. To help yourself get unstuck, you may also want to refer to the Feelings List, which follows.

During the course of this book you will often be asked to identify your feelings. As you do so it's important to keep the following in mind:

- Feelings are neither good nor bad, right nor wrong; feelings just are, they exist. You need not, and should not, judge yourself negatively just because you have or don't have a particular feeling.

- Feelings don't last forever. No matter what you are feeling, eventually it will lift and another emotion will take its place.

- When a strong feeling comes, you do not have to act on it. All you have to do is recognize it and feel it.

- The process of getting at your feelings is important. Try not to block it with excessive self-judgment; save that for your behavior, not your feelings and thoughts. Your actions affect other people. How you feel and what you think is no one's business but your own.

Sad, Mad, Glad, or Scared?—A Feelings List

There are four basic emotions: sadness, anger, joy, and fear. But there are many degrees and shadings of each one; the list that follows gives names to some of them. You may find it helpful to refer back to this list (from Bourne 1990) throughout the book, whenever you are asked, How did you feel?

Words associated with sadness: Defeated, Dejected, Depressed, Despairing, Desperate, Devastated, Disappointed, Discouraged, Embarrassed, Guilty, Helpless, Hopeless, Hurt, Ignored, Inadequate, Incompetent, Inferior, Inhibited, Insecure, Isolated, Lonely, Melancholy, Miserable, Misunderstood, Muddled, Needy, Pessimistic, Preoccupied, Pressured, Regretful, Rejected, Remorseful, Self-conscious, Shy, Sorry, Stupid, Tired, Trapped, Troubled, Unappreciated, Unattractive, Uncertain, Uncomfortable, Unfulfilled, Useless, Victimized, Violated, Vulnerable, Weary, Worn Out, Worried.

Words associated with anger: Annoyed, Bitter, Contemptuous, Distrustful, Enraged, Exasperated, Furious, Hateful, Hostile, Humiliated, Hurt, Impatient, Irritated, Outraged, Overwhelmed, Provoked, Resentful, Stubborn, Touchy, Unappreciated, Uneasy.

Words associated with joy: Affectionate, Alive, Amused, Beautiful, Brave, Calm, Capable, Caring, Cheerful, Cherished, Comfortable, Competent, Concerned, Confident, Content, Courageous, Curious, Delighted, Desirable, Eager, Excited, Forgiving, Friendly, Fulfilled, Generous, Giving, Good, Grateful, Happy, Hopeful, Humorous, Joyful, Lovable, Loved, Loving, Loyal, Passionate, Peaceful, Playful, Pleased, Proud, Quiet, Relaxed, Relieved, Respected, Safe, Supportive, Sympathetic, Tender, Thankful, Thrilled, Trusted, Understanding, Understood, Unique, Valuable, Warm, Witty, Wonderful, Worthwhile, Youthful.

Words associated with fear: Afraid, Apprehensive, Ashamed, Desperate, Devastated, Fearful, Frantic, Indecisive, Helpless, Hopeless, Horrified, Insecure, Panicked, Pressured, Scared, Self-destructive, Self-hating, Terrified, Threatened, Timid, Trapped, Uncertain, Uncomfortable, Victimized, Violated, Vulnerable.

Exercise: *Separating Feelings from Thoughts*

If you're like most people, you probably need some practice in distinguishing your feelings from your thoughts. This exercise is designed to do just that.

For one week, carry a small notebook, and every two or three hours jot down the time and the thoughts and feelings you're having on the left-hand side of the paper. Also make a notation any time you have a particularly strong or troublesome thought or feeling. An example page is shown here:

Sample: Saturday

Time	Thoughts and Feelings	Thought or Feeling?
10:00	I'm angry at myself for staying up too late last night.	Feeling
12:00	He's probably angry at me for what I said last night.	Thought
3:00	I should do better at school.	Thought
3:15	I hate myself for not doing better at school.	Feeling

On the right-hand side, indicate whether what you are experiencing is a thought or a feeling. If you have trouble deciding, reread the preceding sections, and try discussing your dilemma with other people you trust: your therapist, a friend, or family member. The distinction should also become clearer as you read on in the book.

If you have identified your experience as a feeling, try to identify what feeling or feelings you experienced. Talk to others or refer to the Feelings List if you need help.

The next sections in this chapter build on the work you have done here in recognizing and distinguishing your thoughts and feelings, so give yourself some time to become accustomed to the process. If you need more than a week of recording your thoughts and feelings, that's fine. Remember, the healing process is different for everyone. You need to work at your own pace. When you're ready to go on, you will know it.

Remembering the Trauma

In the same way that it is necessary to feel your emotions to be able to have a fully realized life, you will need to remember your trauma in order to heal from it. You may think you already remember more than you want to of the experience, or you may remember very little of the actual event.

In either case, one of the principal tools of this book (or indeed any therapeutic treatment) is to reconstruct what happened. We will be returning to the trauma repeatedly throughout the book, but what you will find is that, as the healing process progresses, your perceptions of the event change as you discover and learn more about the factors that make up your PTSD.

To begin with though, you need to record what you currently remember about the trauma. It's important to be as detailed as you can. For example, in her work with rape victims, S. L. Williams (1990) found that many of her clients tended to give detailed descriptions of what they did before the rape, but failed to truly describe the rape itself. They would write, "I had toast and coffee for breakfast. I wore a blue dress. I walked to the bus stop. Then I was raped."

Dr. Williams had her clients rewrite their accounts to include as many graphic and sensual details as they could remember, including what the rapist looked like, what he smelled like, and the particulars of the room or environment in which the rape occurred (S. L. Williams 1990).

These details are important not because they are or were traumatic in themselves, but because similar details in your present life may be triggers that produce intense emotional—and even physical—reactions. You may even be organizing your life to avoid confronting similar details in the present. For example, if a tornado hit while you were frying chicken, you may now become nauseated as well as sad whenever you smell fried food. You might find yourself leaving social gatherings where fried chicken is being served, or driving out of your way to avoid seeing and smelling fast-food restaurants.

Exercise: Recording the Traumatic Event

In your journal, describe what happened immediately before, during, and after your trauma. (If you have not already done so, be sure to read the introduction to this book, paying particular attention to the sections entitled "Cautions" and "How to Use This Book.") If you have endured more than one traumatic event, describe each one. Since we will be adding to this description several times, you eventually will need 15 to 20 blank pages for each event.

As you describe your traumatic incidents, make them come alive with as much sensory detail as possible. For example, if you are a combat veteran describing a traumatic battle, mention the temperature and terrain, the weapons or other objects you were carrying, your medical and physical condition, the noises and sounds you heard, and any other details you can remember.

As you list the events, describe your thoughts and feelings as the traumatic event progressed. Also describe what others thought or felt about what was happening or about you. You may only "know" what you thought they were thinking or feeling, but write that down.

Take as much time with this as you need. And don't try to do it all at once. If you start feeling overwhelmed, stop. Then come back to it later. If you can't remember everything now, don't worry about it, we'll be returning to it later. You can always add details then, or indeed, at any point between now and then.

Don't be self-conscious about the writing you do in your journal. The idea is to remember and record events, thoughts, and feelings—not to write perfect English. No one ever needs to see this but yourself, unless you choose otherwise.

When you've written down as much as you can remember, do one more thing: congratulate yourself for being willing to look at and deal with these events. It takes a lot of courage.

Self-Blame and Survivor Guilt

The devastating event that occurred to you is important in itself. Also important, however, are your attitudes toward that event. Whether you have survived one trauma or several, your beliefs about why the trauma occurred and the way you judge your behavior during and after the traumatic episode are going to heavily influence the degree to which you continue to suffer.

Do you blame yourself for the traumatic event? Or do you fault yourself for some of the ways you reacted, or did not react, while the trauma was occurring? If you do, once again, you are not alone. It is not uncommon for trauma survivors to blame themselves in some way, large or small, for the event itself, its negative outcome, or both. Certain categories of trauma survivors, for example abused women and children, incest survivors, and rape victims, are known for blaming themselves almost entirely for the abuse they have experienced.

"I'm 55 years old and have spent 25 years in therapy hearing that it wasn't my fault. Yet it still makes sense to me that if Daddy burnt my hand it must have been because I was bad," a child abuse survivor explains. "Blaming myself isn't logical, but logic has nothing to do with it."

Similarly, sometimes dedicated policemen, firefighters, rescue workers, and medical workers berate themselves mercilessly for sometimes being unable to save a life. Like combat veterans, these professionals sometimes perceive their normal human limitations as personal failings.

Even some survivors of natural disasters, concentration camps, and crimes—people almost anyone would view as totally blameless—blame themselves for the traumas inflicted upon them. Some of these individuals conclude it was some mistake or even a sin on their part that caused the event to occur, or that caused its negative outcome to be so serious. Even some cancer patients likewise feel that they are being punished for some misbehavior in their past.

The Origins of Self-Blame and Survivor Guilt

If you blame yourself for the traumatic event or for your behavior during the event, this does not mean you are a masochist. Neither does it suggest that you enjoy mentally torturing yourself.

Instead, self-blame arises in part from the fact that powerlessness and helplessness are two of the worst feelings any human being can experience. Yet being and feeling powerless or helpless in the face of great danger is the very definition of trauma. However, people prefer to think that they are able to control their lives, so it is easier to blame themselves for negative events than to acknowledge that sometimes life is unfair or arbitrary and innocent people can be victimized for no reason.

Consequently, to maintain a sense of being in control you may view yourself, rather than chance, as responsible for one or more aspects of the trauma—perhaps for all of it. In this way, self-blame can be a means of regaining the power that was lost during the traumatic event.

Survivor guilt is another form of self-blame. Do you feel guilty because you made it out alive and others didn't, or because you were less injured than others? It is not uncommon for trauma survivors to feel this way.

Survivor guilt is something other than just compassion for those who have suffered more than you. It is also a way of saying, If I had suffered more, you would have suffered less. Such thinking is not logical, but it makes sense emotionally. It can be a defense against the pain you feel at seeing others hurt.

Survivor guilt can also be seen as hearkening back to atavistic notions about making sacrifices to the gods to assure a desired outcome. With survivor guilt, the idea is that by punishing yourself, you can undo the damage, or at least keep bad things from happening again. But, of course, it doesn't really work that way.

Survivor guilt has one additional aspect: gratitude. It is difficult to accept being grateful that it was someone else who suffered. "It sounds heartless," survivors will say, "but if someone had to die, I'm glad it was somebody else, not me." However hard this feeling is to face, it is nothing more than an expression of the natural and vital instinct for self-preservation.

Accepting Guilt Feelings. If you suffer from self-blame, respect it. Even if you yourself, or others, can easily see that the self-blame is irrational, you need to respect your feelings. For example, you might have self-blame regarding an event such as an earthquake, a hurricane, or some other event that is clearly beyond human control. When you tell others you feel guilty, they may open their mouths wide with disbelief. But your task, at least for the moment, is to simply recognize your own emotion and not disparage it.

Eventually, you will need to examine any guilt you feel, both to see how closely it matches objective reality and to determine exactly where the responsibility for the event truly lies. But for now do not be afraid, in writing in your journal or in talking to your therapist or others who understand PTSD, to discuss the ways in which you feel responsible for the traumatic event or its outcome. Furthermore, try not to blame yourself for blaming yourself. Self-blame and guilt are entirely normal following any type of disaster or loss.

"But what if my carelessness or thoughtlessness did cause (or significantly contribute to) the trauma?" you might ask. "The way I responded resulted in others being injured," you may state with certainty.

If you were raped while walking in what you knew was a dangerous location, or your home was burglarized when you left the door unlocked, or you are a combat soldier who accidentally killed one of your comrades, then you might state with some legitimacy that your actions contributed to the trauma's taking place or to its negative outcome. You may in fact have made a mistake, perhaps several mistakes. However, you need to view your behavior from a trauma perspective.

Looking at the Bigger Picture

In trying to understand your trauma, you cannot look solely at your own behavior; you need a wider, more complete perspective. For example, like many trauma survivors, you may have forgotten or dismissed the conditions that existed at the time.

To work from the preceding examples: if you are a rape victim who feels she set herself up for sexual assault by walking in a dangerous neighborhood, you need to put the rape in its social context. It may be true that statistically more rapes occur in certain neighborhoods than others and that in the future you may choose to avoid those areas. However it is also true that rape occurs independent of location—women are frequently attacked by strangers, in their supposedly secure homes. Fundamentally, rape is the result of sexism and violence, which run rampant in our society, and not the result of individual actions by a particular woman.

Similarly, burglary victims need to remember that even double-bolted doors are often insufficient deterrents to professional burglars. In other words, any reasonable precaution might not have been enough. And, in the case of combat, it is war, not the warrior, that creates the chaos and confusion that make "friendly fire" accidents happen so easily.

If you feel partly, or entirely, responsible for what happened to you, discuss it with your therapist or understanding others. They should be able to help you get a better perspective on your role in what happened.

"I Just Couldn't Think". Some trauma survivors report that during a crime, a vehicular accident, natural or technological disaster, or other traumatic situation, they made a decision that in retrospect was not the wisest. If you feel likewise, you may wonder why you "couldn't think." This impairment in your reasoning powers also needs to be considered from a trauma perspective.

During the traumatic event, you were probably thinking to the best of your ability—under the circumstances. However, the turbulent emotions and high anxiety level that trauma creates sometimes militate against calm, rational thinking. This varies from one individual to the next. Some people, for example, remain remarkably coolheaded during the traumatic episode, but they are not in the majority. They mainly appear on the movie screen, not in real life.

In contrast, during a traumatic episode, most people's judgment abilities are affected, to one degree or another, by the very real dangers involved in the situation and the strong fears such dangers can produce. Thus for many people, it is difficult if not impossible to think clearly under extreme pressure.

Furthermore, there may be biological bases for this "inability to think" under stress. As you remember, when the body goes into an emergency alert during trauma, it normally has available to it three responses: fight, flight, and freezing. Notice that "think and reason slowly and carefully" is not one of these responses.

Perceptual Distortion. Because trauma is by its nature sudden and overwhelming, people are often not able to adequately assess the situation, no matter how intelligent, brave, or physically fit they are. In addition, it is often difficult for trauma victims even to realize that the trauma is occurring.

Tom Williams, a psychologist who has worked with police officers, armed robbery and assault victims, war veterans, and former prisoners of war, has discovered in his work that sensory data often becomes distorted during traumatic events.

"Some victims," he writes, "report perceptual changes in which time is altered and events seem to be happening in slow motion. Visual perceptions may be modified so that people sometimes have a derealized 'out of body' experience, or at least feel that they are simply observing rather than participating in the trauma. Another frequent perceptual alteration is a hysterical-like tunnel vision that focuses on the trauma scene itself to the exclusion of the rest of the environment. For instance, a robbery victim focuses on a weapon directed at him or her and doesn't recollect what the robber was like, what was happening, or who was standing next to the robber."

In this initial denial and shock, it is easy to make "mistakes," or to act in a manner that later confuses you and causes you to doubt and criticize yourself (T. Williams 1987b).

False Guilt. Under traumatic conditions, errors in judgment are to be expected. However, Edward Kubany (1994) found that even people who made remarkably reasonable decisions under conditions of great stress later judged themselves at fault when an unexpected event occurred that caused a negative outcome. The original decision might have been the best decision that could have been made, given the information and resources available, yet because of an unpredictable turn of events, which frequently happens in trauma, the people judged themselves as guilty.

The false guilt these people have stems from the mistaken notion that they could have known better. For example, when his town was under enemy fire, Dimitri had to decide whether to keep his family with him or send them to a safe zone on the next available vehicle. There was little food in the town, the drinking water was contaminated, and disease was rampant. Although there was risk in sending his family away, it was almost certain that someone in the family would die of disease or famine if the family tried to stay together. Painful as the decision was, Dimitri made the wisest choice possible given the information available to him, and his family boarded a truck headed for a safe zone.

Two weeks later Dimitri found out that the truck had run off a mountain road and exploded, killing all the occupants, when the brakes failed. To this day, Dimitri blames himself for the loss of his family. Yet he had no way of knowing that the truck's brakes would fail.

Catch 22 Guilt. A second kind of guilt, Catch 22 guilt, is prevalent in situations where none of the choices are acceptable. "The situation is no-win or Catch 22," writes Kubany (1994), because "all available courses of action have repugnant consequences and involve repudiation of some important value."

For example, in concentration camp situations, typically entire family units are punished for the "misbehavior" of one family member. In such camps, coming to the defense of another prisoner is forbidden and is considered a punishable defense. When Angela observed camp guards beating her grandmother, she was in a Catch-22 situation. If she intervened to help her grandmother, not only would she and her grandmother be severely punished, or killed, but the rest of her family would suffer as well. On the other hand, by not trying to assist her grandmother, she was violating her value system and some of her deepest feelings. Whether she stood up to the guards (putting her grandmother and other family members at risk) or whether she sat by in silence, Angela felt she was betraying her family.

Similarly, a situation that still confronts too many abused children is that the perpetrator threatens to harm another family member or a pet if the child informs the authorities of the abuse. However, if the child doesn't tell about the abuse, he or she is condemned to endure it.

Another example occurs in combat. In many situations, it is difficult to tell friend from foe. To hesitate to kill may mean your death. Yet to react violently immediately may cause the death of an ally.

Exercise: Self-Blame and Survivor Guilt

As a trauma survivor, it is critical that you identify any feelings of self-blame and guilt you may have. This exercise builds on the writing you did earlier about the trauma, so turn to those pages in your journal now. Then, for each traumatic event, do some writing on the following questions. As always, if you begin to feel overwhelmed or experience another of the warning signs listed in the introduction, stop doing the exercise. You can always come back to it.

1. In what ways, large or small (if any) do you blame yourself for the event's occurrence?

2. Do you blame yourself for the way you acted or didn't act during the trauma? If so, why?

3. Do you feel responsible for the extent of the injuries or the damage or other negative results of the trauma? In what ways?

You still may not remember the event completely. However, based on what you do remember, make as complete a self-blame list as possible. Be as specific and detailed as possible. Closely examining these self-blame statements is fundamental to your healing.

Include both rational and irrational thoughts on your list—the "crazy" thoughts may be the most important ones. For example, someone who had been abused as a child might write the following:

"I blame myself for my father beating me because I spilt the milk on his newspaper when I was five years old. I don't know if I spilt it by accident or on purpose because I was mad at him for not buying me a bike for my birthday and I knew that he loved to read his morning paper without any interruptions. I think I spilt the milk by accident, but I may have been just trying to get back at him. I don't know, but I do know that if I wasn't such a sloppy kid, the beatings would have never happened."

Other examples include the following:

"The earthquake happened because I was leading a sinful life and God was trying to punish me."

"When I had to leave my foxhole because of my injured arm, my buddy took my place. A few minutes later he was blown up. I had been ordered to get medical treatment, but I still feel guilty because if I had stayed in my place, he would be alive today."

Remember also to write about the aftereffects of the event. Once again, remember that this is not a writing contest. Your sentences and thoughts can be long, complicated, and garbled.

For example, a battered woman might write this:

> "I blame myself for my son's depression and emotional problems while I was married to John because I blame myself for the beatings because I should have been more mature when I was 19 and seen that John was capable of violence and never married him at all. I blame myself because I didn't measure up to John's expectations and that's why I was beaten. If I had been a better wife, I wouldn't have gotten beaten and my son would not have been affected. The beatings were also my fault because after a few beatings I hated my husband. It's a sin to hate and the rest of the beatings were partly my punishment for hating him and for causing my son emotional damage."

A Closer Look at Self-Blame. As part of the preceding exercise, you need to examine specific behaviors, emotions, or personality traits that emerged during the traumatic event for which you feel guilty or ashamed. The following list identifies some of the common sources of guilt and shame among trauma survivors. (Sexual abuse survivors have additional sources of shame, which will be discussed in more detail in Chapter 13.) Use this list as a starting point. If one of the characteristics applies to you, write about it in your journal.

I believe that the traumatic event or its negative consequences were due, in whole or in part, to

- An innocent mistake on my part

- My general inability to make good decisions

- A one-time act of incompetence

- My general lack of intelligence

- A one-time thoughtless act on my part

- My general carelessness and failure to take adequate precautions

- An impulsive or emotionally immature act on my part

- My general lack of emotional maturity

- My lack of skill in a particular area

- My general inability to learn

- A specific act or feeling that I feel is immoral or not right
- My generally sinful or bad nature

Self-Esteem and Self-Blame

We live in a culture that, in general, values self-confident, socially outgoing people over those who are introspective and full of self-doubt and remorse. But true mental health requires a balance between self-confidence and self-doubt. Self-confidence is necessary for normal functioning, but perpetually self-confident people are usually arrogant and shallow. Those who never question themselves are unable to grow.

Also, no one can be "together" all of the time. Eventually everyone, no matter how fortunate, encounters a situation that baffles or breaks them. Some people seem unaffected by a major loss or crisis, but their apparent solidity is built on shaky ground. Externally, it may seem as if they are handling the situation, but in reality they are either denying or hiding their emotions under a calm facade.

You, on the other hand, are in the process of acquiring skills for handling life's inevitable blows—a process that requires considerable self-examination. The work you have done so far in this book is part of that process, including the realizations you may have come to in the last section—that you see yourself as blameworthy or deficient in some areas.

Having those negative feelings toward yourself can be very painful. So it may be comforting for you to know that the low self-esteem or other bad feelings you may have about yourself are not immutable parts of your personality, and that low self-esteem is, for a variety of reasons, common among trauma survivors.

Origins of Low Self-Esteem

Consider the feelings you had about yourself prior to the traumatic event. What was the state of your self-esteem? If you are like many people, there were probably aspects of yourself you were proud of and aspects you wanted to change. However, you may have suffered from low self-esteem due to a lack of affirming experiences as a child or as an adult. You could, for example, have acquired low self-esteem as a result of a parent devaluing or belittling you in some way.

If you entered the traumatic situation with relatively low self-esteem, then the trauma may have increased your negative feelings about yourself. Alternatively, if you entered the traumatic situation with relatively high self-esteem or with a mixed view of yourself, the trauma may have created serious self-doubts.

In part, as will be explained more fully in the next chapter, this low self-esteem comes from internalizing the attitudes of others. However, it is also largely due to the self-blame trauma survivors feel.

The good news is that since much, if not most, of your self-blame stems from the traumatic event, there is considerable hope that once you better understand the trauma and how it affected you, you can be delivered from some of the negative feelings you have about yourself.

Exercise: Self-Blame and Your Self-Esteem

To begin with, you need to identify the ways in which the trauma has affected your self-esteem. Keeping in mind your writing on self-blame, write in your journal on this issue. You may want to use the following list as a guide.

As a result of the trauma, I now see myself as

- Lacking in intelligence

- Less intelligent than I thought I was

- Evil or bad

- Less desirable sexually

- Unworthy of love or affection

- Ugly, disgusting, or deficient in some way

- Emotionally abnormal

- A very angry, hostile person

- Not as good and honorable as I used to be

- Inadequate in many ways

- Difficult to talk to

- Difficult to live with

- Unlovable

Exercise: The Effects of Self-Blame on Your Present Life

Take some time now to think about how you felt as you did the preceding exercises on self-blame. In your journal, use these questions to summarize your reactions to completing the self-blame and self-esteem exercises.

1. How did it feel to look at and write about the ways you blame yourself and any other negative feelings you have about yourself? Did you feel angry, sad, confused, or afraid?

2. Did the preceding exercises require considerable effort or thought on your part, or were they easy to complete?

3. Were you amazed at the number of ways you took responsibility for the traumatic event or saw yourself in a negative light, or were you already all too well aware of all these thoughts and feelings?

4. Can you identify any of the feelings you had while completing the exercises on self-blame, or did you have no feelings at all? Did completing the exercises put you in a numb state, or did they at any time make you feel hyper, agitated, or even hostile, like you wanted to tear up this book, for example?

5. Now consider whether the feelings and other reactions you had in response to completing the self-blame and negative self-esteem exercises are at all similar to the feelings and reactions you have when someone or something reminds you of the traumatic event, especially of those aspects of the event that tend to make you feel guilty or ashamed.

6. Can you identify three or four situations in which you reacted in such a manner? Reflect back over the past week or month. Did anyone, or anything, touch your "guilt and shame" button? If so, how did you react?

The following are examples of typical reactions to such situations; in this case the speakers are a former battered wife, a survivor of a fire, and a combat veteran:

> "I saw a newspaper article saying that divorce was bad for children, and it touched off my guilt about divorcing my husband. But underneath that guilt was guilt about not having been able to stop the violence. Despite all the therapy I've had, I still feel that if I had been a better wife—prettier, more pleasing, more something—he would have stopped abusing me and we would have had a good marriage. After reading the article, I felt enraged, like I wanted to kill the person who wrote it."

> "The grocery store clerk mentioned that one of her relatives had been in an earthquake in California. She was only trying to be friendly, but it reminded me of the fire. I didn't get hurt, but two of my neighbors and my dog died. I shut down entirely. I couldn't smile or cry. For hours I felt dead inside, and I don't go to that store anymore."

> "I don't know why, but something made me remember how I hit some little children who were begging for food after a firefight. It seemed okay then. Everybody was doing it, but now I can't stand thinking about it. If therapy is going to make me think about these things, I think I'll quit because after thinking about those kids I went around for days as if I was in a black cloud."

In your journal, write about your reactions to events that touched off any of your shame or guilt associated with the traumatic event.

After you have done some writing on this issue, you may begin to see some relationships between the trauma and some of your problems in coping with daily life today. Part of your healing involves becoming aware, little by little, of the ways in which the trauma continues to affect your feelings about yourself and your reactions to people and situations in the present.

Countering Self-Blame

Some of your low self-esteem may stem from "victim thinking"—seeing yourself as having been totally helpless or ineffectual before the onslaught of the trauma. However, you must have had some strengths and survivor skills during your traumas or you would not be alive and sane enough to read this book. You may have been victimized during the trauma, but that does not mean that you were totally passive or totally blameworthy. Nor does it mean that today you are totally unable to meet some of your present-day goals.

In future chapters, you will examine each of the self-blame statements you recorded above to see if they contain faulty thinking. For now, however, you will start to balance some of your critical self-judgments by recognizing some ways you feel you responded positively.

Exercise: Identifying Your Strengths

For each of the traumas you listed in your journal, identify those thoughts and actions on your part about which you feel some pride. Don't worry about seeming conceited. Just make a list of all the positive qualities you can think of.

You may want to begin as follows: "As a result of the way I acted and felt during the trauma, I now see myself as . . ." Consider the following list of possibilities as you write in your journal:

- Brave
- Clever, intelligent, resourceful
- Righteous
- Moral
- Praiseworthy
- Emotionally strong
- Physically strong

What are some of the other positive qualities that were evident during the traumatic event? List these in your journal as well.

It's a Beginning

How did it feel to list your positive qualities? Did you feel you were boasting or immodest? Do you think it is egotistical to take pride in yourself? If you were raised on the virtues of humility and modesty, you may feel that it's wrong to think well of yourself. If that is the case with you, bear in mind that reminding yourself frequently of any strength, endurance, integrity, and intelligence you exhibited during the trauma is one of the few ways you have of countering the negative, self-blaming thoughts you may harbor inside yourself.

"But what if I can't think of any way in which I acted positively?" you might say. If that's the case, don't be devastated by your admission. Many trauma survivors feel as you do. Perhaps as you move further along in the healing process, you will be able to take more pride in how you acted and felt during the incident that changed your life. Do *not* beat yourself up if you can't complete this particular exercise. Simply consider the possibility that you have strengths, and then move on.

You have now taken an initial look at some of your actions, thoughts, and feelings during and since the traumatic event. Your view of yourself will expand and deepen as we look more closely at the traumatic event in the chapters to come. Quite possibly you do not remember all aspects of the traumatic event right now, nor do you appreciate the magnitude or complexity of the stresses you endured. However, as you continue on in this book, especially if you follow some of the suggestions on remembering offered in Chapter 6, your vision of what occurred and how you acted and felt will become clearer and more detailed.

4

The Three Levels
of Victimization

According to the *American Heritage College Dictionary* (third edition, 1993), a victim is "someone who is harmed or killed by another" or "someone who is harmed or made to suffer from an act, circumstance, agency, or condition." A victim is also "anyone who suffers as a result of ruthless design or incidentally or accidentally" (*Webster's Third New International Dictionary*, 1971). The suffering and losses can be physical, psychological, or both.

People raised in poverty and those subjected to racial, sexual, religious, or other forms of discrimination are often viewed as victims of social and historical forces beyond their control. Similarly, people who acquire life-threatening or chronic illnesses or permanent disabilities can also be considered victims. For the purposes of this book however, a victim is someone who has suffered from at least one "particularly negative . . . intensely disruptive" event (Janoff Bulman and Frieze 1983).

Victimization, which means the process of becoming a victim, can be considered to occur on three levels (McCarthy 1986). In brief, the levels are these:

- The traumatic event itself

- Secondary wounding experiences

- The acceptance of the victim label

Level One: The Shattering of Assumptions

Being victimized, whether in a car accident, tornado, mugging, war, or abusive relationship, shocks both your body and your emotions. Even worse, perhaps, is the way it rocks your basic beliefs about yourself, human nature, and the nature of the world. The challenge (or shattering) of these beliefs can greatly increase your psychological distress. Any anxiety, confusion, depression, or disequilibrium experienced after the trauma is heightened by such thoughts as, Whom or what should I trust now? After what happened, I don't know what to believe in anymore.

As psychologists Janoff Bulman and Frieze (1983) point out, victims are usually forced to reconsider at least these three assumptions about themselves and the world: that they are personally invulnerable, that the world is orderly and meaningful, and that they are good and strong people.

Loss of Invulnerability

It can't happen to me, you may have thought. But it *did* happen to you. Therefore, you may no longer feel safe. At the very least, you probably feel less safe than you did before the trauma. And since you were traumatized once, even if others assure you that it can't happen again, you fear it will.

These feelings of vulnerability may develop into two of the classic symptoms of PTSD: a sense of doom or a foreshortened future, and an intense fear that the trauma will repeat itself.

Loss of an Orderly World

Why did this happen at all? And why did it happen to me? you are bound to ask. I thought if I tried to be a careful, honest, and good person, I could avoid disaster.

In answer, you may conclude that life is meaningless and incomprehensible. Or you may conclude that you were singled out for pain and punishment because in some way you deserved what happened—you were deficient, bad, or unworthy. Some survivors interpret the event, or have it interpreted by others, as "God's will," "the work of the devil," or some form of "spiritual warfare." Penny's case is an example of this.

> Penny had been sexually abused by her uncle from the age of 8 and until she was 11. When she was 16, she finally told her parents, who shrugged it off as unimportant. Her uncle's wife accused Penny of lying and trying to break up the family.
>
> When Penny was 20, she was in an automobile accident. She suffered terrible back injuries and was bedridden for over a year as a result. Penny's aunt, of course, said the accident was God's punishment for Penny's lies. But one of Penny's friends from church also saw the accident as punishment—in this case for Penny's having had orgasms during the incest and for Penny's not having fully forgiven her uncle for abusing her. "The accident will bring you closer to God," the friend assured her.

Given the reactions of the people close to her, it is no surprise that Penny felt she was an evil, dirty person who deserved not only the incest, but the accident as well. For Penny, suffering was almost welcome. It was a means of paying for her many sins.

You, like Penny, may have the comfort (albeit cold and probably highly erroneous) of self-blame to explain the trauma's occurrence. However, if you feel you were a decent, responsible person, it may be hard to make sense of what happened to you. Your previous views about human decency and social justice, or your religious or spiritual views, may not be adequate to explain things either. This leaves you in a state of turmoil and confusion.

Loss of Positive Self-Image

In the last chapter you read about, and did some work on recognizing, the ways self-blame and guilt can affect self-esteem. Trauma affects self-image in other ways as well. For example, being victimized or traumatized usually brings to the fore people's feelings of helplessness, vulnerability, and powerlessness. Consequently, they find themselves feeling more dependent on others than ever before. We live, however, in a society that puts tremendous value on self-sufficiency, and that views vulnerability and reliance on others as a weakness. This makes it very difficult to accept "neediness" as a normal, even healthy, part of the response to trauma.

In addition, some trauma survivors find themselves placating their tormentors—for example, the rape victim who offers to mend her attacker's clothing or the battered wife who offers her husband a sandwich in the midst of a beating. These actions, though understandable in the context of the trauma as attempts to survive, can be difficult for the victim to reconcile afterwards. And they can, as a result, negatively affect the survivor's self-image.

Other Common Victim Responses

In addition to the uncertainty, vulnerability, and loss of self-esteem we have already discussed, the first level of victimization also often includes the following reactions:

- Feeling like a child
- A desire to withdraw or isolate from others
- Feelings of anger or rage

Feeling Like a Child. Brutalization, victimization, and losses "make children of us all," writes Frank Ochberg (1988), a specialist in victims of crime and violence. As mentioned above, it is common for trauma survivors to want and need to cling to others for protection, assurance, comfort, and love, like children who have just witnessed something terrifying. The children want to be held and hear someone say "Don't worry. I'm here. I'll help you take care of this and I'll help take care of you, too."

If you find yourself feeling vulnerable and needy in this way, rest assured you are not alone. Experts have found that when people are traumatized, this reaction is normal. At least initially, and to a degree corresponding to the extent of the trauma and the degree of assistance and healing available, trauma survivors tend to forget adult learnings—they return to whatever behavior and coping mechanisms they used when they were children. This makes absolute sense emotionally, since as children they were powerless, helpless, and dependent, as they were during the trauma. It is often less than easy to accept those feelings as an adult.

The high substance-abuse rate among PTSD sufferers can be partly explained as a way of dealing with the increased dependency and security needs normal to trauma survivors. The reasons any particular individual turns to alcohol, drugs, or food are complex, and they vary from one individual to another. However, for some trauma survivors, depending on a substance seems less frightening, more dependable, and less publicly humiliating than turning to other people for help, at least initially.

There are also environments and occupations in which denying feelings of helplessness and dependency is necessary. For example, in the military and in occupations such as police and rescue work, evidence of helplessness and dependency can easily lead to being stigmatized—even being demoted or fired.

Sometimes, too, trauma leaves its victims in need of physical assistance—medical or legal help or financial assistance. Even these nonemotional needs, however, can contribute to feelings of childlike dependency.

Withdrawing from Others. Often the increased need for others coexists with a strong need to isolate and withdraw. For example, you may have begun to isolate yourself from others or to have difficulties with relationships since the traumatic event. But at the same time, you may strongly feel a need for other people. The strong pulls in both directions can confuse you and make you doubt yourself. This increases your need for the reassurances other people can provide.

You may also simultaneously wish to withdraw from others to hide your confusion and self-doubt, as well as simply to pull yourself together. These opposing tensions thus create a vicious circle—a mental state that perpetuates and accentuates itself.

Rage and Anger. Trauma survivors typically experience considerable anger, much of it justifiable. Specific persons, groups, organizations, or governing bodies may have been responsible, in whole or in part, for the trauma itself. Since then, your pride and sense of self-sufficiency may have been further assaulted by your emotional needs and possibly by your need for financial, medical, legal, or other services.

If prior to the trauma you prided yourself on your self-sufficiency, this dependency can be particularly infuriating. Worse is that the lack of control that results from needing others is one of the same feelings that terrorized you during the traumatic event. And if, as happens all too often, you have not been treated with respect, the powerlessness and anger you experience when you turned to someone for help could easily mimic what you felt during the original traumatic event, when you were also helpless and mistreated.

At this point, you may have decided to hide your feelings and needs from others and just pretend you are who you were before the trauma. You may have decided not to seek outside assistance, even financial or other help, fearing denial or rejection—or even being judged as "crazy." Eventually, however, the pretending can become exhausting.

Accepting Help

Difficult as it may be, when the isolation, the pain, or the effort of covering up becomes too great, you need to turn to others for help—emotional, legal, or practical. When that time comes (if it hasn't already) or comes again, it may help to remember the following points.

Needing help is normal. If you felt powerful and dynamic immediately after it was demonstrated that there are forces capable of destroying you, most knowledgeable mental health professionals would consider you delusional, mentally troubled, or at least in a state of massive denial. Consequently, helplessness, neediness, and all the other feelings described above are *appropriate* feelings following traumatization.

Things change. The feelings of helplessness, dependency, and neediness you may experience at times, or even all the time, are temporary. If you are in fact "weak," you will only be weak for a while, as a result of the trauma. Any weakness is not inherent—it only exists because you have been wounded. Even if you fear you will never be strong again, you will. You just need to heal first.

Just as you would not expect someone who broke a leg to immediately start walking, you cannot expect yourself to recover from physical and psychological wounds right away. Until such time as the leg is sufficiently healed, it needs to be in a cast. Crutches may also be needed. Similarly, both before and while you are healing you need the cast and crutches of other people in your life.

Turning to others helps. It has been shown that trauma survivors who have someone to turn to are at lower risk for developing PTSD than those who must or who choose to cope with the trauma all alone. According to trauma experts, trauma survivors who have someone to assure them that everything will be all right, and that he or she will be there to help, are less likely to develop long-term problems such as chronic illness or extreme dependency on others or on institutions for their care.

In sum, the best way to achieve independence is to allow yourself to be dependent when it is appropriate to lean on others. You might want to consider turning to your spouse or partner, your minister, a trusted friend, or an adult member of your family. In general it is not wise to turn to children or adolescents, since your needs can overwhelm them and they are ill equipped to help you. Also, it is not wise to turn to people who are emotionally unstable or extremely emotionally distraught themselves.

If you can, also seek the help of a mental health professional who is trained in working with trauma survivors. Whether you turn to an individual in your family or community or to a professional, that person needs to be supportive and patient, not blaming, for reasons that are explained below.

Level Two: Secondary Wounding

As important to the healing process as other people are, it's an unfortunate truth that often people do more harm than good. You have likely experienced this. Strangers who don't understand your situation can be unintentionally cruel, but so can those who should know better: family, friends, and helping professionals. Instead of being supported, you may have been made to feel ashamed of having been a part of a traumatic event in the first place, of your reactions to the event or symptoms you have developed as a result, or even of asking for help.

You may have heard, for example, "You weren't hurt enough to be entitled to benefits" or "It happened weeks (or months or years) ago. You should be over it by now." Such attitudes exist even in the most obvious and horrendous cases of victimization.

Consider the story of Penny, which you read above. Her parents' indifference to the sexual abuse she had suffered, her aunt's verbal attacks, and her friend's attitude that Penny deserved the pain caused by the accident, are all examples of what is called secondary wounding—the second level of victimization.

Forms of Secondary Wounding

Secondary wounding occurs when the people, institutions, caregivers, and others to whom the trauma survivor turns for emotional, legal, financial, medical, or other assistance respond in one of the following ways.

Disbelief, denial, discounting. Commonly, people will deny or disbelieve the trauma survivor's account of the trauma. Or they will minimize or discount the magnitude of the event, its meaning to the victim, its impact on the victim's life. Consider Sandra, for example.

> After a hurricane, Sandra, a concert violinist, was taken to a makeshift hospital, along with others who were injured. When she was told that three of her fingers would have to

be amputated, she began to cry. "Hush now, you big crybaby," the nurse said. "Look around you. Bed number one lost his arm and bed two has to have both legs removed. Count your blessings and don't upset the others."

Blaming the victim. On some level, people may blame the victim for the traumatic event, thereby increasing the victim's sense of self-blame and low self-esteem. This was what happened to Penny.

Stigmatization. Stigmatization occurs when others judge the victim negatively for normal reactions to the traumatic event or for any long-term symptoms he or she may suffer. These judgments can take the following forms:

- Ridicule of, or condescension toward, the survivor

- Misinterpretation of the survivor's psychological distress as a sign of deep psychological problems or moral or mental deficiency, or otherwise giving the survivor's PTSD symptoms negative or pejorative labels

- An implication or outright statement that the survivor's symptoms reflect his or her desire for financial gain, attention, or unwarranted sympathy

- Punishment of the victim, rather than the offender, or in other ways depriving the victim of justice

Denial of assistance. Trauma survivors are sometimes denied promised or expected services on the basis that they do not need or are not entitled to such services. An example of this is Alvin Jones.

Alvin is a railroad worker who lost his left leg in a train accident. When he sought compensation from the railroad, he was told to wait and see if his leg would "get better." After presenting medical documentation showing that it would not, Alvin's request was again denied because, despite his disability, he had found gainful employment.

Four years later, with the help of an attorney, whose fees Alvin had to pay himself, Alvin was granted compensation. However, he was awarded neither attorney fees nor payment for the four years he had to struggle to obtain the benefits he was entitled to.

Effects of Secondary Wounding

Ignorance and insensitivity can take many forms in addition to those listed above. It is their effects, however, that are often most devastating. Take Claudia's story, for example.

Claudia was trapped in an abusive marriage. Back in her small town, in the early 1960s, there was little awareness of wife abuse and only minimal legal protection for battered wives. Whenever Claudia could, she would call the police when her husband threatened her. Their responses were less than helpful:

"Lady, he's your husband, not mine."

"You're both animals."

"There's nothing we can do about it until he does something. Call us after he actually starts beating or cutting you."

After repeated threats on her life, Claudia took her children and fled.

During the divorce proceedings, mental health experts testified that Claudia was a masochist who also suffered from other "severe psychiatric disturbances" (unspecified), as evidenced by the fact that she had stayed in an abusive marriage as long as she did. On the other hand, they also faulted her for "breaking up a happy home" and subjecting her children to the "horrors of divorce."

And, whether out of sheer incompetence or for some darker reason, Claudia's attorney failed to bring up the husband's own personality problems.

The judge awarded the divorce to Claudia's husband. According to the law in that place and time, Claudia had not been "battered enough"—seven years of hospital reports or other documentation of the abuse was necessary for a battered woman to win the divorce. And because Claudia was labeled a deserter who left her marriage for insufficient cause, the judge allotted the lion's share of the property, including the house, to Claudia's husband, leaving Claudia homeless and almost penniless. He then told Claudia that if she could not adequately support her children, custody would be given to their father.

Claudia's case is a rather extreme example—one we all hope would not happen today. But such things do happen, more frequently than most people would believe. Although some progress has been made in providing legal help for abused wives since Claudia went to court, the laws vary from state to state and county to county. Some areas offer strong protection for abused wives, others do not. Even where good laws exist, however, they are not always enforced.

For example, in one study, the American Psychological Association (1984) found secondary wounding experiences rampant among victims of crime and violence. Some victims reported that their secondary wounding experiences were more painful and devastating than the original traumatic event. Police officers, lawyers, and court officials were cited in the report. However, medical personnel, mental health professionals, and a myriad of others not usually associated with causing psychological injury to the people they serve were also responsible for causing secondary wounding.

Causes of Secondary Wounding

In essence, secondary wounding occurs because people who have never been hurt sometimes have difficulty understanding and being patient with people who have been hurt. Secondary wounding also occurs because people who have never confronted human tragedy are sometimes unable to comprehend the lives of those in occupations that involve dealing with human suffering or mass casualties on a daily basis.

In addition, some people simply are not strong enough to accept the negatives in life. They prefer to ignore the fact that sadness, injustice, and loss are just as much a part of life as joy and goodness. When such individuals confront a trauma survivor, they may reject or disparage the survivor because that individual represents the parts of life they have chosen to deny.

On the other hand, it also happens that trauma survivors are rejected or disparaged by other survivors—those who have chosen to deny or repress their own trauma and have not yet dealt with their losses and anger. When trauma survivors who are not dealing with their traumatic pasts see someone who is obviously suffering emotionally or physically, they may need to block out that person in order to leave their own denial system intact.

The following paragraphs give a brief run down of some of the common causes of secondary wounding.

Ignorance. Some secondary wounding stems from sheer ignorance. Especially in the past, there were few, if any, courses on victimization, domestic violence, or child abuse available to medical, legal, and mental health professionals. Today such courses are available in many locations; however, they are not a required part of the training in any of those fields.

Increasing numbers of police departments are sensitizing their staff to the problems of victims. And where the training is sufficient, the police have been shown to be more responsive to victims. Yet not all police departments are able to devote adequate training hours to this subject.

Burnout. Another major cause of secondary wounding is that many helping professionals (the police, rescue workers, doctors, and other emergency room staff), are themselves suffering from some form of PTSD or burnout. As a result of having worked for years with trauma survivors, they, like those survivors, are emotionally depleted. They may also, like many trauma survivors, feel unappreciated and unrecognized by the general public and by those in their workplace.

Nurses, for example, are notoriously underpaid and undervalued, and paramedics and police officers often feel betrayed by the criminal justice system, which, they feel, frequently releases the criminals they have risked their lives to apprehend all too soon. In some places, the police are ostracized in their own communities.

In the mental health field, social workers and other mental health workers assigned to child abuse or family violence cases, or to public mental health agencies, often stagger under enormous caseloads and are hampered in helping victims by massive amounts of paperwork and red tape, as well as by a lack of support services.

Just world philosophy. Another hurdle victims face is the prevalence and persistence of the "just world philosophy." According to this philosophy, people get what they deserve and deserve what they get. The basic assumption of the just world philosophy is that if you are sufficiently careful, intelligent, moral, or competent, you can avoid misfortune. Thus people who suffer trauma are somehow to blame for their misfortune. Even if the victims aren't directly blamed, they are seen as causing their victimization by being inherently weak or ineffectual.

The just world philosophy arises out of the very human need to feel in control of our lives. Contemplating the possibility that at any moment one's life or health, loved ones, or possessions might be destroyed or damaged, or that at any moment one could become the victim of a malevolent force, is too frightening for most people to bear.

The influence of culture. Our nation was founded by individuals who overcame massive political, economic, and social obstacles by means of hard work, self-sacrifice, and physical and emotional endurance. As a nation today, as in the past, we pride ourselves on our can-do spirit and our American ingenuity—we are certain we can overcome almost any hardship. The American dream tells us that our country is so bountiful and so full of opportunities that anyone who wants the good life can have it; all they have to do is pull themselves up by their own bootstraps.

Abraham Lincoln is quoted as saying "People can be as happy as they make up their minds to be"—implying that in the personal realm, as well as in the economic realm, man can be master of his own fate.

If only he were right.

Overcoming Secondary Wounding

Secondary wounding experiences can be as painful and powerful as the original traumatic event. Just as you need to heal from that event, you will need healing for any secondary wounding experiences.

Healing from secondary wounding experiences requires first that you be able to identify what hit you—what secondary wounding experiences you experienced—and then that you be able to distance yourself from the negative responses of the others involved in these experiences.

The distancing needs to be achieved on both the emotional and the mental level. On the emotional level, the goal of distancing is for you not to be devastated by the experience. In all likelihood, you will still be troubled by others' insensitivity, but you can learn not to allow them to destroy you emotionally. On the mental level, the goal of distancing is to become more resistant to the negative judgments of your worth that secondary wounding experiences deliver.

You need to learn that, generally, the rejection, humiliation, or attack says more about the ignorance, insensitivity, fears, or prejudices of the other person than anything about you, and that it reflects larger societal problems, including the prevalence of blame-the-victim attitudes and the lack of adequate funding for victim-compensation services. Once you learn to view your secondary wounding experiences from this perspective, you will have some armor against the pain involved in many interactions.

Keep in mind that, in addition to the emotional vulnerability resulting from trauma, biological changes can occur that make you exceptionally sensitive to and observant of others' responses. Thus very subtle cues in the behavior of others will affect you much more than they would a nontraumatized person.

A second way to counter the negative messages of those who lack understanding and compassion is with affirming "self-talk" of your own. Together, these two approaches will enable you to gain a measure of objectivity. This objectivity in turn gives you increased control of your life, by acting as a brake on two destructive but legitimate reactions many trauma survivors have to secondary wounding experiences. The first reaction is sinking into helpless-hopeless thoughts and feelings; the second is being overwhelmed by the urge to strike back, verbally or physically.

Even when your desire to retaliate is entirely justified (as it often is), an aggressive response only confirms the other person's belief that you are a "nut case" or otherwise undeserving of assistance—which can lead to that person withholding something that you do in fact deserve and need.

Countering the powerful negative messages of secondary wounding experiences is not done effortlessly or quickly. Such experiences always trouble you to some extent. But you can make progress in affirming your worth as a person and your strengths as a trauma survivor, in addition to increasing your objectivity and control.

Naming the Demon

In certain societies, psychological distress and its symptoms are conceptualized as attacks by supernatural beings. Typically these demons or spirits are given specific names—jealousy, revenge, bad memories, depression—and a healing ritual is performed to rid the suffering person of the particular spirit or demon that is causing the problem.

The efficacy of the healing ritual aside, it is probably helpful to suffering individuals simply to know that their affliction has a name, since for human beings, words are a way of making the unknown knowable, and therefore controllable. Similarly, it may have been helpful for you to learn that your trauma-related symptoms also have a name: PTSD.

For example, because you are aware of what PTSD is, when you experience a PTSD symptom you can tell yourself this: I don't have to panic. I am only having a PTSD attack. What I'm experiencing now is predictable and limited. It will not last forever, and it cannot cause me to lose my mind.

To help achieve some distance from the secondary wounding experiences you have already had and will probably have in the future, you need to learn to name the demons of those experiences. For example, instead of acting on your feelings or allowing yourself to become increasingly hopeless, you can use self-talk to work through the experience: It's not my fault this person is treating me with so little respect and appreciation of my difficulty. But if I lose control of myself, or sink deeper and deeper into depression, I will only be lessening my chances of getting what I need from this person. Maybe if I can figure out this demon's name I will know what I'm dealing with. Just what kind of secondary wounding is this anyway?

Common Secondary Wounding Responses

There are basically six types of secondary wounding responses: those showing denial or disbelief, those that involve discounting, those in which the victim is blamed for his or her problems, those that exhibit ignorance, those involving generalization or labeling, and those stemming from sheer cruelty.

Once you are able to identify the responses of others along these lines, you will be better able to view these reactions for what they truly are. Giving them a name will increase your ability to cope with secondary wounding experiences in a constructive manner, and will lessen, though not eliminate, the pain and humiliation.

Denial and disbelief. When people respond to you with statements such as "You're exaggerating," "That could never happen," or simply "I don't believe it," they are denying the reality of your trauma.

Abusers and criminals are often the first to deny their victims the reality of their experience. "Please don't take my purse," says the victim. "I'm not taking your purse—it's your imagination," replies the thief. Or, "Stop hitting me," says the victim. "I'm not hitting you. You're hitting yourself," the abuser says. Unfortunately, they aren't the only ones who practice denial. Consider this example.

> Sally Brown's three-month-old daughter was raped by
> Sally's boyfriend. When she told the admitting clerk at the

emergency room, he replied, "That's impossible. Nobody would rape a baby. Come on now, Ms. Brown. Tell us the real truth."

How different it would have been for Sally if the clerk had said, "Child sexual abuse is a horrible crime. I will be certain to tell the doctor the information you have given me and remind him to perform all the required tests for victims of sexual assault. While you are waiting, would you like to telephone the rape crisis center or the sexual abuse hotline for further assistance? Here are their numbers; you can use my phone if you like."

Friends and family members also sometimes practice denial, as in the following case.

> When Dan told his mother that his father was verbally and physically abusing him, his mother replied, "Your father is a good man. You've been watching too much TV."
>
> But a nondenying mother might have said, "If you tell me you've been hurt, I believe you. Can you tell me more about what happened? Are you hurt? You need to tell me everything because child abuse is wrong and against the law. I will have to talk to your father about this and maybe take other action as well."

Discounting. In denial, people do not believe your story. When you are being discounted, people do not deny that the traumatic event occurred; however, they minimize its effect on you or the magnitude of the event. Here are three examples of discounting.

> Jane explained to her boyfriend that she sometimes has trouble responding to him sexually because of having been raped three years ago. "How could one little rape have affected you that much? I know some women who have been raped three or four times, but they still like sex," the boyfriend replied.
>
> Jane's boyfriend could have said, "Rape is such a violation. I'm so sorry you had to go through that. I hope you weren't badly hurt, but I understand the psychological scars can be brutal. Thank you for trusting me enough to tell me how you feel. I will do my best to be sensitive to your needs."
>
> Bill, a policeman, shared with a colleague that he has been suffering from headaches and nausea after a shootout in which three people were killed. The colleague replied, "They were a bunch of crooks. They are where they should be—six feet under. You should be in ecstasy, not having headaches."

The colleague could have said, however, "These killings can sure get to you sometimes. Even if they're the bad guys, when their blood and guts are all over the place, it's hard to take. It gets to all of us eventually, even the guys who like to pretend they're made of stone. As much as you've seen in the force, I'm surprised you only have headaches."

Carl Jones, a flood survivor, went to his doctor for "the shakes." "I've been shaking for two years," he said, "ever since that flood washed away my . . . "

"Come on, now, Mr. Jones," the doctor broke in, "that flood wasn't that bad. Only a few people died and about a hundred homes were destroyed. When I was a boy, I was in a flood that wiped out over half the town. Now *that's* a real flood."

But the doctor could have said, "Being in a flood is a traumatic experience. It is natural and normal for you to have a reaction like shaking. Tell me more about the shaking and any other problems you've had since the flood. I know from my own experience of being in a flood as a child that a traumatic event like that can cause people to suffer for years afterwards."

Blaming the victim. The blame-the-victim attitude and the just world philosophy were described above. Penny's story, which you read earlier, illustrates these attitudes. It's not hard to imagine how the responses Penny received could have been improved. Here are some other examples:

After Howard's house was burglarized and vandalized, he took a second job to pay for the repairs and replace his stolen camera gear. When he complained to a friend one day about how tired and upset he was, she replied, "I told you that you should never have moved into that neighborhood. The least you could have done was buy more insurance."

A more supportive response would have been to say, "I can't say I know how you feel, since luckily, I've never had my home broken into. But I do remember how angry I felt when my purse was stolen. The burglars didn't just steal your stuff, they stole your time, energy, and sense of security. I'm angry that they're out on the streets while you're working so much."

Ross, a former serviceman who had been discharged after losing an arm in a training accident, met a cousin at a family gathering. The cousin said, "So you're a lefty now, eh? I guess that's what you get for enlisting."

What he could have said was, "I'm really sorry about your arm. It's one of those things that could happen to any of us. Let me know if I can do anything to help."

Ignorance. Ignorance of trauma and its effects plays a major role in secondary wounding experiences. If people have not experienced trauma themselves, or have not learned about it in other ways, they often do not know what to say or do. Also, as mentioned before, often the fact that you have been victimized threatens other people's defenses against the idea that they too could be victimized.

People are often also ignorant about the possible economic, social, and psychological consequences of trauma. Ignorance can even result in inappropriate medical or psychological treatment methods being applied. These methods may be perfectly appropriate for nontraumatized people, but can be unhelpful, even harmful, to trauma survivors.

Here are a couple of examples of secondary wounding caused by ignorance:

"Jen, I'm sorry, I can't make it to your party. Ever since my accident I try to avoid Route 97 as much as possible. And I can't get to your house any other way," Betty said. "That's crazy," her friend replied, "you're acting like a superstitious nut. And selfish too. You're just thinking of yourself."

But Betty's friend could have said, "I'll miss you, but it's okay. I wouldn't want to subject you to bad memories; you've suffered enough. If I were in your place, I'd probably hate that drive too."

"No more vacations at the beach! After seven months in Saudia Arabia, I don't want to see another grain of sand as long as I live!" said Hank, a veteran of the Persian Gulf war. "You are going to deny your family a trip to the beach just because you had to sit on the sand for seven months?" his father replied. "And don't go claiming you have that PSSD or TSP or whatever that Vietnam thing is called. You didn't fire a shot."

A more knowledgeable response would have been, "I read that even if you aren't in combat, you can still get stress symptoms just from being in a war. Then, afterwards, everything associated with that trauma, even things that aren't traumatic or harmful in themselves, can set off bad memories. It makes perfect sense for you to stay away from sand. Your family can go to the beach by themselves, if they want. Or you can all go to the mountains for a change."

Generalization. One of the social consequences of being victimized is being labeled as a victim. Once you are labeled, there is a tendency for others to interpret most, if not all, of your emotions and behavior in light of that label. For example, the deaf are often assumed to also be blind or mentally retarded. Furthermore once you are labeled, it is very difficult to escape from that label (Taylor et al. 1983).

For instance, it may be assumed that because you have been through a trauma you are now "emotionally scarred," forever and ever. Consider these examples.

Roger lost an eye in a chemical explosion at work. Otherwise, he was not injured. But when he returned to his job, he was offered a wheelchair and told that his company did not employ "cripples."

Clearly, the more humane and logical response would have been to keep Roger on at a job he was fully capable of doing and to offer him any assistance he needed to adapt to his injury.

Juanita, a dental hygienist, confided to her employer that she was seeking counseling for having been robbed and beaten. "That's fine," he replied, "you can take the receptionist's job; she's leaving us anyway," implying that somehow being a victim of crime had impaired Juanita's ability to work. Obviously, this was not the case; a little understanding would have been far more appropriate.

Cruelty. Most secondary wounding experiences *feel* cruel. Therefore it is often difficult to assess whether the secondary wounding actually arises from a desire that the other person has to cause pain, or whether it is caused by ignorance, generalization, or some other secondary wounding process. In many cases, a mixture of cruelty and some other process or processes is at work, as some of the preceding examples demonstrate.

Sometimes the fact of your trauma and PTSD may be used as a weapon by people you know. In the absence of the trauma they would have found something else to use against you. However, perfect strangers are also capable of gratuitous cruelty. A feature of our culture that helps lay the groundwork for these behaviors is an increasing emotional detachment between people, even in families.

According to some observers, contemporary American culture in general is experiencing an "increase in psychic numbing, alienation, isolation and difficulties with intimacy" (Young and Erickson 1988). This generalized numbing throughout the population can be attributed at least in part to economic and social changes that make it difficult for people to empathize with each other's pain, even within their own families, much less with that of strangers.

Exercise: Identifying Your Secondary Wounding Experiences

In your journal, list as many secondary wounding experiences as you can remember, including any current ones, one experience to a page. You will need to leave space for analyzing and commenting on each experience.

When you have finished, review your list and categorize each experience as denial or disbelief, discounting, generalization, victim-blaming, ignorance, or cruelty. Include as many labels as apply; for example, a single experience can contain elements of ignorance, cruelty, and blaming the victim.

After you have completed the labeling for each experience, identify your emotional response. Did you have no feeling at all? Did you experience irritation, anger, rage, hurt, disappointment, disgust, a desire to retaliate, or any other feeling? List as many feelings as apply.

Now take some time to reflect on the process you have just been through. Were you surprised at how many secondary wounding experiences you have endured? Did labeling the experiences help ease the pain, or did it make you more furious or sad?

Did any of the secondary wounding experiences ignite your anger or rage, lower your self-esteem, or make you feel hopeless or helpless? In your journal, write more about those particular experiences.

Once these feelings are faced, their intensity may be lessened. You will likely never feel completely neutral in the midst of a secondary wounding experience—or when you are remembering one. If you are aware enough to feel your emotions, you are going to feel angry, sad, powerless, betrayed, and a host of other emotions. But this does not mean that you are hopelessly bound to the past and will never feel joy again.

Exercise: Secondary Wounding and Your Attitudes Today

In your journal, write about how your secondary wounding experiences are still affecting your life. More specifically, for each experience, consider whether or not that experience had the following effects:

1. Did it alter your views of your social, vocational, and other abilities?

2. Did it change your attitudes toward certain types or groups of people or certain government and social institutions?

3. Were your religious or spiritual views affected?

4. Did it affect your family life, friendships, or other close relationships?

5. Did it alter your ability to participate in groups or belong to associations or affect your attitudes toward the general public?

6. Now look at what you've written and ask yourself, Which of these attitudes do I wish to retain? Which of them are in my best interests to reconsider? Which ones would I like to discard because they hamper my life in the present?

Exercise: Secondary Wounding and Your Activities

Suppose that one of your worst secondary wounding experiences was being treated like the criminal, rather than the victim, in court. Because of this, you have concluded that all judges and jurors are insensitive at best and corrupt and heartless at worst. Yet now someone owes you several thousand dollars, and to get it you need to take that person to court.

If you hadn't had the previous experience, you would probably already have begun the paperwork for the lawsuit. However, because of your hatred of courts and fear of being, once again, denied justice, you procrastinate about pursuing the litigation.

At this point, what do you think is in your best interests—avoiding the courtroom with all its secondary wounding memories and the risk of repeated victimization, or pursuing the thousands of dollars you are due?

The decision is yours. It may be that if you receive some assistance in healing from your courtroom-related secondary wounding experiences you will be able to tolerate the aversiveness of being in court. Counseling can assist you in differentiating your past courtroom experience from the present situation. And with support, you might be able to manage any PTSD symptoms that emerge as a result of placing yourself back in that setting. For example, you could take some friends along, rather than facing the situation alone.

On the other hand, you might decide that you simply can't handle it. You'd rather do without the money than subject yourself to another courtroom experience.

This is not cowardice. Rather it is a respectable life-preserving decision. At all times, it is very important for you to know and respect your limits, and not to be pushed into activities that are emotionally overwhelming or otherwise destructive for you.

Your emotional health comes first, not conforming to some inner voice that says you "should" be able to handle anything (the same voice that has probably been telling you, You should have been able to go through the trauma and everything that's happened since without it getting to you. You just aren't strong enough).

By the time you finish reading this book, you will know beyond a doubt that this "should" has no basis in emotional reality. But even after you have let go of this unrealistic expectation of yourself, others may still believe in it. They may encourage you to do things that you know are not in your best interests emotionally, or denigrate you for letting your "fears and neuroses" or "skeletons from the past" control your life.

Close your ears to these voices and listen to your own inner voice—the one that knows what you have been through and what you can tolerate without arousing excessive anxiety, pain, rage, or other symptoms. In all probability, you will be able to stretch the limits of what you consider tolerable, but you can only do so one small step at a time. Great leaps forward can send you spiraling downward into a depression or flying off into a hyper state.

With that caution in mind, first list the activities that your secondary wounding experiences have taught you to curtail or avoid in your journal. Then for each of them, do the following:

1. Ask yourself whether at this particular time, in your view (not someone else's), you can tolerate the activity. What will be the emotional cost? Is it worth it to you?

   Once again, the main point is to realize that you have a choice. During the original trauma and during the subsequent secondary wounding experiences, you had either no choices or very few, or all the options available were so aversive they were not really choices.

2. For each of the activities you have decided you currently cannot tolerate, or do not feel it's in your best interests to attempt, consider whether counseling or some other form of assistance might make them tolerable. Do you want to make the attempt? If you don't feel you can or want to at present, might you want to in the future, at some point when you are further along in the healing process?

Level Three: Victim Thinking

The third of the three levels of victimization occurs when you internalize the victim status. Even though you are no longer in the original trauma situation, you think and act as if you are still being victimized.

This third level is one of the unfortunate, but natural, outcomes of the first two levels. "The third level of victimization involves the person adopting a lifelong label as a victim," writes Dr. Barry McCarthy. On this level, the trauma survivors in their "general psychological world view . . . play out the victim role." The traumatic event and its aftermath become the "central and dominating events" in trauma survivors' lives, and control their self-esteem. (McCarthy 1986)

In the first two levels of victimization, you have little or no control or personal power. But you can learn to take control of this third level. You do not need to spend your life thinking and feeling like a victim. With some of the help provided in this chapter and in Chapter 10, on empowerment, you can learn to counter the "victim thinking" that may have been forced on you by the traumatic event and the subsequent secondary wounding experiences.

Exercise: Victim Thinking

Victim thinking reflects the feelings of hopelessness, helplessness, defilement, and betrayal often experienced during trauma and afterwards. It can include the low self-esteem that often results from self-blame, survivor guilt, and societal stigmatization.

In your journal, record whether the following thoughts characterize your view of life:

1. I have to accept bad situations because they are part of life and I can do nothing to make them better.

2. I don't expect much good to happen in my life.

3. Nobody could ever love me.

4. I am always going to feel sad, angry, depressed, and confused.

5. There are situations at work and at home that I could do something about, but I don't have the motivation to do so.

6. Life overwhelms me, so I prefer to be alone whenever possible.

7. You can't trust anyone except a very few people.

8. I feel I have to be extra good, competent, and attractive in order to compensate for my many defects.

9. I feel guilty for many things, even things that I know are not my fault.

10. I feel I have to explain myself to people so they will understand me. But sometimes I get tired of explaining, conclude it's not worth the effort, and stay alone.

11. I'm often afraid to do something new for fear I will make a mistake.

12. I can't afford to be wrong.

13. I feel that when people look at me, they know right away that I'm different.

14. Sometimes I think that those who died during the traumatic event I experienced were better off than me. At least they don't have to live with the memories.

15. I am afraid of the future.

16. Most times I think things will never get better. There is not much I can do to make my life better.

17. I can be either a perfectionist or a total slob depending on my mood.

18. I tend to see people as either for me or against me.

19. I feel pressure to go along with others, even when I don't want to. To avoid such pressures, I avoid people.

20. I am never going to get over what happened to me.

21. I find myself apologizing for myself to others.

22. I have very few choices in life.

If you have answered yes to ten or more of these questions, then you probably suffer from victim thinking. Such thinking may have been appropriate during the traumatic event. It may even have helped you to cope with your secondary wounding experiences. For example, if you were suspicious of certain officials, you may have been correct in requiring written documentation of their interactions with you. However, in your present life, victim thinking may be seriously hampering your opportunities for personal growth, vocational development, and the satisfaction of loving human relationships.

But if you are carrying that thinking over today, for example, by continuing to require extensive or inappropriate documentation of interactions with your current co-workers, you will be seen as creating unnecessary work, and perhaps as being hostile to them as well.

Can you identify any areas in your life that are currently being adversely affected by your victim thinking, including but not limited to the personal, professional, family, or creative parts of your life? In your journal, write about the effect of victim thinking on these areas of your life.

Cutting Off Victim Thinking

Once you have decided that some of your victim thinking and other reactions to secondary wounding experiences are hurting rather than helping you, you need to fight back aggressively. It is natural for the feelings and thinking patterns corresponding to being a double victim (of trauma and secondary wounding) to reappear in many life situations, especially in those that are stressful. However, if you would like to approach situations in your life today from a different perspective, devoid of a victim mentality, you can help yourself by doing the following:

- Remind yourself of the original traumatic event or secondary wounding experiences that created your need for the victim thinking. For this you have to determine how and why you acquired the victim thinking in the first place, as you will do shortly.

- Remind yourself of the main reasons that a victim mentality doesn't fit the current situation or doesn't serve you now. Consider that the best revenge, and perhaps the only revenge available to you, is first to survive and second to live well. You might also remind yourself that the negative consequences of following your victim thinking usually outweigh the positive (McKay and Fanning 1987).

Exercises: The Sources of Victim Thinking

Your victim thinking can be traced either to one of four common cognitive mindsets that tend to emerge during traumatic or secondary wounding experiences or to one of the symptoms of PTSD. In the list of victim-thinking statements above, statements 2, 3, 6, 14, 15 are related to PTSD as well as to depression (discussed in Chapter 2).

Many of the other statements are also related to depression. However, they also can be traced to one of the following four mindsets common to trauma survivors (Alford et al. 1988, J. Glover 1988):

- Intolerance of mistakes in others and in yourself

- Denial of personal difficulties

- All-or-nothing thinking

- Continuation of survival tactics

Mindset 1: Intolerance of mistakes. During certain traumatic events (combat, fires, floods, family violence) and in certain occupations that involve injury and death (nursing, rescue work, firefighting, police work), mistakes are anathema. Even the tiniest error can result in death or injury to another person or to oneself. If you have been in such a situation, you have likely seen how the mistakes of others caused needless deaths, injuries, and other losses. As a result, you can develop a mindset of "no mistakes allowed."

The same mindset can develop during secondary wounding experiences in which you feel that if you make even the slightest mistake you will be denied help or mistreated by authorities or others. Or perhaps you attribute the denial, discounting, or other secondary wounding experiences you had to "mistakes" you made in how you presented yourself or how you handled your interactions with others.

This mindset can easily lead to perfectionist values. You may demand perfect performance of yourself, others, or both. Expecting others to be perfect, however, inevitably leads to disappointment and conflict in your relationships. If you also expect yourself to be perfect, you will undoubtedly suffer from endless heartache, low self-esteem, and even depression.

The following list of "shoulds" (McKay and Fanning 1987) commonly creates problems for people, even nontraumatized people. However, for you as a trauma survivor, these perfectionist shoulds impose yet another weight on your already burdened psyche. Do you subscribe to any of the following?

- I should be the epitome of generosity and unselfishness.

- I should be the perfect lover, friend, parent, teacher, student, spouse, and so on.

- I should be able to find a quick solution to every problem.

- I should never feel hurt. I should always feel happy and serene.

- I should be completely competent.

- I should know, understand, and foresee everything.

- I should never feel certain emotions such as anger or jealousy.

- I should never make mistakes.

- I should be totally self-reliant.

- I should never be afraid.

- I should have achievements that bring me status, wealth, and power.

- I should always be busy: to relax is to waste my time and my life.

- I should be able to protect my children from all pain.

- I should not take time just for my own pleasure.

In your journal, first consider each should that you apply to yourself in light of the traumatic event and your secondary wounding experiences. Was this should a necessity during those experiences?

Now consider those shoulds that you attempt to live up to in light of your needs today. To what extent are these standards realistic for you? Do they motivate you to achieve more of your goals, or do they serve as a stick to beat yourself with? Are they truly *your* shoulds, or are they imposed on you by others, for example, your parents, spouse, children, friends, or church?

Which shoulds do you want to keep and which do you want to disregard or modify? The choices are yours.

Mindset 2: Denial of personal difficulties. Certain occupations, for instance, medicine, police work, combat duty, and rescue work, emphasize the necessity for solid thinking, quick action, and endurance, both physical and psychological. There is little room for expression of emotions or for personal weaknesses. Hence, from firefighters to combat soldiers, those who are involved in life-and-death situations tend to keep their personal difficulties to themselves. The legitimate fear of such workers is that if they are emotionally honest they may be seen as cowards, weaklings, incompetents, or otherwise unfit.

Victims of crime, childhood physical and sexual abuse, battering, and natural catastrophes may also deny personal problems for fear of being seen as weak or defective because of their experiences. To avoid this stigma, some trauma survivors put on a macho or stoic facade.

It makes absolute sense for you not to share your personal difficulties with individuals who are apt to denigrate you or who have already done so. However, in intimate relationships, and during the healing process, denial of personal pain, conflicts, and other psychological or physical symptoms is counterproductive and can lead to addictive behavior, psychosomatic problems, or worse. You owe it to the wounded part of yourself to find at least a few people that you can trust enough to share with openly, both friends and professionals.

The mental health field can offer valuable assistance. If you have not sought such help, think about fears or other obstacles that stand in the way of your turning to a qualified social worker, psychologist, or psychiatrist in this, your time of need.

As you consider reaching out for support, take a long-range view of your situation. A few emotional risks taken now with friends or relatives, or time and money spent now on professional help, may save you unnecessary long-term scars and possibly large amounts of money for future help, should your untreated trauma wounds develop into serious psychiatric problems.

Make a list of individuals you feel care about you but who would not be supportive of your sharing with them. Follow this with a list of persons you feel would or could be helpful, indicating for each person the obstacles and personal fears that stand in the way of your making contact with the person. For example, is it too costly in terms of travel time or phone bills to talk to a potential supporter?

Consider which of these obstacles can be overcome. How important is your mental health to you? What risks are you willing to take in terms of reaching out to others to give yourself some relief from the pain?

Always keep in mind that if you take the risk of sharing with someone, and they are not receptive or are nonsupportive, you can bring the conversation to a close as quickly as possible and search elsewhere for solace.

Mindset 3: All-or-nothing thinking. Absolutist, or all-or-nothing, thinking is characteristic of young children, teenagers, and many young adults. It is also characteristic of individuals who suffer from depression. Given that an estimated 50 percent of PTSD sufferers also have biochemical depression, it is not surprising that many trauma survivors tend to view themselves, others, and life situations in simple, "all-or-nothing" terms.

In this mindset, other people are either friends or enemies—there are no in-betweens. For example, you might find yourself thinking, "Either this caseworker is going to take care of all my needs, with no intrusive questioning or mounds of paperwork, or he is just another crook who is out to get me."

When you are plagued with this black-and-white thinking, the caseworker cannot be just an ordinary human being who may know you have already been through the mill but is afraid that he might lose his job or an opportunity for a promotion if he doesn't make you complete all the paperwork.

When applied to yourself, all-or-nothing thinking leads to your judging yourself in the same black-and-white terms. You see yourself either as a total failure or a total success. You make few allowances for partial successes or partial failures. Similarly, life is either all bad and hopeless, or a bowl of cherries with endless possibilities.

If you were traumatized during childhood or adolescence, you may be especially prone to such all-or-nothing thinking, especially if you also suffer from depression. Absolutist thinking is especially strong among survivors who, due to the characteristics of the traumatic event, learned to trust some people almost entirely and some people not at all. Consequently it may be difficult for these survivors today to learn that different levels of trust are appropriate for different people.

In your journal, write about some of the ways you think in absolutist terms. For example, if some of your secondary wounding experiences involved a corrupt attorney, do you now view the entire profession as a collection of thieves? If during the trauma you were assisted by Asians, do you now view all Asians as beyond reproach?

Even though you may be aware that your thinking is not quite rational, in your gut, as a result of the trauma, do you divide people into categories of good and bad? Which groups of people fall into the good category, which into the bad? Similarly, which groups of people do you judge as being incompetent or unreliable?

Also write about some of the ways you view yourself in absolutist terms.

Mindset 4: Continuation of survival tactics. Your survival tactic during your traumatic event may have been anger and aggression, as in combat, or it may have been passivity, as in a domestic violence situation. If you are an incest survivor, perhaps your survival tactic was flirting or acting coy and seductive to avoid a beating or having your abuser turn on another member of the family. Or perhaps you dissociated from your body, pretending the body that was being violated was not really yours or that it had no feeling.

These and other survival tactics during the traumatic event may have saved your life. During secondary wounding experiences, such tactics may have assisted you in obtaining what you needed. Today, however in some ways they may be infringing on your happiness. Can you identify any circumstances in which this may be true? Take some time to write about this topic in your journal.

Your first challenge will be to identify your survival tactics. (The chapters in Part III of this book, on specific types of traumas, may be of assistance in this.) Even if you are deeply ashamed of some of your tactics, it is important to recognize them and come to realize that they served a very important function: saving your sanity or your very life.

Some of these tactics may be difficult for you to identify because they may be such a part of you that they seem more like personality traits than survival tactics. This is especially true if you are a family abuse survivor or have otherwise been severely traumatized. For example, perhaps you had to lie, be very secretive, flaunt your sexuality, act helpless and weak, or be extremely placating in order to survive. You may now think you are a "born liar," a "natural flirt," a "weakling," or a "hopeless wimp." This is not the case. You learned these behaviors to cope, or they were reinforced by the trauma environment.

Do not be discouraged if you cannot identify many of your survival tactics now. As you read this book and think about what happened to you, you will grow in awareness of the many ways you learned to think, act, and feel in order to cope.

After you have listed your survival tactics, write about how they helped you or what would have occurred if you had not used them. For example, suppose you were an abused child who lied. Your journal entry might read like this:

> "I had to tell others the bruises were caused by falls or other accidents because otherwise my father would have beaten me more. I had to lie to my father too, because he could never tolerate the truth that he was the one who hit me. I also lied to him about where I was going, and about stealing money from him and my mother. If I hadn't lied I would never have been able to leave the house and go out with friends.
>
> "Looking back, lying to get out of the house and stealing to have the money to go out was part of my psychological survival. If I had stayed in that dysfunctional household every minute of the day and not maintained certain friends, I would probably have lost my mind."

If you suffer or suffered from an addiction, you might also view your addiction as a survival tactic. For example, you might write the following:

> "I started taking drugs at 13 because that was the only way I could deal with the incest. If I hadn't had taken drugs, I would have had to face the truth and done something about it, like tell the authorities. But if I had told, my family would have fallen apart. As harmful as my family was to me, at the age I was then, I needed to have a family. Having a family, even if it meant that I went on drugs to tolerate it, was part of my survival."

Once you have identified your survival tactics and some of the purposes they served during the trauma or the secondary wounding experiences that followed, write about how you might be practicing some of these tactics in your present life. Which tactics do you replicate today?

For each of the survival methods you have listed, ask yourself whether you use it almost always or only under stress or in certain situations. Be as specific as possible in identifying those situations.

Finally, consider the effects of using your old survival tactics. Ask yourself, Does using a particular tactic help or hinder me in my everyday functioning or in the pursuit of my life goals? What am I afraid would happen if I didn't use the tactic? How realistic are my fears? What would really happen if I didn't use the tactic?

Are there individuals with whom you could check out the reality of your fears? If so, take the time to talk to them.

The next chapter offers insights into the kinds of situations that may be triggering your use of these survival tactics—as well as other of your PTSD symptoms. For the moment though, sit back and reward yourself for hard work well done.

5

Why Am I Acting This Way?—Triggers

Traumatic memories are difficult to study, because they can not be created in a lab. Yet there is ample evidence that traumatic memories may be stored differently from other memories. The current thinking is that when a person reaches a certain level of anxiety of emotional arousal, as happens during trauma, the memories may be encoded in a manner that makes it difficult, if not impossible, for them to be recalled consciously or in full (van der Kolk 1995). Although remembering a trauma in vivid detail is normal, it is also perfectly normal for a trauma survivor to suffer from some form of amnesia. Some aspects of the trauma may be forgotten entirely or recalled only in fragments.

Unlike nontraumatic memories, traumatic memories can bring to the surface not only images of the event, but the feelings, sounds, smells, and bodily states associated with the event. For example, when Alan recalled a violent incident he had experienced 20 years ago, but had forgotten, he not only recalled the incident, but he stayed in state of anxiety and anger for two weeks afterward. The anxiety and anger were the feelings he'd had during the traumatic incident.

In essence, Alan acted and felt as if he were being traumatized all over again. In contrast, when Alan recalls a childhood vacation or his first day in high school, he does not have a major physical and emotional reaction to these memories. Nor do these memories haunt him, as do memories of the violence.

What Are Triggers?

Due to the way traumatic memories are stored, when something arises in the present that reminds you of a past event, you may feel the feelings associated with that past event. (In the case of trauma, the feelings that tend to arise are those of helplessness, betrayal, and victimization.) We call the present-day events triggers, because they trigger the emotions associated with the trauma. Triggers work even with traumatic events about which you have total or partial amnesia. David's story is an example.

Ten years ago David was mugged by two men who had jumped out of a green car. Nowadays, whenever he has to walk past a green car he feels uneasy—even frightened. His body is remembering the trauma because of the association with green cars. Green cars are a trigger for David, so he often goes out of his way to avoid getting too close to them.

You most likely have triggers of your own—some that you are aware of and, perhaps, some you are not. You may be unaware of certain triggers, because you have amnesia about the traumatic events and so can not relate present-day sights, smells, actions, feelings, and people to those involved in your trauma. Often trauma survivors do not know why they react so negatively or intensely to certain situations. It may seem that the situation does not warrant such an extreme reaction, yet there may be a perfectly logical reason for such a reaction if the situation is in some way similar to the trauma. When trauma survivors have amnesia about the traumatic event they may not be able to see the relationship between the present and the past, and may therefore conclude that they are "crazy."

Having triggers, or reacting to them, does not mean you are crazy or defective. However, when you are blind to what you are feeling and why you are feeling it, you may be driven to react in ways that do not serve you well. The purpose of this chapter is to help you become more aware of your triggers and to help you to manage your reactions to them.

Triggers Symptoms and the Adrenal Glands

All people, whether or not they are trauma survivors, have certain triggers to which they react emotionally. However, you as a trauma survivor, have an additional response that makes understanding and managing your reactions both more difficult and more complicated. The emotions that tend to be released are not happy ones, but the traumatic emotions of grief, rage, anxiety, and terror: you no longer feel safe.

In addition, your response is not purely emotional. Your adrenal glands also respond. Their response, which is out of your control, may cause you to react in ways that you later assess are not in your best interests.

As you learned in earlier chapters, being a trauma survivor means you have survived a life-or-death, "emergency" state. This emergency state may have lasted a few minutes, a few months, or many years, during which time your adrenal glands responded with secretions that caused fight-or-flight or freeze reactions.

In the present, one of the main problems you may have is that part of your brain does not know the difference between a real threat and one that is stored in the mind. Therefore, when the adrenals are set off by a situation in the present (a trigger) that reminds you of the trauma or by the anniversary date of a traumatic episode or loss, you may feel as threatened, angry, confused, or bereaved as you did during or after the original trauma.

Furthermore, and this is one of the worst parts of being a trauma survivor, when the adrenals are aroused by a trigger event, your long-term memory tracts, in which memories of the traumatic event and secondary wounding experiences are stored, also tend to be activated. This activation can result in increased nightmares, flashbacks, anxiety, rage reactions, and other PTSD symptoms.

You might not even consciously remember the anniversary date of a trauma. Or you might not consciously associate a certain person, object, or place with the traumatic event. Your wonderfully complex brain, however, does remember and makes the association. Suddenly you are living in the emotional climate of the traumatic event. You may even feel as if you are about to die.

Moreover, as if these reactions are not painful and distressing enough, if you are unaware of your triggers you can be bewildered—even frightened—by your response. When triggers are unexpected, you may feel as if you've been ambushed or unexpectedly "attacked." In this sense, triggers can themselves be traumatizing. You cannot understand why you have so rapidly become angry, numb, disoriented, paranoid, scared, or defensive.

Am I falling apart, or losing my mind? you may wonder. I was doing fairly well, but now suddenly I want to isolate or overwork. I feel so bad about myself too. You might feel hyperactive or self-destructive, or engage in self-destructive activities such as substance abuse or self-mutilation. Or you might become aggressive toward others or emotionally and socially withdrawn.

Whether you respond by becoming hyper or by shutting down, by attacking others or by attacking yourself, usually you are not thinking well. Your reasoning abilities suffer because, due to your biochemical responses to the trigger, you feel threatened. Under these conditions, your thinking abilities might suffer, because after a certain threshold of anxiety is reached, human beings' cognitive functions tend to shut down. The high anxiety level interferes with the ability to remember, think, calculate, plan, or perform other kinds of mental functions.

For instance, in the case of test anxiety, individuals who are well-prepared for an exam find that once they begin the exam they draw a blank or "can't think." Their level of anxiety is so intense that the part of the brain that manages rational thinking and logical functions suffers.

To compound the problem, if you were in an emergency state for too long, your adrenals might be damaged due to the overuse, and thus do not respond properly. The adrenal glands were not made to handle prolonged stress. If they are worn down from overuse, there can be more frequent and more exaggerated fight-or-flight reactions to trigger events and present stresses.

Types of Triggers

Anniversary dates, people, places, and objects, and emotional situations that remind you of the original trauma can serve as a triggers. So can reminders of secondary wounding experiences and present-day stresses—even if they are not similar to the trauma.

Anniversary reactions. Jack's story is a typical example of an anniversary reaction.

> Jack, a combat veteran, experienced increased flashbacks, anxiety attacks, nightmares, and insomnia during certain months of the year, but did not know why. Fortunately, he had at his disposal detailed military records, which indicated the dates he had been sent on dangerous missions.
>
> Looking back through those records, Jack was able to see an almost one-to-one correlation between the dates he had been involved in heavy combat and his increased PTSD symptoms. Establishing a connection between his combat experiences and his present-day symptoms was a relief—he felt less crazy and out of control, and he became able to predict when he would have increased symptoms and to prepare for them.

Current stresses. Jack was puzzled, however, when he had increased symptoms at times that were not related to specific battles.

> "Nothing happened to me in the war during these months. So why am I seeing my dead buddies in the room with me all week? Hey Doc, I thought you said I wasn't crazy?" he said angrily.
>
> As it turned out, in this case Jack's increased symptoms were triggered not by anniversary dates, but by a current stressor. His wife had lost her job and the family was having major economic problems.

Sometimes even the slightest increase in the level of everyday stress triggers increased symptoms of PTSD. Other psychological disorders can be stimulated as well, especially those stemming from untreated PTSD or that are otherwise PTSD related. Consider Loretta's experience.

> Loretta, an incest survivor, developed PTSD as a result of being sexually abused by her father for more than six years. After she left home, her father began to abuse her younger sister. At this point, Loretta reported her father to the authorities.
>
> As soon as her father heard that he would be arrested, he attempted to commit suicide. The attempt failed, but left him

physically and mentally disabled. He lost his job and the family income plummeted. Loretta's mother and older sisters blamed Loretta for ruining the family and "killing" her father, and even managed to convince Loretta's younger sister that her father had not really abused her.

When her younger sister began to call her names and refused to talk to her, Loretta developed a clinical depression that required medication. For several years, Loretta functioned well on antidepressants, even though, as would be expected, she experienced increased PTSD and depressive symptoms on her father's birthday and other dates associated with the abuse.

It was not these triggers, however, that sent Loretta to the hospital. It was stress on the job. Loretta's employer was in danger of going out of business, and all employees were asked to put in overtime without pay. This in some ways paralleled Loretta's situation as a child. She had then had to work "overtime" and gratis ministering to her father's sexual and emotional needs. And at that time, as during the present, she felt that her overtime work was necessary to hold the family together—Loretta's father had told her that if she would not consent to his abuse, he would abandon the family.

Even if the work situation had not symbolized her family situation as a child, the overload at work by itself could have served as a trigger for Loretta. She was also wearing herself out with self-blame for her condition. Due to her work in therapy, she understood and did not condemn herself for increased depressive and PTSD symptoms stemming from secondary wounding experiences and associations with the incest. But this current relapse seemed unrelated to the trauma.

"It is related to the incest," her therapist explained. "Your extra hours at work and the anxiety about the future of the company put you on both emotional and physical overload. These are the exact conditions of your original trauma. While you were being abused, your body and emotions were on overload. On a physical level, you were being overstimulated sexually and deprived of sleep. On an emotional level, you were conflicted in your feelings toward your father and other family members.

"People can recover from trauma, but typically they do not handle subsequent stress the way that 'normal' people do. Trauma survivors like yourself become hyperaroused and are unable to calm themselves down. Or else they go into a total shutdown or severe numbing. For them, present stress feels as if an emergency is going on.

"Can you forgive yourself now?"

Media presentations, conversations, and other reminders. In addition to present-day stresses, media presentations on your type of trauma, or any kind of trauma, may serve as triggers. Furthermore, simply talking to others about your trauma, or listening to others talk about theirs, can serve as a trigger. As part of the healing process, you need at some point to write about, talk about, or draw pictures of the trauma. However, you may react to such disclosure with confusion, anger, or—even more painful—a profound sadness. Even once the healing process is complete, you may still feel that way when you share your story. This is as it should be. Something terrible happened to you. You can learn to live with it, but you cannot, and should not, wipe it away entirely. Along with the rest of your life experiences, it makes you who you are.

Coping with Other People

Your reactions to your triggers, like other parts of your PTSD, can provoke negative reactions from others. Like other secondary wounding experiences, these reactions may result from a variety of causes and take a variety of forms. What's important, however, is to realize that you are entitled to your response to the trigger.

Say for instance, that like David one of your triggers is green cars. You might grow faint, hyperventilate, sweat, or become nauseated when you see them. Or you might become severely depressed or agitated. You might even turn to a substance to comfort you.

Others may label your strong aversion to green cars an overreaction. They may even call you crazy for feeling as you do. "You should be over it by now," they say. "After all, the color of the car was irrelevant." Someone might even suggest that you buy a green car just to help yourself get over it or to prove to the world that you have overcome the past.

But you aren't over it and there is no reason why you should be. Furthermore, whereas the color of the car may be irrelevant to others, it is highly relevant to you. The color is not only permanently imprinted on your mind, but imprinted with it are the terror, disbelief, anger, and other feelings bound up with being traumatized. The color green has come to symbolize an event that perhaps changed your entire view of life. You can erase neither the memory of the event nor the association—no matter how hard you try.

And despite what others may think, your response to green cars is perfectly rational, logical, and understandable. There is nothing wrong or warped about responding to triggers. Indeed, given the way the human brain works, such responses are inevitable.

However, responding to present-day events as if they were events that occurred in the past may not always be quite appropriate for what is going on in the present. For example, if you never leave your home for fear of seeing a green car, or if you exclude from your life anyone who drives a green car or wears green, you might want to think twice.

Such decisions will certainly protect you from the awful memories, but there are clearly costs to such decisions—ones that you may or may not be willing to bear. These costs may, in fact, be greater than the pain and anger involved in dealing with green cars.

The sections that follow are designed to help you, first, identify your triggers, and then to manage them—including helping you decide which ones you want to take control of.

Identifying Your Triggers

In preceding exercises, you wrote down descriptions of the traumatic event you experienced and your secondary wounding experiences. You were encouraged to include as many details as possible, especially sensory details.

A major reason you were asked to form as clear and complete a picture of the trauma and your secondary wounding experiences as possible was so that, at this point, you could go back and identify those aspects of the trauma that could be serving as triggers for you in the present.

Note: If you had difficulty remembering the trauma when you wrote about it in your journal, you might at this time want to go on to Chapter 6, which offers suggestions for mentally reconstructing the trauma. You can then return to this exercise after working through that chapter.

Exercise: Trigger Chart 1

At this point you will make a trigger chart, which can be invaluable to you first in identifying, and later in anticipating, situations in which you might react as if the trauma were recurring.

Give a piece of your journal paper the heading "Trigger Chart 1" and draw three columns beneath it. Label the first column "Trigger," the second "My Reactions," and the third "Traumatic Memory."

In the first column list those times or instances when you feel the adrenaline rush to fight or run or where you shut down or go numb, emotionally, physically, or both. Examples of triggers include smells, sights, sounds, people, or objects that remind you of the trauma or of events associated with the trauma.

Triggers might also include current stresses, such as the following:

- Interpersonal difficulties at home or at work
- Any kind of work or emotional overload
- Financial or medical problems (including premenstrual syndrome)
- Increased crime or other neighborhood problems

- Witnessing or being involved in a current trauma (a fire, car accident, natural catastrophe, crime)

In the second column, indicate your reactions to each trigger situation. Your reactions in each situation will not necessarily be the same. Possible responses include these:

- Anger or rage
- Isolating yourself or overworking
- Self-condemnation
- Increased cravings for food, alcohol, or drugs
- Increased flashbacks
- Self-mutilation
- Depression
- Self-hatred
- Suicidal or homicidal thoughts
- Increased physical pain (headaches, backaches)
- Activation of a chronic medical condition, such as increased blood sugar if you are diabetic, increased blood pressure if you suffer from hypertension, recurrence of urinary tract infections if you are prone to bladder problems

In the third column, try to trace the trigger to the original traumatic event, to a secondary wounding experience, or to an event associated with these experiences. If you cannot remember the original event, do not be overly concerned. The main point of completing this chart is to help you to understand and anticipate when you might be triggered. This understanding is the first step toward change and gaining control.

Take a look at the Trigger Chart 1 examples to get an idea of how the chart works. Consider sharing your chart with your family members and friends. They might be able to help you add instances to your trigger list. Also, sharing this chart will help them to understand you better and ease any stresses in your relationship.

Coping with Triggers and Trigger Situations

"Last week my brother came to town to see the baby. I haven't forgiven him for what he did to me as a kid, and I sure didn't invite him, but I didn't feel okay about refusing to see him.

"So there he is in the living room, mostly just watching TV and eating pretzels—ignoring all of us pretty much—when Tommy, the baby, starts to cry. My brother was on him like that! Slapped him and yelled at him to shut up.

"And I didn't even move, couldn't move. My wife had to tell my brother to leave. I guess the slap and the yelling brought back all those memories of how he used to beat me. I couldn't stop shaking, and I felt so bad that I hadn't helped my kid. I should have been the one to protect him, not Ellen.

"I know it's all part of the PTSD stuff and triggers, but I still wish I had more control over it. I guess knowing helps some though."

As Tom, the speaker above, said, knowledge is one thing, but control is better. The following sections offer not only information but ways to help you deal with triggers and potential trigger situations.

Feeling Safe

As a trauma survivor, feeling safe is a major priority in your life. When you don't feel safe, you are unable to do or give your best in any situation. Trigger situations are threatening because, consciously or unconsciously, they bring up memories of times when you were powerless and therefore vulnerable to attack. They also threaten by bringing up painful and problematic feelings such as anger, fear, and grief.

These feelings are frightening, because they have the power to plummet you into a state of numbing or hyperalertness, or to cause you to otherwise lose control. If you have a history of addiction to a substance, you may know through bitter experience that when sorrow or rage appears, you tend to run for the bottle, the refrigerator, or for some other mood-altering substance. Even sex and work—healthy activities at other times—can serve as a narcotic for these feelings.

Triggers not only give rise to fear of loss of control, they can also make you fear going insane. People who have experienced the terror of wondering if they are mentally ill never forget that experience. It is excruciatingly painful.

You may have made considerable progress in managing your anger and grief. You may even have years of recovery from substance abuse. Yet you may still fear that the next time you are triggered you might not make it. What if you forget to do what your therapist told you to do? What if you are too tired or discouraged to follow the suggestions of your 12-step program?

No matter how much you have grown emotionally, you may fear slipping back into old behaviors. After all, you have practiced the old ways so much for so many years that they have become almost automatic. And, although these new ways of coping are better for you, they require effort, thought, and concentration. They take work. And if you are stressed or otherwise not feeling well, the normal temptation is to resort to the old dysfunctional behaviors, because at the time they seem easier.

Trigger Chart 1—Examples

Trigger	My Reactions	Traumatic Memory
Someone, an authority figure, tells me to do something in a disrespectful, rough, or impersonal tone of voice.	Anger, desire to fight back, desire to run away instead of hitting the person or having to hide my rage.	It reminds me of taking orders from that C.O. who sent us all out to be killed so he could look good.
Trigger Red dresses.	**My Reactions** Fear, anxiety, repulsion. If I can, I avoid people wearing red dresses. If I can't, and someone approaches me, I break into a sweat. I also start feeling guilty, as if I'm causing her to attack me.	**Traumatic Memory** I was wearing a red dress when I was raped.
Trigger Car trips, confinement in vehicles or rooms.	**My Reactions** Sweating, nausea, panic, followed by intense anger. Then numbing and depression for about two days.	**Traumatic Memory** When my abuser was being prosecuted, I was taken to the courthouse over and over. It was two hours from home, and when I got there they didn't believe me. It kept getting more complicated, and each time they treated me worse.

As a result of all these fears, you may find yourself organizing your life to avoid triggers and trigger situations. However, those avoidance behaviors can create problems at home, at work, even within yourself.

This creates a real dilemma. On the one hand you need, and deserve, to feel safe. When you enter into situations that you know trigger you, you are risking emotional and possibly physical discomfort. In some cases, your discomfort can be so extreme that you feel suicidal, homicidal, or out of touch with reality. On the other hand, avoiding situations that have set you off in the past, or that you know have that potential, might be very costly to you. It is one thing, for example, to avoid string beans because they have bad associations, and quite another to avoid your own children, because children are a trigger for you.

It would be wonderful if the world were organized so that you never had to confront any of your triggers, or if you could receive special treatment because of your past suffering. Unfortunately, you are generally going to be expected to cope with life's challenges and stresses just like anyone else. But that coping is going to be more difficult for you than for "just anyone else." To pick a simple example, suppose red dresses are a trigger for you, and your supervisor's favorite color is red. What choices do you have besides quitting your job or suffering in silence? Or perhaps being confined in a car or airplane is one of your triggers. What if someday you need to take a plane to see a dying relative, or need to drive a long distance for some reason?

Social Situations

Special problems arise if you have endured prolonged or repeated trauma. If this is the case with you, your central nervous system may be unable to tolerate a great deal of noise or other stimulation. In that case, even though it is not life threatening, the stimulation of normal socializing or being with your family can irritate and drain you. But what does that do to your relationships with your family and others?

After a day at work or being with others, you may simply need time to yourself to calm yourself, especially if you are experiencing any kind of stress. Sometimes you may need to really be alone—either to practice some of the soothing techniques suggested later in this chapter, or just to think.

If the people in your life can understand, and accept, your needs, any problems may be minimal. But if they do not understand or cannot accept your needs, they may feel rejected or abandoned, and they may in turn reject and abandon you. Thus begins a vicious cycle of misunderstanding, hurt, and anger, the end result of which is mutual alienation.

Even more taxing for some trauma survivors are events such as parties, parades, and other large gatherings. The sheer number of people, the noise, and the confusion involved in such events, can wreak havoc with your central nervous system. Since such events can put you on sensory overload, you might experience panic, anxiety, or, alternatively, numbness.

As a result you might, understandably, decide to avoid all parties and gatherings to avoid the associated discomforts. However, you could pay the price of being branded antisocial by others. You might also brand yourself as deficient because you can't enjoy such occasions. If attendance at some of these functions is an important part of your family life or job, staying away can lead to problems at home or at work. It can also lead to feelings of loneliness and alienation. Yet to attend such functions can feel almost unbearable.

Under these circumstances, what can you do? You are in a double bind, just as you were during your trauma and during many of your secondary wounding experiences (and that feeling of being in a double bind can itself be a trigger, since it emulates part of your trauma). Whether you go or stay away, you lose. Either you participate in functions that cause emotional and physical distress, or you stay away and pay the personal, social, and vocational penalties.

The good news is you can learn to confront and cope with some of your triggers. It is not easy, nor painless, but it is possible. The remainder of this chapter attempts to teach you ways of structuring your confrontations with trigger events so that you feel relatively safe and can begin to tolerate these events.

However, some of your trigger situations may be almost unendurable, and consequently you may need to make your best effort to avoid these situations whenever possible. But bear in mind that over time, as you continue to heal, you may be able to handle more and more situations that at this point seem unbearable.

As with all aspects of the healing process, you need to start small, with baby steps.

Exercise: Trigger Chart 2

Your first task in this exercise is to divide your trigger situations from Trigger Chart 1 into four categories:

1. Triggers you feel might be the easiest to endure

2. Triggers you feel you might be able to handle after a few more months of healing

3. Triggers you feel you might be able to confront in a few years (maybe)

4. Triggers you plan to avoid for the rest of your life

Title a new page in your journal "Trigger Chart 2," and draw lines to make four columns. Label them, from left to right, "Easiest to Handle,"

"Possibly Manageable Within a Year," "Possibly Manageable in the Distant Future," and "Impossible Ever to Handle."

Now, take your list from Trigger Chart 1 and write each trigger in the appropriate category.

Selecting a Trigger to Work On

When you feel you are ready to confront a trigger, select one of the ones you listed in column 1 of Trigger Chart 2—a situation that you judge one of the easiest to confront. Beginning with a more difficult trigger, such as one in column 2 or 3, can be a setup for failure, since no trigger situation, even one you have classified as relatively easy to handle, is truly *easy*. You have to start somewhere, however, so it is best to start where you have the greatest chance of success.

What if it doesn't work? But what if I try and fail? you might ask. What if, after trying some of the coping methods described below, you find that you still cannot handle the situation? This does not mean you are a failure.

In the first place, you need to examine what you mean by the word *failure*. If you can survive the trigger without hurting yourself, harming someone else, or regressing into some dysfunctional state, that is quite an achievement. Just because you feel anxious or otherwise uncomfortable does not mean you have failed. To expect yourself to cope with a potent trigger without any anxiety, anger, grief, or depression is too much to ask. Would you ask it of anyone else, your best friend, for instance?

Your goal is to be able to endure the trigger situation so that you can go on with your life—not to wipe out all your emotional reactions.

For example, suppose your trigger is a certain ethnic group, and you need to work with individuals from that group. In that case, you would be successful if you were able to learn to work alongside people who trigger you with less anxiety, fear, anger, or pain. The point is to get the job done. You can't expect to shed all your discomfort at once.

However, if you continue to have great difficulty coping with one of your "easy" trigger situations, it may well be that you minimized the severity of the trigger. Or it may be that you have limits you were not aware of.

Working within your limits. As a trauma survivor, it is important that you know your limits, respect them, and try not to put yourself in situations that push those limits too far. Knowing what your limits are enables you to prepare yourself for the ordeal of a trigger by making a plan to handle the situation in the best way possible.

For example, if you were a prisoner of war, an abused wife or child, or were otherwise captive, you may tend to be claustrophobic or become anxious when you are or feel confined. If this is the case with you, you should try to structure your life to avoid prolonged confinements. However, there will be times when you have to be confined, such as during a hospitalization or a long trip. Under such circumstances, you can take care of yourself by making a list of all the ways you can give yourself some freedom of movement or take time-outs from the confinement.

For example, suppose you are required to attend meetings all day as part of your job. You know that when you are cooped up you tend to become anxious and depressed, but the meetings are mandatory. Your lunch and other breaks are your own, so during those times, you do not have to go to a restaurant or do what the others do. You can plan to go for a walk or do something else that relaxes you.

Furthermore, after the meetings are finished for the day, you would probably want to avoid activities that feel confining to you. Instead plan something that makes you feel free. It doesn't matter what it is—what matters is how you feel about it and the feeling it gives you. For some trauma survivors who have problems with confinement, going to a movie after a day of meetings is like going from one prison camp to the next. Others, however, experience a movie as a form of pleasurable escape and freedom. Only you can judge what would work best for you.

In sum, as you attempt the following coping techniques with a specific trigger, try not to judge yourself too harshly. Consider each attempt a learning experience—don't judge it in terms of success or failure. This is not a test of your character, moral strength, man- or womanhood, or mental health, but a way of acquiring valuable information about yourself.

Along these same lines, remember that you are not a coward or a weakling if you learn (through your own pain), that certain triggers are so powerful that for now, and perhaps forever, it may be best to avoid them if you can possibly do so. It makes ultimate sense to avoid pain, especially if it is unnecessary. There is no shame in this. Remember, you didn't cause the trauma, and you didn't decide to have PTSD.

Considering medication. In some cases, medication may be helpful in reducing PTSD symptoms upon encountering triggers. To find out, you will need to consult with a psychiatrist who is knowledgeable about PTSD. In general, it has been found that medication is helpful in reducing the intrusive symptoms of PTSD—the nightmares, recurring thoughts, flashbacks, and so on—and the hyperalert symptoms, the startle response and sweating, for example.

However, no medication has been found to help PTSD sufferers cope with the tendency to avoid triggers. Regardless of which symptoms give you the most trouble, or which you desire to work on to improve your life, medication alone is not the answer. Even therapists and physicians who have completed innovative research on the biochemical aspects of PTSD, stress that medication must be accompanied with counseling or therapy for healing to occur (Friedman 1991).

Exercise: Motivating Yourself

In your journal, answer the following questions about the trigger situation you have chosen to attempt to manage. Be as specific as possible in your answers.

1. What are my fears about this situation?

2. How have I usually reacted in the past?

3. What have been the costs of avoiding this situation or of handling the situation with the fear, anxiety, anger, or other emotions associated with the trauma?

4. How would I like to react in the future?

5. What do I stand to gain if I react in a way I feel would be more beneficial?

6. How can I break down this situation so that it is more manageable?

Sometimes even so-called easy trigger situations are too difficult to manage in their entirety. If this is the case, then break the situation down into small parts. For example, if your trigger is a certain object, then break the situation down into being 12 feet from the trigger, then 6 feet from it, then walking toward it. Once you have been able to complete these steps, you can try standing right next to the trigger for 1 minute, then 2, then touching it, and so on.

Only after you are able to take the first step should you take the second. Whenever you are trying to overcome a fear or to change any of your behaviors, it is usually best to start with small, manageable steps.

Writing and sharing. In addition to identifying your fears, spend some time writing about your other feelings about the trigger. You can share some of your writing or thoughts with others if you desire. Consider how Joan used writing to sort out her feelings.

Joan is a 38-year-old woman who suffered from neglect and sexual abuse as a child. Today she has trouble coping with people who let her down in one way or another. For example, if her boyfriend is late arriving (even just a little), or otherwise forgets his promises (including small ones), Joan tends to go either into a rage or a depression. Her reactions are especially intense when she feels stressed for other reasons, such as by overwork, minor illness, or problems with her roommate.

For Joan, being kept waiting and being forgotten are intertwined with a history of gross parental neglect and abuse. Joan's parents used to forget to pick her up from school, church, and parties, as they had promised to. Beatings usually followed.

"I'm know totally overreacting," Joan wrote in her journal, "Jeff is only a half-hour late. That's not anything terrible. It's just that what he's doing is just like what they did to me. I can fly into a rage at him and ruin the evening, or swallow my anger, like I did when I was a kid.

"I know most of my anger doesn't belong to him, but I'm so furious I could explode. I need to keep reminding myself that my fury doesn't belong to him. I don't want to yell at him, but swallowing my anger doesn't work either. All I can do is try to reduce my anger."

Joan tried to reduce her anger by writing about it and doing some exercises in her living room. If you are in an emotional situation that sparks your rage, other methods of reducing your anger may prove more helpful, for example, relaxing, taking a hot bath, talking on the phone to a friend, or resting in bed. Do whatever works for you.

Planning Ahead

Before facing the trigger situation you've chosen to confront, ask yourself these questions:

- What is it I have to do?

- What is the likelihood of anything bad happening?

- If something bad does happen; what can I do?

Try to be as thorough and realistic as possible. Imagine possible eventualities, but don't get caught up in gruesome and unrealistic fantasies. If you become anxious, angry, or otherwise distraught trying to plan for the trigger, counter your anxious or otherwise upsetting thoughts with the following ideas (Veronen and Kilpatrick 1983):

- It's okay if I am anxious, angry, or have other feelings. All my feelings are okay. But I need to focus on what I need to do to confront the trigger.

- I need to make a plan, but I do not need to make a plan alone. In fact, I don't have to do any of this alone. I have the support and encouragement of others. I can call on other survivors, my therapist, and friends for emotional support and guidance. There are people in the world who care about me and who are willing to help me.

Asking others for help. Consider asking others for help. Is there someone you can talk to about how you are feeling either before or after or during your confrontation with your trigger? Ask for suggestions from others, as well as from your counselor or therapist, about how to help yourself cope.

Relaxation Techniques

Before you confront the trigger or trigger situation, consider doing some muscle relaxation exercises, deep breathing, or physical exercise—or some combination of these if that works better for you. The following sections offer some guidelines. Also, throughout the trigger situation, you can use breath control or a modified form of muscle relaxation without anyone else knowing what you are doing.

A note of caution. Before you begin the muscle relaxation exercises suggested here or elsewhere, obtain the approval of your physician, psychiatrist, or other mental health counselor first. Your doctor or psychiatrist's consent is especially critical if you are on medication—either psychiatric or nonpsychiatric drugs. The lowered heart rate and increased oxygen flow induced by deep breathing or relaxation can interact negatively with certain medications. You need to check with your doctor to be sure that there will be no negative side effects for you. Whether or not you are on medication, do not attempt to do deep breathing or relaxation exercises for more than one hour.

For some people the relaxation exercises can bring forth intolerable memories. If this happens to you, stop immediately. If you suffer from multiple personality disorder, if you tend to use dissociation as a means of coping, or you have been told by a mental health professional that you dissociate frequently (even if you don't believe it), do not even begin the muscle relaxation exercises unless you have been given specific medical permission to do so. Also observe the other guidelines listed in the "Cautions" section of the introduction.

Deep Breathing

Your degree of body tension is reflected in the way you breathe. When you are under stress, you breathe shallowly. Conversely, you can learn to calm yourself by practicing deep breathing exercises. Deep breathing increases the oxygen flow to your brain, which increases your capacity to think and concentrate and helps rid your body of many toxins.

The following exercises will be useful to you not only in dealing with triggers, but in other efforts and in any life circumstance in which you want or need to calm yourself. Two forms of deep breathing exercises are offered here: abdominal breathing and calming breath. (Bourne 1990).

Try to practice one of the following techniques regularly. Five minutes a day for two weeks is recommended. Once you've become comfortable with one of the forms, you can use it to combat stress, anxiety, and other PTSD symptoms.

Continuing to practice either of these techniques will make it second nature. You will naturally breathe more deeply, which will promote feelings of relaxation and well-being.

Abdominal Breathing Exercise

1. Note the level of tension you're feeling. Then place one hand on your abdomen right beneath your rib cage.

2. Inhale slowly and deeply through your nose into the "bottom" of your lungs—in other words, send the air as low down as you can. When you're breathing from your abdomen, your hand should actually rise. Your chest should move only slightly while your abdomen expands. (In abdominal breathing, the diaphragm—the muscle that separates the lung cavity from the abdominal cavity—moves downward, causing the muscles surrounding the abdominal cavity to push outward.)

3. When you've taken in a full breath, pause for a moment, and then exhale slowly through your nose or mouth, depending on your preference. Be sure to exhale fully. As you exhale, allow your whole body to just let go. (You might visualize your arms and legs going loose and limp like a rag doll.)

4. Do ten slow, full abdominal breaths. Try to keep your breathing *smooth and regular*, without gulping in a big breath or letting your breath out all at once. Remember to pause briefly at the end of each inhalation. Count to 10, progressing with each exhalation. The process should go like this:

    Slow . . . inhale Pause . . . Slow exhale (count 1)
    Slow . . . inhale Pause . . . Slow exhale (count 2)
    Slow . . . inhale Pause . . . Slow exhale (count 3)

    and so on up to 10. If you start to feel light-headed while practicing abdominal breathing, stop for 30 seconds, and then start up again.

5. Extend the exercise if you wish by doing two or three "sets" of abdominal breaths, remembering to count up to 10 for each set (each exhalation counts as one number). Five full minutes of abdominal breathing will have a pronounced effect in reducing anxiety or early symptoms of panic.

    Some people prefer to count backwards from 10 down to 1 on each breath. Feel free to do this if you prefer.

Calming Breath Exercise

1. Breathing from your abdomen, inhale slowly to a count of 5 (count slowly "1 . . . 2 . . . 3 . . . 4 . . . 5" as you inhale).

2. Pause and hold your breath to a count of 5.

3. Exhale slowly, through your nose or mouth, to a count of 5 (or more if it takes you longer). Be sure to exhale fully.

4. When you've exhaled completely, take two breaths in your normal rhythm, then repeat steps 1 through 3 in the cycle above.

5. Keep up the exercise for at least 5 minutes. This should involve going through *at least* ten cycles of in-5, hold-5, out-5. Remember to take two normal breaths between each cycle. If you start to feel lightheaded while practicing this exercise, stop for 30 seconds and then start again.

6. Throughout the exercise, keep your breathing *smooth and regular*, without gulping in breaths or breathing out suddenly.

7. Optional: Each time you exhale, you may wish to say "relax," "calm," "let go," or any other relaxing word or phrase silently to yourself. Allow your whole body to let go as you do this.

Progressive Muscle Relaxation

Progressive muscle relaxation was developed over 50 years ago by Dr. Edmund Jacobsen as a means of deep relaxation. This technique can be especially effective if you feel anxiety physically, in the form of tightness in your neck and shoulders or back, in your jaw, or around your eyes, or if you experience high blood pressure, insomnia, muscle spasms, or headaches associated with tension.

Progressive muscle relaxation involves tensing and then relaxing 16 different muscle groups. It takes only 15 to 20 minutes to do, and requires nothing more than quiet and enough space to comfortably sit or lie down. Unless you experience overwhelming negative thoughts during the exercise, or some of the muscles being used have been injured so that the exercises are painful, there should be no reason you cannot use this relaxation technique.

Here are a few general guidelines:

- Set aside enough time (you might need 30 minutes at first) at a certain time of day for doing the exercises. When you first get up, before going to bed, and before a meal are the best times. After eating is the worst.

- Make sure you're comfortable: the room should be a comfortable temperature and quiet and free from interruptions, your clothing should not be restrictive, and your entire body needs to be supported. You can lie down, perhaps with a pillow beneath your knees for extra support. Or you can sit in a chair, but be sure your head is supported along with the rest of your body. (Sitting may be preferable if you feel unsafe lying down because of your trauma. Whenever and however you position yourself, be sure you feel safe.)

- Try not to worry or think about outside events. Put them away for the time being. Also, don't worry about your performance of the technique. The goal is relaxation here—it's not a competitive sport.

Aside from helping you cope with trigger situations, regular, daily practice of progressive muscle relaxation can have a significant beneficial effect on your general anxiety level. You can also use the following exercises (from Bourne 1990) before, during, or after completing any of the written exercises in this book, or before, during, or after doing any other kind of work on the trauma, either in a group or in individual counseling.

Muscle Relaxation Exercises. The idea is to tense each muscle group hard (but not so hard that you strain) for about 10 seconds, and then to let go of it suddenly. You then give yourself 15 to 20 seconds to relax, noticing how the muscle group feels when relaxed in contrast to how it felt when tensed, before going on to the next group of muscles. You might also say to yourself "I am relaxing," "Letting go," "Let the tension flow away," or any other relaxing phrase during each relaxation period between successive muscle groups. Throughout the exercise, maintain your focus on your muscles. When your attention wanders, bring it back to the particular muscle group you're working on. The guidelines below describe progressive muscle relaxation in detail:

- When you tense a particular muscle group, do so vigorously, without straining, for 7 to 10 seconds. You may want to count "one-thousand-one," "one-thousand-two," and so on, as a way of marking off seconds.

- Concentrate on what is happening. Feel the buildup of tension in each particular muscle group. It is often helpful to visualize the particular muscle group being tensed.

- When you release the muscles, do so abruptly, and then relax, enjoying the sudden feeling of limpness. Allow the relaxation to develop for at least 15 to 20 seconds before going on to the next group of muscles.

- Allow all the *other* muscles in your body to remain relaxed, as far as possible, while working on a particular muscle group.

- Tense and relax each muscle group once. But if a particular area feels especially tight, you can tense and relax it two or three times, waiting about 20 seconds between each cycle.

Once you are comfortably supported in a quiet place, follow the detailed instructions below.

1. To begin, take three deep abdominal breaths, exhaling slowly each time. As you exhale, imagine that tension throughout your body begins to flow away.

2. Clench your fists. Hold 7 to 10 seconds, and then release for 15 to 20 seconds. Use these same time intervals for all other muscle groups.

3. Tighten your biceps by drawing your forearms up toward your shoulders and "making a muscle" with both arms. Hold, and then relax.

4. Tighten your triceps—the muscles on the undersides of your upper arms—by extending your arms out straight and locking your elbows. Hold, and then relax.

5. Tense the muscles in your forehead by raising your eyebrows as far as you can. Hold, and then relax. Imagine your forehead muscles becoming smooth and limp as they relax.

6. Tense the muscles around your eyes by clenching your eyelids tightly shut. Hold, and then relax. Imagine sensations of deep relaxation spreading all around the area of your eyes.

7. Tighten your jaws by opening your mouth so widely that you stretch the muscles around the hinges of your jaw. Hold, and then relax. Let your lips part and allow your jaw to hang loose.

8. Tighten the muscles in the back of your neck by pulling your head way back, as if you were going to touch your head to your back. (Be gentle with this muscle group to avoid injury.) Focus only on tensing the muscles in your neck. Hold, and then relax. Since this area is often especially tight, it's good to do the tense-relax sequence twice.

9. Take a few deep breaths and tune in to the weight of your head sinking into whatever surface it is resting on.

10. Tighten your shoulders by raising them up as if you were going to touch your ears. Hold, and then relax.

11. Tighten the muscles around your shoulder blades by pushing your shoulder blades back as if you were going to touch them together. Hold the tension in your shoulder blades, and then relax. Since this area is often especially tense, you might repeat the tense-relax sequence twice.

12. Tighten the muscles of your chest by taking in a deep breath. Hold for up to 10 seconds, and then release slowly. Imagine any excess tension in your chest flowing away with the exhalation.

13. Tighten your stomach muscles by sucking your stomach in. Hold, and then release. Imagine a wave of relaxation spreading through your abdomen.

14. Tighten your lower back by arching it up. (You can omit this exercise if you have lower back pain.) Hold, and then relax.

15. Tighten your buttocks by pulling them together. Hold, and then relax. Imagine the muscles in your hips going loose and limp.

16. Squeeze the muscles in your thighs all the way down to your knees. (You will probably have to tighten your hips along with your thighs, since the thigh muscles attach at the pelvis.) Hold, and then relax. Feel your thigh muscles smoothing out and relaxing completely.

17. Tighten your calf muscles by pulling your toes toward you. (Flex carefully to avoid cramps.) Hold, and then relax.

18. Tighten your feet by curling your toes downward. Hold, and then relax.

19. Mentally scan your body for any residual tension. If a particular area remains tense, repeat one or two tense-relax sequences for that group of muscles.

20. Now imagine a wave of relaxation slowly spreading throughout your body, starting at your head and gradually penetrating every muscle group all the way down to your toes.

You might want to record the above exercises on an audiocassette to expedite your early practice sessions. Or you may wish to obtain a professionally made tape of the progressive muscle relaxation exercise. There are many of these available, some of which are to be played while you sleep. However, the sleep tapes have not been proven to be particularly effective, and are additionally not practical for those who have trouble sleeping. Sources of some tapes that help you practice active muscle relaxation are listed in Appendix B.

Physical Exercise

Activities that involve physical exertion, for example, walking, swimming, jogging, and aerobic dance, are highly recommended for dealing with anxiety and trigger situations. "One of the best methods for controlling stress is to exercise. Vigorous physical exertion provides a natural outlet for your body. Exercise releases special chemicals in your brain called endorphins. These act as natural tranquilizers and have tremendous stress-reducing properties. When you experience a state of arousal, exercising can return your body to normal equilibrium, leaving you feeling relaxed and refreshed" (McKay et al. 1989).

Numerous books and programs are available to help you get started on a course of aerobic exercise. It need not be expensive, or complex—walking can be one of the best forms of exercise there is, if it's done right. Just keep a few things in mind:

- Don't start too strenuously or abruptly. Get a checkup and talk to your doctor about what you propose to do. This is especially important if you smoke, are sedentary, or have a family history of medical problems or existing medical conditions of your own.

- Warm up before and cool down after exercise. Allow at least 5 minutes of stretching and light exercise before and after your activity.

- Exercise for at least 20 minutes, three times per week, at a sufficient level of exertion. The Estimated Heartbeats chart shows estimated heart rates by age; 70 percent of maximum is considered the optimal rate at which to exercise (Davis et al. 1988).

- At all times, pay attention to your body. If it screams Stop! then stop. Warning signs include hyperventilation, chest pain, inability to breathe, or any form of acute discomfort (McKay et al. 1989).

Estimated Heartbeats per Minute for Average Man or Woman by Age Group

Age	Maximum Rate	80% Maximum Rate	70% Maximum Rate	60% Maximum Rate	50% Maximum Rate
18-29	203-191	162-153	142-134	122-115	101-95
30-39	190-181	152-145	133-127	113-108	95-90
40-49	180-171	144-137	126-120	107-102	90-85
50-59	170-161	136-129	119-113	101-96	85-80
60-69	160-151	128-121	112-106	95-90	80-75
70-79	150-141	120-113	105-99	89-84	75-70

Quick Fixes

Here are a few suggestions for occasions when you don't have much time or are in a public place or social situation and need a breather (McKay et al. 1989):

- Spend 10 seconds rubbing a tense part of your body
- Take ten slow deep breaths
- Change your posture and stretch
- Talk more slowly
- Get up and get a cold (nonalcoholic) drink
- Sit down and lean back

Positive Self-Talk

Another important component of coping with triggers involves the way you talk to yourself internally. All of us have an internal dialog going on more or less all of the time, and what is said in that dialog can be very important to the healing process and your well-being in general.

You read about self-talk in relation to feelings and thoughts in Chapter 3 and in reference to victim thinking in Chapter 4. Following are examples of how you can get that dialog to be on your side—how you can use it to help you get through a trigger situation.

Several years ago, Claudia was in an abusive relationship. Since that time she has been in group and individual therapy. The following are entries from her journal, but they demonstrate the way positive self-talk works.

February 23, 9 p.m.

"I've been numb with pain all day, but it took me until now to figure out why. This numbness or sadness or whatever it is, is a reaction to telling Tim about some of my traumatic experiences. I felt fine while I was talking to him yesterday afternoon. I guess today I got blessed with the great delayed reaction.

"Now that I think about it, whenever I talk about the past I get like this. Yet I'm always shocked that I react so strongly.

"I thought I'd be over it by now. After all, I've talked about it in therapy and group for years. I've cried about it, raged about it, made my peace with it, even gotten some good uses out of it. Why isn't it over? Why do I have to go through the pain and anger over and over again?

"I guess it's that trigger stuff my therapist is always talking about. When I get triggered, she says I should try to soothe myself as much as possible. So today I talked to friends, tried to eat right and get a little exercise, and tried not to stress myself too much. I also bought myself a little present.

"I did all the right things, but I still hurt. I hurt so bad I can't even cry. Oh God, how I wish I could, crying would be such a relief. It's pretty bad when you're so immobilized by pain that you can't even cry."

February 24

"The pain lifted. I guess doing all the right things helped. I'm also glad I didn't make any major decisions yesterday. When I get triggered like that, I'm not in my right mind. But that's not my fault.

"I have to keep telling myself, 'It's not your fault you were in a trauma. It's not your fault you have PTSD. The only thing you are responsible for is to try to manage your PTSD so that you don't hurt yourself or others.'"

Like Claudia, you need to learn to talk to yourself in a way that is supportive and nonjudgmental. Affirming pep-talks though they may seem silly to you at first, are a powerful tool you can use to deal with triggers and other stressful situations in your life. The following sections (adapted from Veronen and Kilpatrick 1983) give suggestions for things you might say to yourself before and during a trigger situation.

Before the Trigger

As you anticipate your encounter with the trigger event, try to talk to yourself like this:

> Soon I will face a trigger event. In the past, this event has made me extremely anxious. Sometimes my anxiety has turned into rage, sometimes into depression. Either way, I find the situation distasteful, if not unbearable. I am also aware that I tend to react with more anxiety to this situation than other people would. This makes me feel abnormal, deviant, and different in a negative kind of way.
>
> But I need to remember that, though anxiety happens to everyone, to trauma survivors like me it happens very easily, very quickly, and more intensely than to others.
>
> Because of what I have been through, my system quickly responds to certain situations as if an emergency were going on. What for other people sounds like an alarm clock, sounds like a fire engine's siren to me. That's because I was traumatized.
>
> My head knows there is no real emergency, but the rest of me, my emotions and body, don't know. That's why I have to keep telling myself over and over again that this is not *the original trauma*. Nothing terrible is going to happen. It might feel like something terrible is going to happen, but the reality is that I am not in danger.
>
> Yet, in a sense, there is an emergency going on and it's caused by the way my brain reacts to a trigger because I was traumatized. My anxiety creates that emergency. When I get very anxious I can't think well. I don't act the way I want, and I make poor decisions to boot. When people get too anxious or afraid, there are changes in their brain that do not allow them to solve problems as well as usual. The brain just doesn't work as well, and emotions, like fear, anger, panic, and hopelessness, take over.
>
> I hate it when I feel I might become out of control with one of these emotions. What if I get so mad I hurt someone, or myself? What if I become so anxious or scared I act in a foolish or stupid way? Others will think poorly of me. Or what if I get so hopeless and depressed that it shows, and others think of me as needy? That's why I stay away from trigger events—because I fear losing control and can't predict

how I will act.

The bad news is that when I confront a trigger, most likely I will react with fear, anxiety, rage, or depression right away. But that's okay. My crazy way of reacting is perfectly rational for a PTSD sufferer like me. Because I was in a trauma, the neural connections in my body are set up for these kind of emotional reactions.

But the good news is that I can build a new history. I can learn that the anxiety, the anger, the panic, or whatever strong emotion I am having will pass. At first it might take 2 or 3 hours to pass. The next time, 1½ hours to pass. The time after that, ½ hour. Each time I will progress until the trauma reaction becomes shorter and shorter.

I can build a new history in my brain if I keep practicing my coping techniques. Eventually, the new history will be more familiar and powerful than the old history.

In the past I've panicked, then I've panicked at the panic. I don't have to do that anymore. I can use my muscle relaxation and deep breathing techniques. I can take time out from the situation to center myself, call a friend, or do something that will help take care of me emotionally. If the situation becomes unbearable, I should permit myself to leave it entirely and try again another time, if that's possible.

I need to be patient with myself. I need to remember that it only takes a few minutes to become traumatized, but years to get over that trauma. I also need to congratulate myself for trying. At least I am trying. So many trauma survivors isolate from others and from life. They are too afraid to try what I am doing. I understand why they are afraid, but I also need to applaud myself for having the courage to try not to let my past strangle my present.

During the Trigger

When confronting a trigger event, try to speak to yourself as follows:

I need to take this one step at a time. I can't think about the entire event I have to endure. I have to break it down into small segments.

I need to be aware of my fears, anxieties, angers, and other feelings. But I need to focus more on what I am doing than on what I am feeling.

If I am afraid or angry, this does not mean I am a failure. I need to expect to be emotionally uncomfortable. After all, I'm in a trigger situation. Instead of getting mad at myself for my feelings, I need to view these feelings as signals that I need to use one of my coping exercises. For example, it may be time to do some deep breathing exercises, call a friend or sponsor if possible, take time out, or whatever makes sense. I also need to remember the plan I made for handling this trigger and stick with it.

Whenever I become overwhelmed with fear, anxiety, or anger, I need to tell myself, This too shall pass. Eventually I can go somewhere where I feel safe.

Progressing Through Trigger Chart 2

Once you have attempted to use some or all the preceding methods with one trigger situation, you may want to consider choosing another trigger situation to work on. Start with another trigger from column 1 of your Trigger Chart 2, the relatively easy category.

After you have attempted to work with all the triggers listed in column 1, when you are ready—not when someone else thinks you should be ready—you may want to tackle a situation listed in column 2. After you have attempted to confront the situations in column 2, you may then want to proceed to triggers in column 3.

Remember that coping with triggers is psychological, mental, and often physical work. Any kind of change, even positive change, creates a temporary increase in stress. If you are already under considerable stress, wait until your life is less full of pressures to tackle the extremely difficult task of trying to overcome a trigger. Go on to the triggers listed in column 3 only after careful consideration of your psychic energy and resources.

Discuss your decision with your therapist, sponsor, or trusted friends. Although it is important to challenge yourself and try not to let the past inhibit your life in the present, it is also important to be kind to yourself and not overtax yourself.

Acknowledging Reality

Don't delude yourself into thinking that following the suggestions given above will give you an anxiety-free life. These techniques reduce anxiety, but they may not eliminate it entirely. It is natural to have a little anxiety in certain situations—most people do. A very helpful resource in dealing with anxieties is the *Anxiety and Phobia Workbook,* by Edmund J. Bourne (1990). Your therapist will have additional suggestions.

Taking Stock

Over the course of the last five chapters, you have had the courage to look at your traumatic experiences and the equally traumatic secondary wounding experiences that followed. As the result of these experiences, you learned that your psyche is attuned to triggers—situations that remind you of the original trauma. Since you have identified not only the traumas but the triggers that flowed from them, you are no longer in the dark about these important aspects of your life.

You have also had the willingness and courage to examine yourself for any possible depression or addiction. If you have discovered that you indeed suffer from depression or that your "little habits" are, in truth, addictions that could ultimately kill you, you may at first have been shocked, then wanted to deny your findings. However, if you are indeed clinically depressed or addictive in some aspects of your life, and you have been willing to accept these truths rather than run from them, applaud yourself vigorously.

But why? you might be asking. Look at me, I'm a mess. First, I went through a trauma and a series of secondary wounding experiences. Then, instead of coming out a hero, I emerged damaged—depressed, addicted, and full of triggers that can send me into a rage, a crying jag, or a state of numbing that makes me feel half dead, all of which alienate me from others.

Do not despair. Healing is possible. But without the insights you have gained about yourself in these first five chapters, it probably wouldn't be. You must know what your problems are before you can begin to solve them. The time and emotion you spent gleaning the truths about your life in these chapters were not spent in vain. What you have so painfully learned about yourself will form the basis of the healing process, which is the theme of the chapters that follow.

Part II

The Healing Process

Carl Jung, a student of Freud and a famous psychologist in his own right, used the metaphor of a growing tree to describe the client in therapy. The client, he said, is like a tree, naturally growing taller and fuller while its roots spread out wider and deeper into the ground.

When the roots of a tree hit a large stone or other obstacle, do they try to shove the stone away or crack it? No. The roots just grow around the obstacle and then keep going.

The stone may have interrupted or slowed the tree's growth for a while, but no stone, no matter how large, can stop the tree from growing.

In Jung's view, the stones in the way of tree roots symbolize obstacles to personal growth. These obstacles can include an internal emotional conflict (for instance, loving and hating the same person) or an external stressor (for example, a trauma). Jung theorized that certain emotional conflicts are never totally eliminated; they are simply outgrown. They stay a permanent part of the psyche, just as the stones surrounded by tree roots become "part of" the tree. In the same way that roots can move far past the stones in their path into new territory, you can integrate and grow beyond your trauma.

Perhaps today your trauma is, to one degree or another, frozen in time, far away from the rest of you. However, once you have integrated the trauma into your life, you can use some of the powerful energy generated by the trauma to benefit you, to use in pursuing goals of your own choosing. The trauma can become a vital part of your life—just as the stones support and strengthen the root structure of the tree.

How to Use These Chapters

Generally speaking, you will want to work through the chapters in this part in order they appear. However, if (for example) the process of remembering the trauma covered in Chapter 6 raises emotions so great that they must be dealt with before you can continue the work of remembering, then you will want to go on to Chapters 7 through 9, which deal with feelings in general, anger, and grief, respectively. The final chapter of Part II, Chapter 10, discusses ways of regaining control of your life— putting what you have learned from the healing process—and even from the trauma itself—to work for you in your present and future life.

A Growth vs. Deficit Model of Therapy

One of your healing goals should be to rid yourself of the idea that because of the trauma, you are diseased or deficient. Such thinking hearkens to a deficit model of therapy, which assumes that you, the client, are "sick," "wrong," or "inadequate" in some way. The role of the therapist in this model of therapy is to help you discover your deficiencies and purge you of them.

In contrast, in a growth model of therapy, which is used in this book, the therapist's role is to help you discover and develop your strengths. A growth model assumes that you are not deficient or abnormal; instead it was the events you experienced that were (highly) abnormal. As a result, you may have developed certain defenses, certain ways of thinking, and other patterns that may have served you well during the trauma but do not do so now.

As you grow and heal, many of these negative patterns will naturally fall by the wayside, because you won't need them anymore. In addition, the more you are able to look at the trauma directly, the less need you will have for defenses that limit your life.

Healing, as explored in the following chapters, means confronting what you haven't yet confronted, integrating what you have yet to integrate, and binding up your emotional wounds. You don't need to be "fixed," you simply need help in mobilizing your inner healing and creative powers. The following sections describe and give several guidelines for the healing process.

Healing Is a Nonlinear Process

Healing does not run a straight path; it inevitably involves setbacks. For example, in recovering from the flu you may have several days of improved health, followed by a temporary relapse. This setback doesn't mean you won't recover from the flu; all it signifies is that the human body is not an inanimate object. It can't simply be repaired and then be expected to stay that way once and for all. Rather, it is delicate and complex. Yet it has great ability to withstand stress.

Like the body, the human psyche is also not inanimate. You may find yourself taking three steps forward in the healing process, and then two steps back. That is fine; you are still making progress. Sometimes you go backwards because you need to go backwards—if, for example, you have taken on more emotional material than you can handle at a particular time. At that point you may have to retreat so that you can absorb the emotional shock and otherwise make sense of the material.

The Stages of Healing

The healing process can be divided into three stages:

1. Remembering the trauma and reconstructing it mentally—the cognitive stage—covered in Chapter 6.

2. Feeling the feelings associated with the trauma—the emotional stage—covered in Chapters 7 through 9.

3. Empowerment—the mastery stage—covered in Chapter 10. In this stage, you find meaning in the trauma and develop a survivor, rather than a victim, mentality.

Another component that may be important to you involves recognizing any spiritual or moral concerns you have regarding the trauma. Not everyone has such concerns, but if you do, you may want to consider talking to a clergyman, priest, rabbi, or other spiritual advisor. Keep in mind though, that with these individuals, as with others, you need to be on guard against any subtle or overt victim-blaming attitudes.

Whether you come to identify and take a closer look at any spiritual or moral concerns with a religious or spiritual professional, with a trusted friend or family member, or within yourself, it is important that you recognize, rather than deny or minimize, any such concerns. If you do have spiritual or moral concerns, part of the healing process includes learning to forgive yourself for any action or inaction on your part that has caused you shame or guilt.

The stages of healing tend to be progressive. For example, feeling the feelings (Stage 2), will be more intense and meaningful if you actually remember some or most of what occurred during the traumatic event (Stage 1), than if your memory is hazy. On the other hand, you may have feelings left over from the traumatic event without any recollection whatsoever about what happened. This is commonly the case with individuals who were abused as young children.

However, the healing stages do not necessarily flow in a neat progression. You may find empowerment and mastery, for instance, without recalling the traumatic event. Similarly, you may already be in the mastery stage (Stage 3), when suddenly you remember a highly significant aspect of the trauma that changes almost everything you previously thought or felt about it. Much to your surprise, the new revelation puts you back in the role of a helpless, hopeless victim.

Healing Takes Time

Healing is a lifelong process. Depending on the intensity and duration of your particular traumatic experience, it may take months or even years to fully remember or gain perspective on the events that trouble you now. Similarly, it may take a long time for much of the anger and pain to diminish.

If you have been extremely traumatized, it may take 5, 10, or even 20 years. But that's okay; the main point is that you have begun. Your healing process will take its own course and unfold in its own time, not according to some cookbook formula.

You may be in a great hurry to get it over with. If so, you can accelerate your recovery by working harder in therapy and using other aids, such as support groups and books. However, in general, it is better to deal with the trauma in doses. This way, you run less risk of becoming overwhelmed, the way you were during the original traumatic event. Just as you get more out of a meal if you eat slowly and chew each bite, it is more important to take the healing one step at a time, slowly, than to attempt to do too much and understand yourself only superficially.

Restorative Experiences

Your healing process will be heavily influenced by what has happened to you since the trauma. If you were besieged with secondary wounding experiences, your healing process will be longer and more painful than if you had affirming restorative experiences.

For example, battered women who receive some justice in the court system, such as having their abusers jailed, fare far better than those whose batterers are left unpunished. Similarly, the healing process of both abuse and crime victims is facilitated when they feel well treated by court and police officials: when they feel listened to rather than demeaned, when they are informed instead of being kept ignorant of the legal process, and when their cases are handled in a prompt and professional manner.

Restorative experiences can be economic, vocational, political, and interpersonal. To what extent were you financially compensated for any losses incurred during the trauma? To what extent has fulfillment on the job, or the love, approval, and support of others, helped soothe the psychic wounds of the traumatic event? The more restorative experiences you have had, the easier your healing process will be.

Conversely, if you have been retraumatized since the original traumatic event, your healing will be longer and more complicated than the healing of a trauma survivor who was fortunate enough to have escaped subsequent victimization or disasters.

Medication

If you are in an extreme state of depression, anxiety, or hyperalertness, you may need medication to help reduce your symptoms so that you can concentrate in your therapy. For example, if you can't sleep at night and start dozing off at work or during therapy sessions, you may need to consider medication to help you sleep. Similarly, if you are having so many flashbacks and intrusive thoughts that you can't concentrate on your job, you may need medication so that you can function. For such medication, you will need to consult a psychiatrist with expertise in PTSD

The Prerequisite of Safety

In order to begin the healing process, you need to feel and be safe. You cannot begin to heal from your wounds, psychological or physical, if you are still being wounded. If you are in an abusive living environment or are otherwise living in danger, you will need to take steps to create a safer existence. Indeed, creating a safe living environment for yourself is part of the healing process.

The sense of safety is also internal. You need to feel safe with your thoughts, feelings, and behaviors before you can begin to contemplate the trauma. This does not mean you won't sometimes have troublesome thoughts or feelings, but rather that you feel you can manage them.

If some of the symptoms of PTSD, or some of your thoughts, feelings, or behaviors, are making you feel out of control of yourself, those need to be your primary area of concentration.

It is not wise to begin the unsettling process of remembering the trauma and the other stages of the healing process without feeling you can exert at least some control over the symptoms that are creating the most havoc in your life. In some cases, medication may be needed. See Chapter 10 for more on establishing a safe environment and attaining a sense of security.

Cautions: When the Healing Process Is Not Advisable

If you have been severely or repeatedly traumatized or are currently coping with a great deal of stress, the healing process described in this book and certain forms of counseling may not be advisable. In most cases, counseling is helpful. However, in some cases it has been shown to increase symptoms and depression. For example, some Nazi concentration camp survivors have fared much better by keeping their memories in repression and denial than others have by remembering the horror. Similarly, preliminary studies of torture survivors from Cambodia and other Southeast Asian countries indicate that counseling that focused on the trauma made many of these people feel worse, not better. For these survivors, counseling that deals openly with their trauma only deepens their sense of loss and helplessness. For such individuals, supportive counseling for present-day concerns seems to be more beneficial than delving into the past.

If you fall into one of these categories or feel that you, too, are better off not remembering the trauma, then you need to focus on improving your coping skills, rather than on gaining insight. More beneficial to you than the chapters on remembering the trauma (Chapter 6), feeling the feelings (Chapter 7), and understanding grief and loss (Chapter 9), are Chapter 8, "Living with Anger," and Chapter 10, "Attaining Empowerment." You may also want to discuss medication with your therapist or counselor.

Although it is natural and normal for you to experience distress upon trying to follow the healing suggestions in this book, keep in mind the warning signs listed in the "Cautions" section of the introduction to this book (suicidal or homicidal thoughts, disorientation, hyperventilation, shaking, irregular heartbeat, and so on). If you experience any of these signs, seek professional help immediately. It is possible that one of the following statements applies to you:

- You should not attempt to remember the past at all, ever. Instead you can learn means of stress reduction, such as relaxation techniques and deep breathing.

- You have so much stress in the present that looking at the past is best saved for a later point in your life.

- You need some other form of counseling before you tackle the trauma.

- You need to be in a safe, controlled environment, for example, an inpatient ward devoted to trauma survivors, in order to begin the healing process.

The Strength of Survivors

Mary lost two of her best friends and her home in the 1989 Loma Prieta earthquake in Northern California. She came close to death herself, and suffered permanent damage to her legs, which, although not severe, limits her ability to participate in sports and other recreational activities.

To this day, Mary has periods of numbing, alternating with what some of her friends and acquaintances pejoratively call hyperactivity or workaholism. However, those knowledgeable about trauma use more loving words. They say Mary is a high-energy person.

Mary's energy is similar to the high energy noted in other types of survivors, for instance, former prisoners of war. Part of this energy stems from the hyperalert stage of the PTSD cycle, the rest from a sense of gratitude for having survived. Mary feels compelled to live to the fullest and to make her life count by being as useful to society as possible.

Mary serves as a volunteer reader to the blind, in honor of one of her friends who died in the earthquake. Her friend had done similar work while she was alive.

Like other trauma survivors, Mary has a sense of urgency about time that those who have not touched their own death sometimes lack. During the earthquake, Mary's former illusion that she was invulnerable to harm was shattered. As part of her PTSD, she has a foreshortened sense of time. Sometimes she is overcome with fear that she will die young. Therefore she wants to get all she can out of life. Her resulting impatience aggravates her boyfriend, Joel, who is far more casual in his outlook on life.

Joel resents the time Mary spends helping the blind, and when she wants to talk about the earthquake, her losses, and her confusion about the meaning of life, he tries to change the subject. She should forget the past and live in the present, he thinks—she needs to lighten up.

Recently, however, Joel's dog became too old and sick and had to be put to sleep. "He couldn't take it," Mary told her therapist. "Instead of admitting to his feelings, he developed all these psychosomatic symptoms. He had headaches, backaches, rashes, you name it. Yet he claims it doesn't bother him.

"He thinks he's stronger than me because I hurt sometimes and he hardly ever hurts. But if he can't face this, what is he going to do when one of his parents dies or if he's in an accident?

"Because of what I've seen and experienced, I feel prepared for almost anything. I'm not afraid to suffer, or feel any feeling, anymore. The earthquake taught me to deal with emotional and mental pain directly. Even though to other people I might look weak because sometimes I cry and shake a lot, actually I'm stronger than my supposed 'Mr. Macho' boyfriend."

How Will I Know When I Am Healed?

As Mary's story illustrates, healing from trauma does not mean that you will never again remember the traumatic event or never again experience any symptoms. Some symptoms, for instance, sleep disorders, tend to persist for years—even after other symptoms have either disappeared or become relatively insignificant.

If you must measure your progress, try not to think in terms of outcome, but in terms of having made your best effort. Also, think less about eliminating your symptoms and more about the evidence that you are increasing your involvement in the present.

Mental health is sometimes defined as the ability to love, work, and play. If, due to the healing process, you regain or increase your ability to love and care for others (including yourself) and to work and participate in some activities you find meaningful—or you simply become better able to enjoy yourself—consider yourself a great success.

Never mind if you still have nightmares or choose to avoid people or places that remind you of the trauma. Never mind if on the anniversary of the trauma you have flashbacks or nightmares or just sit in a chair, numb or crying. If you are able to know and accept your feelings and not fight them, you are a very strong person. At least you know what you feel and why you feel the way you do. Many people don't know the what, much less the why, of their feelings.

Flexibility and the ability to distinguish present reality from the past are two other aspects of mental health. PTSD sufferers who have not received help are often quite rigid in their thinking and behavior. Because they feel so fragile inside, they may find it difficult to tolerate external changes, for example, changes in schedules. Furthermore, their understandably intense need to protect themselves and their families may lead to a dread of change. However, growth requires the ability to change and adapt. The more you progress in your healing, the more flexible you will become.

Hang in There!

Therapists who work with trauma survivors have observed high dropout rates. After a few sessions, survivors sometimes experience some relief from their symptoms. They tend to sleep a little better at night and feel less anxious during the day. In addition, because the therapist assures them that they are normal people who are simply suffering from symptoms caused by abnormal amounts of stress, there is relief from fears of insanity and abnormality.

I'm feeling much better. Why go anymore? I have so many other things to do, they think. Then they drop out of counseling until some crisis brings them back—as nontraumatized clients also frequently do. Because of some initial relief from symptoms and some emotional support, they think the psychological pain that propelled them to seek help has finally died and been buried, never to rise again.

But the pain is not dead. If you drop out of counseling prematurely, you are only postponing dealing with the problem. If you are truly a trauma survivor, the pain, numbing, anger, or self-destructive behavior will resurrect itself again and again, until circumstances force you to look at it.

In certain extreme cases, untreated PTSD can lead to suicide or homicide. Far more typical, however, is succumbing to depression or addiction. Once these vicious cycles begin to absorb your life energies, you will have greater difficulty than ever facing the trauma. Instead of spending hours with a therapist, you may end up spending years in needless misery and defeat.

With this book, as with any healing effort, you need to hang in there. Don't stop because you feel a little bit better, or because you feel uncomfortable, or because of the agony of confronting the trauma and feeling your feelings. Stop only if you begin to experience some of the warning signs listed in the "Cautions" section of the introduction.

You don't have to be in counseling forever. At some point, it will be time to terminate your sessions or to reduce their frequency. But before you terminate therapy or take a break from it, be certain that you have made progress in the following four areas:

- You have obtained a clearer, more rational picture of the trauma than when you began the healing process.

- You have spent time grieving, raging, or experiencing other feelings associated with the trauma.

- You have acquired some skills and attitudes that help you take back control of your life, as much as is possible and practical.

- You have begun to forgive yourself for the behavior during the traumatic event about which you felt rational or irrational guilt or shame.

- You have mastered some effective stress-reduction skills so you can function better in your day-to-day life.

Be aware that these goals are never completely realized. You do not need to stay in counseling until you are "perfect" or until you are "perfectly healed." The decision to stop counseling, or take a break from it, should be made thoughtfully and discussed with your therapist or group leader.

It is also acceptable, and in many cases extremely advisable, to remain in counseling for many years—as long as is needed.

6

Stage 1:
Remembering the Trauma

On occasion, people may have accused you of liking to dwell in the past. But from experience, you know that remembering is neither easy or fun. In your heart you know that remembering is worse than being there.

Remembering is worse because while you were actually in the traumatic situation, you may have been anesthetized to the physical, emotional, and moral pain. Your body may have emitted a natural emotional or physical anesthetic, or you may have numbed yourself with some substance or compulsive behavior.

Furthermore, during the trauma, your mind was focused on survival. Only later, once you felt somewhat safe, could you begin to comprehend, and feel, the full extent of your losses.

The decision to remember. If the idea of remembering frightens you, and you do not want to take the steps outlined in this chapter, it does not mean that you cannot find relief. By using stress-reduction techniques, you may be able to function as you desire. For some people, learning to manage their stress levels through relaxation, exercise, and other methods is sufficient.

You may be one of those people who simply does not need to examine the past in order to live as you wish. However, if stress reduction methods cease to help you, you will need to consult a qualified therapist, who may recommend working on the original trauma and its aftermath.

Problems Uncovering the Trauma

There are, besides the pain, factors that make remembering the trauma difficult as well. According to Dr. Bessel van der Kolk (1990), a trauma expert at Harvard University, traumatic memories are often stored in a way that does not permit survivors to know or to tell their stories in a narrative form. Consequently, these memories become split off from the conscious mind and exist as fragments on the semiconscious or unconscious level.

Later on, the memories return. However, when they emerge into consciousness, they may not return as coherent stories, but rather in bits and pieces, as fragmentary memories of the event. Alternatively, the memories can return as "terrifying perceptions, obsessional preoccupations, somatic complaints," or as a number of other symptoms (van der Kolk 1990).

When the memories are fragmented and unconnected with one another, survivors sometimes find it nearly impossible to make sense out of their inner life. Until these memories can be pulled together into at least a semicoherent story, trauma survivors may have difficulty understanding themselves. They may not understand or fully appreciate the connection between the trauma and their times of depression, fear, anxiety, irritability, hyperalertness, or emotional shutdown.

As a result, these survivors may feel controlled by "strong, mysterious, and incomprehensible internal forces" (van der Kolk 1990). This feeling of being out of control of their emotions and inner life only serves to deepen the fear, depression, and sense of powerlessness that they are already experiencing. To others, and to themselves, they may seem "crazy." Yet their reactions are eminently rational.

Take Carol, for example, who remembers that while her father was sexually abusing her, her head "went out of the window into the sky (van der Kolk 1990)" She imagined herself neutrally observing the abuse from that vantage, as is common with incest survivors. They often imagine themselves to be flies or ceiling fixtures or bits of dust in the corner of the room—anything but a real person being violated. This process is a form of dissociation.

When incest survivors dissociate during the trauma, as a defense, they later cannot understand why they react to people, places, or objects reminiscent of the abuse with anxiety, fear, rage, or other symptoms.

> Years after the incest, when Carol had a family of her own, her father came into town unexpectedly. During his brief visit, he behaved appropriately and acted as if he had never molested her.
>
> After he left, Carol developed serious leg cramps. Since there were no injuries, the doctor concluded she was suffering from psychosomatic spasms. He suggested aspirin, tranquilizers, and bed rest. The word *psychosomatic* put Carol into a panic; she was more convinced than ever that she had a screw loose.
>
> Years later, in therapy, Carol discovered the origin of her leg cramps. In order to make her submit to the incest, her father had told her that if she wasn't a "nice girl" who would

do what he wanted, he would break her legs. Her mind had forgotten the threat, but her body remembered.

Not just incest survivors but other trauma survivors who have totally or partially repressed their trauma can suffer from symptoms they do not understand.

> Joanne, a 30-year-old secretary, could not understand why she would hyperventilate and sweat anytime she was near an elevator. Although she had been raped in an elevator when she was 13, her mind had blocked out the event. Consequently, she could make no sense out of the fact that she would rather walk up several flights of stairs than go near an elevator. She also could not explain why she became furious whenever her boyfriend wore a blue shirt. If she had remembered that her rapist had worn a blue shirt, she might have been better able to cope with the situation.

In many cases, trauma survivors, especially abuse survivors, turn to substance abuse or addiction in order to cope. However, in my experience with adult survivors of childhood physical and sexual abuse, I have found very few who could link their addiction to the abuse. Instead of seeing the obvious relationship between the abuse and their addiction, these clients tended to view their addiction as yet another indication that they were "no good," and therefore deserved the abuse. One reason for their difficulty in making the connection between the abuse and their alcohol, drug, or food addiction, was this inability to piece together their own personal story.

Helps for Remembering

As explained above, regardless of the type of trauma you endured, it is important for you to eventually be able to recall as much of your story as possible. You may simply be unable to remember some aspects of the story due to psychological amnesia. This chapter is devoted to encouraging you to bring forth the memories you are able to remember. As you complete the exercises that follow, some of your amnesia may also be lifted.

The types of exercises presented below include written exercises, exercises using prompts; storytelling, dancing, drawing, and other forms of art therapy; talking to others; reading; and professional techniques, such as traumatic incident reduction therapy and hypnosis. You will benefit most from these exercises, however, if you first prepare by calming yourself through deep breathing or muscle relaxation exercises, or both, as described in Chapter 5.

Work at your own pace. Some of the suggested exercises may be helpful; others may not. Stay with those that work for you and ignore the rest. Under no circumstances consider yourself a failure because one or more of the suggested exercises are not useful to you.

A Note of Caution

As mentioned in the text introducing this part of the book, you should not attempt any of the following exercises if you or your therapist feel you will be unable to manage the feelings they may bring forth. Remember to consult your therapist or psychiatrist before beginning any such exercise technique—especially if you are currently taking any kind of medication. The same applies to beginning meditation exercises. Also, if these techniques bring forth intolerable memories, stop immediately.

For some trauma survivors, relaxation can be fraught with danger. Prolonged muscle relaxation and meditation may be especially risky if you have psychiatric problems other than PTSD, especially if you have been psychotic or currently suffer from either psychotic tendencies or a full-blown psychosis.

Although in my experience, verified by the work of others in the field, some survivors find great peace and freedom in practicing deep breathing and muscle relaxation techniques, others find such techniques counterproductive, increasing rather than decreasing their anxiety. When these individuals relax, they can only envision the trauma and little else. All the "peaceful, relaxing" suggestions commonly used in relaxation and deep-breathing techniques, which are useful and beneficial to others, are to them just a bad joke.

> Jerry was an emergency room doctor who had seen many deaths. But the week before he came into the mental health clinic for help, two victims of a car accident, a husband and wife, had died on the table before him. This incident shattered his professionally calm, detached front. That night, Jerry dreamed about being four years old and seeing his father murder his mother and then commit suicide. Until then, Jerry's amnestic memories had not been triggered.

Had his counseling begun with relaxation techniques, Jerry might have spent his "relaxation" time having flashbacks of the deaths of his parents. Therefore, therapy began first with talking about the trauma, until the initial shock of recognizing it had abated somewhat.

Before Jerry could even contemplate relaxation exercises, he had to have several counseling sessions. During those sessions, he learned these basic facts:

- He would not die, explode, disintegrate, or cease to function if he dared to remember.

- Remembering would not result in the memories recurring as real-life events.

- The memories would eventually diminish in intensity.
- He could always go back to dissociation, denial, numbing, or whatever other methods he had used before to keep from remembering.

If Jerry's story sounds familiar to you—if you share the same fears of remembering—be sure to share your concerns with your therapist, group leader, or counselor.

Memory Aids

Earlier in this book, you were asked to describe your traumatic experiences in your journal. Reread those pages, adding to your entries any additional memories you may have recalled. Over time, your memories of the trauma will continue to sharpen and unfold. As they emerge, keep writing them down. If you can, keep talking about them also. Consider the exercises in this book as just a beginning. The following sections offer some additional suggestions to help you remember.

Using prompts. Objects can trigger memories. Photographs make excellent prompts. Find photographs of yourself before, after, or even during the traumatic event, or photographs of significant others from that time. With the photographs before you, ask yourself, What was I like then? What did I feel like? What was I interested in? How did I change? If you are looking at pictures of significant others, ask yourself, How did this person change in their attitude or behavior toward me after the traumatic event?

Use your judgment about the photos you choose. For example, what about pictures of people involved in the trauma? If you were abused, is it advisable to look at pictures of your abuser or his or her accomplices? If you are a combat veteran, should you look at pictures of the dead? Or if you are an accident or natural catastrophe survivor, should you read newspaper clippings about the event?

There are no hard and fast rules—you need to trust your gut reaction. If you don't want to look at such pictures, don't. Never push yourself, and never allow others to push you, into "facing the facts" when you aren't ready or when you feel such exposure would be not only pointless but destructive to your serenity.

It isn't necessarily a matter of being ready or strong enough—sometimes it just isn't needed, or helpful. In some cases, the emotional price is just too high to pay. You can grow without ever looking at pictures of the people or places involved in your trauma.

If you do want to take a look, go ahead. Feel free, however, to ask a friend to be with you, or to look at the picture in some other supportive context, for example, in an individual or group counseling session.

Start with one picture and see how you react. If it brings up too much pain, anger, or fear, or starts to create in you any of the symptoms listed in the "Cautions" section of the introduction to this book, stop immediately and follow the directions in that section.

Among other things, photographs may help you identify some aspects of the physical conditions under which the trauma occurred. These conditions, which might also serve as triggers for you in the present, can include the following:

- The season

- The temperature at the time (which may or may not have been consistent with the season)

- The type of room or other environment in which the event occurred

- The colors, textures, and smells of clothing and other physical objects present

You may also want to look at movies, newspapers, magazines, and objects of clothing or other artifacts, or listen to music from the era during which you were traumatized.

Revisiting the scene. You can also stimulate your memory by returning to the original site of the trauma. Under no circumstances should you consider this, however, without obtaining your therapist's or physician's approval first. There have been numerous cases of individuals completely falling apart when they returned to the scene of the trauma without adequate preparation or support. In a few cases of severe and repeated trauma, survivors lost their ability to function on the job and suffered long-term impairment in their ability to relate to others.

Thus it cannot be overemphasized that if you do decide to return to the scene of the trauma, you need to discuss your plan with a qualified helping professional first. Then together you can decide whether it is in your best interest to go there. Together, you can also discuss and prepare for the range of possible reactions you might have.

Talking to other people. Similarly, if you plan to find and talk with people who knew you or who were present during your trauma or otherwise have information about it, you need to talk with your therapist about how you can expect to feel before, during, and after such a venture. For example, if you hope to find the "missing link" or the "magic answer" in your search, you may be disappointed. Even if you do discover valuable information, you may find that the increased knowledge doesn't take away the pain. In fact, you need to be prepared for the possibility that, as a result of this new information, your symptoms will intensify.

Ask yourself if you are willing to deal with additional anger, grief, and possible disappointment at this point in your life. If you have many current stresses, or are feeling vulnerable or overwhelmed for other reasons, you may decide to pursue the plan of returning to the site of the trauma or contacting people from the past at a later time.

If you decide to contact individuals who have knowledge of you or of the trauma, remember your goals. Do not expect these individuals to provide you with unconditional love or emotional support. They may be able to add to the information you have about yourself, the environment, and other people involved with you at the time of the trauma. However, even if these people like you, or love you, it does not mean that they will be able to give you the empathic listening you would expect from a trained therapist or knowledgeable survivor. In fact, you have no guarantees that sharing with them about the trauma will receive any kind of supportive response.

Consequently, in general, it is best to ask neutral questions, such as, I've been thinking lately about my past. I've forgotten so much that I'd like to remember. I wonder if you can help me remember what I was like when I used to live next door to you?

You may also want to inquire specifically about the incident. For example, you could ask, What is your memory of that hurricane we had in 1965? or, Do you remember my Uncle Joe? I remember him as tall, with blue eyes and a lot of charm. Is that how you remember him?

The preceding cautions are not meant to discourage you from taking an active part in your healing. They are included merely to warn you of possible negative effects. Some trauma survivors, in their initial enthusiasm for healing, charge ahead with such plans, only to suffer as a result because they were unprepared for their possible emotional reactions, disappointment, and the potentially negative reactions of others they sought out.

Bear in mind also that seeking out information from others is not the same as confronting those who abused you or who you feel otherwise victimized you. Confrontations such as these are highly complex matters that are well beyond the scope of this book. They require even more thinking, planning, and preparation than does simple information gathering.

On the other hand, it takes much courage and a dedication to one's healing to take the time, effort, and risk involved in returning to people and places from the past to find out what happened. Many survivors have found great peace in finally uncovering some of the missing pieces of their story. "It was worth the pain to find out the truth," is the feeling of many who have been finally able to use the facts they gathered to make peace with the past. And if they did not find out everything they had hoped to discover about themselves and the trauma, they still felt pride in having done all they could to heal themselves.

Talking to other survivors and reading survivor literature. Your memory can also be stimulated by talking to other trauma survivors. They can be found in various support groups, your school, community, or workplace. Also, today there is a wealth of reading material about certain kinds of trauma, especially physical and sexual abuse, rape, and combat.

Less is available on the subjects of natural catastrophe, technological accidents, and crime.

Ask your librarian to help you obtain books and articles on the type of trauma you endured. (Appendix B also lists some books relevant to specific types of traumas.) Not only news articles but literature can deal with your experience. For example, the mythologies of various cultures have numerous accounts of the struggles of incest and rape survivors and those of warriors. These topics are also central to much modern fiction, drama, and poetry.

Storytelling. As an alternative to writing it down, consider recording your story on a tape recorder or telling it to someone you trust. Before you do the latter, however, this individual must be prepared to make three commitments to you. First, he or she must be willing to sit and listen for however long it takes. Second, the person must agree to keep your story confidential. And third, he or she must be willing to listen to your story more than once, if this is what you need. The other person's role is simply to listen, not to make comments.

If he or she commits to listen empathically, but then begins to make critical comments, or comments you feel are critical, stop, say thank you, and then find someone else to talk to—preferably a trained therapist or a knowledgeable survivor. You have enough to cope with in remembering the trauma without also having to deal with the misinformed or short-sighted reactions of others.

Usually it is best to turn to a therapist or another survivor for a listening, empathic ear. However, you must also select these listeners with care. Find a therapist who has worked with trauma survivors (see Appendix A) or survivors who have made sufficient progress in their own healing.

Dancing, painting, and other art forms. Art and dance therapy for trauma survivors is widely recognized as being of extremely high therapeutic value. Some of the emotional aspects of traumatization are beyond words, and are thus better and more fully expressed through other media. In addition, some people simply may be better able to express themselves physically or artistically, through dance, painting, pottery, sculpture, or some other form of art, than they are verbally.

Start by drawing a picture that depicts the trauma, maybe beginning just with a line or circle. You can then go on to draw more if you wish. Draw as many pictures as you like, with whatever tools you like: watercolors or oil paints, colored pencils or crayons.

If you decide to try a dance or movement expression, begin by finding a song or tune that somehow reminds you of the traumatic event or your feelings about the event. Then move your body to the music. If you cannot move your entire body at first, then simply tap your fingers or toes. Then gradually build up to using your arms and legs, until your whole body is involved.

Whether you decide to draw, paint, dance, or sculpt, let yourself go. This is not a talent show. You are not going to be judged for your performance. As you dance or paint you may be able to recall the event and your feelings. Afterwards, you may be able to share the experience with others you trust.

Coping with stuck points. At certain stages of remembering, you may reach blocks, or points where you get stuck—you can't remember anymore or it is simply too painful to go on. When this happens, stop. If you're writing, draw a line underneath what you've written and return to it later.

You should also stop if you start feeling suicidal, homicidal, faint, or experience any of the other danger signs listed in the "Cautions" section of the introduction.

Exercise: Addiction Histories

If you are addicted to alcohol, food, drugs, gambling, or compulsive spending or sexual behavior, most likely your addiction patterns reflect the traumatic event. One way to help resurrect your memories of the trauma is by writing (or recording, or telling another person) your addiction history, as follows:

1. Write at least three pages on how your addiction has adversely affected your life. Go back to the first time you ever used your drug (whether food, alcohol, or drugs) or engaged in a compulsive behavior, and tell how you felt about it. Then go through the rest of your life, noting the times you were practicing your addiction and remembering how you felt about it. You can write less than three pages if that is all you want to do. But the more you write, the more you will learn about yourself.

2. Make a list of all the people in your family who suffer from some form of substance abuse or addictive behavior and/or who are trauma survivors themselves.

3. Look back through your journal, reading what you've written about the trauma and related incidents. What events seem to be related to your practice of your addiction?

4. How did people around you react to your addiction?

5. What was the role of the trauma in creating, perpetuating, or increasing your addictive behavior?

6. Make a list of everything in your life that prevents you from giving up your addiction.

7. To what extent does healing from the trauma play a role in your recovery from substance abuse or compulsive activity?

Professional Assistance

Ideally, you will share your written work, tape recording, or an oral account of the trauma with a mental health professional trained in trauma work. However, professionals can also help you remember by using techniques such as traumatic-incident reduction therapy, eye movement desensitization and reprocessing, hypnosis, and flooding.

Traumatic-incident reduction therapy. In this form of short-term therapy, the therapist asks the survivor to tell his or her story. The therapist remains relatively silent, only asking the client to indicate where the trauma begins and where, in the survivor's view, it ends. The therapist then asks what could be called the "million-dollar question": What is the significance of these events to you? (Figley 1995).

After the client has responded, the therapist asks, Is that all or is there more? Once again, the survivor responds, and then the therapist asks him or her to repeat the story of the trauma. When the survivor feels the story has been told completely, the therapist asks again, What is the significance of these events to you?

The process is repeated several times, providing the trauma survivor with a rare opportunity: to tell the story in full, as many times as needed, to a willing listener. The theory behind this approach is that telling the story repeatedly provides numerous opportunities to rethink the event, to remember details that may have been forgotten but are vitally important to understanding the meaning of the trauma, and to express anger, grief, confusion, guilt, and any other feelings associated with the trauma.

Eye movement desensitization and reprocessing. In eye movement desensitization and reprocessing (EMDR) therapy, traumatic memories are reprocessed both mentally and physically. In the therapy session, the survivor is asked to remember a traumatic experience and then to identify the thoughts and feelings surrounding that experience, including the ways the anxiety and pain associated with the experience are expressed in the body.

For example, as you review your trauma in your mind, you may find that your associated thought is that you were a failure or were guilty of some immoral or incompetent act. You may also find that just thinking about the trauma creates anxiety or pain in certain parts of your body. You may experience nausea, headache, backache, pain in your legs, chest pains, hyperventilation, dizziness, muscle spasms, or tremors.

The therapist then asks you to come up with a more positive view or feeling about the trauma. At this point, you would most likely feel that the positive alternative view of the trauma has little or no validity. Nevertheless, you have acknowledged that there could be a more positive or rational view of the trauma. Later in the session, the therapist will ask you to recall that more positive view.

The therapist then asks you to bring the traumatic memory to mind while he or she moves a finger from side to side in your field of vision. As you watch the finger, you are instructed to keep remembering the trauma and to focus on your negative thoughts and emotions. You are also asked to scan your body and be aware of where you feel the anxiety and emotional pain associated with the trauma.

This procedure is repeated until you can view the traumatic event with only a small degree of anxiety. Once you are able to do so, the therapist asks you to again bring to mind the traumatic memory, repeats the finger motions, and asks you to view the traumatic memory keeping in mind the positive feelings and thoughts that you identified earlier in the session. This procedure is repeated until you tell the therapist you can view the traumatic memory with some kind of positive feeling or thought and with minimal anxiety.

During the therapy and afterward you are asked to keep a log of your anxiety and other symptoms and any reactions or thoughts you have about the session during the week. You then bring this log to the next session for discussion.

Clearly, EMDR is not a form of hypnosis or "mind control." You are in control, in that you can stop the process should it become uncomfortable for you. (The therapist is also to be immediately available to you between sessions.)

The exact reasons EMDR therapy works are unclear. One theory is that the EMDR process is similar to the natural healing process that occurs during REM (rapid eye movement) sleep. During REM sleep we dream, and dreaming is believed to be a way that the stresses and emotions of life are neutralized and processed. It is theorized that the rapid movement of the eyes following the therapist's finger stimulates the body's automatic healing process.

Another theory is that EMDR therapy works because it links the more rational part of the brain to the more emotional, sensual, and physical part of the brain, where traumatic memories tend to stored. By linking the right and left hemispheres of the brain, EMDR helps the individual to see traumas more accurately and more rationally, hence eliminating much unfounded guilt and shame (Call 1995).

Another possible source of EMDR's effectiveness is that, like the exercises in this book and other forms of trauma-focused therapy, EMDR therapy requires that you deal with the trauma directly, rather than avoid the subject. In addition, EMDR requires that you reprocess aspects of the trauma—that you try to identify positive aspects of the traumatic incident or at least reduce the amount of irrational and inappropriate guilt.

Numerous studies indicate that EMDR has been successful in reducing anxiety, nightmares, intrusive thoughts and other symptoms of PTSD in a wide variety of trauma survivors. For example, EMDR has been shown effective with combat veterans and victims of rape, sexual assault, accidents, and severe burns.

Critics of EMDR have attacked what they call "exaggerated claims" made by some EMDR therapists. Given that EMDR is a new form of therapy and that more research needs to be completed, it may be premature to draw definitive conclusions about the experience. However, the ongoing debate about whether EMDR is more effective than other kinds of therapy may not be as important as the evidence indicating that EMDR works—for many kinds of trauma survivors. The degree and type of effectiveness may vary, yet the procedure has been helpful to some. For that reason, it should be considered.

On the other hand, EMDR, nor any other therapeutic method, can be considered a cure-all or the one-and-only guaranteed route to recovery. Some clients have begun EMDR therapy only to withdraw because they found the process too anxiety provoking. These cases do not mean that the client is "weak" or that the procedure doesn't work. It simply means that EMDR, like any technique, can work splendidly for some people and not at all for others.

If you should decide to try out EMDR therapy, keep in mind that it is only one tool for healing. EMDR, if used, should be a part of a comprehensive therapy program conducted by a therapist familiar with you and your circumstances. For more information contact the EMDR Institute, Box 51010, Pacific Grove, California, 93950, (408) 372-3900.

Hypnosis. Hypnosis may sound like "hocus-pocus" to you; if so, you are correct in assessing that hypnosis is not a magic cure. However, hypnosis—the creation of a semiconscious state of deep relaxation—can be useful in helping to bring forth memories that are partially or totally repressed. It can be especially helpful to persons abused as young children, whose memories tend to be more repressed than other trauma survivors.

Nevertheless, hypnosis, like flooding (described below) can be problematic for trauma survivors. In some ways hypnosis may even seem to create feelings of powerlessness that mimic original traumatic situations. Therapists well trained in hypnosis always reassure their clients that the hypnosis will not put them at the mercy of the therapist. Clients are also instructed that all they need do is indicate that the hypnosis is becoming uncomfortable and the therapist will bring them back into a fully conscious state.

Nonetheless, hypnosis requires that the client trust the therapist, and trust is not easy for trauma survivors, especially those who feel they were betrayed by an authority figure. Also, to the extent that hypnosis, like sleeping, requires that the subject let down his or her guard, trauma survivors (who usually have an intense need to feel safe and in control of their environment), may find this difficult. They therefore may not make good hypnotic subjects, especially if they were traumatized while sleeping or in bed. On the other hand, some trauma survivors are so desirous of healing that they are extremely willing to try to cooperate with all hypnosis procedures.

If you decide to seek hypnosis, or hypnosis is suggested to you by your therapist, be sure the therapist is well trained in this area. Also be clear about what you expect from hypnosis. Well-trained hypnotists do not make exaggerated claims about the benefits of hypnosis.

And, although hypnosis may assist you in remembering your traumatic past, recalling the past and processing it are not the same thing. Once you remember a specific memory, you will still have to go on to understand its meaning to you and your feelings about it. Hypnosis is an excellent tool for some, but not all, trauma survivors. In any case, it is only a beginning.

Flooding. Flooding, or implosive therapy, is a relatively new technique that has been used primarily with PTSD-afflicted veterans. During flooding, clients are barraged with stimuli reminiscent of the original trauma. For example, combat veterans may be exposed to vivid war movies or tapes of war sounds. Another technique is to have vets listen to their own most horrible experiences repeated back to them by the therapist. In the presence of memories, sounds, pictures of the original traumatic event, by using muscle relaxation and other techniques, survivors learn to not be anxious or afraid.

Christine Courtois, author of *Healing the Incest Wound* (1988), writes, "Flooding treatment involves two phases: relaxation training followed by repeated presentation of the traumatic scenes. However, this technique might be countertherapeutic for incest survivors, as well as many other types of trauma survivors." Like hypnosis, she says, flooding can recreate the "conditions of the trauma, particularly lack of control and feelings of powerlessness. More research is needed to determine the usefulness of flooding." Thus, given our present state of knowledge about flooding, it should be used only as a last resort.

Reconstructing the Trauma Mentally

Now that you have, I hope, obtained a clearer, more detailed picture of what occurred, you need to begin the process of viewing the trauma from a new perspective. The focus here is on viewing the trauma objectively, rather than judgmentally. Any moral or other concerns you might have are legitimate and important. However, the only way you can deal with those issues is to obtain a clear picture of the trauma, the pressures you were under, and the real choices available to you under those conditions.

Exercise: Visualizing the Trauma

The first step in getting an objective picture involves visualization. To begin, you need to "center" yourself. This may mean taking a few calming breaths or doing a relaxation exercise, or it may mean prayer or going for a long walk—whatever lets you feel calm, relaxed, and at peace.

Next, imagine that you are watching a television show or movie about your trauma, or that you are seeing your story being acted out in the next room, a room from which you are separated by a one-way mirror.

As best you can, pretend the star of this show is not you (even though it is). As you watch, observe what you are thinking or feeling about that person. Make a note of those things he or she is doing to survive that you find admirable. Also make a note of whatever things the star is doing to survive that you find objectionable or of questionable morality or worth. Especially note any inconsistencies in the star's behavior. Is he or she responding one way one minute and another, seemingly contradictory way, the next? Write about why you think the star is behaving in such a manner.

Once the "movie" is finished, you need to spend some time "honoring what you did to survive" (Bass and Davis 1988). In your journal, answer the following questions:

1. What behaviors, feelings, and attitudes did your star develop or use simply to survive the situation?

2. What was the purpose of these feelings, thoughts, or actions? For example, was the purpose monetary gain, power, sexual advantage, or sheer survival?

3. What is your feeling or view of the star's behavior?

4. What might have happened during the trauma if the star had not engaged in these thoughts, feelings or behaviors?

5. What other choices did the star have in each situation?

6. Were any of those choices more acceptable than the choices that were made? Were almost all of the available choices unacceptable? Was the star caught in any Catch-22 situations? If some acceptable choices were available, and your star did not select them, why didn't he or she do so?

7. For which survivor behaviors do you still condemn the star?

8. For which behaviors do you admire the star?

Compare your attitudes toward the star with your attitudes toward yourself. Do you make allowances for the star that you did not, would not, make for yourself? If you are harsher toward yourself than toward the star, do you know why?

Getting Feedback from Others

At this point, it would be extremely helpful for you to take your writing about survival behaviors to a therapist or support group to get feedback. If you are like many trauma survivors, you might have a distorted view of how many options were available while the trauma was occurring. Most likely, you had fewer choices in the situation than you imagined. Others can help point out to you certain realities of the situation that you might have overlooked. You can also share with them your feelings about your survival behaviors, for example, whether you feel proud, ashamed, or sad about doing what you did to survive.

"You're as sick as your secrets," is a common 12-step slogan. However, although it's true that sharing your "secrets" with others can be extremely cathartic and therapeutic, you may not want to share everything you have written. You have every right to be selective about what you share. Under no circumstances allow others—peers, therapists, or your doctors—to pressure you. Being overtly, or subtly, forced into talking only repeats an element of the trauma situation, and so may ultimately be counterproductive.

Exercise: Self-Forgiveness

Forgiving yourself for some of the choices, behaviors, and feelings you had during the traumatic incident is crucial to your healing. You may find forgiving yourself as hard as or harder than making some kind of peace with the individual, institution, or natural force that harmed you. (Please notice I didn't say "forgiving" the person or force that created the traumatic event, but instead "making peace with.")

To begin forgiving yourself, in your journal, answer the following questions:

1. Looking back over the trauma, for which behaviors, attitudes, and feelings do you still castigate or blame yourself?

2. What would it take for you to forgive yourself for some of these behaviors, attitudes, and feelings?

3. Is it possible for you to do whatever you have listed above so that you can forgive yourself? If so, what is keeping you from pursuing whatever you need to make peace with this part of your past?

4. Is there information you need that you might never be able to obtain before you can forgive yourself? If so, your options are to try to forgive yourself anyway or to continue to punish yourself. Who are you helping and what good are you doing in the world by punishing yourself? Who would you harm if you forgave yourself?

Exercise: What If It Were Someone You Love?

Think of the names of family members and friends, people you dearly love. If you can't think of anyone you truly love, imagine a child of about 10 or 11. Now rerun the story of your trauma or your imaginary movie, but make the star one of the people you love or the young child. Have the person do, think, and say exactly what you did during the trauma.

As before, make notes about what you condemn or blame the person for. Are you being kinder to that person than you were to yourself? Would you be able to forgive a loved one for some of the actions or inactions you blame yourself for? If you can forgive that person, why is it you can't forgive yourself for the very same behaviors, attitudes, and feelings?

Making Amends

If you still feel guilty or ashamed about some aspect of your behavior or attitude during the traumatic event, consider making amends to the individuals or organizations you feel you hurt. Punishing yourself helps no one. Instead of self-punishment, is there something positive you can do to make amends?

For example, some abuse survivors are not only victims but offenders. Battered wives who beat their children, or abused children who batter their siblings or neighbors, are cases in point. As part of the healing process, they often come to understand that abusing others was their way of dealing with the anger they felt toward their abuser. They feared confronting their abuser with that anger, so they placed their anger on smaller, safer targets.

But understanding the reason for their abusiveness isn't necessarily enough. These survivors often feel guilty about having hurt others—for good reason. Such guilt is appropriate. However, instead of punishing themselves with alcohol or drug abuse or some other self-destructive behavior, some of these victims who have also victimized have learned to deal with their guilt by getting help for themselves, so that they are not tempted to abuse others, and by volunteering at orphanages or other charitable agencies.

Similarly, some war veterans who feel guilt about having abused women during their tour(s) of duty have made amends by giving time at rape crisis centers or by teaching their sons to respect women. Some who have felt guilt about killing have made donations to orphanages, adopted children from the countries in which they fought, or in other ways tried to make a contribution to their communities.

The next chapters will help you get in touch with your feelings—not only of guilt but of fear, anger, and grief. Unpleasant and painful as those feelings are, acknowledging and coming to terms with them is a vital part of the healing process.

7

Stage 2:
Feeling the Feelings

In the preceding chapter you worked hard to look at your traumatic experiences as a detached observer instead of as an emotionally involved participant. Hopefully, those efforts resulted in the following four gains:

- A clearer, more objective assessment of what your real choices were during the traumatic event

- A greater appreciation of how the trauma itself influenced your thoughts, actions, and feelings

- Reduced self-blame

- A sharper definition of the people, institutions, or forces you feel anger or rage toward

An improved understanding of the traumatic event, however, is not enough. The effects of the trauma cannot be erased simply by rethinking the event. Research has found, for example, that therapies focused on helping survivors view the trauma more rationally are only partially effective in reducing of the symptoms of PTSD. Such therapies are necessary, but they suffer from a major limitation: they only address the mental aspect of the healing process. That aspect is only one part of a greater whole.

Back in Chapter 3, you did some work on identifying your emotions. In this chapter and the two that follow, you will build on that work to come to terms with your feelings stemming from the trauma.

The Necessity of Feeling

For you to heal completely, the trauma must be reworked not only on the mental level, but on the emotional level as well. This necessitates two further processes:

- First, the feelings generated by the trauma that were nor felt at the time need to be identified.

- Second, and more difficult, the feelings must be experienced, at least in part, on a gut level.

No matter how objectively you have come to view the trauma, the fact is that a life-threatening event occurred. Not only did it happen, it happened to you or people you care about—not to strangers on television. You may think of yourself as relatively unemotional or as someone who is cool and collected, not easily rattled. But no matter how self-possessed you are, the traumatic event inevitably generated feelings in you.

The feelings trauma generates are perhaps the most powerful feelings known to human beings, among them fear, anger, grief, and guilt. If you think you don't have these feelings, think again. Do you still have PTSD symptoms? Are you struggling with an addiction? Do you have headaches, backaches, stomach problems, or other physical symptoms of unexplained origin?

If so, this suggests that even though you may not want to deal with your feelings, your feelings are dealing with you.

There are two kinds of courage: courage to act and courage to feel. Many people who have demonstrated incredible courage in their actions, quail at the idea of feeling their emotions. For example, in my work with veterans I have known several who withstood overwhelming numbers of the enemy or endured enormous physical pain, but were utterly panicked at the prospect of confronting their feelings.

If war heroes such as these men can fear their feelings, then it is no wonder that you might also be afraid of feeling your emotions.

Fear of Feeling

Fear of feeling is often associated with two other fears: fear of losing control of oneself and fear of suffering. When you take the risk of feeling your emotions, periods of suffering are almost inevitable. And suffering takes courage.

If you're thinking, I'm not that brave, don't be so sure. You might be more courageous than you think. What about any acts of bravery you performed during the trauma or afterwards? Consider also the courage you have displayed in simply surviving, and in surviving everything you've had to endure since the trauma. Even picking up this book and reading it requires courage.

The other of these two fears, that of losing control, is also common. Even nontraumatized individuals fear that giving in to their emotions will render them out of control. For PTSD sufferers this fear is even more pervasive, and devastating, for two reasons:

- The emotions surrounding the traumatic event (and its aftermath) are extremely powerful, because trauma and secondary wounding experiences, by their very nature, are physically and emotionally powerful events.

- The feeling of being overwhelmed by emotions can recreate the emotional climate of the original traumatic event, in which the survivor felt overwhelmed, not in control, and helpless in the face of an attacking person or force.

But being afraid of losing control and actually doing so are two entirely different things. If you've been successful at "keeping a lid" on your feelings until now, it's likely you will also be successful when you begin to let them out—although it won't necessarily be easy.

In the introduction to this book, an analogy was made between beginning to feel the feelings associated with the trauma (the emergency stage) and natural disasters—earthquakes, floods, fires. And although each insight and revelation may bring a strong surge of emotion, especially if you are a multiple-trauma survivor or a survivor of child abuse, not every one will be as intense as the initial emergency stage. Subsequent feelings may emerge as tremors, as small trickles of pain and sadness, or as flickers of anger rather than infernos of rage.

It's also important to remember, as you pass through the emergency stage and at other times of strong feeling, that the emotionality you are experiencing is temporary. It will pass. The human organism simply cannot sustain a state of such intense feeling for a prolonged period of time without shutting down for a rest.

Don't be surprised, therefore, if after an emotional day or two, you suddenly feel numb and exhausted. For hours, perhaps even a few days, you may be able to feel very little. The strong feelings have drained you, and you need time to recuperate.

Take Your Time

Don't push yourself to feel, or allow others to push you (not even your therapist). Allow your own internal healing process, not outside pressures or sources, to bring your feelings to the surface. If you become overstimulated emotionally, the emotions may emerge too soon, before you are ready to handle them. Your emotions should come forth when they are ready, not when your therapist, family members, friends, or even you think that they should be ready.

Some of your feelings regarding the trauma, like some of your memories, may need to stay buried for the time being, for many months, maybe even forever. Even if you diligently complete every exercise in this chapter and work hard in therapy, your feelings will not necessarily surface. You cannot will them to do so. Your feelings will manifest themselves in their own time, in their own way.

If some feelings never surface, perhaps this is what is best for you. Healing does not necessarily require that you remember and become emotional about every single aspect of the trauma. In fact, you can read this entire book and not have any of the emotional experiences described—and still benefit.

Most likely, however, someday some of the feelings will emerge. For now though, they may be staying in the background for one of four reasons:

- You are already on overload—emotional, physical, or otherwise—due to present life stresses, and it would be nonproductive, if not destructive, for you to also be dealing with the trauma.

- For one reason or another, you are not emotionally ready to handle these feelings.

- You do not have an adequate support system to help you when you start to hurt.

- You have fears and concerns about your emotional side or about specific emotions that are preventing your growth in this area.

Just as you cannot will or force yourself to remember the trauma or to get over it within a certain time period, you cannot force yourself to feel the feelings and get rid of them by such-and-such a date. You can, however, aid yourself in the emotional aspects of the healing process by reading about how other trauma survivors in your situation have felt, as well as by building a support system. For example, you can begin to search for a mental health professional with whom you feel comfortable and in whom you have confidence. Similarly, you can also search out other survivors and friends you can share your experiences with and can expect to be supportive.

When the feelings do begin to emerge, it may mean that your routine is temporarily interrupted. For example, spending an hour, an evening, or even an entire day crying or angry, unable to concentrate on anything but your emotions, is to be expected. However, if the following symptoms appear, you should seek immediate professional attention:

- Fainting spells

- Hallucinations

- Total immobilization for more than 2 to 3 hours

- Feelings of being out of touch with reality

- The urge to hurt yourself

- Suicidal or homicidal thoughts or behavior

- Being unable to function at all for more than a day

Keep in mind that if you become low on courage during the healing process, you can always "borrow" it from others. For example, your family, friends, or your therapist or support group might be glad to encourage you if you ask. In addition, you may turn to a spiritual source for guidance and courage, if such is your belief.

Managing Your Emotions

Feeling your emotions may seem a little less frightening to you once you realize that experiencing an emotion does not mean that you necessarily have to act on it. Any emotion can temporarily dominate your consciousness. Yet this does not mean that you have to act on this particular emotion or give it the power to control your actions. All you have to do when you feel an emotion is to feel it. You don't even have to share it with anyone unless you choose to do so.

Many people fear that if they have an emotion, it will take over. While this may sometimes happen, it is a temporary condition. In most cases, the opposite is true: only when emotions stay denied do they exert massive control over human behavior.

Mastering your emotions does not mean that you can make them go away. Neither does mastery imply that you can reduce or lessen the intensity of your emotions at will. In the emotional realm, mastery means that you can tolerate the intensity and duration of your feelings without abusing yourself or others. It also means that you can decide which emotions you wish to do something about, and which you wish simply to experience and nothing more. In fact, the more you identify and "surrender" to your emotions—allowing yourself to accept that you have them and feel them—the more you will ultimately be able to exert control over your life.

You may be repelled by the word *surrender*. In your work, perhaps even in your mind, strength is equated with victory and success, not surrender. However, unlike the world you work in, in the emotional world surrender leads to victory. Not surrendering to emotional truth leads to defeat in the form of crippling symptoms, life-threatening addictions, or a chronic anxiety that can permeate everything that is meaningful to you—from your work to your love relationships to your self-esteem.

Preparing Yourself

Even if you are desperate for the healing to begin (and to be finished), you cannot force yourself into an emotional experience. However, you can prepare the way for your emotional healing by identifying and critically examining any fears or obstacles you have regarding the emotional side of your personality. The following exercises are designed to help release you from any unnecessary fears you might have regarding your emotional side.

Exercise: Identifying Your Fears About Feelings

Although you cannot force yourself to feel, you can prepare the way by beginning to identify some of the fears you have about feelings. In your present life—at home, at work, and in social situations—you will be required at times to interact with others on an emotional, as well as an intellectual, basis. Therefore, awareness of your fears about emotionality and overcoming some of those fears is critical, not only to your emotional healing from the trauma and its aftermath but to the entire quality of your life.

Begin by reviewing the Feelings List in Chapter 3 and your journal entries on distinguishing feelings from thoughts. As you proceed through this chapter and throughout this book, remember that feelings are rarely pure. At any given moment, you are probably experiencing not just one but several feelings at a time.

Now, in your journal, take time to list some of the fears you have come to associate with feeling or showing emotions. As you write, consider the following questions:

1. Were you ever told by someone important to you that being emotional or showing your emotions was wrong, shameful, weak, sinful, slothful, unpatriotic, or a sign of mental or emotional instability or a lack of faith in God?

   You could have been given this message as a young child, teenager, young adult, or at any other time in your life. The important persons could have been either authority figures or nurturing ones, for example, a parent, teacher, caregiver, friend, lover, or a religious, military, police, or court authority.

2. Are emotional reactions for you associated with a loved one or caretaker

   - hurting you or someone close to you?

   - hurting themselves?

   - damaging or destroying property or pets?

- making threats?

- entering a mental ward or seeking psychiatric medication?

- committing suicide?

- committing homicide?

3. What emotions did this individual display? Was he or she angry, sad, or afraid, or was some other emotion dominant? Did you as a result come to fear certain emotions?

   If the answer is yes, which emotions have you come to associate with the negative events surrounding this individual's emotional expression or display?

4. Was that person's behavior an expression of his or her true feelings, or rather of

   - a mental or emotional disturbance, for example, an organic brain tumor that caused memory and other problems, or a psychotic condition such as paranoia or hallucinations?

   - an addiction, such as alcohol or drug abuse, pathological gambling, compulsive overeating, bulimia, or anorexia nervosa?

   - a medical problem? (For example, hypertension or hyperglycemia can create extreme irritability, even violence.)

   - a display of anger that covered up the person's true feelings of grief, hurt, disappointment, sense of failure, sense of powerlessness, or frustration with life?

5. Were you ever verbally abused, physically punished, abandoned, rejected, or otherwise shamed for being emotional or showing your emotions?

   If so, did the verbal or physical humiliation follow your expression of any emotion at all or certain specific emotions? For example, were you punished for being angry, but not for crying, or punished for crying, but not for being angry? Or were you punished for showing any feeling whatsoever, even joy?

   List the ways in which you were punished. Be specific. What type of physical punishments were used? What names were you called? Did you internalize (come to believe) the names you were called? If you were physically abused as well, did you eventually come to believe that you deserved physical abuse because you committed the "sin" or displayed the "weakness" of showing emotion?

6. Are you afraid of losing control? In the past have you actually lost control, or is this a possibility that so far has not materialized? Just because this fear has not materialized does not mean your fear is unfounded.

Have you ever come close to losing control? Can you specify which emotions, or mix of emotions, you feel would contribute to or cause you to lose control?

Examine your fear of losing control closely. What are your fantasies or thoughts about what you would do or how you would feel if you did indeed lose control? How dangerous or costly would it be if you lost control that way? Consider the emotional, social, vocational, and financial costs not only to you, but to your family or others you care about.

7. If you have actually lost control of yourself when you allowed yourself to be emotional, what forms did the loss of control take?

   - Did you suffer memory loss, inability to concentrate, fainting, dizziness, paralysis, or unexplained, unexpected, or intense pain in some part of your body?

   - Did you cut, burn, bruise, or otherwise mutilate yourself?

   - Did you hurt yourself by abusing alcohol, drugs, food, or some other addictive substance or behavior?

   - Did you attempt to or succeed in damaging property or pets or in hurting another person?

   - Did you make rash decisions, forget to show up for an important appointment, or act in ways that betrayed your moral values or resulted in lowered self-esteem?

8. Under what circumstances did you lose control? Were you alone or with others? Were you practicing an addiction? Were there other stresses in your life besides the trauma or a secondary wounding experience? Do you think you would have lost control if you had not been in these particular circumstances? More specifically, do you think you would have lost control if you were with supportive individuals, if you were addiction-free, or if you were not burdened by multiple stressors?

9. Can you identify what feeling or feelings seemed to trigger the loss of control? (Refer to the Feelings List in Chapter 3, if necessary.)

10. Do some of your fears of feeling stem from the trauma? From your perspective, did something negative or terrible happen during the traumatic incident because you became emotional or showed your feelings? Consider also your secondary wounding experiences. Do you believe that you were in any way unfavorably treated or otherwise the object of victim-blaming attitudes because of your emotional state? What evidence do you have that your emotional state or actions caused or contributed to any negative outcome during the traumatic event or a secondary wounding experience?

Exercise: Reexamining Your Fears About Feelings

Respect all your fears, both those you think are rational and those you believe are not—the distinction between rational and irrational is almost irrelevant when it comes to fear. Fears grounded in emotional threats, such as rejection and shame, may seem trivial compared to fears grounded in threats to life and limb; however, those grounded in emotional issues can be just as controlling and destructive as threats to physical survival.

For example, emotional fears can lead to addictions or other self-destructive behaviors that, in the final analysis, can cause physical disease and even death. According to 12-step programs' philosophy, fear is one of the major roots of addiction. Untreated addiction ultimately leads to emotional, if not physical, death.

Your task in this section is to critically examine each of the fears you listed in the preceding exercise for the purpose of determining which of them are realistic, on the basis of either psychological or physical threat, and which are dinosaurs from the past. With some assistance, you may choose to discard some of these "dinosaurs."

For each of the fears listed in your inventory, consider the following questions:

1. To what extent does this fear reflect your fear of rejection, abandonment, disapproval, or some sort of punishment by others, as opposed to a genuine fear of emotionality or of a specific emotion?

    Imagine, for example, being in a situation in which the people around you accepted or even applauded, rather than rejected or disapproved of, your emotional state. Would you still be afraid of your feelings?

    If your fear of feeling seems primarily based on the negative responses of others, rather than in some internal fear of emotionality itself, your task is to find people who will be supportive of your emotional life.

2. If you showed your emotions today, would you be punished physically, emotionally, or financially? Are you still living with an abusive person who verbally or physically hurts you when you show certain feelings? Do you have an employer who is intolerant of emotional expression?

    If so, then you need to adjust your behavior accordingly. For example, you need to find a safe place to get in touch with your emotional self. However, if you are still being abused by a family member or caretaker, it may be difficult for you to find the necessary privacy.

    If you are in an abusive relationship, there are no easy routes to obtaining privacy, just as there are no simple means of eliminating the abuse without also terminating the relationship. If the abuser is rigid and not amenable to discussion and compromise, sometimes a seemingly simple matter, such as obtaining the minimum of privacy and dignity within the relationship, may involve much larger and more serious issues, such as considering the option of leaving the relationship temporarily, if not permanently. Chapter 13, on domestic violence, considers some of these issues in more detail. (Additional resources for abused persons are listed in Appendix B.)

3. If you were taught that being emotional or having certain emotions is shameful, wrong, weak, sinful, or a sign of mental or emotional instability, make a list of all the persons who taught you these views. As best you can, write about why these individuals hold such attitudes. Do their attitudes stem from their personal fears and difficulties with emotions, from certain religious or cultural traditions, from some other outside force or necessity, or from some combination of these factors?

    In some cases, fear of showing emotions arises for reasons of survival. For example, according to psychologist Erwin Parsons (1985), historically slaves learned to keep their thoughts and feelings to themselves to minimize the extent that they could be manipulated by their masters. Also, in many instances, the inner life of a slave was the only possession that could not be taken away. This historical necessity for "wearing the mask," as Parsons calls it, can persist into the present among formerly enslaved groups such as African Americans.

    You may or may not have a clear idea why the individuals on your list held such negative views toward emotionality. However, the goal in trying to understand their reasons is not so that you can judge these people or become an amateur psychoanalyst. Rather, the goal is to help you distance yourself from their attitudes. Once you realize that their attitudes may stem from their own personal considerations or outside pressures, not from some inherent truth about the negativity of emotions, you can give yourself the freedom to make your own decisions. In the present, unless these individuals can still harm you, you can work toward choosing which of their values regarding emotionality you would like to keep and which you would like to modify, or even discard.

4. Is your fear grounded in an expectation based on a sex role? We live in an age of women's and men's liberation, yet traditional sex role stereotypes die hard. Some men and boys still feel they need to always be strong and never cry. Some girls and women feel they must always be "sweet" and never get angry. Yet the male survivor needs to grieve his losses, and the female survivor to experience her anger and rage.

    If you are a man, do you fear that others will see you (or that you will see yourself) as a "weakling" or a "sissy" for expressing emotions? Do you have special problems acknowledging and coping with sadness, tenderness, or self-doubt? If you are a female, do you fear that someone will label you (or that you will label yourself) as "unfeminine," "aggressive," or "masculine," if you experience the power of your anger?

5. If you indeed lost control when you became emotional or had specific emotions, can you identify the source of the loss of control? Did it stem directly from the emotional experience itself, or did it instead come from your fears about how others might react to you if they knew (or saw) how you felt?

    When you lost control, did you experience physical symptoms: hyperventilation, dizziness, or any of the warning signs listed in the "Cautions" section of the introduction?

    Did you become disoriented, out of touch with reality, destructive toward yourself or others, or otherwise undergo significant psychological or physical distress during your last emotional experience? If so, you need to discuss your situation with a mental health professional before continuing on in this book. For example, if the last time you truly felt your pain you lost consciousness, became delusional, wandered off for days at a time, sat immobilized in your bed for a week unable to eat, or found yourself incoherent, stop reading this book *immediately* and seek help.

    However, if your loss of control stems from anticipated rejection, shame, or punishment from others, or from internalized prohibitions against being emotional, you may continue.

You have just examined your original list of fears in terms of some additional considerations. Now review your revised list and decide which of your fears are so unfounded that you can discard them, and which you feel are realistic or strong enough to warrant further discussion with a qualified therapist or supportive, knowledgeable friend.

PTSD—Anger, Grief, or Helplessness?

On the psychological level, PTSD is basically a problem of unresolved anger, unresolved grief, and feelings of helplessness. Some experts feel that the fundamental issue is the grief. Others argue that it is the anger or the helplessness. To date, the debate has yet to be settled.

In my view, the relative importance of grief versus anger versus helplessness varies from one trauma survivor to the next. You may be volcanic in your rage but have yet to shed a single tear over your losses. Or you may have grieved profoundly but have yet to confront your rage. Perhaps you are still stifling it with alcohol, drugs, or some other substance, or distracting yourself from it with overwork or some other compulsion. Feeling helpless can generate both anger and grief, and feeling intense anger and grief can also make you feel helpless to cope with the power of these emotions. Or you may be out of touch with your grief, feelings of helplessness, and anger, along with many of the rest of your feelings. If your numbing is this pervasive, for you, reading this book is more of an intellectual exercise than an emotional experience.

In any case, wherever you are emotionally today is fine. Do not fight or berate yourself for feeling or not feeling angry, for grieving or not grieving, for feeling helpless, or for feeling very little. Accepting yourself as you are emotionally is the first step toward moving on. Don't you have enough to cope with without going to war with yourself too?

Anger and Grief—The Intimate Connection

For trauma survivors, anger and grief are intimately related. The losses endured as a result of the trauma inevitably generate a lot of anger, especially if the trauma involved some form of social injustice. Hence, on one level, the anger is pure rage at whatever force caused damage or death. On another level, however, the anger reflects grief for personal losses, as well as sorrow and disappointment over the failure of certain government, religious, or other institutions to live up to their stated purposes and standards.

For example, a decade ago drunk drivers who were responsible for the deaths of pedestrians or other motorists frequently received ridiculously light sentences by today's standards. Relatives of the victims were consequently enraged not only at the drunk driver but at the court system. Even more infuriating was that sometimes the courts did not even order the guilty drivers to receive treatment for their drinking problem. Many drunk drivers would leave the court free to drink and drive again, perhaps to kill more innocents, and themselves.

As with relatives of victims of drunk drivers in the past, some of your anger may be a legitimate response to victimization and secondary wounding experiences—and some of your anger may be a defense against your grief.

Isn't it easier to be angry than to be sad? When you are angry you feel powerful and full of energy. In contrast, when you are grieving, you feel weak and helpless. Grieving involves mourning not only specific losses but your helplessness. In grieving, you are acknowledging the devastating reality that nothing you do can resurrect the dead or give you back what you lost. Your anger, no matter how intense, is impotent. Some of your losses, if not all of them, are permanent.

In the next chapter you'll take a look at your anger. You will work on identifying the sources of your anger and learn to acknowledge and feel it. Then, finally, you will learn how to take control of it—to prevent it from negatively affecting your life.

After that, in Chapter 9, you will be asked to review your writing about your anger and make the connection between anger and grief. You will learn about the process of grieving and explore some strategies for coping with it. Chapter 10, the final chapter in the healing process, offers guidelines for overcoming helplessness by attaining empowerment.

8

Stage 2 Continued: Living with Anger

As discussed at the end of the last chapter, you may be unaware of the ways anger affects your life. You may not feel any anger at all, or very little. Alternatively, you may be all too aware of your feelings of anger—even rage—and the impact those emotions have on your life and the lives of those around you.

This chapter is designed to help you cope with your anger, whether or not you are conscious of it. (Even if you are not aware of your anger at the moment, you may become aware of it in the future. At that time, this chapter can be helpful to you.) This chapter helps you cope with your anger in three ways: by helping you to identify sources of your anger, by assisting you in acknowledging the importance of those feelings, and by offering strategies for coping with anger so that it does not dominate your life.

The Problem of Anger

If you are one of those people who feel a lot of anger, you may be at a loss as to how to deal with it. Do your present means of coping with anger seem inadequate? Do you spend a great deal of energy trying to squelch it in order to better fit in with others? Do you sometimes hold yourself hostage in your own home, not daring to go outside lest you be triggered into lashing out at someone?

Or have you chosen, instead, to vent your anger? If so, how did others respond? Did they listen intently, or did they minimize or discount your feelings? Did they want to hear more, or did they find excuses to get away? Did sharing your feelings alienate family members, friends, employers, or others?

As a result of your anger, have people close to you slipped—or stormed—out of your life? As they departed, did you say to yourself (or shout to them), Go ahead. Leave me. You never understood me anyway. Why should I care?

But is that the truth? Underneath it all, did you care? Do you want some of these people back, or at least some new relationships? Is your rage a formidable barrier to forming relationships that work—not just with sexual intimates, but with your children, parents, neighbors, co-workers, and others?

Unacknowledged and unexamined trauma-related anger can color every aspect of your life: your work or school performance, your daily habits, and most important of all your self-esteem and relationships with others. Anything that might provoke irritation will have the additional charge of your unresolved anger related to the trauma. This can result in those old, familiar feelings of being out of control—and the attendant fears and anxiety—because your response is out of proportion to the current situation.

Given that you are a trauma survivor, the intensity of your reaction is perfectly understandable. The strength of your reaction belongs in part to the past, not to the present. Also, feeling out of control of your emotions can create a new anger, and new pain in your heart. If others label you as "overreacting" or "crazy," and you feel they are correct in their assessment, your self-esteem will plummet, which will only sadden you more. In addition, their assessment—whether you agree with it or not—may cause you to respond with more anger or withdraw from the relationship.

No matter how you or others react to your anger or grief, if you do not understand the role of the trauma in your emotional responses, you can easily feel confused, drained, and somewhat powerless over your emotions. These are the same uncomfortable feelings that plagued you during the traumatic event and afterwards. Hence you are reliving the trauma over again. Only this time it is being replayed in your own head.

As a trauma survivor, you may always carry some trauma-related anger (and grief) in your heart. However, you can definitely increase your understanding of your emotions. By looking at these feelings more closely and learning some anger-management techniques, you can take from your anger much of its power to control your behavior and damage your life.

Dealing with Anger in Doses

Are you afraid to experience even a flicker of your anger for fear that it might suddenly turn into a raging fire that will destroy your life or hurt someone else? This fear is prevalent among PTSD sufferers, especially multiple-trauma survivors and abuse survivors. Typically, abuse survivors have had to stifle their anger at the abuser out of fear of retaliation. The longer the abuse continues, the larger the mountain of suppressed anger the survivor accumulates. Combat veterans also have special difficulties with rage. As part of their military training, they not only learned to automatically react to anger with violence but were rewarded for doing so.

The ideal way to handle anger and rage is in doses. Dealing with all your anger at once will overwhelm you and is not an effective means of resolving it. You need to try to examine one piece at a time, in small, manageable doses. In the sections that follow, your anger will be divided into two parts: anger at yourself (which you may sometimes project outward onto others), and your justified anger at the people or institutions that created or perpetuated your traumatic experience.

Although the first of these sections concerns self-blame, you may not be able to look at your self-blame until you first deal with your rage toward others. If your dominant feeling is anger at others, proceed to the "Anger at Others" section. Then return to the "Anger at the Self" section.

Conversely, you may not be able to experience your anger or rage toward others until you first examine your self-blame. In that case, complete the exercises in the order they are presented. It is equally likely, however, that for you the two forms of anger are connected, and thus it will make no difference which set of exercises you do first.

Anger at the Self: Self-Blame and Survivor Guilt Revisited

Are you saying, Oh no! Not self-blame and survivor guilt again! What's going on here? Is the writer running out of topics?

Self-blame and survivor guilt are repeated themes throughout this book because they permeate the lives of many trauma survivors. Long after the trauma has stopped, some survivors continue to subject themselves to emotional pain and various forms of deprivation and self-punishment precisely because they have not adequately dealt with their self-blame or survivor guilt. Hence it is critical that, as much as possible, you come to understand self-blame and survivor guilt and the extent to which you suffer from them.

One, two, or even three assessments of your self-blame and survivor guilt may not be enough. Understanding these feelings is so fundamental to your recovery that with each new insight into the traumatic event and its aftermath they need to be reexamined. Healing from trauma, like any form of personal growth, is like an onion. After you peel off one layer, there's another one beneath to contend with.

Assuming you did not cause the trauma, self-blame and survivor guilt should not even be a consideration: you were simply in the wrong place at the wrong time or were the victim of someone or something more powerful than yourself. Therefore, you should not blame yourself for what happened, how you acted, or for surviving when others did not. However, even when logic dictates that you have no reason to be experiencing either self-blame or survivor guilt, you may be burdened with these feelings.

Despite their illogical nature, self-blame and survivor guilt seem to be inherent to trauma. Even people who any objective observer would deem innocent of any wrongdoing or mistake have been found to blame themselves.

A major source of this self-blame is the helplessness inherent to traumatic experiences. To be smacked in the face with the awareness that you are helpless to save yourself, or others, violates your fundamental human need to feel competent and masterful and able to control your life.

For example, I have seen self-blame among former prisoners of war. Some of their self-blame stems from feelings of powerlessness: trapped in a POW camp, there was nothing they could do to improve their situation. They experienced intense hatred—not only toward their captors for the deaths of their comrades, but toward themselves for being unable to help. To have attempted to help a comrade would have meant their own death in addition to his. Although it is easy to understand the anger of these POWs, their self-blame defies all reason. Yet their reactions to being POWs illustrates that deep anger at having been victimized can coexist with intense self-blame. Anger and self-blame may seem to be contradictory feelings—and in some ways they are. But in the context of trauma they are not.

Aside from your experience with powerlessness, another possible source of your self-blame is society's blame-the-victim attitude. You may have internalized that attitude and now consequently continue to victimize yourself, even though the trauma and secondary wounding experiences are over.

Additional sources of self-blame include the shattering of certain illusions. Perhaps you, like many other people, consciously or unconsciously, feel that you are special, that you are all-knowing or all-powerful, and that therefore bad things can't or shouldn't happen to you. Self-blame can also result from childhood teachings. A prevalent idea is that if you are good enough you will be rewarded with a good life. Yet safety and security cannot be purchased with morality or even with religious dedication.

Your self-blame and survivor guilt may also be rooted in your analysis of and judgments about what you did or did not do during the traumatic event or its aftermath. In previous chapters you completed some preliminary thinking and writing about your self-blame. It is now time for you to review the lists of actions and behaviors you feel guilt and shame about, and to see whether they accurately reflect your present view of the trauma.

Exercise: Reviewing Self-Blame

Turn to the pages in your journal where you recorded the things for which you blame yourself. Are there any incidents on that list that you now wish to exclude? Are there any incidents you recall now that you did not recall when you began this book? Include these in your journal.

Then, for every instance about which you still feel guilt or shame, consider the following questions:

1. To what degree did your behavior reflect the physiology of trauma, in that you responded with a fight, flight, or freeze reaction?

2. Given your real choices in the traumatic situation, how could you have reacted differently? Where is the evidence that if you had acted in a different way the outcome would have been better?

3. If you are judging yourself as having failed in meeting some moral standards, would you hold the same standards for someone else or for the others involved in the trauma? Are you taking into account the emotional shock of being in trauma as well as the specific pressures that were operating in your traumatic situation?

4. Where is the evidence that your actions during the trauma truly did make the situation worse? Have you compared your perceptions with those of others who were present during the event or who have endured similar traumas? Have you examined newspaper reports or other materials that might provide more information about what actually occurred?

5. Do you have an all-or-nothing view of your behavior during the traumatic event? Are you overgeneralizing or exaggerating? Is your self-blame based on a general pattern of unacceptable behavior, or on one or two mistakes?

    If you must rate yourself, think in terms of percentages, for example: About 30 percent of me was scared to death, but 70 percent was holding on and coping. About 10 percent of the time I was selfish but 90 percent of the time I did my best to help the other survivors (McKay et al. 1981).

6. Do you suffer from I Should Have Known Better Guilt or Catch 22 Guilt? See Chapter 3.

7. Since the trauma, have you generalized your trauma-related self-blame or survivor guilt to the rest of your life?

8. Is your self-blame balanced with an appreciation of your positive behaviors and attitudes during the event, for example, ways in which you exhibited courage and good judgment?

Anger at Others

This section will help you define the people, institutions, or other entities toward which you harbor anger, if not rage. You may not even realize or acknowledge that you have anger. Or you may feel some anger but only have a vague idea of who or what you are angry at. Alternatively, you may know intellectually that you are angry but have yet to experience it emotionally. Whatever the situation, healing involves identifying those people and institutions that you feel contributed to your pain or to the pain of others. Recognizing your anger and other feelings, and taking from that some control over how you respond to these people or groups in future interactions, is also an important part of healing.

Exercise: Identifying the Sources of Your Anger

To begin to discover, or clarify, who you are angry at, return to the list of traumas in your journal. For each one, list whomever or whatever (besides yourself) you blame for the event. You may blame a specific group of people; a certain religious, governmental, societal, financial, or other institution; a commercial company. Even if you aren't sure whether certain individuals or groups are actually responsible, if you feel anger toward them, put them on your list.

Now go back over the list of traumas and add to your anger list any additional entities you think you might be angry at, even if you can't feel that anger.

If you can't think of any additional instances, walk through the traumatic events and secondary wounding experiences as if you were someone else. Who or what might have made that person angry? Document your responses in your journal.

Exercises: Obstacles to Acknowledging and Feeling Anger

The following pages list obstacles you may have to acknowledging or experiencing your anger. If you have difficulty getting in touch with your anger, read through this material to see which ones apply to you.

Pretrauma problems with anger: past training. You may be having problems identifying or experiencing anger due to what you learned about anger from others. Ask yourself the following questions and jot down your responses:

1. How did my mother deal with her anger, and my father with his? What was I taught by my parents, grandparents, teachers, schoolmates, siblings, and others about anger? Did I receive any contradictory messages about anger? What were they? How did I deal with the contradictions?

2. How did I deal with my anger as a child? As a preteen? As an adolescent? As a young adult? What happened as a result (at each age level)? How do I deal with anger today with respect to my spouse (or partner), my children, other members of my family, co-workers, friends, strangers? What are my major problem areas when it comes to anger?

3. What was the role of anger in my trauma and secondary wounding experiences? What messages did I receive from other survivors, from my attacker(s), or from agency staff or others about anger? What happened as a result of my expressing (or not expressing) my anger during the trauma or afterward?

4. How have I dealt with my anger regarding the trauma and its aftermath so far? What are my fears about acknowledging my anger?

Did you grow up with idea that anger was bad or sinful? You are entitled to your religious or moral convictions; however, even if you believe that anger is sinful or immoral, the following statements are also true and do not contradict your position:

- Anger is a normal human emotion.

- Anger is an emotion, not an aggressive act.

- Anger need not lead to acts of aggression. Although in our society anger frequently makes people feel like committing aggression, there are many other ways of coping with anger.

- Anger is important because it can be used to improve your life. Anger can be a signal that you are living in a way that does not meet some of your basic needs. Some of these needs may be physical, others psychological. For example, a common cause of anger is inadequate sleep or poor nutrition.

Viewing anger as a character defect: 12-step programs and anger. In *Twelve Steps and Twelve Traditions*, the handbook of 12-step programs such as Alcoholics Anonymous, Narcotics Anonymous, and Overeaters Anonymous, anger is described as a "character defect" and the "dubious luxury of normal men" (Alcoholics Anonymous 1953). The philosophy of those programs is that addicted personalities cannot handle anger without resorting to their addiction. Therefore, anger must be eliminated by means of the 12 steps and program suggestions: going to meetings, talking to a sponsor, meditation, writing, and so on.

These suggestions are excellent. However, labeling anger a character defect implies that anger is bad or somehow sinful. In the case of trauma and secondary wounding experiences, anger is inevitable.

Being misused or traumatized creates a different kind of anger than the anger born of selfish, childish, or less-than-noble wishes. Trauma survivors did not choose to be in life-threatening situations, or injured, or witnesses to the death and injury of others. The resulting anger is perfectly normal and need not be negatively labeled as some type of personal inadequacy.

Permitting that anger to develop into a life-style or to otherwise dominate one's life, however, when the means of help are available, could be considered a personal inadequacy. It could also be considered a tragedy, or a form of self-punishment born of self-blame and survivor guilt.

Although 12-step programs have saved thousands of lives, they were not designed or intended to be healing programs for trauma survivors. The anger and rage some trauma survivors feel is often beyond the scope of such programs. Nevertheless, 12-step programs have provided tremendous support and recovery to trauma survivors as they attempt to give up the addictions they have developed, at least in part, to cope with the trauma.

If viewing your trauma-related anger as a character defect hinders you from looking at your anger and getting help with it, then that label is not assisting in your healing process. Before you can "let go" of the anger, as your program would have you do, you have to know what that anger is all about.

Amorphous, diffuse, or absent targets. Another reason you may be having difficulty identifying or experiencing your anger is that the true target of your anger may be unavailable to you, or because the target is so amorphous and diffuse you cannot focus your anger on any specific person.

For example, it is harder to feel anger at abusers if they are dead (or sick or elderly) than if they are alive, healthy, and still abusing. Similarly, how you do "get back at" or express anger at an earthquake, a tornado, a hurricane, or a flood? Or, if you are a combat veteran who is angry at governments for supporting the institution of war, at whom or what can you vent your anger? It is more difficult to direct anger toward impersonal institutions—where to some degree everyone is to blame, yet no one is to blame—than at a specific person.

Freshness of the trauma. If the trauma is recent, you may be in an acute reaction state. In this state, you can be so distraught, anxious, and confused that you cannot concentrate on dealing with any one emotion in depth. If that's your situation, concentrate for now on surviving the acute stage and obtaining as much emotional support as possible.

Clinical depression. Suppressed anger often underlies clinical depression. If you have a clinical depression, you may not be able to get in touch with your anger because it is so deeply suppressed. On the other hand, you may have so much repressed anger that you fear getting in touch with even a little of it. Your underlying fear may be that you will suddenly be flooded with all the angers you have stored up over the years, and you will "explode." (Refer to Chapter 2 for further information on depression.)

A qualified therapist can help you with this and other fears regarding anger. The therapist should also help you deal with one anger at a time.

Chemical imbalance. As explained further in Chapter 2, if you were severely traumatized or if you suffered repeated or prolonged victimization, you may as a result be suffering from certain chemical imbalances. These imbalances often lead to all-or-nothing thinking or fight-or-flight or freeze reactions. A fight-or-flight reaction can trigger intense rage, and a freeze reaction the opposite, an almost complete emotional shutdown.

The depletion of various catecholamines (for example, dopamine), serotonin, and other stabilizing neurotransmitters, results in a tendency toward irritability and aggressive outbursts, intense moods, and mood swings. As a defense against such painful and uncomfortable states and fearing lack of control over your anger, you may shut down emotionally as well as physically. Medication may be needed to help restore the depleted neurotransmitters.

Murderous fantasies. You will have trouble unearthing your anger if it contains conscious or unconscious homicidal or sadistic fantasies. You may fear that if you allow even a small portion of your anger to rise to the surface, you will lose control and seek revenge by torturing, killing, or destroying the property of those who have injured or offended you.

If some of your anger is directed toward a parent or someone who symbolizes a parent, you will have special obstacles in recognizing your anger. It is a normal part of childhood to fantasize (usually unconsciously) about hurting or murdering one's parents. Often this fantasy arises when they frustrate us in some manner. However, the murderous or vengeful fantasies are usually suppressed.

If the parent is abusive, the fantasy may become conscious or semiconscious. Or perhaps some vengeful feelings may emerge. Yet even in an abusive situation, the taboo against expressing anger and hurting one's parents persists. The idea that one should honor one's parents, or at least respect them as parents, pervades our culture. This moral code makes it difficult for abused children to deal with their legitimate anger toward an abusive parent.

Retaliatory fantasies are normal among trauma survivors, especially abuse survivors. However, if you find yourself obsessed with such fantasies, or if they are in any way bizarre, elaborate, or delusional, you need help beyond this book, in the form of counseling. You should also seek help if you have gone so far as to obtain the weapons or other means of destruction, planned a date for the murder, and so on.

Under these conditions, the anger-management exercises that follow are insufficient to help you. You may need some medication for relief, or even hospitalization.

Taking Stock

Stop and congratulate yourself. You've done a tremendous amount of work—not physical, but emotional. Never forget that dealing with your emotions can be just as difficult and taxing as laboring on a construction site.

Emotionally, you have been working on a construction site, or rather a reconstruction site. You've been reconstructing your memories and feelings regarding the trauma and your secondary wounding experiences to enable you to, bit by bit, discover the reality of those experiences. You've had the courage to face your fears about emotions, particularly the difficult emotion of anger. And you've shown both humility and courage by being willing to look at your self-blame and survivor guilt. As a result of all your efforts, you are now better able to identify the individuals, institutions, and other forces that aroused your anger during the traumatic event or afterwards.

Exercise: A More Complete Anger Inventory

Review your list of angers in your journal, adding to it any additional sources of anger you are now able and willing to acknowledge. Consider also the following possible sources of anger.

1. Are you angry at your PTSD symptoms? Consider how those symptoms have affected or hindered your career, your social life, your spiritual life, and your relations with the opposite sex.

2. Are you angry at any physical disability you suffered as a result of the trauma and its aftermath?

3. Are you angry that you became addicted or developed a compulsion as a way of dealing with the trauma? How do you feel when you look back on all the time, money, and effort you spent on your self-defeating behavior?

4. Are you angry that you have not been adequately compensated for having been victimized or traumatized? Do you feel you suffered so much as a result of the trauma that you are entitled to recognition, comfort, financial compensation, or justice? Are you angry because these compensations have been inadequate or completely lacking?

5. Are you angry at society, or life, because in addition to having been victimized, you still must suffer normal life stresses and perhaps even subsequent victimization or traumatization? Did you feel, hope, or wish that having been traumatized once would immunize you or your loved ones against future pain and loss?

Connecting anger and self-blame. Do you see any relationship between your self-blame and your anger at others? While your journal entries regarding self-blame and anger are fresh on your mind, see if you can make a connection between some of your self-blame and your anger toward certain other people, institutions, or forces. Make note of these instances.

Managing Your Anger

If you have become so angry about what happened to you that you feel you might explode, or if you, in your anger and frustration, have lashed out at someone you love, destroyed property, hurt a pet, or damaged your own body, you would probably benefit from learning ways of managing your anger.

The following sections offer concrete suggestions about how to manage your anger. They are just that, however: suggestions. Some will be more helpful than others. Use the ones that work for you and disregard the rest.

A Note of Caution

If you suffer from clinical depression, chemical imbalances, or severe homicidal or suicidal thoughts and tendencies, the anger-management suggestions offered here are insufficient. You will need professional help as well.

Anger Is a Feeling—Not an Action

Anger affects your body. When you get angry you may feel hot, start breathing hard, and become tight and tense. It may also cause a rush of adrenaline, an increase in heart rate, blood pressure, blood sugar, and other physiological changes that energize you to act. However, this does not mean you *must* act.

Feeling angry is not the same as acting on your anger. You can feel so angry you feel like punching, or killing, but you do not have to verbally abuse others, hit them, tear up their belongings, or hurt yourself. ("hurting yourself" includes bingeing, drinking, using drugs, gambling compulsively, or acting on some other compulsive or addictive impulse).

The first step to taking control of your anger is to tell yourself, and keep telling yourself, I'm okay. All that's happening to me is that I'm feeling angry. All I have to do with my anger today is feel it. I can figure out later what to do about it. All I have to do now is ride with it. If I can just feel the anger without hurting myself or someone else, I am a success.

Then promise yourself that you will do something about it later, after you've had a chance to think it over.

Taking Time Out

Imagine the intensity of your anger as ranging from 1 to 10, with no anger being point 1, mild irritation point 2, and near murderous rage, point 10. The midpoint of the scale, at point 5, is where your adrenaline tends to take over and you can no longer think. It may take only a few undesirable occurrences or frustrations before you find yourself hovering at that dangerous 9 or 10 level on the scale, ready to snap.

You can save yourself (and others) considerable heartache if you can catch yourself before you reach the danger point. With the help provided below, you can learn how to monitor your anger level. If you can deal with your angry feelings at the lower levels—for example, at level 2 or 3, or at least before you reach the midpoint of the scale—you may be able to diffuse it. Once you reach levels of 5 and above, however, you are almost over the brink. When you become that angry, you lose the capacity to listen to others or your rational self.

One way to arrest your anger before it reaches the danger point is through "time-outs." When you're really angry it is difficult to think rationally. At such times, consider calling a time-out. Leave the room or the immediate situation and do something else, preferably something physical, such as walking or other exercise. Wait until the intense anger has subsided before you take action on the situation at hand. Give yourself whatever time you need to center yourself. Once you have centered yourself, you will be able to think about your goal in the situation before you decide on a plan of action.

If you are living with someone, it is best to let them know well in advance about your possible need for time-outs or any other strategy you might have for coping with your anger. For example, you could say something like the following:

> I have a problem with anger. Sometimes I become so angry I can't think rationally. My anger level is so high I'm afraid I'll say or do something I don't mean. When this happens, I need some time to myself to calm down.
>
> I need your help for this. What I plan to do is to take a time-out. I'll simply leave the room and go off by myself to do whatever I need to bring down my anger level. If I walk away from you, it doesn't mean I'm rejecting you or refusing to deal with whatever issue we are talking about. It just means I can't handle it at that moment.
>
> You are not the problem. My anger is the problem. I'm trying to cope with it as best I can. I don't know how long a time-out I will need. It's unpredictable. But I do know that if I try to talk with you when I'm overflowing with anger, my anger will make our discussion totally unproductive. If you ever need a time-out, you can take one too.

Some trauma survivors have an "anger room" in their home. No one else is allowed in this room. This room is theirs. There they can write, rest, read, relax, or do whatever they need to do to calm themselves. In this room, they can be assured of the privacy they need to deal with their anger as best they can. The following was the experience of Betty, the wife of a child abuse survivor.

"At first I objected to Tom's anger room. Why should he have a whole room for himself in our little house, when I didn't even have a desk for myself? When he told me he didn't ever want me in that room, I nearly hit the roof. After all, it was my house too. Then he bought weights and an exercise bike, and I was furious. They seemed to me like unnecessary expenses.

"I couldn't understand why he still had all that anger. After all, he'd been in counseling for over two years, talking about being abused until he was blue in the face. He was angry when he started counseling, but the counseling only made him angrier. I was angry that I had to deal with his anger and that it wasn't going to go away overnight. But finally I just had to accept that my husband had this mountain of anger inside of him and there was nothing I could do about it.

"Sometimes Tom would go into his anger room for hours at a time, lifting weights. I resented the time it took away from the family, but obviously Tom needed that room. He spent less time with the family, but when he was with us, he was really with us, not trying to fight his anger. Before, he'd try to be calm, but he wasn't. Even the children could tell that he was trying hard not to erupt into a tirade.

"Now when Tom goes in his anger room, I'm glad. Better that the weights get his rage than that he vent it on me or one of the children."

Heading off your rage. Time-outs do not resolve the underlying tensions, disappointments, hardships, or other problems that make you feel as if you will explode with rage. But they can help you control your anger so that you do not create additional problems for yourself by verbally degrading or physically striking another human being, by injuring or destroying property or animals, or by harming yourself.

However, time-outs can be misused. If you are planning to use time-outs as a technique for controlling your anger, you need to consider the following suggestions.

Human beings do not suddenly "fly into a rage," with no warning. Usually there are indications that it's approaching, although you may not be aware of them. Your first task then, is to become aware of your emotional and physical feelings that generally precede an angry outburst or the desire for such an outburst. For example, do you experience muscle tension, nausea, rapid heart rate, sweating, hot flashes, rapid breathing, headaches, body tremors, or other physical symptoms when you begin to get angry?

Matthew McKay, Peter Rogers, and Judith McKay, authors of *When Anger Hurts: Quieting the Storm Within* (1989), stress the following:

> Notice where and when you begin to feel tension. For some people it's a tightness in the gut that signals the beginning of frustration. For others, the tension might be located in the neck and shoulders. "Hunching" the shoulders might be an attempt to protect the neck, or even to cover the ears from hearing painful messages. Tension in the legs, calves, and thighs is often associated with the "fight or flight" syndrome. Tension in the jaw indicates an effort to stifle some response. A particularly telling sign is tension in the hands resulting in a clenching of the fists.

In 12-step programs, recovering members are urged to "HALT" when they are H (hungry), A (angry), L (lonely), or T (tired). If you have a substance abuse or addiction problem, one of your signs of impending anger may be an intense urge to revert to your addiction. For example, do you have an overwhelming desire to drink alcohol, use your drug, or spend money unwisely? Alternatively, do you start experiencing negative thoughts about yourself or someone else, or start thinking about becoming violent? Are there certain trigger events that almost always lead to your becoming enraged?

You need to know yourself and take the time necessary to identify and catch the early warning signs of an angry outburst. Then, long before the outburst becomes almost inevitable, you need to take action, such as calling a time-out.

Calling time out. To announce a time-out to your partner, spouse, family member, or friend, you could say, I'm getting angry, so angry I can't think straight. I'd like to call a time-out. However, sometimes telling someone you are angry is a trigger for their defensiveness or retaliatory anger. Using a nonverbal means of communicating the need for a time-out may be a better idea. For example, you could agree ahead of time that the letter "T" made with the hands by either party would signal the need for a time-out.

You need to take responsibility for your own anger and behavior—not for the other person's. Even if he or she is obviously angry, refrain from saying, You're so angry, we need a time-out, or If you keep that up, I'm going to burst. Make any statements in terms of "I." Better yet, wait until after the time-out has cooled your temper and you have had a chance to think before you make *any* statements.

Once you have calmed yourself, you may want to review your anger with a clearer head. See the exercise "Looking at Your Anger Objectively" at the end of this chapter.

Timing time-outs. You and your partner need to have a previously agreed-on duration for the time-out. Generally 1 to 1½ hours is recommended. If you don't agree on a time span in advance, then the time-out can easily be interpreted by the other person as a personal rejection, as your way of not dealing with the problem at hand, or as some other form of irresponsibility. You need to show up after the agreed-on time and tell your partner whether you are willing or able to talk about the issues at hand. Similarly, the person who is left behind should also be there and not try to escape the situation by being somewhere else at the scheduled reunion time.

During the time-out. During the time-out, consider doing something physical to reduce your tension. For example, you could take a walk, go running, or take a hot bath. You might also find relief in writing down your thoughts or sharing them with a friend. Or you might want to practice relaxation exercises (see "Planning Ahead" in Chapter 5).

Do not drive, drink, drug, or binge eat. Also, try not to use the hour to make a list of everything that is "wrong" with the other person. Focus on calming yourself, using the methods that work for you, whether it's jogging or lying in bed.

Practicing time-outs. You may want to practice time-outs when you aren't angry. You may also want to make a contract with your partner regarding time-outs. The following form is a suggestion (from McKay et al. 1989; adapted from Deschner 1984).

Time-Out Contract

When I realize that my (or my partner's) anger is rising, I will give a "T" signal for a time-out and leave at once. I will not hit or kick anything and I will not slam the door. I will return no more than one hour later. I will take a walk to use up the anger energy and will not drink or use drugs while I am away. I will try not to focus on resentments. When I return I will start the conversation with "I know that I was partly wrong and partly right." I will then admit to a technical mistake I made.

If my partner gives a "T" signal and leaves, I will return the sign and let my partner go without a hassle, no matter what is going on. I will not drink or use drugs while my partner is away and will avoid focusing on resentments. When my partner returns, I will start the conversation with "I know that I was partly wrong and partly right."

Name_____ Date_____

Name_____ Date_____

Sabotaging time-outs. Time-outs can become a weapon, rather than a peace-keeping tool. If you don't come back when you agreed you would, if you consistently use time-outs to avoid dealing with painful or difficult problems, or if you return from time-outs so inebriated or high that you cannot spend time talking with your partner, you will not be achieving the purposes of a time-out. You will only be further alienating your partner and exacerbating the situation, thus defeating the purpose of the time-out.

Venting Your Anger

Do not vent your anger indiscriminately. Some popular psychology books laud the merits of "letting all your feelings out," including your anger. However, venting anger is best saved for your therapist, therapy group members, or others who can tolerate strong feelings.

Releasing the full force of your anger toward the people who are the object of your rage will seldom bring about better communication or help you obtain your desired goal, unless your goal is to alienate those people. In most cases, when people hear or see an angry person, they hear the anger rather than what the person is saying.

Your anger will probably frighten them, make them defensive, or cause them to "tune you out" or disparage you. Some may retaliate in kind, which could lead to an escalating verbal or physical fight. What displays of anger usually do not do is bring about long-term solutions to problems, especially in the area of relationships, including work relationships.

"The boundaries for safe and legitimate anger are simple," writes Carol Staudacher in *Beyond Grief: A Guide for Recovering from the Death of a Loved One* (1987):

> First your anger should not be directed at someone who
> will predictably retaliate with greater anger and aggression.
> You will only escalate your own frustration and anger when
> you try to defend yourself. This does not mean [you should]
> pick on people who can't defend themselves. It means . . .
> don't inflate the cause for your anger by antagonizing
> someone who may use verbal or physical tactics which will
> intensify your rage and anguish.
>
> Second, your accusations or revelations should not
> be directed toward someone who could suffer unjustly
> from them. That is, it would not be appropriate to be
> accusatory toward your mate who was driving the car
> in which your child was killed. It would, however, be
> appropriate to focus and channel your anger toward a
> judicial system which allowed your daughter's assailant
> to be released from prison.

In summary, nothing is gained by exerting anger which has at its base cruelty, or by publicly venting anger which could provoke cruelty toward yourself.

Staudacher goes on to suggest that you ask yourself two questions: Is my anger giving me temporary energy, or is it depleting what small amount of energy I have? and Am I using my anger or is it using me? She concludes with this: "If your answers indicate that you have an anger that drains, consumes, or 'manipulates,' you would benefit by sharing your feelings with a professional counselor."

Giving Anger Its Due

Establishing boundaries for your anger does not imply that your anger is "wrong" or that you shouldn't be angry—quite the contrary. Your anger is telling you something, something important. Pay attention to your anger and try to understand what it means and represents. Your anger can serve as a powerful motivation to help you find the solutions to the concerns that trouble you. Your anger may be a signal that you are feeling powerless, lonely, abandoned, or stressed. Or it may signify that you are being victimized by someone or some institution.

When you are in a situation in which your anger is provoked, acknowledge it rather than deny it. However, before you act on it, think in terms of your long-term goals instead of your short-term emotion.

Ask yourself, for example, the following:

What do I want out of this situation (or person)? Is this person truly responsible for what is causing my anger, or am I displacing my anger from some other situation onto this person?

How is it in my best interest to behave now? Will venting or some other display of anger truly help me achieve my goals? If I need to ventilate my feelings, I will respect my need—it is a legitimate need. However, it might serve me better to save my verbal explosion for ears that will appreciate and understand me.

If I blow up now, I may ultimately lose whatever power I have in this situation. I may even wind up worse off than I am as a result.

Immediate Anger-Management Techniques

Instead of venting your anger when it is not in your best interests to do so, do something safe. For example, try some form of physical exercise or the deep breathing and muscle relaxation exercises described in Chapter 5. You might also review the section entitled "Quick Fixes" in that chapter for ideas.

Venting is one way of externalizing your anger or, as it is commonly called, "getting your anger out." However, there are other ways to do so. For example, you can talk to someone, write down what is making you mad on a piece of paper, speak your anger into a tape recorder, or draw a picture about it. Afterwards, you can throw away the paper or the picture and erase the tape. If you believe in a higher power, you can tell that entity how angry you are.

You can also play the piano, bang on a drum, hit a pillow, stomp your feet, push against a wall, yell or scream. In general, it is not wise to hit a punching bag, since the bag somewhat resembles a person. Do not injure pets or other living things, even plants.

Caution: If muscle relaxation or any of the other suggestions given here release homicidal, sadistic, or otherwise aggressive fantasies, you may become frightened. In that case, stop what you are doing and find someone supportive to talk to. Call your therapist, if necessary. Or, if you are in a 12-step program and have a sponsor, call that person.

Taking Life Stresses into Account

As a trauma survivor, your rage may become so intense that you feel like you are going to explode. You need to take that feeling seriously.

It is not unheard of for trauma survivors, especially child abuse survivors and combat veterans, to lash out and seriously hurt themselves or others. Murders, suicides, self-mutilations, and substance abuse binges (which often set the stage for murder or suicide) can occur when a survivor reaches the point of feeling, I'm so angry I can't stand it anymore.

If you find yourself at the explosion point frequently, you need to examine your life carefully. Are some of your basic needs not being met? You may be overextending yourself in one or more areas of your life. Is there any possibility that as a result of the trauma you have developed a self-denying or self-punitive life-style? Are you, to any extent, overcompensating for the low self-esteem born of trauma or of trauma-related self-blame or survivor guilt by trying too hard or giving too much at work or at home?

Has overcompensating or overworking in one or more areas of your life resulted in emotional or other forms of deprivation? Given that anger can be a means of reducing stress, is your anger a coping mechanism for the pressures of your life? Are there any ways to reduce those pressures so that you are less stressed and as a result less angry?

Another possibility is that your anger is the result of ongoing victimization. If this is the situation, you need to find ways to stop it from happening. Depending on the nature of the victimization you are experiencing, you may need to contact authorities, lobby for legal changes, organize support groups and other efforts with similar survivors, or in some other effective way *fight back*.

Frequent explosions or near explosions suggest one of three possibilities: you are in a situation of great stress, you have a nonfunctional life-style, or you have considerable unresolved anger regarding the past. If one of these is the case with you, then give yourself the support you need to deal with these issues.

Rest and Recreation

Another possibility is that you need some "R and R," a vacation, for example. *When Anger Hurts* (McKay et al. 1989) offers the following suggestions for dealing with stress and anger:

> It is vital that you allow some space in your life for doing things that are fun.
>
> **Hobbies.** It doesn't really matter whether you collect stamps or samples of barbed wire. The important point is that you are focusing your attention on something that gives you satisfaction.
>
> **Music.** ". . . has charms to soothe a savage breast." It doesn't matter what you prefer, just spend a little time each day listening to your favorite kind of music and your stress will decrease automatically. There's something about music which takes us away from our everyday troubles. Beatles or Bach, Miles or Mantovani, sit back and relax and feel your stress float away.
>
> **Nothing.** This is the most difficult, yet most rewarding kind of time to take. In this world of hectic doing, working, being productive, accomplishing, achieving, we rarely allow ourselves the ultimate luxury of simply doing "nothing." Even if you only manage 5 minutes a day, this small pleasure will give you great rewards in terms of controlling stress and enriching your life.
>
> **Humor.** A good laugh is probably worth as much (or more) than an hour of psychotherapy. Less expensive, too! If you can learn to look at the funny side of life, stress will diminish automatically. Clip favorite cartoons from the Sunday paper and tack them on the fridge. Learn to hum refrains from old Tom Lehrer songs, or recite Abbott and Costello's "Who's on first" routine at inappropriate moments. Norman Cousins (author of *Anatomy of an Illness*) was able to cure himself by watching Marx Brothers movies.

Exercise: Looking at Your Anger Objectively

Start keeping an anger diary, noting the people, places, and situations that make you angry in the present. Then, at some time when you are not angry, examine those entries and ask yourself the following questions:

1. What was it that really made me mad?

2. Were there any other feelings present besides anger? Was I also sad, lonely, disappointed, fatigued, stressed out by my job, school, or marriage? (Consult the Feelings List in Chapter 3 if necessary.)

3. Which of my angry episodes are related, to one degree or another, to the trauma or my secondary wounding experiences? (Refer back to Chapter 5 for specific help in handling trigger situations.)

4. Are there any positive actions I can take to meet my needs or stand up for myself?

When Anger Hurts (McKay et al. 1989) offers additional information about anger and anger management techniques. A wide variety of topics are covered, including, "Anger as a Choice," "Combating Trigger Thoughts," "Combating Stress Step by Step," "Anger and Children," and "Spouse Abuse." Also offered are many practical suggestions and exercises for handling anger-provoking situations, including handling angry, irrational people.

The next chapter presents a topic that is intimately connected with anger: grief. Although grief is often more difficult for survivors (and others) to deal with, grieving your losses is absolutely essential to the healing process.

9

Stage 2 Continued: Understanding Grief and Sorrow

Give sorrow words: the grief that does not speak
Whispers the o'er fraught heart, and bids it break.

—William Shakespeare,
Macbeth, act IV, scene iii

Grieving is perhaps the hardest part of the healing process. Indeed, grieving and coping with losses are among the most difficult aspects of human existence. Emotionally, grieving is such a challenge that most people, both trauma survivors and others, tend to avoid it at all costs.

How much easier it is to be angry than sad! When you are angry, you surge with adrenaline and rage. You feel so powerful and strong that you are certain all you have to do is vent your rage and you can finally get what you want.

But when you are grieving, you feel like a collapsed balloon. The pain of loss engulfs you and you feel vulnerable, defenseless, and weak. And you hurt. You hurt so much you feel like you are dying inside.

You never thought it was possible to suffer so. You'd give anything, pay any price to end the suffering of remembering what you lost and will never have again.

But, if you are to be healed, you need to grieve. You need to surrender to the sorrow and let yourself feel it.

The Benefits of Grieving

Grieving may be one of the most difficult challenges of your life, yet it may well be worth the struggle and the pain. Unresolved grief has been found to be a factor in the development or perpetuation of a wide range of psychological problems, including anger or outbursts of rage, restlessness, depression, addiction, compulsion, anxiety ranging from mild to severe, and panic disorders. Unexpressed grief has also been implicated in the development or worsening of medical problems such as diabetes, heart disease, hypertension, cancer, asthma, and a variety of allergies, rashes, and aches and pains.

If you are willing to at least attempt to mourn your losses, the risk of these medical and psychological problems can be lessened. Sometimes the grieving might feel like absolute devastation. However, the benefits of grieving will include not only a lessening of your PTSD symptoms but ultimately a sense of freedom.

Grieving does not go on forever. Once you fully grieve a loss, you are free to move on to new involvements. This does not mean you will never think of, or feel, that loss again. However, the grief will no longer stand in the way of pursuing whatever life goals and dreams you may have.

The Three Levels of Loss

Grieving is not simple. When you grieve, you experience loss on at least three levels. The first level is grief over the specific person, object, or physical, emotional, or spiritual aspect of yourself that you have lost. For example, you may have lost a friend or relative, a home, a limb of your body, or a certain physical or intellectual ability. Equally damaging, you may have experienced the tarnishing of a cherished value. For example, as a trauma survivor, your faith in a spiritual being, loyalty to a government or institution, or belief in the integrity of certain people or agencies may be damaged beyond repair.

The second level of loss involves grieving the fact of your powerlessness. Part of your sadness stems from acknowledging that no matter what you do, you cannot replace what has been lost. No matter how smart, powerful, successful, or rich you are, you cannot resurrect the dead, satisfactorily replace the part of your body or brain that was injured, or totally restore your faith in the people or institutions that have disappointed or betrayed you.

The third level of loss involves grieving your mortality. The fact that you are going to die is the ultimate expression of your powerlessness. At the same time you are grieving a specific loss, you are also, consciously or unconsciously, to one degree or another, grieving your own mortality. Like all humans, you know you are going to die someday. However this is probably not a reality that you, like most people, care to think about very much. The awareness of your own death that comes with grieving the deaths of others or the death of a part of yourself is one reason that grieving is so hard.

The Importance of Identifying Your Losses

Just as you cannot deal with your anger without knowing what you are angry about, you cannot deal with your grief until you identify your losses. The same way that you might sometimes find yourself furious, but don't know how you became so enraged, you may sometimes find yourself feeling exceptionally sad, without understanding why the happiness you were feeling an hour earlier suddenly faded.

As you complete the following written exercise, you may be surprised to discover how many losses you have sustained. The human tendency is to deny painful experiences such as loss. However, as you make a detailed list of your losses, it will be harder to maintain this denial.

In answering the following questions, you should expect to feel some pain and anger. But once you identify your losses and begin to grieve them, you can then use your understanding of what you have lost to empower you and enrich your life. For example, once you know what you have been cheated of, you can begin to make plans to compensate yourself as much as possible, if you choose to do so. You might also begin to make some adjustments in your life so that, as much as possible, you can prevent these losses from recurring. Or you might use the insights you have gained from your losses to otherwise help yourself or others, as discussed in the following chapter.

Exercise: Identifying Your Losses

Set aside a section of your journal and entitle it "Losses." There you will itemize your financial, emotional, medical, or physical losses, and your philosophical, spiritual, or moral losses. Take some time to complete this exercise; it's far more important than it may at first appear.

Financial costs. Make a list of all the financial losses you have sustained as a result of the trauma or any secondary wounding experiences. Consider both direct and indirect costs.

Direct costs include money and property that were stolen, medical bills, relocation expenses, legal fees, babysitting and transportation costs (to go to court, doctor's appointments, and so on), days lost from work, and the costs of mental health care to cope with the trauma. Include in your direct cost list any financial costs borne by relatives and friends.

Indirect costs include the cost of lost opportunities, for example the loss of career opportunities you were unable to pursue due to medical, psychological, or other conditions stemming from the trauma. Perhaps you had to go to court to prosecute your offender several times. And while you were busy with attorneys and the court system, you missed out on applying for a new job or working on a new project that could have led to a promotion.

Emotional costs. From what emotional symptoms have you suffered and for how long? How have you had to limit social, vocational, and other aspects of your life because of the symptoms resulting from the trauma or secondary wounding experiences? These are all losses.

Other aspects of the emotional cost of the trauma are the costs to your family members and friends. How did the trauma affect your relationships with the significant others in your life? What emotional costs did they have to bear as a result of your trauma or secondary wounding experiences?

Medical and physical costs. Have any of your physical or mental abilities been negatively affected by the trauma or by secondary wounding experiences? If so, list which ones and how they have been impaired. How have these medical or physical limitations affected other aspects of your life: your job, relationships, sex life, creative pursuits, and so on?

Philosophical, spiritual, and moral costs. What cherished beliefs about yourself, specific people, people in general, and specific groups, organizations, or institutions were negatively affected by the trauma or by secondary wounding experiences? Be as specific as possible in your listing.

The Grieving Process

The Five Stages of Grief

In her landmark book, *On Death and Dying,* Elizabeth Kubler-Ross (1981) explains that the grieving process consists of five stages: denial, anger, bargaining, depression, and acceptance. Not only those who are dying but anyone who suffers major losses in life usually experiences the five stages of grief.

These "stages" do not always occur in precise order. A person can be in more than one stage at a time, and the length of time spent in each stage varies from person to person, as does the depth of feeling. Throughout the five stages, feelings of fear, despair, disorganization, guilt, and anxiety, and even adrenaline surges, may be experienced (Staudacher 1987, 1991).

Denial. In the first stage—denial or shock—the loss created by the trauma and its aftermath is not acknowledged. For example, an abused wife would most likely go into denial or shock the first time her husband beat her. So disbelieving would she be that someone she loved and trusted could turn on her, that she probably would not be able to identify her losses. But those who have been abused have many losses: their hope for protection and care from a loved one and the physical injuries they have suffered among them.

Similarly, those who have seen others die as a part of their trauma—whether in a war, hurricane, car accident, or technological disaster—would be likely to go into denial regarding the deaths they observed. They might feel they were dreaming instead of living real life. Some individuals deny the reality of the deaths around them by unconsciously hoping for miraculous resurrections.

Anger. Once your denial is cracked, expect to be flooded with anger. You may be angry at life for giving you such hardships. If you are religious, you may be angry at the deity of your understanding. If you have been abused, you may experience an intense rage at the individual who abused you. You may also be angry at yourself for seemingly accepting the abuse. You have yet to learn that perhaps you had no choice but to accept it. (For help in dealing with your anger, refer to Chapter 8.)

Bargaining. The bargaining stage of grief is characterized by fantasies of "what if" and "if only." It is also characterized by excessive and irrational self-blame. If you were carelessly driving a car that caused a ten-vehicle crash on the highway, killing a dozen people, then you have every right to hold yourself responsible for the trauma. Similarly, if you killed or abused others, and in the process were abused or hurt yourself, then you need to take responsibility for your actions.

However, it's more likely that you did not cause the trauma or its aftereffects. Continuing to punish yourself for the what-ifs and if-onlys serves little purpose other than to wear you down and perhaps ultimately destroy you.

Depression. There are many kinds of depression: the normal fluctuations in mood experienced by almost everyone, clinical depressions (described in Chapter 2), and the depression associated with the grieving process. You may be experiencing this last type. If so, remember that this is a normal response to an extremely stressful situation.

As a trauma survivor, you are under severe stress. Not only are you coping with your everyday feelings and needs, but you are coping with the trauma, as well as the reactions of others. You are also probably making complex arrangements for reordering your life and obtaining medical, psychological, legal, and other help for yourself and perhaps even for others who were involved in your trauma.

At the same time, you are also suffering the loss of yourself as you once were, the disruption to your marriage, family life, or career caused by the trauma and its aftermath, and the loss of your belief that the world is a safe and just place and that you are automatically protected and safe from harm.

Depression is a natural response to all these stresses and losses. Even though the depression associated with the grieving process is temporary, it can still be intense and painful. You may also suffer some of the symptoms associated with clinical depression: difficulty concentrating, low self-esteem, changes in your eating and sleeping habits, feelings of futility and hopelessness, or various physical problems such as backaches, headaches, vomiting, or constipation.

Extreme fatigue, and its opposite, physical agitation, are common to depression. You may find every task an overwhelming burden, see little hope for yourself or your situation, feel tired all the time, and receive little or no pleasure even from people or events that normally would please you.

Review the section entitled "What Is Depression?" in Chapter 2 to ascertain whether you are suffering from more than the depression associated with grief.

Acceptance. Acceptance is the final stage of grief. After you have passed through the other stages, you will feel less depressed and enraged about the trauma. You will simply accept it and the emotional toll it has taken on you, your family, and any others involved. Acceptance does not mean that you are happy, but rather that you have stopped fighting your own limitations and the reality of what has happened to you.

You can compensate yourself to some extent for what you have lost. However, part of acceptance is realizing that whatever compensations you arrange for yourself are partial, at best. There is no way to restore what you have lost. In the acceptance stage, you accept those losses. You accept your scars. And you accept that all you can do is seek support for yourself when you go through periods of remembering the trauma. You learn to be as kind and loving to yourself as you would be to a wounded child who is in the process of healing, but realize that even your self-love cannot take away all the pain.

What You Can Expect

As mentioned above, conceptualizing the grieving process as consisting of five stages does not mean that you will progress neatly from stage to stage. Human emotions never come in neat packages. There are transitional states, where you move from one stage to the next. But you can also be in more than one stage at a time. For example, the acceptance stage is often colored by anger, depression, and bargaining.

Or you may reach the acceptance stage, only to have the anniversary date of the trauma, another major life loss or trauma, or some other trigger set you back to an earlier stage.

Because grieving is a process, it takes time. You cannot sit down one day and decide that you will set aside a few hours that week to grieve and be done with it. There is no timetable or schedule for grieving. Some therapists talk about six months to two years to recover from the death of a loved one and five years to overcome the effects of a divorce. However, there are no published statistics about how long it takes to finish grieving the losses inherent to a trauma. Much depends on the nature of the trauma itself.

The depth and length of your grieving process will depend on the extent and meaning of your losses. It will also depend on your cultural background, your personality, and the number of other demands that are placed on your time and energies.

You should not be surprised if your period of mourning is longer or more intense than those of nontraumatized people. Your grieving is different from theirs in that it involves images of horrific events, which have a stronger impact on the heart and mind than ordinary losses. There is a vast difference, for example, in grieving the loss of an aged parent due to illness and losing that parent as the result of multiple stab wounds incurred in a robbery attempt. In the former case, you are dealing with the pain of the normal grieving process, which is overwhelming for most people, even so-called normal people. In the case where the loss is infused with horrible images, such as a bleeding, disfigured loved one and thoughts of the events that led to that person's death, the grieving process is understandably even harder to bear and tends to be longer lasting.

Because you have PTSD, you can also expect to have recurring times of grieving. People and situations that remind you of the trauma or of secondary wounding experiences can trigger a renewal of both grief and anger. You can also expect that when you have new losses, you may react more intensely than you feel is warranted. You may be correct in your assessment.

Without beating yourself over the head for "overreacting," you need to acknowledge that trauma survivors are more reactive to subsequent grief and loss than are individuals who have not been traumatized. It is as if new wounds open up the old wounds and you feel both at once.

Consequently, if you were traumatized once, then subsequently involved in a minor car accident, you might find yourself reacting with more depression and sorrow than the others who were present. Your strong reaction can be accounted for by the fact that the trauma has expanded your ability to feel intensely.

However, you should also be aware of the difference between true grief and chronic self-pity. Self-pity, along with anger, guilt, and depression, are all parts of the normal grieving process. But if self-pity, anger, or guilt come to dominate your personality, then you may be suffering from more than grief. For example, if you are suffering from neurotic grief, you will be unable to let go of the bereaved or accept your losses no matter how hard you mourn. Or you might be using your losses as an excuse to stop functioning. If you are concerned about your feelings of grief, review Chapter 2 on depression and talk to a therapist to help you obtain a better definition of your emotional status.

Strategies for Coping with Grief

Does the phrase "coping with grief" make you angry? Are you sick and tired of being told that if you complete a few little exercises in some self-help book that you can cope with an event or series of events that nearly devastated you?

"How am I supposed to 'cope' with seeing young men split in half?" says a combat veteran. "How do I 'cope' with losing my arm in a car accident?" says a teenager. "I'm supposed to 'cope' with being beaten and raped?" asks a mother of four. "Is it possible to 'cope' with seeing a fire destroy your home and community?" asks a severely shaken business-man. "Is there truly any way to 'cope' with feeling like an orphan in your own family?" asks a formerly abused child.

The anger and questions of these survivors are legitimate. Coping does not mean "overcoming" or "whitewashing" the very real losses trauma can create. As has been stated repeatedly throughout this book, if you are truly a trauma survivor, you can never forget what happened and you will have scars.

Instead, consider coping, in the context of this book, to mean that you are willing to do these things:

- Take some steps toward dealing with the trauma directly and constructively, rather than indirectly and destructively

- Make an effort to confront and try to ease your emotional, physical, and spiritual scars

- Take some steps to make your life in the present as fulfilling and meaningful as possible

- Begin to accept, rather than deny or fight, the limitations the trauma has imposed on your life

In essence, coping means that you do not allow the past to totally destroy the present. Coping means that despite your extremely negative experiences, you have preserved part of your heart, soul, and self-respect.

Coping with grief, and with the recurring sense of loss that so often afflicts trauma survivors, means that you learn to live with the sorrow. You learn to accept the grief, without allowing the fact that you are grieving to plummet you into depression, self-hatred, or despair.

Grief is so unfamiliar to most people that when they first experience it, they feel as if something is wrong with them. However, people who have had a major loss, even a loss not of the proportion of a trauma, soon learn that grief and sadness are natural and permanent parts of life.

Nevertheless, there are actions you can take to help lighten the burden of grieving. They do not erase the pain, but they do help. These actions include creating the time and space to grieve, overcoming cultural barriers to grieving, expressing the grief, giving dignity to the grief, using positive self-talk, developing a support group, and nurturing yourself.

Creating a Time and Place to Grieve

Grieving requires psychic energy, as well as the time and a place to grieve. If you are in a life situation in which you are besieged with many external demands, you may have little time and no place to do your grieving. Usually an office or other place of employment, where certain amounts of emotional composure are expected, are not appropriate places for you to weep or grieve in other ways. You may need to take time off from work, go for long walks at lunch, or find some quiet spot so that you can have the freedom to feel your feelings without being stared at, reprimanded, or considered odd.

Even in your home, you may need to create a particular space for emotional expression. If, however, economic and other realities make such privacy nearly impossible, then your grieving process may be forestalled. It is not uncommon, for example, for trauma survivors whose circumstances involve significant economic, legal, or medical problems to—by necessity—be so involved in responding to these problems that the grieving process is postponed. Only after these other problems are resolved is their grief free to arise, at the point when they have the time and energy to grieve.

Surmounting Cultural Barriers

To expedite the grieving process, you need to allow yourself to feel the grief. The more you fight your grief, the longer it will take for you to go through the various stages and obtain some degree of inner peace regarding your losses.

However, in trying to allow yourself to grieve, you may find yourself shackled by the American cultural ideal of emotional coolness. Whereas in other societies it is perfectly acceptable, even expected, for people to openly grieve their losses, in our society a display of strong emotion is considered a sign of weakness or mental instability. To grieve "too long" is considered a sign of self-pity or dwelling in the past.

In contrast, in other societies, individuals are permitted to rant, rave, and wail for as long as they need to. But in the dominant American society, the response considered appropriate to loss is usually a form of stoicism. One is expected to "get over it" as soon as possible, and show as little emotion as possible in the meantime.

For example, when President John Kennedy was shot, Jacqueline Kennedy was widely praised as a loyal wife and a brave and strong person for not shedding a tear during his funeral. However, had she been living in some other society, she might have been considered heartless, and a disgrace to her husband. In other societies, the bereaved are permitted, if not expected, to cry openly, moan, to scream, and even to try to jump into the casket.

In these societies, the bereaved are also helped by religious and other rituals that acknowledge their losses and permit them to receive the support and consolation of others. For example, certain Christian groups hold memorial services at specified intervals after a death. It is a Jewish tradition to read prayers for the dead at every Sabbath service. These prayers, called *Kaddish*, do not speak of death itself, but serve to comfort the mourners.

Also in the Jewish tradition, the bereaved are not expected to do much for a year following the death of a significant loved one. This tradition acknowledges the psychological reality that grieving takes time and energy, and that one cannot truly engage in grieving and maintain a normal routine. Furthermore, the time spent grieving is not considered misspent or wasted, as it might be in the dominant American culture. Traditional Jewish culture acknowledges that the more progress an individual makes in their "grief work," the freer that person will later be to live in the present.

In certain Native American and other cultures, crying is forbidden for men. Yet these cultures provide acceptable and helpful ways for men to express grief through music, dance, and artwork, or through periods of fasting, solitude, or meditation.

Sex-role stereotypes and grieving. Part of the stigma that attends emotionality in our culture stems from the fact that emotionalism is associated with women, who are presumed to be weak, hysterical, irrational, and needy partially because they are inherently "emotional." In contrast, men are endowed with the presumably superior traits of rationality, intellectuality, and self-control. Men who are heavily invested in the traditional male sex role, which equates strength with emotional control, and women who need to distance themselves from the denigration now attached to the traditional female role, will do their best to suppress their feelings and appear cool, calm, and collected, regardless of the situation.

The irony here is that recognizing and grieving a loss is the first step toward restoring emotional control.

Expressing the Grief

Just as you need to express your anger in a safe, constructive manner, you need to express your grief. To the best of your ability, you need to ignore cultural messages about the inappropriateness of deep grieving, especially if you are male.

If you can cry to express your grief, you are fortunate. Cry, scream, and wail all you want, for as long as you want (in a safe, accepting environment). Not everyone can cry, however, and even if you are able to cry, you can still gain further insight into your grief by expressing it through writing, drawing, or otherwise.

Writing about how you feel. Weeping is only one outlet for grief. Writing, drawing, dancing, and other art forms can also serve as outlets. For example, you can write a letter to or about the individuals you lost or to those you now feel alienated from. (You needn't mail it.) You can also write a letter to the parts of yourself that were lost, as well as to any agencies or institutions you feel failed you. You don't even need to show these writings to anyone, although you may if you want to.

For example, the following is what Anne, a formerly physically abused child, wrote about the death of her trust in others.

Dear Little Anne,

Remember when you were just a little baby and your mommy and daddy were the most wonderful people in the world? Remember how happy you were when daddy would come home and play with you? He always had a toy in his pocket and would call you his special girl.

You felt so safe and protected then, because there was a daddy who would be there for you. But then daddy started yelling and hitting and hardly ever said anything nice.

Then you died. And when you died, Little Anne, my little girl, trust in the world died too.

I'm so sorry you are dead. I wish I could bring you back to life. But I can't. You were too young to die. It wasn't your fault you were killed. Maybe it isn't even your dad's fault that he killed you. He probably didn't mean to do it. But he did do it.

I can see you lying on the floor. Where is everybody? Can't somebody help you, save you? How could they leave you like this?

I'm screaming for help for you, but nobody hears me. Little Anne, I want to save you but I can't. Please come back to life. I need you. I need you so I can play, so I can love. I need you so I can feel young, even though I am growing old.

Can't you at least move your hand or blink to show me you aren't completely dead? I don't care if you are scarred and crippled, as long as part of you is still alive. I promise to take care of you. Just don't leave me.

After writing about Little Anne, the adult Anne found that there were parts of her trust that were not dead and that she could work on regaining some trust in the world and in other people.

Additional suggestions on writing about grief can be found in *Beyond Grief*, by Carol Staudacher (1987). "Some survivors" she writes, "find that talking about their feelings and writing about them are equally beneficial. Others prefer writing to talking because they are less comfortable with verbalizing their thoughts. 'When you write what you need to say, nobody can judge you or talk back to you, or get uncomfortable,' explained a male college student whose father and brother were killed in a private plane crash."

She goes on to suggest taking several sheets of paper—one for each emotion you have felt during the day. At the top of each page, write a word or two describing the feeling. "Next write about how that feeling makes you act and think. You may also write about why you think you have the particular feeling. . . . If writing is a comfortable outlet for you, it could be more helpful in resolving personal issues than you would imagine."

If you do not like writing about your feelings directly, you might want to write a poem or a short story that expresses your grief indirectly.

Other ways of expressing grief. If writing is not a helpful medium of expression for you, you might prefer to sing, draw, paint, or make a piece of sculpture that expresses your grief. Or you might want to express your grief through movement to music.

Even gardening can be a form of expressing grief. One survivor of an airplane crash, for example, bought several new kinds of vegetable plants, one for each person who died in the crash. He tended to his plants lovingly, pretending they were the deceased, and gave away the produce to the needy in honor of the dead.

Giving Dignity to Your Grief

You can give dignity to your grief by remembering that the people, qualities, or values you are mourning are worthy of your grief. One way to both express your grief and give dignity to it is to create a memorial for it. If your grieving involves the loss of one or more people, you may want to hold a religious service, if you feel this would meet your needs. Alternatively, you may want to hold an informal service with others who understand your pain, or raise funds for a memorial contribution honoring the deceased.

Some people set aside a corner of their home or a special drawer where they keep mementos or writings about the trauma as a form of memorial.

Another way to think of an appropriate form of memorial is to consider what the deceased might have wanted as a commemoration. However, if your grief involves intangibles, such as the loss of certain qualities within yourself—your innocence, for example, or the loss of certain mental or physical abilities—you may need to create a personal memorial service for yourself. You might want to invite a few select friends to your home one evening and ask them to be with you as you share about your losses. Alternatively, you may want to make a memorial for your grief by finding a survivor mission, as outlined in the next chapter.

Talking to Yourself Positively

When you are in the midst of grieving, divest yourself of such thoughts as, I am going crazy, Why can't I control this? or There is something wrong with me. Look at so and so. She went through the same experience, yet she shows no feeling at all.

Don't listen to people who say that you are in danger of falling apart or that you are weak because you cry or otherwise grieve. The idea that it doesn't do any good to grieve or that you should just forget about it is wrong. Talking about the grief and feeling the grief do help. You are not going to collapse if you feel the grief. In fact, you are more likely to collapse or become destructive to yourself or others if you don't allow yourself to feel.

You have enough pain to deal with in your losses without also berating yourself. Instead, talk to yourself in the following way.

> I am grieving now. I need to be grateful that I can grieve, but that doesn't make it any less painful. I hate grieving, and I hate the anger I feel, too. I wish it would all go away and I could keep up my normal schedule like a normal person.
>
> But I am a normal person. Any normal person who saw what I saw and suffered the losses I suffered would be grieving too. I've worked hard to get in touch with my feelings, and this sadness is one of them.
>
> Just think, I used to [go numb, overeat, space out, drink, do drugs] instead of feeling this grief. I can see now why I wanted to escape it; the pain is so bad and I don't know when it will end. I feel trapped by it, like there's no way out.
>
> But I've made progress. I can face it all without running away. I must be very strong to be able to tolerate all this suffering without trying to escape. I need to congratulate myself instead of putting myself down.
>
> Also, I need to stop thinking of this grieving as a sign of my emotional weakness or mental instability. I need to remember that my grief is a mirror of my love for the [people, qualities, values, abilities] I lost. They are worth my tears. My grief gives dignity to their death. It's okay if I grieve them over and over again. They are worth it.
>
> Would I criticize others if they were grieving for me? If someone else had lost what I lost or had symptoms like mine, would I think something was wrong with that person

because they felt sad about it and cried sometimes? I'd be compassionate with them, wouldn't I? I have to treat myself with as much gentleness and understanding as I would someone else in a similar situation.

I can't help it that I have PTSD. I didn't choose what happened to me. Because I have PTSD, I can expect that I will experience this grief again, but I don't have to be afraid of it. Grief is only a feeling. I won't die from it. I can cry for five minutes, five hours, or five months, and I still won't die. Even though I'm always afraid that once I start crying I won't be able to stop, I always have stopped.

Most likely I won't cry for five hours or five months. I should know by now. My fears about giving in to the sadness have always been worse than the sadness itself.

I can't keep comparing myself to other people who don't seem to grieve much. Either they hide their grief in public and feel it in private, or they deny their sorrow. Just because they don't share their grief, doesn't mean I am wrong to feel mine. Because of what I went through, I have much to be sad about, so it's appropriate that I grieve.

Developing a Support System

Grieving is the time for sharing with other people, not isolating from them. No one can take away your pain, but talking to others can help to mitigate it. You may feel as if no one wants to listen, but this is not the case. You need to find someone with time, energy, and sensitivity to listen to you. You do not need a critic or a judge but someone who is accepting and not afraid of grief, anger, or any other form of negativity.

No single individual, however, can meet all your needs for sharing and caring. Your time with your therapist, if you have one, is limited. Consider sharing your grief with several people. If you give away a little of your sorrow to each of them, you will run less risk of feeling you are burdening any one person.

Also, search for a survivor's group in your area. (Appendix A offers some ways to get started.) You may also find support among family members and friends. But do not assume that your immediate or extended family will automatically function as a support group. Your friends and family may love you and want to be supportive. However, some of them may be unfamiliar or uncomfortable with grief. They may discount your pain by telling you to look at the bright side or dry your tears and get on with life, because they are frightened or do not know how to deal with emotional pain, especially the intense pain involved in grief. Particularly if they have unresolved grief issues of their own, your grieving will be threatening to them.

Alternatively, your friends and family members may want to be supportive, but feel inadequate in knowing how to help. If they also feel some survivor guilt or other form of guilt regarding you and your trauma, they may find themselves avoiding you or feeling angry with you for grieving, even though they may truly be concerned about your sadness and losses.

Carol Staudacher's two books, *Beyond Grief: A Guide for Recovering from the Death of a Loved One* (1987) and *Men and Grief: A Guide for Men Surviving the Death of a Loved One* (1991) might also be of help to you. These books describe the characteristics of grief, personal coping strategies, and self-nurturing techniques. They are intended for the bereaved and those assisting the bereaved. The first book also provides assistance for the following types of specific losses: the loss of a spouse, parent, or child; loss during childhood; loss due to suicide; and loss due to murder. The second book discusses the special problems men may have with grieving due to cultural prohibitions against male grief and bonding.

Accepting Grief

In an ancient Greco-Roman myth, the goddess of the Dawn, Aurora, loses a son in battle. She then rushes to the king of the gods, Zeus, and says, "Zeus, even though I am not one of the most powerful goddesses and the loss of a son may seem minor to you, my heart is broken. Insignificant as I may be compared to the other gods and goddesses, grant me two favors: that my son's death be honored, and that it never be forgotten."

Zeus granted her requests. On the day of her son's funeral, the sky became dark. The next day, when Dawn arose, the world was covered with dew. But the dewdrops were not dew; they were Dawn's tears for her dead son. From that day on, every morning Dawn would shed tears for her son and the whole world would remember her loss, as she did.

But the daily tears of dewdrops did not stop Dawn from doing her job or put her in a helpless or degrading position. Instead they were an expression of her sorrow, and when people throughout the world saw the dewdrops they knew they were Aurora's tears for her dead son. In her tears, they saw their own sorrows, and they honored her tears, as they did their own sorrows, and then proceeded to go about their lives.

In societies where myths such as that of Aurora and her son are well known, grieving is not a private matter. It is a communal event, and there is much support for those who grieve. In contrast, in our society, grieving can be a lonely business.

You may feel that others shun you because you are sad, or that you need to hide your grief from others to fit in or be acceptable. And these perceptions may be accurate, given that American society tends to value success and happiness and disdain pain and loss (which are often illogically equated with incompetence and weakness).

Therefore, unless you are from a culture that understands and permits grieving, or you had been in counseling for personal issues prior to the trauma, you may have been almost totally unfamiliar with grieving up until now. For instance, your understanding of grieving might have been limited to the few tears people shed at a funeral.

Now, however, if you are grieving financial, physical, psychological, existential, or other losses inherent to trauma, you are at least aware that the sad, sometimes angry, sometimes numb feelings you have are simply part of the grieving process. Hopefully, you also now understand that your grieving is not only perfectly normal, but absolutely *necessary* to your healing. The more progress you make in grieving your losses, the more free you will be to be open to present and future life opportunities. Conversely, frozen or repressed grief is a major contributing cause of many of the symptoms of PTSD, many psychosomatic problems, and a host of other psychological problems.

If your losses have been many or profound, your grieving may be lengthy and deep. But you do not have to suffer alone. Make sure you take active steps to develop a support group that will give you the assistance you need and deserve.

The next chapter deals with the last of the three stages of healing: empowerment. There you will learn to evaluate your progress and read about ways to continue healing and growing in the future.

10

Stage 3:
Attaining Empowerment

During the traumatic event and your secondary wounding experiences, you were rendered powerless. However, you can use what you have learned in healing from your wrenching experiences to exert increasing mastery and control over your life. Much of the work you have completed so far in this book has been an effort to understand, and through understanding exert some control over, the psychological fallout of your traumatic and secondary wounding experiences. The purpose of this chapter is to help you find ways of turning the trauma around—making it work for you, rather than against you.

To become empowered after having been traumatized means to regain your strength. This may include physical strength, but the main ways you will empower yourself lie in the arenas of making healthy, independent choices for yourself—rather than allowing other people or "ghosts" from the trauma to make the decisions for you. (These ghosts can include negative thinking, low self-esteem, and the many fears that are the natural result of having been traumatized.) Your ghosts may never disappear entirely, but once they are understood, their power over your life can be reduced.

Appreciating Your Progress

Although there are obvious limits to what you can control in life, you may not be fully aware of all the areas over which you can develop mastery. You may not even be giving yourself full credit for the degree to which you have already gained control. You have come a long way since you first began the healing process. You have taken the risk of looking at your trauma and your secondary wounding experiences, rather than running from them. And you have made the effort to gather additional information about what happened to you and to share your experiences with others.

Armed with this new information and the feedback from knowledgeable and sympathetic others, you have begun to be able to view your experiences more objectively. Perhaps you now understand how some of your perceptions of the trauma, and your emotional reactions to it and the events that followed, were based on understandable distortions of what actually occurred. Your perceptions and reactions were also grounded partially, if not totally, in well-intentioned but nevertheless unrealistic notions about your true options under the life-threatening conditions of trauma.

Most likely you overestimated what you could have done and underestimated your utter powerlessness. Added to this may have been a shock reaction at seeing firsthand the effects of human error, cruelty, or helplessness in the face of a catastrophe.

Emotional and Spiritual Progress

You have also taken the risk of looking at your feelings. In contrast, many people are only half alive emotionally because they are too afraid to acknowledge, much less deal with, their fears, angers, losses, or any of the other emotions that you experienced so powerfully during your traumatic and secondary wounding experiences. Sometimes these people "wake up" at midlife, or later, realizing that they have lived an emotional lie. They have spent much of their life ignorant of their true feelings and reacting to them blindly.

Perhaps they desired to stay "in control" of themselves and felt they could achieve this goal best by denying or suffocating their emotions. However, this strategy for self-control is based on a faulty assumption. The more they ran from their feelings, the more their feelings ran them.

"The unexamined life is not worth living," said the Greek philosopher Socrates. The suffering imposed by your PTSD, or by the addiction or other problems you developed in attempting to cope with it, forced you to confront your feelings. Yet you were probably thrust into the healing process by more than the desire to eliminate pain.

Were you also searching to grow? Were you also grasping for a fuller, more satisfying life? Were you also seeking to rediscover who you were and what you wanted before the trauma irrevocably changed your life and personality in so many ways?

Dealing with the feelings has been painful. So much so that the pain seemed to be unending and you often wondered if it was worth the trouble. But today you probably understand your emotional workings on a deeper level than those who have not been forced by circumstances to confront their emotional selves. As a result, you have more, not less, control over your behavior and your life than if you were blind to your emotions.

In this sense, the trauma strengthened, rather than weakened you. For example, you may feel, justifiably, that having triggers to deal with poses obstacles to living your life. Furthermore, if some of your triggers are almost intolerable to you, they limit the activities in which you feel you can comfortably engage. However, as the result of having had to learn to cope with those triggers, you have at your disposal some skills for dealing with a variety of other life stresses and problems.

In one sense, having PTSD is a disadvantage: because of your symptoms you have to work harder at "normal life" than do nontraumatized people. In another sense, however, you have a distinct advantage. Due to your PTSD, you have learned some constructive ways of coping with feelings and with stress. For example, you can apply the deep breathing exercises, the positive self-talk, and all the other techniques you have learned so far to the normal kinds of frustrations and obstacles even nontraumatized people must deal with. You are also capable of carrying on with life while enduring great emotional pain. These skills are invaluable in dealing with the expected challenges of life.

In addition, the trauma has also enabled you to grow existentially or spiritually. During the trauma, you touched your own death. This experience made you acutely aware of your mortality. The knowledge that you, too, will someday die, no matter how smart, rich, competent, careful, or good you are, can plummet you into despair. But it can also encourage you to take greater control of your life and push you toward pursuing your dreams and goals more vigorously than ever before.

Exercise: Taking Stock of Your Progress

To appreciate more fully how much you have grown, you can take stock of your progress. Entitle a page in your journal "My Progress," and use the following questions to summarize your progress in the three areas: mentally or cognitively, emotionally, and existentially or spiritually. (Note that these questions are not meant to imply that what you thought and felt before were distortions. Many of those thoughts and feelings were based in reality.)

Mental or Cognitive Growth

1. What have you learned about how the conditions of trauma distorted your view of what occurred during the trauma, your role in causing the trauma or influencing its outcome, your self-esteem, and your view of other people?

2. What have you learned about how the victim-blaming mentality of certain people and institutions affected your view of what occurred during the trauma, your view of your role in causing the trauma or

influencing its outcome, your view of yourself, and your view of other people and institutions?

3. What have you learned about reality? More specifically, what have you learned about how people react when their lives are threatened? What have you learned about how bureaucracies and other organizations operate? What have you learned about human error, human cruelty, or human indifference?

4. What have you learned about your ability to control your life? In what areas can you exert control? In what areas are you not able to exert control?

Emotional Growth

5. What have you learned about yourself emotionally?

6. Which emotions do you still struggle with?

7. What are your most trying emotional situations today?

8. Do you have any unfinished emotional work to do regarding the trauma or secondary wounding experiences? If so, what?

Existential or Spiritual Growth

9. How did the trauma change your view of the meaning of life?

10. How did the trauma change your view of human nature?

11. How did the trauma confirm or change any of your previous spiritual or moral beliefs? How did it change your views of right or wrong, of sin, or of injustice?

12. What have you learned about the personal meaning of the trauma? Did you view it as a punishment of sorts, or from inside some other personal framework? Has the healing process changed your original views of the personal meaning of the trauma? If so, how?

13. Do you now see the trauma (and any secondary wounding experiences that followed) as purely random events in which you just happened to find yourself trapped for reasons having very little to do with your personality, morality, or any other aspect of yourself? Or do you still attach some personal meaning to these experiences? If the trauma still has a special personal meaning for you, what is that meaning?

The Great Trauma Brain

You cannot change your past, but you can learn from it. As part of the healing process, you have learned that the trauma and the secondary wounding experiences caused you to develop ways of thinking and feeling that, although appropriate for the trauma, often did not serve you well in the present. These ways of thinking and feeling can be called the Great Trauma Brain.

In Chapter 4, in the sections on victim thinking, you learned some ways that the Great Trauma Brain tends to think. For example, it tends to view situations in absolutist or black-and-white terms: They're either for me or against me, and there's nothing in between. The Great Trauma Brain also tends to react to frustrations and challenges with either rage or passivity, with an anger too intense or fears too great for the present situation. The Great Trauma Brain also is plagued with negative thinking and a sense of doom. It prepares itself for the worst possible outcome and can grieve losses even before they occur.

Sometimes the Great Trauma Brain provides valuable information and helps to save the day. Other times it is totally off base and can cause you endless troubles in solving problems and dealing with other people.

To make rational decisions and observations about your life, you need to recognize and take into account the observations and reactions of the Great Trauma Brain. However, you also need to distance yourself from those observations and reactions and consider alternative points of view.

For example, suppose you are a family abuse survivor. Over the years you have learned to associate yelling and anger with being physically abused. For you, anger is a trigger signifying the pain and humiliation of the abuse. Prior to the healing process, you might have reacted automatically to an angry person the way you did to the family member who hurt you. However, as a result of the healing process, when someone is angry at you, you can stand back and judge the situation for its present reality, not its past meaning. For instance, suppose your boss becomes angry at a staff meeting. He is not necessarily angry at you, but as a family abuse survivor, you almost automatically assume it was something you did that caused his wrath.

As a result of the healing process, however, you can stand back from your Great Trauma Brain reaction and tell yourself the following:

> Look at me. I'm not even sure the boss is angry at me, but I'm positive he's going to hit me. That's the little child in me afraid of Daddy reacting, not the adult me. Yet I feel nauseated and numb, just like I did when I was a kid.
>
> But these are just my Great Trauma Brain thoughts and reactions. They don't really apply here. Realistically, my boss isn't going to hit me. I don't have to get on my knees and beg him not to hit me, and I don't have to run and hide. Yet a part of me feels I must do something to

protect myself.

I know I'm overreacting, but it's okay. It's okay that my first reactions to my boss are like the reactions I used to have to my dad when he got angry. After all the years I spent being the target of Dad's rage, it would be pretty amazing if I didn't react to an angry male authority figure with some fear.

When my boss gets red in the face, I'm afraid he's going to fire me. My father would always threaten to kick me out of the family whenever he would get red-faced. On the other hand, my fear of being fired is not totally unrealistic.

I should thank my Great Trauma Brain for teaching me that angry people can make snap decisions that they later regret, but may have too much pride to retract. Therefore, it's perfectly possible that this boss of mine, who flies into rages quite easily and quite often, is capable of firing even good workers like me.

If he upbraids me for something, it's in my best interest to stay cool. If I try to defend myself or challenge him in front of the staff it would only aggravate him more. To save his pride, he might just fire me on the spot.

I won't be a wimp. I will talk to him—but later. If there's one thing I learned in life with my father, it's that trying to talk reasonably to people when they are in the heat of anger is useless. They're much more approachable and rational after they vent their anger.

I'm grateful to be able to separate the past from the present, but also glad that I can use what I learned from the past to help me in the present. I can also give myself time to think about how I want to react.

How different this is from when I was a child. Then I had to react right away. If I didn't think of something to say or do real quick, my dad would beat me horribly. But in this situation, I can take an hour, a day, or a week to respond to my boss's fury—if in fact, he is angry at me. He may not be upset with me at all, in which case I don't have to do anything.

Self-Care and Safety

Empowerment begins with safety and taking care of yourself physically and emotionally. The essence of your traumatic experience was being, or feeling, helpless in the face of danger. Your prime need now, as a trauma survivor, is to feel secure by making your environment as safe as possible and by taking care of yourself so that you feel comfortable in your own body and with your own emotions.

Feeling Safe in Your Environment

The sense of safety begins on a very basic physical level. In particular, if you are a crime or family abuse victim, be sure you have done all you can do to protect yourself from further crime and abuse. Specific safety suggestions are included in the chapters devoted to these subjects (Chapters 11 and 13, respectively). These suggestions range from informing yourself of various forms of legal and police protection to arming your home with protection devices with which you feel safe and comfortable.

Self-defense courses are also useful to help build your sense of personal safety. You may feel you would never have the courage to use any self-defense tactics against an attacker however, it is still empowering to have these techniques at your command.

Some therapists and therapy programs for trauma survivors include time in the wilderness or outdoors as an exercise in facing danger in moderate doses. The philosophy of such programs is that trauma survivors can increase their life options if, instead of avoiding all dangerous situations, they learn to modulate their responses to danger. These programs hope to teach, for example, that there are levels of danger, that one can survive the initial anxiety reaction to danger, and that one can even learn to control some of the anxiety or panic reactions to threatening situations. You might want to consider one of these programs. However, do not undertake such a program unless you truly want to and your therapist feels it is safe for you to do so.

Even if you are not a family abuse or crime survivor, you may want to secure your home, automobile, and other property as much as possible. For example, are parking areas and entryways well lit and windows secure against break-ins? Do you have a fire extinguisher and smoke detector? Are there hazards in your home that could be avoided, for instance, piles of newspaper or other flammable materials? Is the electrical wiring in good condition? Are stairs and banisters sturdy? Do you check the tires, brakes, and otherwise maintain your car so that you have the assurance it is in good running order?

The list of precautions you can take is endless, but you owe it to yourself to take the time to make sure your immediate environment is safe, including your work environment. You may want to ask others, such as safety inspectors at your work, auto mechanics, and home inspectors and safety officials, for specific ways to make your world as safe as possible. Also talk to your neighbors. Neighborhood crime watch and other community efforts have proven to be one of the best ways to ensure a safe environment.

Physical Health and Safety

Your body needs to be safe. Critical to empowerment is taking care of your physical and medical needs. Survivors who struggle with survivor guilt, low self-esteem, or even extreme self-hatred sometimes unconsciously neglect their bodies as a form of self-punishment. Because they feel responsible for others' deaths or injuries in the trauma, or because their self-esteem was crushed, they often do not feel they deserve to take the time or spend the money on their medical and physical needs.

Even if this does not feel comfortable, natural, or necessary to you, check out your medical concerns. Permit yourself adequate sleep and take the time necessary to exercise and eat properly. These suggestions may sound elementary, but it is common for individuals with PTSD, depression, or addiction problems to neglect their bodies because they experience anxiety in taking care of themselves medically or physically.

Emotional Self-Care

To feel safe with your emotions, you need to understand your posttraumatic stress disorder or other responses to the trauma and, for as long as necessary, avail yourself of the help of mental health professionals, family members, and friends. Such assistance will help you to further clarify your feelings and thoughts and provide you with the necessary emotional support so that you can bear the intensity of your reactions to the trauma and other life stressors.

Another way to take care of yourself emotionally is to ask for help with tasks that overwhelm you—either at work or at home. Regardless of your occupation, you will at some point or another be given tasks that cause you intense internal pressure. *It's too much for me,* you may feel, yet you may hesitate to share that feeling with your co-workers. That is the same feeling you had during your trauma experience.

Perhaps no help was available during the trauma, or for other reasons you felt that survival was all up to you and your limited resources. But you can ask for help now. Depending on your circumstances, you may be able to share with your co-workers that a particular assignment is creating confusion or stress for you, and ask them for suggestions in handling the task. This does not mean you are asking them to do your work for you, but rather that, as co-workers, they probably have insights that could lighten your task.

Avoiding Revictimization

Another important part of taking care of yourself is to avoid revictimization. It is an unhappy, but well-established fact that people who have been traumatized or victimized once are frequently traumatized or victimized a second time. In psychological terms, these survivors are said to have been retraumatized or revictimized. Revictimization rates are especially high among family abuse survivors, for example, abused children, incest survivors, and battered wives.

In many instances, revictimization is directly related to the original trauma and its secondary wounding experiences. Trauma and the secondary wounding experiences that follow can so incapacitate people that they are literally set up for future misfortunes. For example, survivors who become physically or psychologically disabled or who lose much of their property due to the trauma, frequently suffer a significant decrease in their standard of living. The lower their standard of living, the greater the probability that they will be victimized by crime. The less money they have, the greater the probability of receiving inadequate medical and mental health care, police protection, and other services.

Furthermore, the psychological distress caused by having to adjust to a lower standard of living can exacerbate PTSD, other stress symptoms, and any medical problems. Such psychological dehabilitation, in combination with economic need and possible physical disability, makes survivors of a variety of traumas vulnerable to financial, psychological, and other forms of exploitation.

Reviewing the Three Levels of Victimization

As you will remember from Chapter 4, those who work with trauma survivors point out that survivors are victimized on three levels: first, the original traumatic event; second, secondary wounding experiences; and third, internalization of society's negative view of them.

Due to this socially imposed low self-esteem and low social standing, trauma survivors may experience greater difficulty than most people in asserting their rights, pursuing their goals, or putting a halt to further abuses or exploitations. Learned helplessness can also play a role here.

As discussed in Chapter 2, on the biochemistry of PTSD, experiments have shown that when animals are subjected to shock that continues no matter what action or inaction they take, they learn to become passive. They give up, in effect. And once the animals have learned this, when subsequently a means of escape is provided, they have become so defeated that they cannot take advantage of it. Similarly, Lenore Walker (1979) found that battered women often learn to become helpless, since no matter how they change their behavior or try to control the situation, the beatings still occur. Furthermore, the learned helplessness acquired in these women's domestic lives spills over to their professional and social lives, where they are not in fact helpless or powerless.

As a trauma survivor, you had little or no control over the first two levels of victimization, the trauma and secondary wounding experiences. But you do have some control over the third level. You do not have to be like Bob, a trauma survivor who so deeply adopted society's negative attitude toward him that he became exceptionally passive in situations where passivity was an invitation to be scapegoated or misused.

> Because of what happened to me, I got the idea I didn't deserve a good life. When things go wrong at the office, I don't speak up. When my supervisor gives me her work to do, I say nothing. When my ex-wife asks me for too many favors, I have trouble saying no. I'll spend a hundred dollars on my kids in a minute, but it takes me an hour to decide to spend fifteen dollars on myself.
>
> Other people say I'm letting myself be taken advantage of. I guess it's true. But I feel so worthless sometimes it's hard for me to feel I have any choices.

But Bob does have choices. So do you. You do not need to allow yourself to be revictimized in the present. In this book you have been repeatedly asked to examine the feelings of self-blame you have as a result of your trauma. One of the purposes of this repeated examination of your self-blame was to help eliminate or reduce any unfounded or exaggerated sense of guilt you might have been suffering from; such guilt can contribute to the acceptance of further victimization.

In the exercise that follows, you will be asked to think about situations in the present in which you feel misused or maltreated and in which you are, consciously or unconsciously, acting as powerless as you did during the original trauma. Once you identify these situations, you may or may not choose to act to rectify matters. However, you need to be aware of all the instances in your present life, large or small, in which you assume the role of the victim.

It cannot be overemphasized that when you assume a passive role, it is not necessarily because you are "sick" or masochistic. You may be doing so because such a position was a survival tactic during the trauma, or because you were psychologically beaten down by secondary wounding experiences after the trauma.

No situation is too minor to consider, even one as seemingly petty as having loaned a co-worker five dollars that was never returned. A lot of little victimization and abuses can result in one big depression.

A special note to family abuse survivors. You are a domestic violence survivor if you are now or were in the past physically or sexually abused by a member of your family or a caretaker. Emotional abuse is harmful, but it does not qualify you as a victim of family violence. You must have experienced a violation of your body or the threat of injury or death to be considered a survivor of family violence.

In violent homes, typically one child or person in the family is singled out as the victim. This is not always the case, however. In some homes, almost all the children or family members are beaten by the abuser. In homes where one individual is the prime victim, that individual, whether a child or an adult, is often mistreated by other family members as well. The other family members may not hit or sexually molest the victim, but they frequently demean or exploit him or her emotionally, financially, or in other ways.

Even after the victim has left the family home or the original site of the abuse, other family members may perpetuate the exploitation of the victim through verbal abuse or other means. Some of the subtler forms of mistreatment include treating the abuse survivor as the "black sheep" of the family or assuming that the abuse survivor will always be available to do favors for the family.

If you are a family abuse survivor, be sure to closely examine ways in which family members or caretakers other than the abuser might be exploiting you. These people may not be aware of their behavior because it was or is a part of a family system that they perpetuate unconsciously or semiconsciously. An added complication is that these family members may also be sources of kindness and love towards you. Yet at the same time they automatically treat you like a second-class citizen. These complex factors make it that much more difficult for you to demand respect.

Exercise: Avoiding Revictimization

In your journal, answer the following questions:

1. In what ways have you internalized the blame-the-victim attitude of certain people and institutions in society?

2. To what extent, if any, did the victim-blaming attitudes of others reinforce any low self-esteem or self-doubts you had prior to the trauma and your secondary wounding experiences?

3. Did your trauma or secondary wounding experiences subject you to the learned helplessness syndrome? If so, in what ways are you manifesting the learned helplessness syndrome in the present?

4. To what extent has the healing process helped you to overcome the low self-esteem and negative thinking that being victimized created or reinforced in your life?

5. In what ways are you being victimized or misused in your present life? (List all the situations in which you feel mistreated or ignored, if not outright victimized.)

6. Which of those situations can be changed?

7. Of the situations that can be changed, which situations do you want to work on changing?

8. For each situation you choose to work on, list at least three constructive steps you can take towards rectifying matters.

For example, you might want to lighten your load at work, but until recently you felt you had to accept whatever tasks were given to you. You now realize you may be being revictimized at work, and you want to change the situation. To do so you could begin by rereading your job description to ascertain whether or not the tasks you are being given fall into your job category. If the tasks are not part of your job description, you can choose to discuss the matter with your supervisor, delegate work whenever possible, and/or ask for help with difficult assignments.

Harnessing Your Rage

Have you ever desired revenge against those who hurt you or who you felt did not adequately assist you during your traumatic experiences? Or are you a saint?

Saints are rare in this world. Unless you are an exceptionally spiritual or religious individual, you probably harbor at least a few vengeful thoughts and feelings toward whomever or whatever you feel was at fault in your trauma and secondary wounding experiences. You may be only dimly aware of these feelings—or you may be all too conscious of them.

The rage born of injustice has ignited nations into massive political and social changes. Some of that rage lies in you. You are entitled to be angry at whatever injustices you suffered, either at the hands of others or from the hand of fate. And you wouldn't be human if you didn't want to strike back at whomever or whatever wounded you.

Although it is never in your best interest to strike back violently, it *is* in your best interest to at least be aware of your vengeful feelings and thoughts. In fact some of your nonviolent revenge fantasies might well be worth considering as a basis for positive action. Consider the following example:

> Several years ago in New York City a woman was assaulted by her husband. Still carrying the knife he had cut her with, he chased her into the streets and continued to beat her, in front of a number of witnesses.
>
> Fearing the woman would be murdered in front of their eyes, the neighbors telephoned the police. The police arrived, but did nothing. Claiming there was insufficient evidence of assault, they refused to arrest the abuser. They also did not assist the woman in getting to a hospital.
>
> The woman swore revenge. Marshaling her profound rage and hatred toward the police, she found dozens of abused wives in her area who had had similar experiences with the police. Together, they filed a class action suit against the New York City police department. It was the first such

class action suit in New York's history.

These woman had seemingly unlimited anger at the injustices they had experienced at the hands of the police. Their anger and desire for revenge empowered them to withstand the numerous obstacles thrown in their way. Eventually they won, and the results of their victory are still benefiting women today. By directing their anger in a prosocial manner, rather than in an antisocial or self-destructive way, they were able not only to help themselves, but to change history.

A Note of Caution

Soon you will be asked to list your vengeful thoughts, feelings, and fantasies. Under no circumstances, however, is this exercise intended to suggest that you automatically act on any of the ideas you list. Do not even attempt this exercise if you fear it may trigger you into harming other people, property, animals, or yourself.

Acknowledging your revenge fantasies is a far cry from acting them out. In fact, one reason you are being asked to list your revenge fantasies and then discuss them with a qualified counselor or support group is to diffuse the destructive fantasies and prevent them from becoming reality.

Remember, at all times your priority is your own well-being, safety, and advancement. In many instances, following through on any violent or destructive revenge fantasies will hurt *you*—possibly without punishing or hurting those who made you suffer.

Once again, if you don't feel you can make this list without becoming violent, don't even attempt it. Instead seek professional help as soon as possible.

A further note of caution. If you fall into one of the following categories, do not attempt this fantasy exercise without the help of a therapist or support group:

- You are a combat veteran or a police officer.

- You have formal or informal training in fighting, killing, sabotage, or another form of destruction.

- You have beaten or otherwise physically abused others, or have sexually abused, others.

- You like to torture animals.

- You have killed people.

- You are currently or have frequently been suicidal, homicidal, or both.

- You suffer from severe depression, hallucinations, a psychosis, or psychotic episodes.

- You enjoy watching others suffer or property being destroyed.

- You are afraid that if you dare to think about your revenge fantasies, you will act on them.

If you fall into one of the above categories, you need to discuss with a qualified mental health professional or counselor whether you should attempt the following exercise. If it is decided that you can handle the exercise, your counselor needs to stay with you as you talk about or list your revenge fantasies.

Not talking about the fantasies won't make them go away. However, you do not want thinking or talking about your vengeful dreams to trigger a violent response. If you fall into one of the above categories, a violent response may be almost automatic because of your training, mental suffering, or history.

All forms of violence, from arson to assault to murder, are wrong. Because such forms of violence are so common in our society, and because they are even glamorized in many media presentations, it is quite easy to view such acts as "normal." They are not normal, however; nor are they legally acceptable, except in certain cases of self-defense.

Exercise: Revenge Fantasies

Use the following statement as a beginning for your list of revenge fantasies. List those fantasies you have on a recurring basis first, then go on to those you think about less frequently. You can even go ahead and make up some new ones if you like.

I am still angry at _____ and _____. Sometimes when I become really angry, I fantasize that I _____ or _____.

Your fantasies need not be realistic, nor do they have to be particularly vengeful. They might simply be dreams of becoming successful and admired while those who have hurt you do not. Be sure to write down as many fantasies as you can think of.

Now review your list of fantasies. First, go through and put a check mark by those that, if you acted on them, would cause physical harm to someone or something. Put two check marks by those that, if acted on, would harm you or people you love. Under no circumstances act out those fantasies. Now, review your list again. Be sure that those fantasies you have not checked are in fact nonviolent.

Of those nonviolent fantasies you have listed, put a star by those that might promote your well-being or perhaps spare others from suffering what you suffered. Then think about which of these might you consider pursuing. Make a list of the pros and cons of pursuing each fantasy you have selected.

For example, suppose one of your revenge fantasies is writing a letter to an organization that failed to respond to your needs as a trauma survivor. You would want to consider how the organization handles such grievances and follow its established procedures. If you strongly suspect or have evidence to support the idea that the organization might retaliate against you for writing such a letter, you might decide not to pursue that course of action—or you could postpone acting until some time when there would be less risk. Similarly, if your revenge fantasy is to publicly expose an official of the organization who was particularly demeaning to you, weigh the consequences in terms of your self-interest as well as in terms of what you feel compelled to do out of a sense of justice.

Depending on the organization in question, following established procedures for filing grievances may or may not bring about quick results—or any results at all. Nonetheless, such procedures are available and should be used as a starting point.

Getting Even—Weighing the Pros and Cons

After being victimized or traumatized, it is possible to fall into one of two extreme modes of reacting. The one extreme is to continue the victim/trauma role of being powerless and allow others to abuse or take advantage of you without protest in many current life situations. An example would be the rape victim who overworks at her job, overgives to her boyfriend, and volunteers to take care of her elderly parents and others at the expense of her own social life. Because she is giving so much to others and doing so little for herself, she finds herself depressed much of the time. She attributes her depression to the rape, which is valid.

However, some of her depression is also the result of her present self-sacrificial life-style. If she could only remove the sense of guilt and defilement she has as a result of the rape, she might feel less obligated to cleanse herself and prove her goodness through self-denial.

At the other extreme are trauma survivors who are determined to never again be taken advantage of or exploited by anyone or any force. Determined to rid themselves of the victim role, they are unwilling to give to anyone or any cause unless they are assured of getting back at least an equal return. If they feel their rights are threatened in some manner, they will fight for those rights regardless of the cost.

A former victim who desires to shed the shackles of passivity and negativity and makes efforts to do so is worthy of admiration. It is truly heroic to fight for one's rights against many odds. However, in making decisions about how far to push for your rights, your physical, emotional, spiritual, and financial well-being also need to be considered.

In *some* situations there comes a point where it is self-defeating to stand up for yourself or seek revenge or retribution even through legal means. I am not advocating that you give up or remain a victim in your thinking. However, sometimes trauma survivors need to put themselves first, before any cause or fight for justice or anything external to themselves, however important these may be.

For example, Joe lost one of his children and his home when, without adequate warning, a tornado hit the town he lived in. Other residents also lost property and family members. Joe, like many of the town's citizens, was justifiably enraged at the town council, since they had known months before the disaster that the city's tornado warning equipment was in need of repair. In addition, the council then procrastinated on distributing compensation. Joe describes the ensuing battle this way:

> I started out the fight determined to win. Like many of my neighbors, I blamed myself for not pressing the council harder to get that warning equipment fixed. We had petitioned a few times, but then we lapsed into thinking, Oh, it will never happen here.
>
> Well, it did happen here, and even though technically it wasn't our fault, we did sort of blame ourselves for not sticking to our guns and insisting on the repairs. So then we had a new battle—getting what is due to us as compensation. None of us wanted to give up just out of fatigue like we did last time. I've worked on my case 10 to 15 hours a week, hired two lawyers—even read law books myself. I was determined the town council wasn't going to win this time just by hemming and hawing and using legal mish-mash.
>
> But it's been over a year now. I've spent a small fortune on lawyers, with no real results. If I had taken a part-time job instead of working on my compensation case so hard, I'd have money in the bank instead.
>
> My wife is still grieving our son. She needs me, and I have two living children who need me too. But I've been so caught up in my desire for revenge that I've ignored them.
>
> The town council only wants to give me half of what I feel I'm due. But I'll take it and run. At this point, I'd rather have my sanity and the well-being of my family than the money.
>
> Some of my neighbors are angry with me, calling me "quitter" and other names, but I have to do what I think is right for me.

This story is not meant to imply that you should not fight those institutions or persons who hurt you using legal channels. On the contrary, it may be critically important for you personally to do so, as well as for the survivor group you represent. Indeed, if survivors of various injustices had given up pursuing their rights when they met the first obstacle, we would not have civil rights legislation, health and safety regulations, battered women's shelters, and many other protections.

Consulting others—and yourself. Before you follow through on any actions you are considering, discuss them with qualified others, for example, your therapist, your survivor group, and other objective parties. They might have suggestions to offer that would make your actions more effective. They might also have warnings as to possible dangers. Use their feedback to evaluate your decision and to better plan your strategy should you decide to proceed. If your decision to act could affect friends or family, you need to discuss it with those people as well.

Obtaining feedback from others is helpful, but don't neglect your own gut feelings. Take your time deciding what to do. The trauma is over. You don't have to put yourself on emergency-alert status as you did during that time.

You also need to prepare yourself for possible failure in your attempts to be heard or to effect change. The familiar feelings of powerlessness that failure often causes can be devastating. Only you can assess whether you can tolerate yet another secondary wounding experience. Only you can decide if proceeding with your plan is worth the risk of losing or being discounted one more time.

Other Ways of Getting Even

Giving up on, or deciding not to pursue, a course of action does not of course mean that you will no longer be angry or have revenge fantasies involving people or organizations that hurt you. It just means you've decided not to channel your energies in that direction. It could be that getting even in some symbolic way will be safer and ultimately more productive for you.

For example, you might express your anger in a letter, which you then—instead of mailing—share with your survivor group (if you choose). Since you won't be mailing it, the letter can contain as many of your thoughts and feelings as you like—you can be as nasty as you want without worrying about it backfiring on you.

More constructive in the long run, may be to join (or begin) an organization dedicated to victims' issues or to preventing what happened to you from happening to others.

Survivor missions. Because you have been wounded by life, you are in a unique position to help others who also have been wounded. Furthermore, you may have acquired insight into the social, political, or economic conditions that contributed to your trauma. Others who have never been traumatized may not have such insights. At the very minimum you are most certainly an expert on what it feels like to suffer from PTSD and other psychological reactions to the trauma and from secondary wounding experiences.

In more ways than one, you can use the various understandings you have acquired to help rectify deficits in your community and prevent your trauma from happening to others. For example, Mothers Against Drunk Drivers (MADD) was founded by Candy Lightner, whose daughter was killed by a drunk driver. Similarly, the first rape crisis centers and battered women's shelters were begun and staffed by former victims. Some war veterans lobby against war. Others do volunteer work for disabled veterans at hospitals or through veteran's service organizations.

There are countless ways to use your grief for good in the world. Even if you suffer from an impairment, there is usually something you can do. For example, Susan lost both legs in a car accident. Today she spends several hours a week reading to an older woman who was blinded in a similar accident. Joshua suffered brain damage due to combat. Today he spends a day a week assisting at a nursing home, wheeling patients from one clinic to another.

Go to your local library and spend some time doing research. Look for newspaper and magazine articles (if and when you feel strong enough to read such material) about those who have experienced traumas similar to yours. Often these articles will include commentary from a survivors' organization you might want to become involved with.

There are books available on some topics, and they will often reference these organizations. Appendix B lists some as well. Finally, people can often be your best resource. Talk to your counselor or therapist and other members of your survivor group to find out what organizations they're aware of.

A well-spent life. As a trauma survivor who has been battered by life, one of your major goals needs to be taking better and better care of yourself emotionally and physically (and spiritually as well, if this is important to you).

It is sometimes said that the best revenge is a well-spent life. Merely surviving the trauma and its secondary wounding experiences can be a monumental form of revenge in certain situations. In addition, further revenge is to develop yourself—to go on to enjoy life and make a contribution to it. Whether you try to get back at those who hurt you, or you determine that it would be more rewarding to compensate yourself for your losses, rather than spending valuable time, money, and energy in getting compensation from others, your well-being needs to be your primary concern.

The next section is devoted to encouraging you to compensate yourself. Self-compensation is a major form of empowerment, because you are in control. Generally, compensating yourself for your losses is much more reliable than expecting the persons or institutions that harmed you or demonstrated little compassion for your pain to give you something, even what you are entitled to legally.

Working Toward Compensation

"I've been through so much," says one trauma survivor. "Will I ever get back even part of what I lost?"

Just as you might secretly (or not so secretly) have revenge fantasies, you probably have some notions about what you think you deserve as compensation for all the hardships and heartaches you have survived.

In the following exercise you will list all that you feel entitled to as compensation for having suffered the trauma and the secondary wounding experiences that followed.

Exercise: Compensations

In your journal, set aside at least three pages. Label the first page "Compensations I am entitled to by law," the second page "Compensations I should be entitled to by law but am not promised," and the third page "Compensation fantasies: what I would receive in the best of all possible worlds."

On the first page list all the compensations you are entitled to by law. For example, combat veterans are entitled to certain benefits by law. Survivors of natural catastrophes in this country are also legally entitled to certain types of assistance. Crime victims have certain legal rights as well. You may need to do some research to find out what your legal rights are. Many communities have free or sliding-scale legal aid services. Refer to Appendix B for information on locating these services.

On the second page, list all the compensations you feel should be provided to you but are not legally guaranteed.

On the third page, list all the compensations you would like to have, but which, at this point, you feel are simply not available in the real world. As you complete this part, do not let reality inhibit you. This is a wish list, pretend you can have anything you want.

Do not limit yourself to material objects. For example, do you ever wish you could have back certain years of your youth or certain mental faculties, such as the ability to concentrate? Would you like a banquet or parade in your honor, or the apology of your abuser? How happy would it make you feel to receive a proclamation from the head of some institution or agency that you were right and the organization was wrong? Do you also desire validation or apologies from other sources?

Let your imagination run free. From your compensation fantasy you can evolve a more realistic list of experiences, attitudes, and objects that can serve as forms of compensation for your sufferings.

Before you begin writing, you may want to reread the list of losses you made in Chapter 9. There you were asked to list your financial, emotional, spiritual, and other losses, as specifically as possible. Reviewing this list may spark your imagination about what you would like in compensation for these and other losses.

Pursuing Legal Rights and Promises

The following is a list of things you should consider when pursuing legal claims and compensations:

- Think about how much time, energy, and money you are willing to put into the fight for your rights. Is it more difficult and stressful for you to fight for your rights against an obstinate or complicated bureaucracy then to give up and accept an unfair settlement to your case?

- In all likelihood, a large amount of paperwork and delay will be involved. To get through it you may need the support of your family, friends, or other survivors. Can you ask for and receive that support?

- Other survivors' knowledge and advice can be invaluable in pursuing your rights. What have they tried in order to obtain their lawful rights? Could you possibly unite with other survivors to claim your rights?

- If you are not receiving a response to an application or other inquiry, try to find out why. Telephone or write to the proper authorities. If they are unresponsive or have frustrated your attempts to obtain your lawful compensations, there may be a grievance board or committee to which you can appeal.

- Can you allow yourself to give up the struggle to obtain what is legally yours if the struggle becomes too costly to you emotionally, socially, vocationally, or financially?

Self-Compensation

Using what you have written for the second and third parts of the compensations exercise as a guide, what can you realistically give yourself as a form of compensation? Although you certainly may include material items, such as clothing, jewelry, books, or a new car, and experiences such as vacations and entertainment, such compensations may be beyond your means.

Many trauma survivors find that, although it is important to give themselves material goods and pleasurable experiences, it is also important to treat themselves with loving kindness on a daily basis. It has also proved important to them to respect the impact of the trauma on their personalities and habits, as the following stories indicate.

Loretta, an incest survivor, allowed herself six years to go through college rather than the regular four years. "I was so pressured during my childhood," she says, "I didn't want to repeat that experience in college. Also I wanted to make time for both individual and group incest therapy. If I carry the regular workload, I'll never take the time necessary to heal myself."

Mike, also a family abuse survivor, compensates himself by trying to retrieve what he can of his childhood:

My father left my mother when I was six. After that, my childhood ended. My mother became an alcoholic and began to beat me at least twice a week. I was so busy recovering from the physical abuse and taking care of younger brothers and sisters, I hardly ever played.

Today I am trying to compensate myself for my lost childhood by being on a baseball team. I also play games with my sons, realizing that I'm vicariously enjoying being a kid by being with kids. Last week I bought myself a train set, and I'm considering joining a pool and taking swimming lessons.

I realize I could be making money, going to night school or doing good works instead of playing so much. But the good works I'm doing now are for myself. At least for the present, I need to make up for the past any way I can.

Joanne, a hurricane survivor, compensates herself by taking the anniversary day of the hurricane off from work every year and holding a small memorial service for her friends who died in the storm. She also makes a point of not pressuring herself at work. "I'm a trauma survivor. I can't handle as much stress as others. Maybe I'll achieve less than others in life. But I simply cannot, or refuse to, recreate the trauma by exhausting myself as if some catastrophe were going on."

You can also compensate yourself emotionally by trying not to punish yourself for the reemergence of symptoms in the presence of trigger events or at anniversary times. "Each time, the stick I beat myself with gets smaller and smaller. And I use it for a shorter time," says one survivor.

Another way of taking emotional care of yourself is to keep a daily journal of your feelings and allow yourself time to talk to others about your problems and concerns. You can carry the load alone if you want to, but why suffer needlessly? If help is available, take it.

Spiritually, you may want to give yourself the time to meditate, pray, or engage in other activities you find rewarding.

The above ideas are only suggestions. Only you know what will help you feel compensated. Over time, the experiences and objects you desire as forms of compensation may change. That's fine, just be sure to continue to compensate yourself.

Refinding Yourself

"I lost my heart in Vietnam," more than one veteran has said. "He killed my soul," abused women have lamented. "I'll never be the same," catastrophe survivors moan in a state of shock.

Do you ever feel the same? Do you ever wonder who you were and what you wanted before "it" came and shattered your life? Empowerment includes refinding yourself, the person that existed before the trauma. Is any of your pretrauma self salvageable? Do you want to revive any part of that self or any of your pretrauma goals?

In the following exercise, you will write in your journal about who you were before the trauma. You may want to center yourself with deep breathing exercises or muscle relaxation before beginning.

Exercise: Who Was I Then?

Try to recall where you were living at the time the trauma occurred. Who were you living with, and what were you doing? Did you have a job, or were you in school or raising a family? Try also to recall your physical self. How did you wear your hair? What did you weigh? What kind of clothes did you like?

Form as vivid and detailed a picture of yourself as possible. Use photographs of yourself from that time if you have them. As you look at the photographs or concentrate on the vision of yourself in your mind ask, Who were you? What were you like? What would you be like and what would you be doing right now if the trauma hadn't happened?

To further activate your memory, you can review the list of losses you made in Chapter 9. Examine your list to see if it contains aspects of your pretrauma self that you feel were killed or wounded during the trauma. These may include your faith in certain people or institutions, your innocence, your sense of humor, your illusion of invulnerability, as well as some of your intellectual, vocational, or recreational interests.

As you write about your pretrauma self, consider the following questions:

1. What did you do for fun?

2. What were your major worries and anxieties?

3. What did you like about yourself then?

4. What didn't you like about yourself?

5. Who were your friends?

6. How were you getting along with your family?

7. Did you have any religious or spiritual beliefs? If so, what were they?

8. Did you have any firm philosophical or existential convictions? If so, what were they?

9. What dreams or goals did you have for your life, and what were your interests?

10. Of the goals and interests you had prior to the trauma, which ones would you like to pursue now or in the near future?

11. Of the pretrauma goals and interests you are still drawn to, which would you realistically be able to pursue? What obstacles would stand in your way?

Salvaging the Past

If the obstacles are insurmountable, some past goals cannot be considered resurrected. However, if the obstacles are not insurmountable, what stands between you and what you want? Even if you cannot achieve all of a certain goal you may be able to achieve part of it.

For example, you may have loved dancing at parties prior to the trauma. Then the trauma occurred. Your interest in socializing diminished. You became so depressed you did not have the desire, nor the energy, to go to parties, much less dance at them. If you were severely injured you may no longer be able to dance as you once did. Or perhaps your body was spared, but your face was disfigured, or you may feel so scarred on the inside that you have trouble mixing with others.

As a result, you may lack the confidence to attend parties and have a good time like others. Yet in your heart, you still love music and the part of you that enjoyed dancing is not quite dead.

What can you do? If your physical condition permits, you could simply go dancing somewhere that you need not interact with others if you choose not to, and only stay for as long as you are comfortable. If you are disabled, you can still sway or otherwise move in time to the music. I have seen double amputees dancing by moving their wheelchairs to the beat. Others take jobs as disc jockeys. Although they cannot dance, they love music and dancing so much, it brings them joy to be near it.

What if one of your pretrauma ambitions was to pursue a certain course of study? Could you go back to school now? If you cannot return full time, is it possible for you to attend part-time or to take one course at a time? If even that is too costly in terms of time and money, are there any local county or city classes or seminars sponsored in your field of interest? Usually such classes are low-cost or even free of charge.

If you cannot attempt to pursue a certain interest right away, perhaps you can plan to pursue it in the future.

The main question to keep asking yourself is, Is there a piece of my dream that can be turned into reality? Even if all you can salvage is a sliver of your dream, grab it and nurture it to the best of your ability.

Rewriting the Trauma

Another way to refind yourself is to rewrite the story of your trauma with a different ending. Give your trauma story the outcome you desire. You can write as many fantasy endings to your story as you like, as long as the endings are ones you wish had taken place in real life.

Do any of the desired outcomes reflect some of your wishes for your life? List these wishes in your journal. Afterwards, review this list of wishes and eliminate those that could never come to pass; put a check mark by those that could realistically happen, at least in part, if you decided to work toward them. On this list of realistically attainable objectives, are there any you truly wish to pursue? What is keeping you from taking action along these lines? Are those obstacles realistic?

Accepting the Scars

Did you read the sections on self-compensation and refinding yourself and think, More Pollyanna talk? Did you want to shout, Don't you know I'm scarred—scarred for life!

Your scars are deep. Whether psychological, physical, or both, they hurt. Some may be permanent. There is no way to think, compensate, or wish-list them away. You cannot talk your way out of them either. They may not be in the forefront of your mind every minute of the day, but they are still there.

As a trauma survivor, you are subject to unwanted, recurring thoughts of the trauma, to nightmares, and perhaps even to flashbacks. You may also have times of rage, emotional pain, numbing, anxiety attacks, physical pain, and other symptoms related to the trauma. All the positive actions in the world cannot make these go away entirely either.

Yet, *not* taking positive action in the present, *not* finding ways to compensate yourself, *not* pursuing your dreams, and instead treating yourself badly will not remove the scars either. There seem to be few choices other than either giving up and letting your wounds crush you or accepting the scars and going on with your life.

Support Systems

As has been repeatedly stated in this book, it is critical that you get support and continue to get support as long as you need it. It is hard enough being a trauma survivor with support, but being without support is an unnecessary and lonely battle.

If you already have a support system in family or friends, you may or may not need to be involved in counseling or with a survivors' group after you have undergone the healing process. However, if you are not so fortunate as to have an existing support system, you will probably need to find one outside your family or peer group. In either case, you may need to be involved with a therapist or group for many years, just as you are with your family and friends.

There is no need to feel ashamed of your need for support. Most people need emotional support in life. Those who claim they don't usually have serious emotional problems or are in denial of a basic human need.

Think of getting support as a form of preventive medicine. Why wait until you feel so overwhelmed or depressed that you require intensive therapy or hospitalization, or develop an addiction, psychosomatic illness, or other psychological symptom to cope with your scars and feelings? Would you berate diabetics for needing insulin all their lives? Would you ridicule heart patients if they needed to do some exercise every day for the rest of their lives? Then why begrudge yourself what you may need for your mental and physical health?

The more intense and prolonged the trauma you endured, and the more harmful and numerous your secondary wounding experiences, the more support you deserve.

Even though you can't make the scars go away, you can realistically hope that over time they will diminish. You can also hope that as you carry on, doing more and more for yourself, the scars will seem less important.

You can also expect that eventually, with continued effort on your part to acknowledge how you feel, to share openly with trusted others, and to be loving to yourself the best you can, you will find some of the promises of the healing process fulfilled.

The Meaning of "Healing"

Part of healing includes ridding yourself of the idea that to be "healed" means you no longer have any PTSD symptoms—or even that the symptoms become infrequent or very mild. While this may occur, it is more likely, depending on how severely you were traumatized and the kind of support you have had since, that you will have some symptoms forever and will have some periods of intense symptoms.

All PTSD symptoms cannot disappear because PTSD symptoms are constantly being triggered by anniversary dates, current losses and disappointments in your life, and by therapy or counseling itself. Also, since the world is still full of traumas, including wars, crimes, auto accidents, and family violence, if you have had such a trauma in your past you run the risk of being retraumatized in the present by current events. As a result, holding to absence of symptoms as a standard of mental health is holding to an impossible standard.

At a recent meeting of trauma experts, the idea was rejected that healing from trauma meant an overall mental state of positive thinking and positive action—as was the idea that healing can be measured by permanent reduction or elimination of PTSD symptoms. Instead, the experts suggested that trauma survivors consider their progress along the following lines (Harvey 1995):

- Do you panic less at your PTSD symptoms? Are you able to recognize a PTSD symptom more quickly than in the past?

- Are you increasingly able to comfort or soothe yourself in nondestructive ways when you are suffering from a PTSD symptom or from depression?

- Are you increasingly able to cope with or manage your PTSD symptoms and the strong emotions that accompany remembering or being triggered without harming yourself or others?

- Are you growing in self-respect? Are you increasingly willing to take care of yourself physically and emotionally? Do you spend less and less time and energy deceiving people? Are any of the areas of your life becoming increasingly free from the trauma and its effects?

- Are you able to have nondestructive relationships with friends, co-workers, and intimates? Are you increasingly able to speak up in relationships or to otherwise negotiate in relationships so that you can both have the relationship and get your needs met?

- Are you increasingly able to derive some meaning from the trauma, or your life?

Notice that in many of these criteria the word *increasingly* is used, indicating that these standards are not absolute. Progress is measured by growing toward the goals implied in these questions. Reaching such goals may be humanly impossible.

The Promises of Healing

The promises of healing include, but are not limited to, the following:

- Reduced frequency of symptoms
- Reduced fear of the symptoms
- Reduced fear of insanity
- Rechanneling of the anger and grief in positive directions

- Change from victim to survivor status

- Change from rigidity to flexibility and spontaneity

- Increased appreciation of life

- A sense of humor

- A profound empathy for others who suffer

Before you began the healing process, you probably viewed your traumatic experiences as a major earthquake—one that irrevocably affected your entire life. Now, although the scars are real and some permanent, you have learned some ways of turning the ordeal of the trauma into a source of strength and empowerment.

To be empowered by the trauma does not mean sugarcoating your losses, but rather learning to appreciate your emotional and spiritual growth and your increased understanding of the trauma. All of this progress helps to make you a survivor, rather than a victim.

Empowerment also means learning to take increasing control over your own life, including the power to reward yourself. Rather than waiting for others to make your life pleasant or to compensate you for your losses, you have learned some ways of rewarding yourself.

Strength and power come with accepting the emotional aftermath and psychological scars of the trauma, rather than denying that they exist or punishing yourself for having them.

You can find ways to use your newfound strength and power to get more out of life than has seemed possible since the trauma (or even before it happened). You may even use your new knowledge to change other areas of your life where you thought yourself powerless, in addition to those aspects directly related to the trauma. That is deep empowerment—the lasting gift of the healing process.

Part III

Specific Traumas

The purpose of Parts I and II of this book is to familiarize you with the nature of PTSD and the PTSD cycle. Hopefully, if you have already read those chapters you have gained some understanding of what happened to you and some possible reasons for your reactions. You should also have learned some useful techniques for managing stressful situations and increasing control of your life in general. Better yet, Parts I and II may have helped you develop your self-awareness and discover some of the new strengths your life experiences have brought you.

The chapters that follow can help you build on that strength and self-awareness.

How to Use These Chapters

These final chapters offer information and exercises specific to particular types of trauma. Just as it is necessary to view your PTSD symptoms in light of the psychological and physiological changes trauma can cause, it is also important to look at your traumatic and secondary wounding experiences and your coping mechanisms in the context of the particular type of trauma you experienced.

Different aspects of PTSD are more common and more intense with different types of trauma. For instance, in general combat veterans are more likely to be troubled by survivor guilt than are rape victims; someone injured in a car accident may be unable to bear riding in a car, but a formerly abused child may not have any such trouble. These chapters offer additional material and exercises on the aspects of PTSD that have been shown to be the most troubling for each of seven different types of trauma:

- Crimes committed by strangers (Chapter 11)

- Rape and sexual assault (Chapter 12)

- Domestic violence, including sexual abuse (Chapter 13)

- Suicide of a family member or a close friend (Chapter 14)

- Natural catastrophes (Chapter 15)

- Vehicular accidents (Chapter 16)

- War and combat (Chapter 17)

In addition, these chapters place the trauma in a social and sometimes political context, which can be a useful and empowering way of viewing your experiences.

These seven types of trauma were chosen because they are the most common in our society. If your trauma is of a different type, you may still benefit from reading some, or all, of these chapters.

These chapters refer back to earlier reading and exercises in this book. You need not have read all of Parts I and II before reading the chapter about your type of trauma. (However, you should have completed Chapters 1 and 2, including the questionnaires.) You may want to read the appropriate chapter in this section first, then work through Chapters 3 through 10, and then return here and do the exercises.

One advantage to using these chapters in this way is that at the beginning of each of these chapters is a section called "Guidelines for Using This Book"; it tells you which of the preceding chapters you should concentrate on most. (Bear in mind though, that healing requires that you pay attention to *all* aspects of recovery. Even if an issue is not particularly troublesome to you now, it may become so in the future.) If you have already worked through Chapters 1 through 10, the guidelines sections can be used as suggestions for areas you may need to devote further attention to.

If you have survived more than one type of trauma, you will want to read the chapters pertaining to each type. Similarly, some traumas have aspects of two or more of the types described here. For example, sexual abuse is sometimes also rape, so a survivor of sexual abuse might want to read the chapters on both sexual assault and domestic violence.

One final note: The chapters in this section will provide you with basic information, but entire books have been written about many of these types of trauma. You may want to seek out some of these books. Appendix B lists some, and your local library may have many more. The more you can learn about your trauma, the greater will be your understanding and self-knowledge—your most powerful tools.

11

Crimes Committed by Strangers

Guidelines for Using This Book

As a crime victim, you may need to pay special attention to the exercises on self-blame in Chapter 3. Self-blame may be totally irrational in your case, yet you may still need to carefully examine the ways in which you believe you caused the crime. You are also encouraged to assess yourself for depression, as outlined in Chapter 2.

As you work through Chapter 5, on triggers, be sure to note details of your experience that on the surface may not seem relevant, for instance, your thoughts or emotional state immediately before the crime, what you were wearing, or what you had just eaten. If you were thinking about going to a football game before you were mugged, football games, although irrelevant to the criminal act, may now be a trigger for a fear or anxiety reaction. Also, when you approach or are involved in trigger situations, be sure to make use of one or more of the relaxation techniques described in Chapter 5.

If the person who victimized you was not apprehended and brought to justice, you may not have readily available the appropriate target for your anger: the criminal. In these cases, crime survivors often turn their anger at the criminal on themselves, in the form of depression, or onto family members. To learn techniques for identifying and coping with anger, give special attention to Chapter 8.

Note: Chapter 12 is devoted to the crime of sexual assault, including date or acquaintance rape. If you are a survivor of a sexual assault, you will want to read both this chapter and the next. If you are a victim of sexual abuse in a family setting, you will want to read both Chapter 12, on sexual assault, and Chapter 13, on family abuse; you may want to read this chapter as well. See Appendix B under "Crime" for resources that may offer additional assistance. Other sections there may prove useful as well.

The Prevalence of Crime

According to a 1991 Senate Judiciary Committee report, since the 1960s the crime rate in our nation has increased 516 percent, while the population has risen by approximately 41 percent (Fyfe 1991). Between 1983 and 1993, there continued to be marked increases in all categories of crime—violent crimes and property crimes (U.S. Bureau of the Census 1995). Improvements in recording procedures and greater public willingness to report crime probably contribute to these increases. However, the increase is substantial enough to indicate that there is far more crime today than 20 or 30 years ago.

According to the most recent data available, approximately 746 out of every 100,000 Americans are victims of violent crime, which includes murder, rape, and aggravated assault. Nine out of every 100,000 Americans were murdered; 40 out of every 100,000 were raped, and 440 out of every 100,000 were subject to aggravated assault. Property crimes affected approximately 4,800 out of every 100,000 Americans (U.S. Bureau of the Census 1995). These statistics do not include white collar crime, fraud, and so on. Moreover, these statistics are based only on reported crime. Our national picture becomes even more grim when you realize that, overall, most crimes go unreported (U.S. Department of Justice 1988).

Although the exact frequency of crime is uncertain, what is certain is that crime is a serious problem in our society, that the crime rate is continuing to escalate, and that the nature of crime is changing.

The Changing Nature of Crime— How It Affects Victims

Not only has violent crime escalated since the 1960s, but the nature of the violence has changed. Violent crimes today are often more brutal, more impersonal, and more senseless than ever before. Consider, for example, the phenomenon of "wilding" seen in numerous American cities— gangs of youths attacking and beating strangers for no motive other than the thrill of the violence itself. Or take the numerous incidents in which a gunman has opened fire on a group of strangers (or acquaintances) because they symbolize something he is angry at.

Combined with the rising crime rate, the changing nature of crime has increased the degree of depersonalization, mistrust, and alienation in our society as a whole. For crime victims, who after the crime often feel more like objects than like individuals, this sense of depersonalization can be especially intense. Being a crime victim is hard enough to accept when there seems to be a comprehensible reason for the crime. But when the crime seems to be an expression of senseless evil, the victim's feelings of exploitation and humiliation can be exceptionally severe. Depending on the particulars of the case, the degree of depersonalization can be so intense that victims begin to lose their faith not only in society but in themselves.

These are but a few of the psychic wounds of criminal victimization. Although these wounds are intangible, they can exert great power over a crime victim's life. Yet such wounds are not well respected in a society that better understands broken bones than broken spirits, and often seems to consider property as more important than human life. Although trauma survivors and some empathic others can understand the crime victim's feelings, people who themselves have never been victimized in any manner may have great difficulty comprehending the psychological aftermath of criminal victimization.

The Psychological Aftermath of Crime—Acute Stress Reactions

If you have been victimized by crime, you can expect to experience what mental health professionals call *acute stress reaction*. Acute stress reaction includes many of the symptoms of PTSD: numbing, sleep problems, mood swings, rage, amnesia, and depersonalization. If these symptoms persist for over a month, they can develop into PTSD (T. Williams 1987b, Bard and Sangrey 1986, *DSM-IV*).

According to Morton Bard and Dawn Sangrey, authors of *The Crime Victim's Book* (1986), immediate stress reaction involves several stages. The first stage, often called the shock stage, occurs while the crime is actually taking place and immediately afterwards. Its symptoms include shock, physical or emotional numbing, and denial.

During the second stage, often called the recoil, or impact, stage, the shock and numbing lift. At this point, the victim begins to absorb the reality and full meaning of the crime and to experience the feelings associated with it. These feelings include fear, anger, grief, resentment, dependency, powerlessness, desire for revenge, and perhaps shame and guilt. Victims may experience troublesome mood swings, mental confusion, and hypersensitivity to the reactions of other people and to noise.

Physical symptoms not directly caused by the crime may also appear. These symptoms reflect stress put on the body and central nervous system by the psychological stress of the victim's realization that he or she has been criminally victimized and is not immune to harm. These symptoms include (but are not limited to), headaches, backaches, and other body pains; nausea and other gastrointestinal problems; and intense shaking. In addition, the crime can intensify any medical, physical, or psychological problems that existed prior to the crime.

During the third stage, the attribution stage, the victim (and perhaps friends and family members) tries to figure out what caused the crime. Blame may be pinned on the criminal, the victim, or both. The victim may even take responsibility for the crime, rather than acknowledge the important role of chance in determining who is victimized and who is not.

The fourth stage is the resolution or recovery stage. During this stage, the victim's emotional equilibrium returns, because to one degree or another, he or she has worked through the emotions pertaining to the crime and perhaps feels empowered by having taken measures to avoid becoming the victim of future crime.

Lack of resolution can lead to the development of phobias and fears, acute psychosomatic problems, and the intensification of any preexisting psychological problems, as well as to PTSD.

PTSD and Crime

Being a victim of crime does not automatically mean you will develop full-blown PTSD. Since PTSD is only now becoming understood and appreciated by mental health practitioners, there are no statistics available indicating what percentage of crime victims develop PTSD as opposed to other possible consequences, such as acute stress reactions, phobias, or psychosomatic problems.

These problems, however, can develop into PTSD if they are left untreated or if they are exacerbated by subsequent trauma or other major losses closely following the crime. Preliminary work that has been done in the area of crime-related stress indicates that the psychological consequences of criminal victimization are far more widespread than had been previously thought. It also indicates that the severity of these consequences and the possibility of developing PTSD or PTSD symptoms are strongly related to the severity of the crime (Chambless et al. 1990). For example, PTSD symptoms can develop even after a nonviolent crime, in which nobody is injured; however, full-blown PTSD tends to develop primarily when there is physical injury or a threat to safety and life.

In a study completed in the late 1980s, between 2 and 9 percent of the civilian population was estimated to be suffering from PTSD, primarily as the result of automobile accidents or violent crime. Another study of crime victims found that the development of PTSD had nothing to do with the crime victim's age, sex, race, religion, or social class. Neither was the development of PTSD related to any previously or currently diagnosed mental problems. For example, people suffering from depression, panic disorders, or other mental health problems before they became crime victims were no more likely to develop PTSD than people who had no history or current diagnosis of a psychiatric illness.

The determining factors in the development of PTSD were found to be, first, physical injury as the result of the crime, and second, a perceived threat to life. If the person felt his or her life was endangered during the crime, then regardless of whether that person was actually injured or truly endangered, the fear of injury or death contributed to the development of PTSD (Chambless et al. 1990).

Violent crimes. Crimes involving attempted or completed physical assault are traumatic for more obvious reasons. These crimes, usually called violent crimes, include robbery, rape, and other forms of sexual assault; physical assault; and, of course, homicide. In the case of murder victims, acute trauma reactions can occur among the victim's friends and neighbors, as well as among the victim's family members. In some cases, the trauma reactions of family members of homicide victims can reach PTSD proportions.

PTSD is more likely to develop if the homicide victim is a child or if the incident involves multiple deaths. For example, in 1984 outside of San Diego, California, James Huberty entered a McDonald's restaurant, killed 21 persons, and injured 15 others. Afterwards, PTSD as well as acute stress reactions, developed not only among those who witnessed the event and family members of the homicide victims, but among members of the community who did not even know the victims (NIMH).

Property crimes. Psychologically, a threat to life may be necessary for the development of PTSD. However, crimes against property and other crimes that do not involve fear of injury or death can also cause intense psychic pain, as well as acute stress reactions.

Our property is an extension of ourselves, and certain objects have irreplaceable sentimental value. As with anything in life, it is not just the particulars of an event, but the meaning the event holds for the individual that determines its impact. For example, a widow who is robbed of her wedding ring, her husband's silver-framed photograph, and other mementos of her marriage, could find herself plummeted back into the depths of the grieving process by these losses. The cash and camera equipment stolen from her next-door neighbor, though of greater monetary value, would cause their owner far less suffering than the widow experienced.

Provided there was no life threat involved in these burglaries (if, for example, neither woman was at home during the burglary and the burglar was quickly apprehended, which put to rest any fears that he might return), neither of them would be likely to develop PTSD. Nevertheless, both women, especially the widow, could experience acute stress reactions to being burglarized, resulting in large part from the sense of having been violated.

The Sense of Violation

Whether you are a victim of a robbery, assault, rape, attempted homicide, a purse snatching, burglary, or auto theft, you have been violated. Some of your belongings may have been taken or destroyed. You may have been injured, or someone who was with you may have been injured or killed.

Even if you or others involved were not significantly injured or your financial losses were small, you may still have an extremely negative reaction to the crime. This negative reaction may persist for a long time. You may not understand why you continue to feel so bad. Others may not understand either. Often people have seen so many brutal crimes on television or read so much about them in newspapers, that any but the most vicious of criminal acts seem ordinary.

You weren't bruised that badly. Why are you so upset? people might say, or, So you were raped. You came out alive, and in one piece. Think of what could have happened. You should be grateful, not depressed. Perhaps they are trying to comfort you, but such responses only serve to make light of your pain and fear—maximizing your sense of isolation and abandonment. Their comments make you feel that because you were not injured, or not injured "enough," or the amount stolen was not significant, you are not entitled to be afraid, sad, or otherwise upset.

Although the degree of injury and the value of any items stolen are certainly important, there are other losses in crime besides the physical. What you and those who trivialize your experience may fail to appreciate is that aside from any physical or financial losses, your inner self has been violated. You no longer feel safe in the world. Your sense of trust in others and in your community has diminished, if not evaporated entirely. Furthermore, the sense of autonomy and control over your life that is so essential to your functioning has been shattered.

The disorientation, fear, self-doubt, and heightened sense of vulnerability that can follow this shattering of your trust and sense of autonomy can affect every area of your life. Even if you emerged from the crime without a single scratch and with all your belongings intact, you may have to deal with these psychological losses and other violations to your inner self. The next several sections are designed to help you do that. One section is devoted to each of the four stages of immediate stress reaction, so that you can understand what has happened since the crime occurred and thus evaluate your feelings and actions in that light.

The Shock Stage

During the crime or immediately afterward you may have been in a state of shock, disbelief, emotional or physical numbing, or have experienced other forms of disorientation. Although you'd seen crimes on television and in the movies, read about them in the paper, and knew how prevalent crime is in our society, nothing really prepared you for this.

In fact, it is impossible to be prepared to be criminally victimized. There is a vast difference between reading or watching a movie about a crime and being a crime victim yourself. Nothing in those presentations could possibly have prepared you for the shock and trauma of being attacked or having your belongings stolen.

While the crime was happening, you may have been unable to believe it was really occurring. It frequently takes a while for the reality of the situation to register. For instance, a mugging victim describes her experience this way:

> I was just walking down the street when suddenly I felt a pounding on my back. The pounding continued, but I kept walking as if nothing was happening. I don't know how long it took for me to realize that someone was hitting my back with a club.
>
> Maybe it was only a few seconds, maybe more, but as soon as the awareness that I was being mugged began, it shut off again. For a while, everything shut off, even my brain. I saw blood on the ground, but it took a few minutes for it to register that it was my blood. Maybe I would have fallen apart or something if I realized I was bleeding.
>
> Looking back, it's hard for me to remember how I felt or what happened. A part of what happened is crystal clear; other parts are extremely muddled. But one thing I am certain of is that I definitely had no emotion during the mugging. No physical pain either. Even though my face was cut, my back bruised, my arm broken, I didn't feel a thing.
>
> A part of me was dead, but this other part of me screamed and fought and held onto my purse. I had always fantasized that I would willingly turn over all my belongings to a thief. I had no idea that I would end up acting like an animal, yelling louder than I had ever yelled in my entire life, trying to protect the couple of dollars I had in my purse.
>
> Only after the mugger started pounding my head into the concrete did I realize I might die. This can't be me. This can't be real, I thought. Someone should be helping me now, but no one is. I'm all alone and I'm going to die. Then I remembered all the things I wanted to do but never did. And all the while I was still crying and screaming, but physically feeling nothing. Yet blood was all over.

Adrenaline Reactions and Tunnel Vision

Under assault, human beings experience adrenaline reactions, which can lead to fight, flight, or freeze reactions. However, human beings are so complex that they can have more than one of these reactions in the same episode. The mugging victim above, for example, became so full of adrenaline that she ended up fighting her attacker, even though he was much larger and stronger than herself. This was a fight reaction.

At the same time, however, she had temporary freeze reactions in terms of her emotions and her ability to acknowledge reality. She also experienced a continuous physical numbing of pain. Only afterward did she begin to feel the pain of the injuries.

During the attack she also suffered from a mental equivalent of tunnel vision—a perceptual distortion of physical reality. This reaction is common during criminal victimization (T. Williams 1987b). Like many crime victims, the mugging victim above could not, and still cannot, recall all the details of the event. For example, even though she fought with the mugger for quite some time, she cannot remember what he looked like, or even what color shirt he wore. "He had on a plaid shirt and a hat, but that's all I can remember," she told the police.

Looking back, you may be confused about how you behaved during the crime or immediately afterwards. You may not recall details about your attacker, or you may not remember how long the attack occurred or the exact sequence of events. Perhaps you thought of calling the police, or pushing the panic or alarm button, or screaming for help, but you were too physically numb or paralyzed to do so. Or maybe you attacked the criminal even though a silent panic button or some other safer recourse was available.

Similarly, if the attacker asked you to do something—unlock a drawer or a car, open a safe or a cash register, turn over your credit cards—you may have experienced a physical or mental numbing that prevented you from cooperating.

"My brain turned into dead meat," a robbery victim relates. "I would have been more than happy to let the burglar have my credit cards, but I couldn't remember where they were. My mind just wasn't working. I was also perfectly willing to open my safe, but I forgot the combination. I use it every day, but with that gun pointed at me, I couldn't think. I couldn't answer his questions or anything, which enraged him."

During the shock stage, any kind of reaction is possible. Numbness, adrenaline highs, and hysteria are all normal, as is serenity. Some victims remain amazingly calm and rational. They even attempt to talk to their assailant.

However you reacted or behaved, try not to judge yourself. Remember, everyone's crime experience is unique. Most likely you did the best you could under very difficult circumstances.

Secondary Wounding and the Reactions of Others

During both the shock stage and the subsequent recoil stage, you may have found yourself especially vulnerable to the reactions of others. Like survivors of other types of trauma, immediately after the traumatic event, crime victims are physiologically aroused and emotionally jarred.

Their defenses are also down. For example, the belief that, It can't happen to me, one of people's major defenses against acknowledging their vulnerability to harm and death, has just been shattered.

Yet at that point you had not had time to build up a wall of denial or to crawl into a psychological cave for comfort and rest. In this state, questions—such as, What do you mean you don't remember what the mugger looked like? Why were you going to a party alone anyway? Why did you leave the door open? Why were you carrying such a bulky wallet?—can easily feel like personal attacks.

You may have been able to defend yourself against this questioning, or you may not. You may have reacted with great anger, or you may have just sat there in silent shame. Maybe crime so defeated you psychologically that you found it hard to say anything at all; so much of your energy was going into absorbing the shock of being victimized that you had little left over for arguing or standing up for yourself.

Some of the individuals who ask such questions actually are being insensitive, hostile, and demeaning. They take advantage of people's emotional vulnerability to humiliate them and thereby make themselves feel superior and powerful. However, others who ask such questions are not intending to attack at all. Yet their words can certainly feel attacking and critical.

For example, some of your family members and friends may feel grief and anger over what happened to you. Yet they may have difficulty channeling those emotions appropriately. Therefore, they may discharge their anger at the criminal (or themselves for failing to protect you) by criticizing and attacking you. Or, as has been commonly observed, they might have confronted the rescue personnel, the hospital staff, or other officials involved—which could result in further secondary wounding experiences.

Ideally, your friends and family would say, I'm sorry this happened to you. I feel sad and angry that you had to go through this. Are you all right? How can I help?

One reason for people's inability to express empathy or support may be the guilt or responsibility for the crime that they feel—even if it's irrational. They might be thinking of all the "if onlys" that could have averted the crime. Perhaps they feel they should have stopped you from going where the crime took place, should have been with you, shouldn't have argued with you the day before, and so on. But instead of acknowledging and dealing with their own guilt, they may be projecting it onto you.

For example, the mother of a rape victim might say, I told you a million times not to walk home from the bus stop alone. You foolish girl. You deserved it! Or Why don't you pay attention to where you are going? What were you doing, daydreaming again? This wouldn't have happened if you had been watching where you were going.

But in her heart this mother is feeling, It's my fault. I should have gone to pick her up. She usually calls me from the bus stop. But this morning I told her I was very busy so she probably didn't want to bother me. It's my fault.

Nevertheless, if for whatever reason helping professionals, police officers, family members, or friends fail to support you, their lack of support can create even more emotional pain. Your trust in society has just been violated by the criminal. Now someone who is supposed to help you is talking to you in a way that seems to violate your trust.

Both immediately after the crime and later, you need support, not anything that smacks of criticism or blame. You want someone to ask, or at least acknowledge, how you feel, or offer you some comfort and reassurance, rather than asking what the criminal did or didn't do. If you don't get this support, once again you may feel uncared for, unloved, and abandoned, just as you may have felt during the crime.

Exercise: Reexamining the Crime, Your Initial Reactions, and Secondary Wounding Experiences

Return to your journal entries describing the crime and the secondary wounding experiences that followed. Are there any details of the crime you wish to add to make the description more complete? Are there details of the crime you do not remember? List those events, smells, sights, and other aspects of the crime that you cannot recall. Have you contacted any witnesses? Sometimes speaking with others who have knowledge of the crime can help you remember.

Next, review your writing on self-blame. Also, if you have not covered the following questions already, consider them carefully:

1. Prior to the crime, did you ever think that you would be a crime victim someday? Research shows that people who expected to be criminally victimized someday, or at least entertained that possibility, tend to have fewer difficulties coping with the emotional aftermath of being a crime victim than people who expected to go through life without ever being the victim of a criminal attack.

2. If your answer to the above question is yes, how did you believe you would act if you were suddenly the victim of a crime? How did your actual behavior compare to your expected behavior? If there are discrepancies between how you thought you would feel and act and how you actually felt and acted, how do you feel about those discrepancies?

3. How much was your fantasy about how you would act influenced by movies, books, or other media portrayals of crime? Now that you have firsthand experience with crime, to what extent do you think these media portrayals are realistic? In what ways do you feel having been

exposed to media portrayals of crime helped you cope with your crime experience, if any? In what ways has the prevalence of depictions of crime in the entertainment media done you a disservice?

4. In assessing your reaction to the criminal event, can you identify ways in which the surge of adrenaline influenced your behavior? What about the ways in which noradrenaline, or the numbing response, influenced your thoughts and behavior?

5. Did anyone criticize or negatively comment on how you acted while being victimized, or immediately before or afterward? Did anyone deny or undercut your fear or other feelings? Did a part of you agree with these critics? If so, where is the evidence that the views of these other people are accurate? Even if they are experts in criminology or a related field, why do you think they know more about your crime experience than you do?

6. If you were criticized, how did you respond? How do you feel about how you responded? Why do you think you responded as you did to your critics? If one of your children, or someone you love dearly, was the victim of the crime instead of yourself, how would you feel if others criticized that person the way they did you?

The Recoil, or Impact, Stage

The second stage of immediate stress reaction starts when the shock and numbing have subsided and your feelings begin to emerge. In this recoil, or impact, phase, the feelings you experience can range from anger at the perpetrator to intense self-hatred, guilt, and shame. You may be brimming with fantasies of revenge one minute, only to have your fire melt into feelings of utter helplessness and dependency the next.

The result can be confusion. Your feelings keep changing, and they do not emerge in neat packages or in any particular order. Some feelings may contradict others. You may have mood swings: sometimes you feel intensely emotional, other times numb.

This waxing and waning of emotional awareness, like the confused and contradictory emotions, is normal. You need the numbing periods to recover from periods of emotional intensity.

Also, if you are relying on movies or television for models of how you should feel, you may think you shouldn't feel much of anything. Victims on screen are usually portrayed as recovering quickly, and the injuries to their ability to trust, their sense of autonomy, and the rest of the emotional turmoil that follows criminal victimization are largely ignored or downplayed (when the victim is included in the plot at all).

However, these portrayals are far from accurate. Experiencing a wide range of emotions is normal, and the feelings usually persist for quite a while. According to Bard and Sangrey (1986), even people who have suc-cessfully passed through the resolution phase may be subject to periods when the feelings of helplessness, dependency, and vulnerability experi-enced during the impact and recoil phase return at unpredictable mo-ments.

Moreover, even if crime dramas and literature were to accurately reflect the emotional reality of victimization, each individual's response to the threat of death or injury is unique.

Fear and Phobias

Fear is perhaps the dominant emotional consequence of crime. For example, researchers in one study found two-thirds of crime victims (both male and female) reported elevated fear levels, increased feelings of insecurity in their own homes and communities, and increased anxiety. Increased nightmares, insomnia, increased use of tranquilizers, and in-creased health worries and fatigue have also been noted as part of the immediate stress reaction (Katz and Burt 1985).

During the impact stage, you may begin to feel the fear that was suppressed or minimized during the criminal attack. You may also de-velop phobias or fears connected to specific objects, places, or the time of day that the crime occurred. For example, if you were wearing white pants at the time of the crime, you may avoid that color. Or if the crime happened at 9:00 p.m. on the streets, you may find yourself at home be-hind locked doors every night at 9:00.

You may find the idea of feeling afraid frightening in itself. And this, combined with the notion of feeling the strong emotions and mood swings of the impact stage for the rest of your life, may make your situ-ation seem hopeless. But it isn't.

The entire point of this book is that healing is possible—if you can begin to rethink the event more objectively, have the courage to feel the feel-ings associated with it, and develop compassion for yourself as a survivor.

Critical Voices

Others may respect your fears, or they may discount them. You're overreacting they may say. Or, You had nothing to worry about during the attack and you have nothing to worry about now. If you were beaten or severely injured, or if the criminal was apprehended and confessed to intending to cause you bodily harm, you stand a greater chance of having your fears validated.

However, whether or not other people judge the crime to have been dangerous, it probably felt that way to you. Anyone approached by a criminal would feel endangered. When a stranger enters your home or business, or moves to physically attack you, your life is on the line. You cannot know what the criminal will or will not do. In many types of crimes, a threat is implicit—you don't need to see a weapon or even hear a verbal threat to know you are in danger.

Think back on your experience. Was there any way to tell if your assailant was hiding a knife, gun, or some other weapon? How could you have known whether others who might have harmed or even killed you were waiting in the background? Was there any way to truly predict how the criminal would have responded if you had resisted—or if you hadn't?

The criminal was a stranger to you. Even if you know now, how could you tell then whether your attacker was a professional criminal, mentally disturbed, or had his or her thinking and behavior distorted by alcohol or drugs? Some drugs, for instance PCP, create paranoia, delusions of grandeur, and certain other mental distortions. If your assailant was on a potent drug (or even a mixture of drugs), he or she might have easily been capable of great irrationality, impulsivity, and cruelty. Alcohol can also cause violent and unpredictable actions. Your assailant could easily have been under the influence of some substance without your being aware of it.

Regardless of the particulars of your experience, you do not have to defend your fear. You have every right to be afraid. No matter how nonviolent the criminal appeared to be or how minimal the danger perceived by others, the truth is that when you are being robbed or attacked, injury and death are always possibilities.

The Issue of Fighting Back

Has someone criticized you for not "standing up for yourself," "not fighting back," "acting like a sissy," or "letting him get away with it?"

Don't listen to such talk. You need not harbor any shame about having surrendered to the criminal. Confronted with someone who wants to hurt you, or who is at least capable of hurting you, there is nothing heroic about trying to be a hero. Forget the movies and the television programs. In real life you may be safer submitting than fighting back.

Some research shows that there is a greater possibility of injury when victims resist rather than submitting. Some research studies, however, have come to the opposite conclusion—that resistance is better. The data is inconclusive, at best. In general, though, the police advise that you be as "cooperative . . . polite . . . and accommodating . . . as possible," and that you "act calmly but quickly to meet the robber's demands and keep the transaction time at a minimum" (*UFCW* 1991).

Those who belittle or mock your fears, or who seek to humiliate you for having given in to the criminal's demands, simply do not understand. They probably would have reacted in similar fashion if they were surprised by a criminal attack.

Alternatively, you may have been one of those crime victims who fought back. Perhaps you are being applauded for taking a stand. On the other hand, particularly if you were injured as a result, others may be calling you "foolish" or "immature." But like your fellow survivor who gave in without a fight, you reacted the best you could in most difficult circumstances.

Whether you surrendered or your adrenaline flow or training propelled you to strike back, your behavior is not there for others to judge.

Exercise: Identifying Fears

In your journal, answer the following questions:

1. What were your fears during the crime? Be as specific as possible. Did you fear rape, mutilation, death, scarring of your face, or some other injury? Did you fear injury to your children or other loved ones? Did the criminal make any specific threats? Did he or she behave erratically? In what ways did the attacker threaten or appear to be dangerous? Even if the criminal did not act as if he or she was dangerous, what were your fears about the potential danger?

2. What are your fears now, after the crime? Crime survivors commonly fear that the crime will somehow be repeated or that the criminal will come back and harm them. If the criminal escaped, you may fear he or she will find out where you live and hurt you worse next time. If the criminal is arrested and put in prison, you may fear retaliation. Such fears are not unrealistic. Criminals, especially rapists, do sometimes return to assault the same victim again, even after years of imprisonment.

   List your current fears regarding the criminal. Be as specific as possible. Did he or she threaten to come back and find you? Do you know someone who was victimized more than once by the same person?

3. What do you think is the real probability that your attacker will come back to harm you? What information are you almost certain the criminal has about you? What information do you think he or she might have? What measures can you take against that probability? What prevents you from acting on your fears and seeking to make yourself and your loved ones as safe as humanly possible?

Countering Fear with Positive Action

Bard and Sangrey (1986) write that there is no such thing as crime prevention. Crime is so rampant today, they argue, that there is little one can do to prevent becoming a crime victim other than hiding in an armored room with an armed bodyguard. Security measures, such as alarm systems, may reduce the risk of crime, but they cannot prevent it.

Nevertheless, part of your healing may involve doing what you can to reduce the risk of being victimized again. Research shows that individuals who take active measures to protect themselves make greater progress in the emotional healing process than persons who throw up their hands and say, It's hopeless. There's nothing I can do to protect myself.

Fears that the crime will recur or that the criminal will return may propel you to drastically improve the security of your home or office or even to change where you live or work. According to some studies, approximately one out of four rape victims changes residences after the assault, one out of five gets an unlisted phone number, and approximately one-third of rape victims change or quit their jobs within two months. Elderly crime victims who have the means also have been noted to change residences (Katz and Burt 1985).

It is also not unheard of for rape and other victims, especially victims who live alone, who are elderly, or who are physically handicapped or otherwise relatively defenseless against crime, to not only change residences, but to move to another neighborhood. Some individuals even move to other cities, although this is less common.

If you find you are taking absolutely no action toward reducing the risk of being victimized again, you need to ask yourself why. Spend some time writing about this. Think about the possibility that you feel powerless and hopeless because of the crime or other circumstances in your life. If it is financial assistance you need, consult the list of resources under "Crime" in Appendix B.

Consider the following questions regarding your security needs:

1. Are you at all willing to restrict your activities to reduce the risk of being a crime victim? If so, which activities are you willing to restrict? Can you modify your activities instead of giving them up (walk with a friend, for example, instead of alone)?

2. Are you interested in purchasing or using any self protection devices, such as mace, or property protection devices, such as a home or car alarm? What prevents you from finding out more about these devices or using them? Be advised that there are strong pros and cons to using any type of crime-risk reduction device. For example, using mace on a would-be attacker might give you time to escape. On the other hand, mace canisters have frequently been taken away from and used against their owners.

3. Have you considered taking a self-defense course? Such training can improve your physical strength and self-image, and that increased confidence can itself be a deterrent to criminals searching for an easy target. But this is not to say that self-defense training can make you invulnerable. It is no protection against a gun, for example, and some criminals are sufficiently crazed or desperate that no potential victim will appear strong enough to deter them.

4. Is there a civic-action or crime-watch program in your neighborhood? Are you interested in finding out more about it and perhaps joining it? If there is no such group, would you consider starting one?

The above questions are not endorsements of chemical sprays, alarm systems, self-defense classes, or any particular restrictions on your activities. The suggestion to consider these options is just that: a suggestion. Discuss your options with your family members and others who are knowledgeable and who care about you. Also discuss your options with your local police department or with a civic-action or crime-watch program in your area.

Anger

Anger is always an issue for trauma survivors, but especially for crime survivors. Your anger might have begun the moment the shock lifted and you realized you had been victimized. However, the target for your anger, the criminal, was probably nowhere to be found. Only rarely is the criminal apprehended on the spot, or even soon after the crime has taken place. When the criminal is not available, your anger has no tangible target, no place to go.

But it needs to go somewhere, so you could find yourself taking it out on yourself in the form of depression or some self-destructive activity. You may have unleashed it on friends and relatives, or you may have displaced anger that belongs to your victimizer onto the police, medical staff, and others involved in your case.

Because you are angry, even the smallest error or insensitivity on the part of any these people can feel like a punch in the stomach. And if you have cause to be angry at any of these people because they are downright insensitive, unhelpful, or insulting, your anger may become enormous.

After you have been victimized—especially if you are physically injured—you need and truly deserve exquisitely sensitive care. Such care, however, typically is not sensitive. Your angry response to the deficiencies in the way you have been treated is nonetheless legitimate.

You may, however, be experiencing a double anger. The first level of your anger is a direct response to any mistreatment or any mismanagement of your medical, legal, or other care. The second level of your anger may be the anger you harbor toward your assailant.

The judicial system. Another source of anger involves police and legal procedures. If you have had the satisfaction of learning that your assailant has been apprehended, you are fortunate. According to the U.S. Department of Justice (1988), "For most crimes, no one is apprehended. For every five offenses reported to the police, there is approximately one arrest." Serious violent crimes are more likely to be cleared by arrest than are property crimes.

However, "cleared by arrest" does not mean the offender is prosecuted, sentenced, or even indicted for the crime—it simply means an arrest has been made. The offender may or may not be taken to trial.

Even if your offender is tried, you may have to wait a long time for the trial to take place—anywhere from weeks to months, even years. Frequently there are numerous delays and many forms of red tape that have to be endured before justice is done, if it ever is.

If you feel the offender has been adequately punished, at least part of your desire for justice may be satisfied. However, if you must witness the courts giving your assailant a much lighter sentence than you feel is deserved, expect to feel enraged. If your losses are irrevocable, for example, the loss of a limb or someone you loved, your rage toward not only the criminal, but the court system, could reach mammoth proportions.

If you are a member of a minority group, you may also encounter racism in the courts. For example, according to an article in the Washington Post (8 June 1991) a study of New York courts revealed that some minorities received "basement justice" in terms of the routinely less-than-thorough manner in which their cases were reviewed. Although the report stresses that not every minority person is treated unfairly, the inequities found highlight the fact that racism in the court system is far from dead.

Sexism is still thriving as well. Concerned attorneys, both male and female, are now conducting studies of sexist practices, sexist attitudes, and sexist interpretations of the law in the courts.

If you feel that you are being victimized by the courts because of your race, sex, or for some other reason, your anger regarding the crime will only be intensified. Added to your anger at the criminal will be your legitimate fury at the socially imposed injustices you encounter as you seek to have your assailant apprehended and adequately punished.

Exercise: Anger and the Costs of the Crime

Once your anger begins to surface, you may want to refer back to Chapter 8 on anger and anger management. Reviewing that material can help you obtain insight into your anger and guide you in making your anger work for you, rather than against you. Reread your journal entries on anger, and spend some time writing about any additional angers you have discovered that you bear toward either the criminal, the legal system, or those involved in any secondary wounding experiences.

Consider also the following possible costs of having been victimized. The more complete a picture you can obtain of the financial, physical, emotional, and personal costs of the crime, the more causes for your anger you will be able to identify.

1. What was the amount of money or the value of any items stolen?

2. What were the financial costs of the emergency room or other medical bills, of the time you lost from work in recovering from the crime,

of transportation to any police or court proceedings, of childcare, and so on?

3. What were the financial costs of any locks, security devices, weapons, insurance, self-defense training, and so on you have purchased as a result of the crime?

4. Were any preexisting medical, psychological, or family problems exacerbated by the stress of the crime?

5. Are there any restrictions placed on your activities as a result of the crime?

6. Are there any pleasures, events, or activities you are sacrificing in order to feel safe?

7. What are the financial and emotional costs of any life changes you have made as a result of the crime, for instance, changing jobs, moving, and so on?

8. What are the emotional costs of the victimization to you, to your family, and others in your life?

9. What is the cost in terms of time spent replacing or otherwise dealing with any loss of property, coping with your emotions and the reactions of others, and dealing with the police and other authorities?

The Attribution Stage

Due to the crime victim–assistance movement, which began in the early 1960s, many of the blame-the-victim policies of government and other institutions have been exposed. Some have even been altered. And victim-blaming attitudes may be waning somewhat as a result. This does not, however, mean that such attitudes are in any danger of extinction.

Attributing the crime to the victim, rather than the criminal, is utterly irrational. However, it helps people dispel the guilt and anxiety they feel when confronted with a crime victim. It also allows them to feel as if they have some control over their lives.

You yourself, like most human beings, want the world to make sense, want events to have a reason for happening. Consequently it may be easier for you to conclude that the reason for the crime was your behavior, attitude, or personality than to think the crime was completely random.

You may find family members and friends reinforcing this notion—either overtly or subliminally. And whether you accept their attitudes or not, such blaming can destroy or severely disrupt those relationships. As a result, you may be deprived of or alienated from your support system. Yet this is the very time that you, like most crime survivors, need your family and friends most.

The Masochism Myth as Applied
to Crime Survivors

Criminals as a group tend to be impulsive in their behavior. If they use or abuse alcohol or drugs, their behavior is even more likely to be erratic and unpredictable. In your particular case this means that a criminal decided to rob or assault someone, and you just happened to be available.

If you have been a victim of more than one crime or trauma, you need to be on guard against the word *masochism*. Some people may be quick to label you a masochist and interpret your misfortunes as stemming from some inner need to be miserable. They may say, for example, that you are "accident prone," or that you unconsciously "provoked" or "set yourself up" for the crime.

Even some mental health professionals misuse the theory of masochism to explain a wide variety of traumas. In general, the theory holds that if you are a masochist, you have an ongoing yearning to be punished and suffer. As a result, you consciously or unconsciously create a painful world for yourself.

The masochism theory is highly questionable under any circumstances, but in terms of crime, it has no basis. If you really were a masochist craving suffering, you wouldn't pick an unpredictable, chancy type of victimization like crime. You'd become involved in something predictable and longer term, such as a job where you allowed yourself to be used or a life-threatening addiction. True masochists would not waste their time trying to lure some stranger into attacking them or their property.

Never forget, the criminal chose you, not the other way around. As Bard and Sangrey (1986) stress, even people who have been criminally victimized more than once are not masochists. There are many alternate reasons that explain why some people have the extreme misfortune of being criminally victimized more than once in their life. Perhaps they are poor: it is a proven fact that the poorer you are, the greater your chance of being a victim of crime. Other people are victims of multiple crime because they lack the information and finances with which to buy protection against crime.

People also vary in the degree to which they are willing to restrict their life activities or use protection and security devices to reduce the risk of being victims of crime. Some people are unwilling to go to extreme measures to protect themselves. Others will not venture away from their immediate neighborhoods. And still other people take the middle ground and try to avoid risky places. Everyone draws their own line about such things, but the fact remains that criminal attacks occur in homes on Sunday mornings at 8:00, on busy streets at 3:00 in the afternoon, as well as in alleys at 2:00 in the morning.

If people are attacked as they go about their lives, this does not mean they provoked or caused the attack. The criminal attacks the victim, not the other way around, no matter what the circumstances.

Exercise: Self-Blame

Review your journal writing on self-blame regarding the crime. Add to your journal entry any additional insights you may have on how you blame yourself for the crime. Keep in mind that many crimes are impulsive and unpredictable. Even if you left your car door unlocked, this does not mean you are responsible for the subsequent theft. You could have locked the car door, only to have vandals smash the windows or enter your car in some other way.

The Resolution Stage

In the resolution stage, your victimization experience does not disappear. It simply loses much of its power over you. You are less controlled by your fears, your anger, and your self-blame or the blame others may have heaped upon you.

It is easier to reach the resolution stage if your victimizer has been apprehended and adequately punished. However, if the criminal received too light a sentence or was never caught, you will indeed struggle to make peace with your experience.

Making peace with the past will also be difficult if you are facing a prolonged court case or other procedures, or if you continue to need medical or psychological care for injuries. For example, if your health or physical abilities are now seriously or permanently impaired, you will probably think of the crime every day. "How can I forget about it?" a crime victim asks, "Every time I put on my prosthetic arm, I'm back on that street again with those thugs all over me."

For this crime victim, as for you, resolution means going on in spite of the memories and the pain. It does not mean you will never feel rage, fear, helplessness, or hurt again. It simply means that you have stopped the criminal from robbing you of the rest of your life. Even if you have suffered minimal physical hurt, it may take weeks or even months for you to feel emotionally stable again.

Difficulties Reaching the Resolution Stage

If you have not reached the resolution stage, do not consider yourself a failure. Someday you will, at least in part. Allow yourself sufficient time and permit yourself the experiences that promote your healing.

Your difficulties in resolving your crime trauma probably do not reside within you. They are more likely to be related to the severity of the crime, the severity of your subsequent secondary wounding experiences, the lack of support from others, or the particular meaning of the crime to you. You may need to work through the exercises in this book more than once or even seek additional help. Do whatever is necessary. You are worth it.

If you are a multiple-trauma survivor and the crime is one of a string of traumas you have endured with minimal reaction, then the crime may be the proverbial straw that broke the camel's back. If this is the case, then you are dealing not only with the crime but with all the traumas that preceded the crime. As would be expected, if you are dealing with more than one trauma, your healing period will of necessity be longer and more complex than if you were dealing with only one episode.

When Acute Stress Reaction Becomes PTSD

Emotional support from friends, family members, or others may be enough to help you through your acute stress reaction. However, if such support is not available, or if the symptoms persist for over a month, consider professional mental health counseling. The dangers of not attending to the emotional aftermath of criminal victimization include the development not only of PTSD but of phobias or psychosomatic problems that can severely restrict your life.

12

Rape and Sexual Assault

Guidelines for Using This Book

Our culture is full of confusing messages about sexual behavior. As a result, especially in cases of rape, many individuals and institutions tend to blame the victim for her, or his, trauma. As a rape victim you need to look within yourself and evaluate the extent to which you have internalized society's victim-blaming attitudes. Chapter 3, which examines self-blame in trauma survivors, and Chapter 4, which describes the different types of secondary wounding experiences they endure, may be especially relevant and important in your healing.

Self-blame among rape victims can easily turn into self-punishment, therefore you need to thoroughly assess yourself for the presence of depression or addictive or compulsive behavior, as described in Chapter 2.

Having been raped creates confusion in many victims regarding their sexuality. Hopefully your experience has not robbed you of being a sexual person, but your sexual expression may be tainted by memories or other effects of the rape. Thus what is for most people one of life's pleasures, may be for you a trigger for fear, anger, anxiety, or other painful or otherwise troublesome emotions. These feelings might appear at some times more strongly than others, and may sometimes not come up at all.

To cope with your anxiety in sexual relationships or other trigger situations, you may need to pay special attention to the relaxation exercises in Chapter 5. Your anxiety also can be diminished by focusing on empowering yourself through physical exercise and some of the means suggested in Chapter 10.

You might also need to make some special effort to get in touch with your anger. The exercises in Chapter 8 are designed to help you understand prohibitions against anger you might have internalized from childhood experiences and other learnings.

Chapter 13 covers domestic violence, including sexual abuse. If you were raped or sexually abused in a family context you will want to read that chapter as well as this one.

> **Note:** Because women are the primary victims of rape and other sexual assaults, the rest of this chapter, *in gender*, addresses women. This is not intended to exclude or discount men who have experienced such an assault. For the most part, the issues and problems discussed here apply equally to men and women. Men will find the section entitled "Myth 8: Men Don't Get Raped" of particular relevance.
>
> Legal definitions of rape and sexual assault vary from one state to the next. However, in this book *rape* is defined as any unwanted sexual act, whether between male and female or between members of the same sex. Rape and sexual assault can include vaginal, oral, or anal sex, or any other forceful taking of another person's body, including coercion and contact while the victim is unconscious.

The Prevalence of Rape

Mentally, you know you are not the only person who has ever been sexually assaulted. If you listen or watch the news on radio or television, or if you read the newspaper, you know that reports of rape and sexual assault in this country are increasing at an alarming rate. You may even have a friend or relative who was raped too. But emotionally you may feel as if you were the only one who has ever experienced this fear and humiliation. You probably never felt more alone and scared in your life than when the assault happened.

But, as you know, you are not alone. According to the *Washington Post* (15 March 1991; 29 March 1991), between 1981 and 1991 the rate of rape in the United States increased four times as much as the overall crime rate. American women are eight times more likely to be raped than European women, as a whole, and the United States' rape rate is 20 times higher than that of Portugal, 15 times higher than that of Japan, 23 times higher than that of Italy, and 46 times higher than that of Greece. Some 40 to 80 percent of college women report being sexually assaulted by dates or friends.

More recent studies confirm these statistics and indicate that, on an international level, anywhere from 10 to 50 percent of women have experienced some form of sexual assault. The more specific the questions about the sexual assault, the higher rates of assault found by the studies. Another unhappy finding is that, while about one-fourth of persons exposed to trauma in the U.S. develop PTSD, the rate of PTSD among rape and sexual assault survivors is much higher. (Green 1994)

These grim statistics can have two effects: either additional fear and hopelessness about ever feeling safe, or a perspective on your experience as part of the larger problem of sexism and violence in our society.

If these statistics have the latter effect—that is, if you are enraged about having been assaulted—you are in a sense lucky. Your fury probably leaves you little room for the shame, guilt, and sense of defilement many women experience strongly after being sexually assaulted. If you are angry, you are putting the blame for the rape exactly where it belongs: on the rapist and on the social forces that produce and support rape and other crimes against women in this country.

However, your anger may not yet have emerged. And even if you do feel anger, you may still be afraid. Your fear may be profound. In no other crime is the violation so great. Not only was your person attacked in the most terrible way, but the feeling of security you had in your own body and perhaps your home or neighborhood was violated as well. Your fears are entirely appropriate under the circumstances (Scheppele and Bart 1983).

The Myths of Rape

Aside from fear, one of the most common emotions rape victims feel is shame. Unless you were spared traditional teachings, you may find yourself feeling like "spoiled goods." A part of you may even blame yourself for the assault, especially if the person who violated you was not a stranger, but a friend or acquaintance.

The United States has come a long way toward placing the responsibility for sexual assault on the perpetrator rather than on the victim. As an American woman, you are not in the same position as many women in, for example, Islamic societies, in which rape victims are blamed for not having fought off their attackers and are subsequently treated as outcasts.

Thanks to the women's movement in this country, such blame-the-victim attitudes toward rape and sexual assault victims have been exposed and debunked for what they are—cruel sexist lies. Nonetheless, such attitudes die hard. Most likely you will encounter these attitudes at one time or another, in other people, in official policies, and even in yourself. The sections that follow outline the various forms the attitudes take— "myths," for our purposes—and show the flaws in such thinking.

Myth 1: Only Bad Girls Get Raped

Were you ever told that good girls don't get raped, only bad girls do? Have you heard it said that the only women who get raped are those who consciously or unconsciously "ask for it"? Such attitudes betray a double standard of sexuality.

According to this double standard, sexual feelings and expression are acceptable for men, but unacceptable for women—"good women," that is. Although the sexual double standard is not as widespread as it used to be in our country, it has not vanished. According to surveys, two-thirds of American citizens feel women provoke rape by their appearance or behavior, and that women engage in intercourse voluntarily and then cry rape later (Allgeier 1991). This myth is closely related to Myth 2, that women enjoy being raped.

Myth 2: All Women Enjoy a Little Rape Now and Then

Hopefully none of the important people in your life, male or female, still believe the myth that women enjoy or need "a little rape now and then." Yet this myth persists.

Does a part of you believe this myth also? Don't be ashamed if your answer is yes. How could you not partially believe it? It's almost impossible to escape images of women enjoying sexual victimization in our society. Such messages are plastered on billboards and magazine ads, acted out in the movies, and written up in novels, short stories, and even psychology and psychiatry books.

In fact, some mental health professionals claim that "unconsciously" every woman desires to be raped. This allegation may even sound true to you because at times you have fantasized about being carried into sexual bliss by a powerful lover. If so, do you now assume that your fantasies about being overpowered by a highly sexual male led to the rape?

Such thinking is fallacious. As Diane Russell explains in her book, *The Politics of Rape* (1975), the fact that some women fantasize about rape has more to do with the sexual oppression of women in our society than with any inherent characteristic of being a woman. If there was no double standard for sexuality and women could feel as sexually free as men, women would not need to think about rape as a means of obtaining sexual gratification. Like men, they could enjoy their sexuality free of guilt, as often as they desire.

However, because women are saddled with the idea that "good girls" don't or shouldn't like sex, women sometimes fantasize about rape. In this context, rape fantasies serve as a means for some women to enjoy their sexual selves without taking responsibility for their sexual desires. In the vast majority of cases the cause of a woman's rape fantasies does not lie in her desire to be harmed or victimized, nor in her supposed masochism. Rather, the cause lies in the sexist notion that having sexual desires is bad and degrading to women.

As Russell stresses, "Having voluntary fantasies of being raped and wanting to be raped in actuality are two entirely different things." When you fantasize about rape, you are in control. In real-life rape, you are not in control. On the contrary, you are subject to physical injury, even death.

"But in my rape fantasies I was beat up and hurt," you might be thinking. Don't be alarmed. Other women have such thoughts as well. If your fantasies include some pain, this does not mean you are neurotic or that you asked for the rape or any brutalization that accompanied it. The pain in your fantasies may simply be a means of punishing yourself for having sexual desires.

Think about it. Was your actual rape, as opposed to any fantasies you may have had about rape, a sexually enjoyable experience? During your rape, wasn't your dominant reaction fear rather than sexual pleasure? What about the many ways, verbal and nonverbal, the rapist might have humiliated and terrorized you?

Myth 3: Men Rape for Sexual Release

Rape involves sexual behavior and sex organs. However, rape is not a sexual act; it has very little to do with sexual passion. In fact, rape has been called a pseudosexual act, because in the majority of cases it is committed in order to fulfill nonsexual needs.

Research has shown, for example, that very few rapists fit into the category of lonely, socially inadequate men who rape because they cannot find a sexual partner. The majority of rapists already have a sex partner. Many have more than one sexual partner (Fortune 1983).

Acts of rape and sexual assault fall into three categories: power rape, anger rape, and sadistic rape.

Men who feel powerless or frustrated in life may rape in order to feel powerful. Rape has been related to economic conditions in that negative economic conditions, place men in positions of relative powerlessness. Try as they might, they cannot find a job that meets their vocational or economic goals and dreams.

As a result, they may resort to the most primitive, but also the most available, way of proving their power—abusing a woman or a child. Because women and children are perceived as being smaller and weaker, they are easy targets. Also, until recently, the legal rights of women and children have been minimal, so they could not fight back through the legal system.

Men who are angry at life or who are angry for other reasons may also act out their anger by assaulting women. Included in this group are men who are specifically angry at women due to some negative personal experience with a particular woman. It has been found, for example, that men who were sexually abused by a female relative were more likely to commit crimes against women than men who had not been so abused (Condy et al. 1987).

In sadistic rape, the goal is to humiliate and hurt. Sadistic rape can include mental and physical abuse, the use of objects to penetrate the vagina and the anus, and many forms of nonsexual torture.

Myth 4: Rape Is a Sign of Virility

In our country, rape is part of a virility mystique in which maleness is equated with sexual aggression (Russell 1975, Tieger 1981). In other societies, however, men who rape are not considered masculine at all. Instead they are deemed deficient in masculinity and seen as weaklings.

In Italy, Greece, and many Spanish-speaking nations, for example, men who need to resort to physical force to win a woman are often pitied or mocked. In those cultures "real men" don't need to stoop to blows to entice a woman to bed. Instead, they take pride in using their sex appeal, their intellect or wit, and their personal charm to win a woman's favors. (This is not to say that there is no sexism or no rape in these countries. However, neither is rape glamorized or seen as some form of initiation rite into manhood as it is in some segments of our population.)

Myth 5: Date Rape Isn't Really Rape

Were you raped by a stranger, or by a friend or acquaintance? Even if it was your husband, your boyfriend, a date, or a friend who forced himself upon you, his violation of your body is just as much a rape as if he were a total stranger. Acquaintance or date rape is real and can hurt as much, if not more in some respects, than being raped by a stranger.

Some research shows no difference in the reactions of women who have been raped by strangers as opposed to women raped by friends or dates. However other research suggests important differences. For example, women raped by strangers are more fearful for a longer period of time. Yet women who are raped by a date or a friend suffer from more self-doubt. They may seriously question their judgment and their ability to take care of themselves (Katz and Burt 1985, Katz 1986).

If you were raped by a date or a friend, you may wonder, What's wrong with me that I accepted a date or became friends with a rapist? Why didn't I see that he could be abusive?

Also, as a victim of acquaintance rape, your trust in men may have taken an even greater blow than that of a woman raped by a stranger. You were betrayed and deceived, not by some unknown character, but by someone you loved, liked, or at least trusted enough to go out with or be with socially. Furthermore, you may have more trouble being believed than women who have been raped by strangers. This is especially the case if you were at all sexually or romantically involved with the rapist.

Basically there are three kinds of date or acquaintance rape: beginning rape, early date rape, and relational date rape. Beginning date rape occurs on the first date. Often the rapist has a personality problem and made the date specifically to rape his victim. In early date rape, the rape occurs after a few dates. The victim typically wants to be "just friends," but the man wants to sexualize the relationship and forces the issue.

In relational date rape, the couple has already engaged in kissing and light sexual activity, but not intercourse. The man may feel that intercourse is his due because of the money he has spent or for some other reason. For example, he may also feel that having intercourse will prove that the relationship is "going somewhere" (Wade and Cirese 1991).

If the victim and rapist have already had intercourse prior to the rape, it is still rape if on a particular occasion the victim does not desire sexual contact and the rapist forces himself upon her or uses psychological manipulation (such as threatening to end the relationship or find another woman) with some minimal force to achieve that contact. Just because a woman has willingly had intercourse with a man before, does not mean he has the right to coerce her into having intercourse again.

Myth 6: Only Attractive Women Get Raped

Do you blame the rape on your looks? Being attractive is not an invitation to rape; rather, it is an expected part of the female role. Our society highly values physical attractiveness, and women are expected to make themselves appealing to men. In some circles, considerable attention and praise are given to women who dress provocatively—there is even social pressure to do so. Yet even blatantly seductive clothing is not an invitation for rape.

Women that hardly fit the cultural stereotype for attractiveness—including overweight and elderly women—frequently become the victims of rape. But when it happens to these women, they are sometimes accused of having provoked the rape in order to get attention or be seen as sexually desirable. In fact in one study, "unattractive" rape victims were more often blamed for their rape than were others (Tieger 1981).

Clearly, since both attractive and unattractive women can be blamed for being raped, attractiveness or lack of attractiveness cannot be considered a cause of rape.

Even if you flirted with the rapist or were feeling sexual, it doesn't mean you were "asking for it." At all times, you have the right to say no to any form of sexual activity you do not desire. Others, due to their own prejudices and preconceptions, may not consider it rape. In your heart, however, you know you were violated. Your own understanding of the event is all that matters, not the understanding of others who have never been wounded in such a profound manner.

Myth 7: If You Didn't Resist,
You Must Have Wanted It

Did you resist the rape, or did you submit? If you resisted, are you chastising yourself for not resisting "enough"? If you didn't put up a fight, are you wondering what is wrong with you? Are you thinking, Maybe I did want it? Or, I have no backbone; I'm a failure.

One of the most terrifying aspects of rape for women who did not fight back is confronting their own passivity. Therefore, it's important to realize that if you were passive during the rape, your passivity was probably a combination of sex role conditioning and a defensive noradrenaline reaction, resulting in a freeze or numbing response.

In evaluating your response to the rape, consider that, in general, men are stronger than women, and you have probably had little or no training in physical fighting or self-defense. Without such training, how could you have fought off a rapist who was probably both larger and stronger than you?

Have you also taken into account the factor of surprise? The rapist may have planned the attack and so was mentally and physically prepared to fight. Whereas if you, like most rape victims and most victims of crime in general, were caught off guard, by the time you got over the shock and numbing of being attacked the rapist probably already had the advantage. That hardly means you "really" wanted to be raped, does it?

The obstacles that inhibit women from fighting back are not only physical ones. Psychological obstacles can be equally—or even more—powerful. Unless you have somehow miraculously escaped sexism in your life, you were probably exposed to the female sex role stereotype. This stereotype teaches women not to fight or compete with men, or even to show anger toward them. From childhood on, girls are taught to please and obey, not to display (or experience) physical strength, assertiveness, and independence.

If you went limp during the rape, you were only reacting the way you were trained to react. In addition, you may have hoped to avoid injury by being submissive. Although there are no conclusive statistics, many rape victims do sustain physical injuries.

There is no conclusive evidence regarding whether it is better to fight back or to submit, probably because each rape is unique. Some women who have fought back, pleaded with the rapist, or offered him money have managed to escape or dissuade him. Other women who tried the same approaches found that their fighting or pleading only seemed to earn them more savage beatings.

On the other hand, some women who submitted without a fight feel their surrender saved their lives. Others found that their passivity angered the rapist. "He wanted a woman with 'spunk,'" one woman reports. "He beat me because I was 'no fun'."

Rape survivors, policemen, and others who work with the problem of rape on a daily basis cannot truly say what is the best way to stop a rapist. If these people, who have had considerable experience with rape, do not know the "right thing to do," why do you, for whom the rape was a total shock, think you should have instantaneously known what was the best course of action?

Sexual pleasure and orgasm during rape. You may have felt that your body betrayed you in other ways than just not being able to fight back. Did you lubricate during the rape, or experience sexual arousal or orgasm? Were you shocked to find your body responding in such a manner? Are you now ashamed to admit your level of arousal?

You may have not been sexually aroused at all (which is no comment on your sexuality). However, if you were, you need to know that a sexual response during rape is not at all an uncommon experience among rape victims. If you did respond sexually, you may feel deeply guilty, as if the response of your physical self somehow indicates that you "liked it."

Before you chastise yourself for one more minute, remember that your sexual organs do not have a brain. They cannot distinguish between a mauling rapist and the gentle touch of a lover. They simply react to stimulation the way they were physically designed to respond.

If you climaxed or had some other sexual response to the rape, this does not mean that you enjoyed it. Even women who climax several times during a rape say, Yes, I climaxed. But I hated it. If the rapist insisted on stimulating you, demanded a sexual response from you, you had little choice in the matter.

Or perhaps you responded physically simply because you are sexually alive. Sexual aliveness is a positive quality, not a curse. Unfortunately, your sexual responsiveness was abused. However, this does not mean that your ability to enjoy sex is "wrong," that it caused the rape, or that it will cause future rapes. Women who don't respond that way also get raped.

Placating behavior toward the rapist. After the rape, did you agree to see the rapist again? Did you cook him dinner, mend his clothing, talk with him at length, or in other ways act as if he were your friend or lover, not your assailant? Are you ashamed to admit to such behavior?

If so, perhaps your shame and self-doubt can be reduced by appreciating that when the rapist overtook you physically, he also crushed your spirit and sense of autonomy. Your behavior following the rape was simply an extension of his crime, not an expression of something inherently wrong with you.

It may even be that you had a very powerful reason to engage in friendly behavior toward the rapist: to avoid physical harm not only to yourself but to your children or other loved ones.

Myth 8: Men Don't Get Raped

In the majority of rape cases, the male is the offender and the female, the victim. Yet men are raped too, more than has been commonly thought.

Most male rape victims are raped by other men, in the sense that they are forced to submit to anal intercourse, oral sex, mutual masturbation, masturbation of the offender, or other sex acts. Fear of bodily harm can also cause a man to have an erection. In this sense a man can be raped by either a man or a woman. In addition, men can be raped by women in the sense that they can be coerced or intimidated into sexual behavior they do not desire. Furthermore, a percentage of sexual abuse is perpetrated by adult females on young boys.

Information on male rape victims is extremely scarce because male victims, like their female counterparts, feel deep humiliation and shame at having been victimized in such a manner. Their shame stems in part from fear of being seen as passive victims of rape, as homosexual, or both. In our society, victims and homosexuals are not perceived as being masculine.

Consequently, men are more reluctant to report rape to the police, to prosecute, or to in any manner speak openly about their experiences. Only very recently have a few brave men begun to admit and talk openly about their experiences. As a result, it is likely the coming years will reveal that sexual assaults on men are more common than was previously thought.

Exercise: Recalling the Rape in Detail

Go to your journal now, and review what you wrote there about the rape in light of what you've read above. Did you go into great detail about what happened before the rape but fail to describe the rape itself? For example, did you write a narrative something like this: I was on my way to the grocery store after having finished the laundry when someone jumped out of a car, grabbed me, and then I was raped?

Your description should include the events that preceded the rape, especially if they are relevant to the rape or your feelings about the rape. However, your description also needs to be as detailed as possible about the rape itself, including the following:

- What did the rapist look like, smell like?

- What did he say?

- What did he do?

- What did you say?

- What happened first?

- What did you think then?

- What did you feel then?

- What happened next?

- What did you think and feel then?

- Were any weapons or objects involved?

Be as specific as possible, not only about the sensory details, but about your feelings and reactions. For example, if you were sexually aroused by the rape, at least note it mentally. You don't have to write it down if you don't want to. And you don't *ever* have to tell anybody. You just need to acknowledge it to yourself. Hopefully someday you will not feel guilty about it.

Exercise: Reexamining Self-Blame

In earlier chapters, you wrote at length in your journal about the self-blame you feel pertaining to the rape. But in the preceding sections in this chapter you have learned more about the normal reactions to rape and about the common misconceptions that may have contributed to your self-blame. In light of this new information, reexamine your list of self-blaming statements. Cross out those you no longer believe or that you have learned to see as unreasonable, and add any additional sources of self-blame you may have discovered. As you review your revised list, ask yourself the following questions:

1. Where is the evidence that your self-blaming statements are true?

2. If a man were raped, would he come up with a list of self-blaming statements like yours? (If you are a man, would a woman come up with the same list?)

3. If your mother, daughter, best friend, or someone else you truly loved was raped and came up with this list of self-blaming beliefs, how would you respond? Would you agree that she was correct in all her self-blaming judgments, in only some of them, or in none of them?

4. How would you react if you heard her blaming herself so much?

5. Can you apply the same perspective and compassion to yourself as you would to her? If you can't, why can't you?

Exercise: Reexamining Secondary Wounding Experiences

Review your list of secondary wounding experiences pertaining to the rape. Add any additional experiences you may have remembered as a result of reading this chapter.

For example, if you have a husband or boyfriend and have openly shared the details of the rape with him, how did he react? Was he tender and supportive? Or did he become so engrossed in his own guilt for not being there to protect you, or in his own desire for revenge, that you ended up helping him with his feelings rather than him supporting you?

Did he become sexually aroused by your story? Was it obvious that he was getting turned on, even though he tried to hide it? Did any other important men (or women) in your life—father, brother, cousin, therapist, or a colleague at work—have a similar reaction?

Were you asked questions such as, Was he good? How long was his penis? Did you secretly enjoy it? Did you climax? Did he do anything weird?

As angry and wounding as such responses probably make you feel (and justifiably so), these important men in your life are not perverts, but merely products of male sex role conditioning. Studies show, for example, that convicted rapists and other men often hold similar attitudes towards women. Furthermore, researchers have found that as many as 35 percent of college men indicated that they would like to rape women, provided they could be certain they would not be caught (Scott and Tetreault 1987, Tieger 1981, Malamuth 1981).

Given that these attitudes are the "norm," you may have had secondary wounding experiences that range from the so subtle as to seem almost imaginary to megaton scale. Don't discount any of these experiences—you didn't make them up. They are all real, and they all affect your life.

Dealing with the Emotional Aftereffects of Rape

The most common symptoms reported by women after rape include fear, depression, anxiety, sexual disinterest, reduced pleasure in life, and sleeping problems. Some women have physical problems, such as irritated throats, vaginal infections, gastrointestinal upsets, and skin rashes. Many women make drastic changes in their life-styles. They increase their personal security, restrict their activities so as to feel safer, or change neighborhoods, jobs, or phone numbers.

Researchers have found that for about a year after the rape, victims tend to decrease their sexual activity. If they do engage in sex, they report less satisfaction than before the rape. Often their sexual experiences are interrupted by flashbacks to the rape and feelings of fear and depression.

Getting Help as Soon as Possible

The immediate stress reactions that tend to follow a crime such as rape (see Chapter 11) do not need to develop into PTSD. Yet they can and frequently do. With good help, however, the long-term consequences of rape or other sexual assault need not occur.

An individual's speed of recovery depends on the nature of the rape and on any history of previous trauma. However, preliminary research indicates that within six months to a year after a rape, women who have received qualified help report that much of their emotional equilibrium has been restored. Although they may still feel scarred by the rape, they feel better able to function.

Some victims, however, wait years before they seek help. Don't you be one of them. If you have been raped, find someone with whom you can talk about the rape as soon as possible. The exercises in this book may be helpful to you, but usually a validating, supportive human response is also necessary. The sooner you go for help, the shorter the recovery period will be.

Pseudorecovery and Delayed Reactions

Therapists have found that many rape survivors show up for treatment five to six years after the rape. These women might have had some immediate stress reactions after the rape, but then quickly swept the rape and its impact under the rug. They urgently desired to return to normal life as soon as possible. Some need to prove to themselves, and perhaps to others, that even though they may have been helpless victims during the rape, they are no longer victims, but strong, capable, healthy women. You may have done this yourself.

But I don't have any symptoms, you might protest. I went back to work two days after the rape. My sex life is fine. I don't stay behind locked doors, and I feel just as confident and happy as ever.

My reply is, That's wonderful. I hope you never have any symptoms in the future either.

The possibility exists however, that you are having a pseudorecovery—a partial or superficial recuperation after the rape. *Pseudorecovery* refers to a quick bouncing back to normalcy without having processed the feelings associated with the rape.

Perhaps you were too busy taking care of other people's reactions to the rape to pay attention to your own. Or maybe you haven't even told your parents, your boyfriend or husband, or other significant people in your life. You may fear being blamed for the rape, or even being punished for it (if, for example, you have a possessively jealous husband, boyfriend, father, or brother).

Or maybe you have family members or friends who are just so old-fashioned that you know they wouldn't understand. You may fear upsetting some people in your life, especially if they are elderly or ill, or if you feel they are emotionally fragile or already have too many problems of their own.

Who you tell about the rape is your choice. For a myriad of good reasons, you may decide not to tell certain family members or friends about it. However, it is important that you find someone to talk to—and that you not stuff your feelings away and never talk about them.

If you never develop a symptom, that is fine. But someday you may, perhaps when you experience some other loss in your life or when you are under severe stress at work or in some other difficult situation. If this should occur, spare yourself unnecessary misery and get help as soon as possible. Appendix B lists some resources that may help you find the assistance you need.

Viewing the Rape as a Challenge

For a while after the rape you may "crumble," but you do not have to stay that way. The rape may have created such fear and shame in you that you want to retreat from life. And you may *need* to retreat for a while to have time and room to experience your sadness, grief, anger, fear, and other feelings, without distraction.

However, it is also important that you continue to function as best you can. The more you can continue to be involved with life, the braver, stronger, and more capable you will feel.

Rape crisis experts sometimes tell rape survivors this: Now that you have been raped, you are at a crossroads. There are several things you can do. Some of these things restrict or limit your freedom. These include accepting subtle blame for the attack, limiting your physical movement (not going out at night, discontinuing certain activities, never being alone), and limiting your growth and positive potential. By doing other things, you can take control of your life. You can set your own schedule. You can explore new avenues for personal growth. You can help other survivors. You can overcome what has happened (Veronen and Kilpatrick 1983).

In dealing with your feelings and the aftermath of the rape, it may help you to practice saying the following affirming statements.

- I am more than a rape victim. The fact that I was raped does not define my personality.

- I have a right to be a sexual person and enjoy sex.

- I have the right to not enjoy sex, to be asexual, to not always be interested in sex.

- I have a right to choose my sexual partner.

- I have a right to choose my sexual activities.

- I am a victim of a sexist society; I did not cause or ask for the rape.

- No matter what I was wearing, or how flirtatious I was acting, or where I was, I am not responsible for the rape.

- The rape is not a punishment for some sin on my part. The rape was an act of violence and power on the part of a misguided, inhumane person who used me for his own purposes.

- My past sexual history has nothing to do with the rape.

- I don't need to punish myself for somebody else's crime.

- Punishing myself won't change the rapist.

- Punishing myself won't make the memories go away.

- I may not be able to control my fear, anxiety, depression, or other stress symptoms, but I can take positive steps toward comforting and healing myself. I can find supportive friends, see a therapist, and otherwise be kind to myself. I can also take steps to increase the control I have over my time.

The Decision to Prosecute

After the rape, you have many decisions to make: whether to report the rape to the police, who to tell about the rape and who not to tell, and whether to press charges and proceed with prosecution. These decisions should be yours, not someone else's.

If you want to take legal action against your rapist, the first step is to file a report at your local police station. You can do this by calling the police, who may come to your home to take the report, or by going directly to the police station yourself. The police will then investigate the case and present a report to the district attorney's office. This office will decide whether there is enough evidence to warrant taking the rapist to court.

Decide whether to pursue legal actions according to *your* best interests. You may feel it is wrong to allow the crime to go unreported and the criminal to go free. Yet you may also hesitate to commit yourself to such a time-consuming, energy-draining process as criminal prosecution. Prosecution will probably subject you to some additional secondary wounding experiences, and will force you to think about and relive the rape again several times.

On the other hand, filing charges and seeing your case through to the end can be an excellent outlet for your rage and need for revenge. You will also be helping to fight rape; one reason rape persists is precisely because so many women hesitate to prosecute. They fear the criminal justice system, and depending on who they are and where they live, their fear may be justified.

You will need to take many factors into account in your decision. First, however, you need to obtain a clear picture of the laws and court procedures in your area. What exactly will be involved? How many hearings? What kinds of testimony are permitted? Talk to rape-crisis counselors and former victims who have prosecuted, as well as to an attorney who specializes in sexual assault. These people may be able to help you understand exactly what you are committing to in terms of time and process.

You also need to estimate what the prosecution will cost you in time lost from work, transportation and babysitting costs, and other financial expenses—not to mention an attorney, if you decide to hire one. Also take into account the emotional costs of, for instance, seeing the rapist again, hearing his lawyer present him in a favorable light, listening to a distorted account of the rape, and hearing lies about your character. Consider what might happen if the media were to become involved.

Keep in mind, however, that even if you gather all the information you can from the most reputable sources, court proceedings are highly unpredictable. Court dockets tend to be overcrowded; frequent delays and postponements are common. In addition, what begins as a relatively small case may mushroom into a long and complex one. Most important of all, you need to be prepared for the possibility that you will not be believed in court or that the rapist will receive an extremely light sentence. Under such circumstances, you could feel victimized all over again.

On the other hand, even if you lose in court in terms of having the rapist adequately punished, you can win in other respects. You can make the rapist at least suffer the embarrassment and financial costs of a court involvement. And you will have the satisfaction of having stood up for yourself and showed the rapist and others that, although you weren't able to defend yourself at the time, you are certainly going to fight back now.

When the Rapist Threatens to Retaliate

But what if the rapist threatened to harm me, or someone I care about, if I reported the rape or took him to court? you might ask.

If this is the case, you need to seriously assess the threats. Some rapists have acted on their threats. Others have not. For example, there are verifiable accounts of rapists who served time in prison for rape, only to on their release immediately find the victim and rape her again. According to an FBI report, rapists who seek out the same victim upon release from prison usually do so within 90 days (*Washington Post*, 16 June 1991). In most cases, however, the offender does not attack the same victim (*Washington Post*, 17 June 1991).

You may not like the idea of being controlled by the rapist's threats. But those threats cannot be dismissed as meaningless either. There are no easy answers.

Making Your Own Decision

Only you can make the final decision whether to press charges and testify—after you have discussed your concerns and options with people you trust and who respect you, as well as with people who have information and experience with the court system and with rape issues in your area.

Don't be swayed by people who call you a coward for not prosecuting. Close your ears as well to the opposite: people who call you unfeminine for prosecuting or accuse you of being "out to get men." As much as possible, ignore the voices on both sides. There is no perfect or one right decision. There are risks whether or not you prosecute. Whatever you decide, the decision won't be painless or cost free. But it will be *your* decision. You will have taken back that much power over your life.

13

Domestic Violence and Sexual Abuse

Guidelines for Using This Book

There is perhaps no form of violence in which the victim is more emotionally conflicted—both toward the abuser and toward him- or herself—than in cases of domestic violence and sexual abuse. Secondary wounding experiences, in both the family and the larger society, are likewise more frequent and more grievous for domestic abuse survivors than for survivors of other types of trauma.

As a victim of domestic violence, you will need to read all the chapters in Parts I and II not just once, but many times. In Chapter 1 you will need to read the definition of trauma carefully. In many domestic violence situations, the abusers have so brainwashed their victims that abuse seems normal, and victims are often so traumatized that they live in a state of emotional numbness and denial.

When you are asked to list your traumas as part of the self-assessment for PTSD (also in Chapter 1), your list may be long. Do not attempt to detail all you have experienced; you do not want to be overwhelmed. Jot down the major traumas first. Then add to your list as you feel ready, as memories surface, or as you increasingly recognize that what you thought was normal behavior on the part of your abuser was, in fact, abnormal.

You may complete the self-assessment and determine that you do not have PTSD. However, it is possible that your PTSD is masked behind depression or addiction. Therefore you need to carefully assess yourself for depression and addiction using the questionnaires in Chapter 2. Some of your PTSD symptoms may not emerge in a clear fashion until you have received help for depression or addiction.

If there is violence in your home but you do not meet the criteria for PTSD, depression, or addiction it does not mean you are not being traumatized. Instead of developing PTSD, depression, a substance-abuse problem, or an eating disorder, you may be dissociating or somatizing.

If you are dissociating, you may not remember the abuse, or you may recall it only in part or minimize its extent. In these forms of dissociation, you are suffering form total or partial amnesia.

Alternatively, you may be fully aware of the violence, but have no emotion about it. In this form of dissociation your senses and thoughts are disconnected from your feelings. You may have little physical pain when you are injured and experience minimal emotional pain when your integrity and feelings are trampled upon by your abuser.

Rather than dissociating, however, you may be somatizing, especially if, for any of a host of reasons, it is dangerous for you to talk about your life. Not uncommonly, abused women suffer from severe headaches, back problems, and other physical problems.

Like your list of traumas, the secondary wounding experiences you are asked to inventory in Chapter 4 may also be extensive. You will need to especially focus on how family members, friends, and other persons who may have sincerely cared for you may also have been agents of secondary wounding experiences. Like yourself, they may have been ignorant about family violence, fearful of the abuser, or caught up in a family system in which the victim was blamed or where alcohol or some other substance dominated family interactions.

You need to pay special attention to Chapter 5, on triggers, since almost every aspect of living may have been colored by the abuse you experienced. The "anniversaries" of your abuse may include many holidays, as well as everyday occurrences such as mealtimes, bedtime, and weekends.

The chapters on identifying angers and losses are particularly relevant. You may have difficulty getting in touch with your anger, since in your household perhaps only the abuser or certain select other individuals were permitted to feel and express anger, whereas you, as victim, were punished for expressions of anger. Or, in contrast, you may be destructively lashing out at peers or co-workers, present family members and friends, or others with the anger you feel toward the original abuser. Whether you are suppressing your anger, expressing it inappropriately, or both, it is critical that you begin to discover the true sources of your anger and learn to manage it as constructively as possible. Chapter 8 offers help in both areas.

Especially painful for you will be the chapter on grieving, since a little at a time, you will have to grieve the family life and relationships you never had. Thus, Chapter 9 is critical to your healing. Only after you have grieved can you go on to empower yourself as described in Chapter 10. At times, it may be difficult to see how the devastating experiences you have had to tolerate can become sources of strength, but they can. You may need to read Chapter 10 more than once, as well as seek professional help and the support of a survivors' group or some other form of supportive counseling.

If sexual abuse, including sexual overstimulation, was or is part of your domestic violence experiences, Chapter 12, on rape, is also relevant to you.

It is impossible to live in a violent home without sustaining some damage to your emotional and physical health. Regardless of whether you can assess yourself as having PTSD, depression, somatization, or dissociation, you are encouraged to seek help. You do not need to fit into any of the psychological categories described here to begin to find a way to live in safety.

If you were severely abused by a parent or caretaker who was psychotic or otherwise severely mentally ill, or by a parent or caretaker who was a member of a cult that advocated or permitted ritual torture, sexual exploitation of children, or other forms of child abuse, and if this abuse occurred before the age of five, the possibility exists that you may be suffering from a severe dissociative disorder or multiple personality disorder (MPD). Although this book may be of assistance to you, if you have a severe dissociative disorder or MPD, you need special help from a therapist specifically qualified to assist individuals with multiple personality disorder. Neither this book, nor an ordinary therapist, nor even a trauma specialist is enough. At this point, relatively few therapists or hospitals are trained in assisting persons with your problem.

If you have MPD, do not despair. It is a much more common disorder in our population than is commonly thought. Having MPD does not mean you cannot participate in survivor groups or other forms of counseling. However, therapy specifically directed at your MPD is essential.

For assistance in removing yourself from an abusive situation and for a list of some of the other resources available, refer to Appendix B under the headings "Battering" and "Child Abuse," and the section entitled "Ways Out" at the end of this chapter.

What Is Abuse?—Definitions

For the purposes of this book, *abuse* is a broad term that encompasses any kind of physical cruelty in a domestic situation. *Sexual abuse*, whether of an adult or child, means unwanted sexual contact of any kind, regardless of the victim's age, sex, or relationship with the abuser. Emotional abuse and manipulation also play a role in both physical and sexual abuse.

Women and children are those most often victimized in these ways, but increasingly, cases of the abuse of elderly people and grown men are coming to light.

Battering

Physical abuse of adults, or battering, is a multidimensional phenomenon. Physical assault must exist in order for the relationship to be considered a battering one; emotional abuse in itself, without the assault, does not constitute a battering relationship. However, battering often includes not only emotional abuse, but economic, social, and sexual abuse as well. Economic battering refers to the use of money as a coercive tool by the abuser. Social battering refers to the abuser's attempts to isolate the victim and severely limit or control the victim's public interactions.

In addition to bodily assault, battering includes any statements or actions that indicate the intent to assault. (In many states, the *threat* of violence is a crime.) Battering ranges from slapping to punching to threat or attack with a weapon, including burning, biting, and shoving. For a pattern of battering to be shown, there must have been at least two deliberate, severe physical assaults.

Police officers and judges tend to consider only black eyes, broken ribs, and burns as acceptable evidence of battering. Similarly, vaginal lacerations are often needed to prove marital rape. However, psychological humiliation and degradation are just as devastating as physical aggression. Surveys of abused women show that psychological abuse goes hand in hand with physical attacks, and many battered women remember the psychological injuries they have endured more than the physical ones. Given the damage inflicted on the psyche as well as to the body, battering might best be defined as any violation of the physical or psychological space of another person within an intimate or bonded relationship.

Note, however, that a battering relationship is not one in which an individual simply feels unhappy due to lack of love, respect, or appreciation. Rather, the individual must have experienced at least one life-threatening situation and know that the abuser is capable of killing him or her. It is not necessary for the abuser to continually beat the victim. What is relevant is that the victim has been terrorized or humiliated into a submissive posture by the threat of injury or death. Even threats of violence, accompanied by minimal physical abuse, are sufficient to establish a pattern of domination by force.

If you are controlled by your spouse's, lover's, or caretaker's anger and your fear of that person's violence or potential for violence, you are being abused. It cannot be overemphasized that you need not be beaten every Saturday night to have been battered. Once you know your partner or caretaker is capable of hurting you, even to the point of death, and you come to live in fear of his or her anger and what it could lead to, you become metaphorically a prisoner of war.

Child Abuse

Child abuse, like battering, does not refer to a one-time assault, but to the repeated battering, neglect, or sexual molestation (see "Child Sexual Abuse," below) of a child by a parent, relative, or other caretaker. Just as a woman need not suffer repeated fractures and knife wounds to be considered battered, a child need not be covered with burns and scars to be classified as abused. The definition of child abuse used by the National Center on Child Abuse and Neglect (NCCAN 1983a, b), includes many forms of maltreatment not considered in the definition of battering typically adopted by mental health professionals. For example, emotional abuse by itself is an official category of child abuse. There need not be the violence or threat of violence that is necessary for an adult relationship to be considered battering.

Officially, an abused child is a person under the age of 18 whose physical or emotional health is harmed or threatened with harm by acts of omission or commission by parents or other persons responsible for his or her welfare. The specifics of what legally constitutes child abuse vary from state to state. In general, however, four types of abuse are considered (NCCAN 1983a,b):

- Physical abuse
- Neglect
- Emotional abuse
- Sexual abuse

Physical abuse includes assault with a weapon, burns, fractures, or "other actions leading to possible injury of a child. Spanking for purely disciplinary reasons is generally not seen as child abuse."

Neglect can be physical or educational. Physical neglect includes "abandonment; refusal to seek, allow or provide treatment for illness or impairment; inadequate physical supervision; disregard of health hazards in the home; and inadequate nutrition, clothing or hygiene where services are available." Educational neglect includes knowingly permitting chronic truancy, keeping the child home from school repeatedly without cause, or failure to enroll a child in school.

Emotional abuse includes "verbal and/or emotional assault" and "close confinement," such as tying or locking in a closet; inadequate nurturance, such as that affecting failure-to-thrive babies; knowingly permitting antisocial behavior, such as delinquency, serious drug or alcohol abuse; and refusal to allow medical care for a diagnosed medical or emotional problem (NCCAN 1983a,b).

Child abuse, like battering, is rampant in our society, and has been for centuries. It has also been assumed to be normal in almost every country in the world. In recent years, however, much publicity has been given to both these forms of domestic violence, and there has been much public outcry against the archaic laws and attitudes that support the abuser rather than the victim.

Today, child abuse in any form is considered a crime, and due to child-protection legislation, teachers, therapists, clergy, and other professionals are legally mandated to report suspected child abuse. In contrast, there is no law mandating reports of suspected battering or other domestic violence not involving children.

Despite child-protection legislation, however, much child abuse goes unreported, for the same reasons that battering does: denial, fear of retaliation, and aversion to getting entangled in the legal system.

Emotional abuse, although an official category of child abuse, is rarely considered grounds for legal action unless it is accompanied by severe physical abuse, sexual assault, or neglect.

Agencies designed to assist abused children are often understaffed or hampered by the conflicting rights of the parents or caretakers and the rights of the child, and by the confusion and complexities inherent in most domestic violence situations. As a result, there have been cases in which children have been removed from the homes of nonabusive parents because of physical injuries resulting from legitimate accidents. However, in other instances severely burned or battered children have been allowed to remain in life-threatening environments.

Child Sexual Abuse

According to the NCCAN (1983a,b), child sexual abuse includes "sexual molestation, incest, and exploitation for prostitution or the production of pornographic materials." A child is defined as any person under the age of 18; the abuser, however, can be any age. Even individuals who are under 18 and therefore considered children themselves are defined as perpetrators of sexual abuse if they are considerably older than the victim or have some degree of power or authority over the abused child.

If against your will you were fondled, penetrated, or made to engage in oral sex or other sexual acts by an elder person before you were the age of 18, then you were sexually abused. In addition, if you were made to pose for pictures in the nude or in provocative poses, if you were made to observe or touch adult genitals, if you were made to expose your genitals (even if you weren't touched), then you can consider yourself sexually abused even if no stimulation or penetration occurred.

The Structure of Abuse

Being physically assaulted by a stranger is traumatic. However, being abused by someone in your own family is even worse. The horror of being a victim of family violence is that you are being hurt by someone who claims to love you or who has promised or is obligated to take care of you.

Regardless of your age, sex, race, or sexual orientation, whether the abuse you suffered was physical or sexual, occurred in the past or is on-going, if you are being physically hurt or sexually abused by someone you love, or once loved, you can expect a variety of reactions to the trauma: self-hatred, guilt, and shame among them. You probably have many of the same feelings experienced by victims of stranger crime and rape, for example, the rage and humiliation that go along with being physically violated. However, you can also expect to feel a deep sense of personal betrayal.

The following sections delineate the emotional and physical dynamics common to abusive families.

Denial

Denial is a common phenomenon in violent homes. Both the abuser and the abused person (as well as other family members) tend to deny, discount, or trivialize the abuse. Take Albert's account of his childhood, for example:

> You psychologists are all the same! You're all a bunch of softies. I don't feel betrayed, humiliated, or any of those other things you say I feel. My father only whipped me to straighten me out. I was always acting up. He just used his belt to keep me in line.
>
> Yeah, he drew blood and left welts on my legs. But I never felt betrayed. Personally, I don't think there's anything wrong with what he did. He was only trying to make me obey. You're making a big deal out of nothing, lady. These things happen in families. They're normal.

The key word here is *normal*. Albert lacked appreciation for the various traumas he had endured as a child, because for him they were normal.

For Albert, not showing his feelings was also normal. As a child, he had been punished viciously for expressing even the slightest emotion. For example, if he so much as whimpered while he was being beaten, his father called him a sissy and hit him harder. "I'm not hurting you. I'm making a man out of you," his father would say. And just as Albert's father had denied being abusive to his son, Albert denied that he had been abused.

Both the abuser and the abused may discount the violence by calling it "nothing" or "a scratch" or "just a little roughing up." Sometimes the violence is rationalized as discipline: She had to be taught right from wrong, an abusive caretaker might claim.

Sometimes other family members take it upon themselves to try to rescue the victim. But more often they share in the denial, numb themselves to the violence, or imitate the aggressor. If they come to identify with and copy the aggressor's behavior, they may also begin to abuse the victim, another family member, or people or property outside the home.

Along with denying and discounting the violence comes a denial and discounting of the feelings that go along with abuse. Albert denied having any feelings of betrayal, anger, or disappointment stemming from being abused by his father. In part, however, he simply didn't know the words. Like many formerly abused children, Albert lacked adequate language for his emotions. If you share this problem with Albert, review Chapters 3 and 7. These chapters offer vocabulary and other help in identifying and accepting your feelings.

As a family abuse survivor, the first step toward healing is acknowledging that you were abused. Such an admission may be painful and difficult for you. It means relinquishing the illusion that your caretaker or partner was normal and "really loved you." Perhaps this person did truly love you, but he or she also abused you. You need to look at that abuse square in the face, in all its gory details, before you can fully understand yourself.

In many cases, childhood physical or sexual abuse is the missing piece in self-understanding. It is not unusual for individuals who have suffered trauma as adults—for example, in a war or natural catastrophe—to undergo therapy for their adult trauma but still be plagued with PTSD or other symptoms. Sometimes they interpret the persistence of the symptoms as signs that they are hopeless cases or destined to be losers. Their physicians and therapists, too, may view them as especially resistant cases. Instead, however, the problem may be childhood abuse that has not been recognized. Or if it has been recognized, it may be discounted or minimized, as in Albert's case. In other instances, adult trauma brings childhood trauma to the fore.

Denial is both wonderful and horrible. It enables people to endure the unendurable, but it can also prevent them from living full lives. In the following exercise, you will be asked to take the risk of lifting the blanket of denial regarding any abuse you experienced from a partner, a parent, or a caretaker.

Exercise: Overcoming Denial

Review the definitions of battering, child abuse, and sexual abuse. For each category that applies to you, make a list of the specific ways you were abused. If possible, indicate the frequency of the abuse and the age at which abuse occurred. For example, if you are a formerly abused wife, you might have entries under physical, emotional, sexual, and economic abuse. Look over the following examples before you begin:

Physical Abuse

Shoved down stairs four times in three years.

Threatened with a gun once a week.

Threats of violence every weekend.

Two beatings this year, one the year before, four the first year we were married.

I wasn't allowed to go to the doctor until my temperature was 103 degrees for a week straight.

Emotional Abuse

He called me "ugly," "flat-chested," and "rhino-skinned."

I was "compulsive" if I was on time for him, but when I was late he called me "defiant." If I was early, he called me "neurotic."

He wouldn't let me go to my niece's birthday party because he didn't like my sister.

Sexual Abuse

He made me pose nude in front of mirrors.

I had to wear a bikini in public when I didn't want to.

Economic Abuse

I wasn't allowed to call my grandmother after my grandfather died because it was long distance.

If I didn't give my paycheck, he would hurt the kids.

After you finish this exercise, you may feel depressed, angry, or both. If you have these feelings, do not berate yourself. Instead congratulate yourself on not being numb anymore. If, on the other hand, you have no feelings, do not berate yourself. You are using numbing to protect yourself. When you are ready, your feelings will begin to emerge, in their own way, at their own pace, at a time that is right for you.

Guilt and Shame

Along with denial, guilt and shame are hallmarks of family abuse survivors. This guilt and shame is based on two myths: abused persons often feel that they deserved the abuse, and that they should have been able to prevent it.

Myth 1: It must be my fault. If only I had been better or more lovable, I wouldn't have been beaten, many formerly abused children think, consciously or unconsciously. If only I were a better housekeeper, or if I was sexier or smarter, my husband wouldn't beat me, many abused women think.

Do you feel responsible for the abuse? Are you certain that it is inadequacies or failures on your part that caused the violence? If your answer to either of these questions is yes, you need to be aware that the opposite is true.

It is the abuser, not you, who uses force. You are not shoving, kicking, hitting, or sexually abusing yourself. These are the actions of the abuser. All abusers are responsible for their own behavior. By now it is widely known that battering, child abuse, and elder abuse are against the law. If you are a victim of abuse, you are guilty of causing abuse only if you are abusing someone else, not because of the abuse you have suffered.

In addition, it is not your personal inadequacies and failures that cause the abuse, but the abuse that creates feelings of inferiority and exacerbates any preexisting sense of inadequacy or failure. The abuse and the lack of validation, affection, and respect that underlies the abuse can almost permanently implant in its victims a sense of unworthiness and shame. The abuse insistently gives the message that you are so unworthy that you deserve to be beaten.

Writer Andrea Dworkin (1978) calls these feelings "a bruise that does not heal." Children who are beaten by a parent or caretaker can only assume they are being beaten because they are bad or unwanted. Similarly, if an adult is abused by the very person who has pledged eternal love, he or she will typically assume that the violence reflects his or her own failings. In addition to the physical abuse, your abuser probably filled your head with derogatory comments about you as a person. These negative messages constitute an "old tape" that may never be fully erased from your mind. New learnings gained from therapy and positive life experiences may be able to diminish the power of that tape most of the time, but the old tape will still sometimes play.

Furthermore, the very existence of this old tape can make you feel ashamed and inferior. Margaret, who was abused as a child, explains it this way:

> It's not fashionable to lack self-confidence these days. Our society likes winners, not losers, and if you aren't brimming with self-esteem, you're seen as a loser who's not worth hiring, or dating. Try feeling inferior on a job interview and see how far it gets you.
>
> I can't just deny the old tape that says, You are bad, you are bad, Mommy beats you because you are bad. But it's like my mind is a television. If I accidentally tune in on the old you-are-bad channel, now I can—thanks to therapy and AA—switch to a new channel. Sometimes I can even laugh

at that channel like it's an old comedy show. But other times it still hurts, and I sure as heck don't tell many people about it. They would think I was crazy for still thinking about things that happened 40 years ago.

In general, both the violent incidents and the emotional abuse that goes with them have more to do with the *abuser's* feelings of inadequacy and failure than any "failure" on the part of the victim. Violence in the home reflects the emotional temperament of the abuser, not the actions or personality of the victim.

Myth 2: I let it happen. The second myth underlying guilt and shame revolves around the victim allegedly having allowed the abuse. Although the abuser betrayed you by being abusive rather than loving, you may also feel as if you betrayed yourself—your dignity, your self-esteem, your worth as a person—by staying in a situation in which you were being harmed.

If you were abused as a child, you had no choice but to stay with your parent or caretaker—you were too emotionally and financially dependent to consider other options. However, as an adolescent, young adult, or adult, you may wonder about your sanity if you are still in a violent situation, or if you stayed in one longer than you felt you absolutely had to.

Am I a masochist? you may wonder. You may especially ask this question if you have been exposed to psychological theories that contend that you are only victimized or hurt if you allow yourself to be.

Such theories are unrealistic and inaccurate. They fail to take into account the multitude of ways in which even a bright, financially independent, and psychologically well-balanced individual can become entrapped in family violence. Such theories blame the victim as blatantly as if they alleged that victims of family violence cause the abuse through some overt action.

The following exercise will help you begin to overcome the destructive messages these myths of self-blame perpetuate.

Exercise: Pinpointing the Rage

Consider the following questions:

1. To what degree do you view yourself as responsible for the abuse or for being unable to stop it?

2. Are you more angry at yourself for supposedly precipitating or allowing the abuse than you are at your abuser?

If your answer to either of these question is yes, then you need to refer to the exercises on self-blame in Chapters 3 and 8 and be sure you have carefully noted all the ways in which your abuser had you entrapped. If you have trouble with this, the following section explains some of the many traps that operate in abusive situations. Read that section and make note of those traps that apply to your situation.

As you review your work on self-blame, jot down the ways in which your abuser or other individuals in your family or circle of friends blamed you for the abuse. In other forms of trauma, much of the self-blame stems from high standards people place on themselves from a desire to be in control of the situation. However, in family abuse situations, there are other sources of criticism. The message that "you are to blame," is not just internal, but external.

Also consider these questions:

3. How did your abuser blame you for the abuse?

4. How did others in your family hold you responsible? Specifically, what did these people say or how did they act to affirm the idea that the abuse was your fault?

Traps

There are numerous complex and powerful forces that keep people stuck in emotionally and physically destructive situations. Due to these forces, many times adolescents and adults can be as entrapped in their battering relationships as a preschool child would be.

If you are an adult man or woman currently in a battering relationship, whether heterosexual or homosexual, you may be or feel yourself to be stuck in it for reasons that have nothing to do with your alleged masochism. If you are being abused by someone you love, the ways they trap you may be physical, financial, or psychological. If you were battered or abused in the past, the same traps probably operated to keep you in the relationship.

Physical traps. Abusers often threaten to physically harm or kill their victims, other people, pets, or even themselves if the victim protests or reports the abuse or tries to leave the relationship. In some cases, the abuser prevents the victim from avoiding the abuse or leaving the relationship by literally locking the victim in a room or by using handcuffs or other means of confinement. If the victim is disabled, the abuser may threaten to exploit the disability in order to make the victim stay.

Financial traps. Abusers often financially imprison their victims by taking control of or squandering the victim's income or property or by threatening financial warfare or ruin should the victim decide to protest the abuse, leave the relationship, or otherwise "make difficulties." It is part of the pattern of control in abusive situations for the abuser to come to hold all the financial power in the family—either by psychological manipulation or through other forms of coercion. Such financial control is as powerful, if not more powerful, than the weapon of physical abuse.

Emotional traps. Still other traps are virtually invisible. These are the emotional traps. They can be even harder to overcome than the physical and economic chains that the abuser may have wrapped around you. Often these emotional traps revolve around love and need. Although you might be ashamed to tell your therapist, support group, or others, a part of you may still love the very person who has abused you. Abused children frequently have both intense love and hate for the abusive caretaker or parent.

One emotional trap is that the abuser may have brainwashed you into thinking that you are incompetent, inferior, and unable to live without him or her. Hence, even if you were in other ways able to leave the situation, the abuser has demoralized you so that you lack the confidence to face the world alone. (The irony is, however, that in many cases the abuser is more dependent on the victim, either emotionally or financially, than the victim is on the abuser. Even if the victim is a preadolescent child, the abusive parent or caretaker may be extremely emotionally dependent on that child.)

An abusive relationship becomes especially entrapping when the abuser is one of those who truly does love the victim. Even though the love may be mixed with unhealthy dependency and the abuser is using the victim as a scapegoat for present or past frustrations in life, the abuser may be genuinely bonded to and have real positive feelings for his or her victim.

On the other hand, your abuser may seem to be purely sadistic in behavior. He or she may not even pretend to love you, or may be ambivalent toward you and any other victims. In some cases, the abuser both loves and hates his or her victim.

Another force that keeps people in battering or sexually abusive relationships is the abuser's threat of suicide. Some abusers' extreme emotional dependence on their victim may "cause" them to threaten to kill themselves if the victim leaves. Such threats may be sincere or they may be attempts at manipulation. But even manipulators sometimes commit suicide. (In other cases, the abuser threatens not only suicide, but murder. Such murder-suicides are unfortunately not rare.)

Lisa describes her bind this way:

> I can't have my husband's blood on my hands. I just buried my parents. I couldn't take another funeral right now. Plus, he's told our children that if I leave him, he will kill himself and it will all be Mommy's fault if they don't have a daddy.
>
> I feel I have no choice but to stick with him at least a few more years, until the kids get older and can understand. I also have to feel I could handle it if he does kill himself.

In a similar type of emotional blackmail, perpetrators of sexual abuse threaten to abuse another family member should their original victim leave. Such threats are frequently followed through on, and the former victim blamed (by the abuser or others) for the new abuse. "My dad said he would stop abusing my younger sister if I would come back home. So I did," explains one survivor.

There are many strong reasons why both battering and incest victims have difficulty simply abandoning their homes or exposing their abuser. Incest victims, for example, often have roles as family caretakers. Many feel as if the continuity of the family depends on their caretaking services as well as on keeping the secret. Indeed, they are often correct. Numerous case studies have shown that when the incest survivor speaks out or when the battering victim leaves his or her abuser, the family can disintegrate emotionally, economically, and otherwise.

The Battering Cycle

One powerful emotional trap is the battering cycle. Lenore Walker (1979), the first psychologist to systematically study violent relationships, found that battering is neither random nor constant, especially when abuse occurs in the context of marriage or a sexual relationship. Instead, in many but not all cases, battering occurs in a repeated pattern, a cycle with three distinct stages:

1. The tension-building stage

2. The acute battering incident

3. The phase of kindness and contrite, loving behavior—the "honeymoon" stage

In stage one, the tension-building stage, tensions arise between the partners that ultimately lead to stage two, the acute battering incident. Then follows stage three, the honeymoon stage. Typically, in this stage the abuser is loving and kind and promises never again to hurt the victim or in some other way implies that the violence may be over. The abuser's repentance is totally believable, and the victim has true faith that there will be no more violence.

Stage three is powerful. In the case of the abused spouse or lover, it is in this stage that the victim's dream of love and romance is renewed. In hopes that the marriage or relationship is not really dead, the battering victim forgives his or her partner and stays. In the case of an abused child, it is in this stage that the child's dream of an attentive, affirming parent is revived. Feeling as if a miracle has occurred, the abused child excuses the parent and allows him- or herself to fully love and be open to that parent. Without the shield of hate and anger born of the abuse, the child is vulnerable to the abuser, who can use the child's vulnerability to psychologically manipulate the child for selfish goals.

This stage accounts for the enigmatic ability of abuse victims to quickly forget painful episodes, sometimes almost as soon as they occur, or to minimize them.

The battering cycle disproves the theory that battered adults are masochists who stay in abusive relationships because they like the violence. Most battering victims stay for the kiss, not the fist—for the love and attention of stage three, not the anxiety and physical and emotional pain of stages one and two. Similarly, incest victims who have difficulty breaking away from their abuser or who have mixed feelings toward their abuser should not be considered "sick."

Both battered women and incest victims may have protective, loving feelings toward their abuser because of the stage three affection the abuser has showered upon them.

Social isolation. The power of stage three is magnified by the fact that violent homes tend to be isolated. The abuser does his or her best to cut the victim off from other people and relationships, lest the victim realize that abuse is not normal and consequently try to leave. In addition, once violence begins in a home—whether physical, sexual, or both—the violence itself creates isolation. Other people tend to shy away from families where there is tension.

Furthermore, since much of the time and energy of the abuser and victim are spent on the many tensions and crises involved in their relationship—relatively few resources are left for involvements outside the home. Other family members also spend time and energy recovering from the episodes. In addition, they may be afraid to invite others to their home because they fear what an outsider might witness.

Deprived of the affirmation and validation of others, the victim of abuse becomes that much more vulnerable to the "attentions" of the abuser. The violence fosters or increases the victim's dependence on the abuser. Children already have a natural emotional and economic dependence on parents or caretakers, and many adult women (in particular) have been trained into such dependency. However, once the violence begins and then escalates, even someone who was fully independent before the relationship became abusive can become emotionally dependent on the abuser.

Exercise: Identifying and Defusing the Battering Cycle

Does the battering cycle described above describe your relationship with your abuser? If so, take some time to recognize and write about the specific forms the battering cycle has assumed in your experience. (Note that though these questions are phrased in the past tense, they apply equally to ongoing abuse.)

1. **The tension-rising stage.** During the tension-rising stage, what happened between you and the abuser? How did the tension rise? What kinds of incidents seemed to escalate tension? For example, was your abuser predictably angry when bills arrived, when dinner wasn't

ready on time, when the home was messy, when your grades were low, or when he or she had been drinking or taking drugs?

2. **The acute battering incident.** What happened during the battering? How long did battering incidents tend to last? Note what the abuser said as well as what he or she did. How did you react, both in terms of your behavior and your feelings?

3. **The honeymoon stage.** What kinds of gifts did you receive from the abuser? (Consider both gifts of affection as well as material gifts.) What promises did the abuser make? How long were these promises typically kept?

4. **Defusing the cycle.** Now that you have identified the cycle, can you see how the gifts, promises, and attentions of stage three served to entrap you? Are there ways you can give yourself the positive aspects of stage three or obtain the same gifts, promises, or attentions from other, nonabusive people?

Generation to Generation:
Inheriting Violence

After several counseling sessions, Albert (the formerly abused child you read about earlier in the chapter) finally shed some of his psychic numbing and began to become aware of his feelings. For example, he recalled that as he was being beaten as a little boy, he used to think to himself, When I grow up, I'm not going to be like you, Daddy. I hate you. I hate you.

But as Albert grew up, no one taught him the skills with which to handle anger or life frustrations appropriately. As a result, whenever he became frustrated or felt emasculated by a situation, at work for example, he would lash out at his wife, the same way his father had done toward him. It pained him greatly to find himself acting the way he had sworn he never would—like the man he had despised all his life, his father.

Hitting his wife did not solve Albert's problems; it only made them worse. Albert felt out of control, not only on the job and in other life situations, but out of control of himself. He was also aware that he was alienating his family:

> I've ruined my family, just like my dad did. My
> daughter calls me a monster, and she's right. I'm just like my
> dad. Is it genetic? Please tell me it isn't genetic.

Family violence is not genetic. However, it can be multigenerational, seemingly passed down from one generation to the next. For instance, little girls who grow up seeing their mothers being abused can learn to accept violence as a "normal" part of marriage. Little boys who see their mothers being beaten can learn that it is "okay" to hit one's wife. Children who are beaten or otherwise abused themselves learn that maltreatment is part of child rearing.

However, it is *not* true that most abused children grow up to be child abusers themselves. Nor do most children who witness violence between their parents become either the abuser or the victim in their marriages. In fact, some children growing up with violence become so repelled by any form of violence or harm that they fear to engage in even the mildest forms of discipline of their children or to express the gentlest forms of reproach or anger toward their partner.

On the other hand, there are individuals who grew up with violence who find themselves unable to refrain from practicing violence themselves, despite their sincere desire to not repeat the torment of their earlier years. Because their home was violent, they had little opportunity to learn nonviolent means of resolving interpersonal conflicts or managing stress. They also were never taught (or were poorly taught) the language of feelings. Consequently violence became their prime means of communicating their strongest feelings, rather than language or other forms of expression.

Parentified Children

In addition, children growing up in violent homes are rarely properly or sufficiently nurtured. In many cases, there is a role reversal in which a child takes care of one or both of his or her parents. The child may be abused him- or herself, and "parents" the abuser. Or one of the parents may be the victim, and the child is responsible for nurturing either the victim, the abuser, or both of them.

Such children are called *parentified* children in that they are prematurely forced to act like a parent or caretaker. At an age when the parents should be taking care of the child, the child is instead taking care of one or both of the parents. When the parentified child later becomes a parent, he or she may expect to be nurtured or parented by his or her own children (or spouse). And when that family member fails to provide the love, support, or help necessary, he or she may strike out.

Ways Out

All questions of morality aside, the battering of adults and children and child sexual abuse are illegal. Legal remedies are available and should be explored. These legal remedies may be limited and are sometimes not enforced properly or are unenforceable, but they do exist and should be considered.

Abused Adults

Since the majority of adult victims of battering are women, shelters and hotlines are geared primarily toward women. Abused women need to contact their local battered women's shelter or community crisis center for help, as well as the police.

Since law enforcement policy and social services vary not only from state to state, but county to county, your local authorities, local help hotlines, and local women's programs can provide you with the most accurate information as to what types of protection are available.

Generally, you can seek relief through either the civil or criminal court. From most civil courts you can obtain a protection order, a peace bond, a divorce or separation, child custody and visitation rights, child support, and money damages for personal injury. See Appendix B, under "Battering," for other sources of assistance.

Abused Children

If you are an abused child or one of your children is being abused, you can report the abuse to the local child protective services office. Since the states, not the federal government, have been given the responsibility for investigating child abuse and neglect, each state has its own child protective service reporting system. Some states have hotlines and toll-free numbers. The police, public library, or a mental health hotline can provide this number, as can your local city or county mental health or social services department.

If you are an abused child, you will not *automatically* be taken from your parents or caretakers. Although it used to be the case that authorities took the children into protective custody first and asked questions later, as of the writing of this book there is a new emphasis on keeping families together. However, this varies from place to place, and child abuse legislation and philosophies are constantly changing. For complete and updated information, contact your local child protective services agency. See Appendix B, under "Child Abuse," for other sources of assistance.

14

Suicide of a Loved One

Guidelines for Using This Book

This chapter is written for suicide survivors—not those who have attempted suicide and survived, but the relatives, friends, co-workers, and other associates of suicide victims. The exercises in this chapter are designed to help you understand the significance of the suicide in your life, clarify your feelings of guilt and shame, reduce unwarranted self-blame, and guide you through the special grieving issues that affect suicide survivors. Since clinical depression is prevalent among suicide survivors, you will need to assess yourself for clinical depression and follow the suggestions regarding depression in Chapter 2. You will also need to pay special attention to and complete the exercises in Chapter 4 regarding victim thinking, and those in Chapter 9 on grief.

The Emotional Aftermaths of Suicide: PTSD and Depression

In some cultures, suicide is an act of heroism; in others, an act of cowardice. Our culture generally views suicide as shameful, for both the victim and the survivors. Those who commit suicide are often judged to be emotional weaklings, moral failures, or otherwise deficient. They are blamed for not being "strong enough" to endure the pain of living and those associated with them tend to be blamed, shamed, and stigmatized as well.

Not so long ago, it was believed that suicide ran in families and that some families had a "suicide gene" or hereditary defect (Victoroff 1983). Today, a suicide in the family is seen by some as indicating that the family failed the victim or that individual members of the family failed to function as competent spouses, parents, siblings, or children. In some religious faiths, suicide is seen as a sin. Given such attitudes, it is no wonder that many families keep the suicide of their loved one a secret, calling it death by heart attack, accidental poisoning, or unknown causes.

Along with the feelings of shame and guilt such attitudes foster, often even more severe effects are felt: a prolongation and intensification of the grieving process, clinical depression, and post-traumatic stress disorder.

Suicide and PTSD

If you witnessed the suicide, discovered the body, or were in some way exposed to violence or aggression concerning the suicide, you are at risk for developing acute stress disorder or long-term post-traumatic stress disorder (Grossman et al. 1995, Brent et al. 1995). You are also at risk for developing PTSD if the suicide brought to the surface a previous trauma in your life that prior to the suicide you had been able to manage with minimal stress symptoms.

If you had been previously been traumatized, the suicide of a child, spouse, sibling, or close friend may have tipped your internal balance, bringing forth all the feelings and reactions that belonged to your original trauma. In that case, you will be coping not only with the suicide, but with the traumatic feelings and memories belonging to the past. This double trauma prolongs your adjustment to the suicide and make it more painful and complex.

PTSD following a suicide also tends to develop when there is family history of depression, substance abuse, or suicide; when survivors themselves have a history of depression, substance abuse, suicide attempts; or when the survivor is a child who either discovered the body or witnessed some domestic discord prior to the suicide of a parent (Grossman et al. 1995, Brent et al. 1995). In such cases, children tend to blame themselves not only for the parental fighting but for the subsequent suicide. In cases of marital suicide-homicide, where one parent kills the other and then commits suicide, the emotional scars on the child are even more devastating.

Clinical Depression and Suicide

While PTSD is one possible consequence to survivors of suicide, more common is the development of a clinical depression or an intensification of the depression stage of the grieving process. A growing body of research suggests that suicide survivors often have a longer and more agonizing grieving process than those who are mourning the death of a loved one due to accident, illness, or natural causes (Smith et al. 1995; Brent et al. 1993a, 1994).

Unlike other mourners, suicide survivors have to deal with the issues of shame and social stigma. Their self-blame and guilt tend to be more intense than that of other mourners, as does their anger towards the deceased. It is often difficult for anyone grieving the loss of a loved one to admit feeling anger at the dead person for leaving or abandoning them, but it is especially hard for suicide survivors. Yet unless this anger is confronted the grieving process is arrested.

At highest risk for developing a clinical depression following the suicide of a loved one are mothers, siblings, and children of the suicide victim, adolescent friends of the victim, and individuals who already suffer from PTSD or other symptoms of depression due to previous trauma (Brent 1993b, Valente and Saunders 1993, Rappaport 1994, Van der Walk 1989–90).

Rising Suicide Rates

Every 20 seconds someone in the United States commits suicide (Heckler 1994). In 1985, suicide was the ninth leading cause of death in the United States (Bhatia, Khan, and Sharma 1986). Today, it is the eighth leading cause of death (Heckler 1994). Between 1960 and 1991, the annual suicide rate of rose from 16.6 to 18.7 per 100,000 persons (Seltzer 1994).

One of the most noticeable trends in these statistics is that the suicide rate among adolescents and young people up to the age of 25 has almost tripled (MMWR 1995). There is also a striking rise in suicide among young African American men and those of other minorities. The suicide rate reached an all-time high for white males in 1988, but has been relatively stable since. However, the rate for minority males has escalated since 1986, substantially reducing prior differences between white and nonwhite teen suicide rates for males (MMWR 1995; Shaffer, Gould, and Hicks 1994).

Since 1960, suicide rates have also risen among elderly men in general (Seltzer 1994).

Homicide, Suicide, or Accident?

Despite the preceding statistics, the true rates of suicide are unknown. Whether a death is a suicide is not always clear. For example, some one-car collisions and other vehicular accidents are undoubtedly suicidal—but which ones? It is impossible to interview the victim to determine whether the cause of death was a driving error or a sincere wish to die. The same problem arises regarding certain poisonings or drug overdoses. Were they accidental, or intentional?

Along similar lines, alcohol and drug abuse, as well as other forms of self-destructive behavior, can be seen as "minisuicides," which for some people ultimately lead to death. Such deaths, however, are typically not included in suicide statistics.

Likewise, if an individual provokes another person—a spouse, the police, a drunken or armed stranger or attacker, or a violent known enemy—into murder, the death will probably be listed as murder, not suicide. Wolfgang, who studied spouse murders, theorizes that men who view suicide as "unmasculine" or "passive," but who nevertheless harbor serious suicidal wishes, may achieve their death wish not by killing themselves directly, but by placing themselves in dangerous situations where they invite another person's attack (Wolfgang 1956, 1969).

Are you wondering if your loved one committed suicide or whether the death was an accident? Is there a possibility that the victim arranged circumstances so that he or she, would be killed? Answers to these questions may not be available to you now; they may never be available. Yet your need to know may be urgent. For example, if you were certain the death was due to an accident or homicide, you would be delivered from a considerable amount of self-blame and social stigma. But if you don't know the facts, it is hard to make sense of the death or know how to respond to it emotionally. The agony you may be experiencing due to not knowing the truth may be yet another source of the anger you have regarding the suicide.

Causes of Suicide

Not everyone who commits suicide does so for the same reason. They kill themselves for a variety of reasons, often for more than one. Some of the classical reasons for suicide include revenge, the wish to end pain, and the desire to reconnect or unite with a deceased loved one—a child, parent, or buddy. In Shakespeare's *Romeo and Juliet*, Juliet kills herself to be reunited with Romeo. Some combat vets speak of suicide as a means of rejoining their dead buddies.

Suicide can also be an act of self-assertion or a means of taking control over one's life. History brims with examples of men and women trapped in horrible circumstances in which they had little or no control over their fate. Their only means of escape and self-determination was to take their own lives. They killed themselves to preserve their dignity and self-respect and to defy those who had enslaved them.

Suicide can also be an act of self-hatred as well as an act of hostility toward others. In many cases, suicide is the result of untreated or inadequately treated clinical depression or depressions so severe that individuals can no longer resist their suicidal thoughts.

In his book *Waking Up Alive*, Dr. Richard Heckler (1994) discusses additional causes of suicide, including the following:

- Penetrating hopelessness—The person's state of mind is such that feelings of hopelessness penetrate every or almost every aspect of his or her life.

- Inner chaos—The person experiences so much ambivalence about so many aspects of himself or herself and feels so indecisive in matters large and small that he or she feels without identity and unable to relate to others.

- Unbearable or unending pain—An emotional or physical condition of so much agony exists that death seems like the only remedy.

- Acknowledgment—The person hopes to find in death the recognition and appreciation he or she did not receive in life.

- Desire for peace and calm—The person has exhausted his or her ability to cope with stress and sees death as a means of obtaining love, peace, and relief for current exploitation and suffering.

Precipitating Events

Notice that the above list does not include reasons such as failing an exam, being served with divorce papers, losing a job, being forgotten on one's birthday, arguing with a friend or relative, being slighted by a relative, or losing a lover to a best friend—although such events are often perceived as the "cause" of someone's suicide.

Therapists term them precipitating events, yet a single occurrence seldom causes a person's suicide. (Exceptions include instances of catastrophic trauma. For example, in war and refugee situations, people may commit suicide after witnessing family members being slaughtered or witnessing or being forced to participate in other atrocities.)

Unhappy and traumatic events can push an individual further into depression or closer to a suicide state. However, in general, suicide does not occur because of a precipitating event but because this event occurred in the context of a chain of numerous other negative events that are interpreted by the individual in despairing or vengeful ways.

As an example, if a woman commits suicide soon after her husband leaves her, her husband's departure may be seen as the precipitating event. He will undoubtedly feel guilty, as if he caused the suicide, and family members and friends might also point the finger at him, disregarding this woman's history, mental status, or current life stressors totally unrelated to her marriage. Yet clearly, by itself divorce causes relatively few women (or men) to kill themselves. However, the loss of a love relationship can lead to addiction or other self-destructive behavior, even suicide, if some of the following conditions contribute to the situation and the person does not receive adequate help:

- The woman erroneously interpreted her husband's departure to mean she would never love or be loved again, while also believing that life was not worth living without love or marriage.

- The woman suffered from low self-esteem, depression, or other problems in addition to the breakup. The departure of her husband simply confirmed her deep belief that she was evil or worthless and life wasn't worth living.

- The woman did not have access to a support system or professional help. Either she had no friends or family she could turn to or she could not afford or was not aware of available professional support.

- The woman had easy access to a means of committing suicide. (Higher suicide rates tend to exist in areas with easier access to handguns or among professionals who have access to medications [Richard and Young 1995].)

- The woman was coping with other major losses or stressors at the same time; for example, she had just lost her job and both of her parents recently died in a car crash.

- The woman did not know how to communicate her feelings. Killing herself was her way of telling the world how she felt.

- The woman's therapist, physician, or other health care worker did not monitor her properly.

- The woman needed antidepressants or other medications to help her cope with her losses, but she did not have access to them.

These are but a few of many examples of factors that contribute to suicide. But no one of them by itself would probably be enough to cause a suicide. Likewise, while precipitating events are often blamed for the suicide of an individual, they are also not sufficient to cause a suicide.

Suicide and Self-Blame

Every person who commits suicide leaves behind parents, family members, friends, neighbors, and others who are beset not only with grief but with a multitude of agonizing, often-unanswerable questions: Why did it happen? Did I miss some of the warning signs? Why didn't I pay attention to the warning signs I did see? What could I have done to prevent it? What could others have done? Who is really to blame? How much am I to blame?

As a suicide survivor, you need to gain a clearer picture of the suicide of your loved one and any part you may have played in it. Completing the following exercise will give you a more accurate picture of what, if any, aspects of the suicide you are responsible for, and what aspects were out of your control.

No written exercise can erase the survivor guilt. Such guilt can last a lifetime, and some of it is beyond any "rethinking" process; for many survivors, this guilt is a gut phenomenon. However, the following exercise will help you obtain a more complete and global view of the suicide, and come to see that the suicide of your loved one probably cannot be accounted for by a single precipitating event or a single action on your part or anyone else's.

It bears repeating that you may carry some guilt, founded or unfounded, and the self-loathing that such guilt can breed, to the grave. However, after completing this exercise, you will have a clearer idea of what you feel guilty about, and you may find some relief from unnecessary or unfounded guilt and shame.

In this exercise, you will attempt to distinguish your actions (or inactions) that may have truly contributed to the death of your loved one from those actions that did not, even thought you, due to extreme guilt and shame, irrationally or illogically feel that they did.

Exercise: Clarifying Survivor Guilt

1. Pretend you are a newspaper reporter. Write a life history of your loved one, including the story of the suicide. Be as detailed as possible. If you need more information about your loved one or the suicide itself, try to get it from relatives, friends, doctors, or other health care providers. When you cannot ascertain the truth, indicate this in your report.

2. As part of your newspaper article, pretend you are interviewing those who knew your loved one. Or if you can, actually speak with these people. Ask each person what they thought of the deceased, why they think he or she committed suicide, whether they feel responsible, and if so, in what way?

   Ask the respondents to be as specific as possible. For example, if Aunt Mary feels she contributed to the suicide by frequently criticizing the victim, ask Aunt Mary to specify in what ways she was critical, how often she criticized the deceased, and how the deceased reacted. Also inquire of Aunt Mary how the supported or otherwise interacted positively with the deceased.

3. When you feel you have a fairly complete picture of the victim's life, examine that life in terms of the causes of suicide discussed above, and review the criteria for post-traumatic stress disorder in Chapter 1 and the criteria for clinical depression, alcohol or drug addiction, and eating disorders in Chapter 2. If your loved one suffered from one of these maladies, he or she was already at higher risk for suicide than most persons. To blame yourself for your loved one's suicide would then involve blaming yourself solely or largely for his or her PTSD, depression, or addictive behavior, Is this, really the case?

4. To further obtain a more balanced perspective of the life of the suicide victim, review the various reasons each relative or friend of the de-

ceased thinks contributed to the suicide. For each reason offered, ask them to provide you with evidence proving their assertion.

5. Still trying to stay objective, interview yourself. What was your relationship like with the deceased? Do you feel you contributed to the suicide or could have prevented it? If so, specify in detail how you feel you are to blame.

   Then, as with the others you interviewed, put in writing the positive aspects of your relationship with the deceased. Once again, be as specific as possible in documenting the ways that you showed love and acceptance and had positive experiences with the deceased.

6. As with the other suicide survivors you interviewed, review the reasons you feel you contributed to the death of your loved one, and provide solid evidence for each point.

The purpose of this exercise is to obtain an overall view of the suicide victim's life. Hopefully, you will see that what you did or did not do was only part of a large, complex picture. You were probably not the only person who was important to the suicide victim. Also, if many of the individuals whom you interviewed feel responsible to some degree for the suicide, then it probably is impossible that you are the sole or major cause of suicide.

False Guilts

In Chapter 3, two types of false guilts were discussed: "I should have known better guilt" and Catch 22 Guilt. Suicide survivors can suffer needlessly from one or both as the following stories illustrate.

> After Tom, age 15, lost his girlfriend, he began spending long periods of time alone and stopped socializing with family and friends. When Tom told his parents that he planned to kill himself, they told him that many young people felt that way when they lost their first love and that soon he would find a new girlfriend and forget about the one who left him. When Tom told his parents a second time that he was going to kill himself, his parents told him he didn't know what he was talking about and that he should be grateful for all he had in life.
>
> Tom continued to keep to his room and to talk about suicide. His parents recognized the warning signs at that point and rushed Tom to a psychiatrist, who hospitalized Tom immediately. After two months of inpatient therapy and a few weeks of outpatient treatment, it seemed as if the suicidal crisis has subsided. Tom no longer looked forlorn and no longer talked about death.
>
> Several months later, however, Tom went into his

bedroom and killed himself with a handgun.

Tom's parents were fraught with guilt. Had they missed a warning sign? No, they had not. In fact, there was no indication that Tom was once again suicidal. After the suicidal crisis had subsided, Tom had appeared calmer and happier. The therapist was convinced that Tom's depression had lifted and that he was out of danger. But, unknown to Tom's parents or his therapist, Tom's apparent improvement was the result of his inner decision to commit suicide at some future time, and thereby terminate what he perceived to be an unbearably painful and hopeless existence.

Tom's parents blame themselves for not keeping him in inpatient treatment longer and for not keeping a more careful watch on him once he came home. They also blame his therapist for not perceiving Tom's suicidality. But Tom had deceived his therapist and his parents into thinking all was well. Tom's parents suffer profoundly from "I should have known better guilt," yet they could not have known better.

Until Marilyn received help, she was burdened with Catch-22 guilt.

Marilyn's boyfriend, Barry was heavily addicted to drugs and stole money from her. Marilyn tolerated the stealing, but when Barry's drug-addicted friends began harassing her teenage daughter and threatened to rape and prostitute her if Marilyn did not provide them with funds for their drug habit, Marilyn quickly left, taking her checking account and her child with her.

Six days later Barry committed suicide. In his suicide note, he stated that he had killed himself because Marilyn had abandoned him. Marilyn felt both guilty and angry at Barry for making her feel guilty. Yet staying with him would have put her daughter in danger, and she would have felt guilty and angry about that. Marilyn was clearly in a Catch-22 position.

Another example of a Catch-22 is Carol's story.

Carol was being incestuously abused by her uncle. The uncle said that if Carol told anyone he would commit suicide. Carol remained silent until she saw her uncle make advances to her younger sisters. At this point Carol informed her parents and they called the police. Before the police arrived, Carol's uncle committed suicide and left a note blaming Carol for his death.

If Carol had not reported the abuse, her sisters would have been molested, but by turning in her uncle, she took the risk that he would act on his promise to commit suicide—a classic Catch-22 bind.

Childhood omnipotent guilt. Another form of guilt is childhood omnipotent guilt—a well-documented tendency of young children to think that the world revolves around them and that they control everything that happens. Young children think that if they wish something it might come true. For example, when children become frustrated with a parent or sibling, they often think or say, I hate you—I wish you were dead, which is a perfectly normal expression of aggression. But, if for some reason that parent or sibling subsequently becomes ill, dies, or leaves the family, the child thinks that he or she caused this person to become ill, die, or leave.

This is called magical thinking, because hating one's parent, sibling, spouse, or friend, or even wishing another person dead, does not cause these people harm unless the aggressive wish is acted upon.

No matter how old or how mature we may be, a part of us—consciously or unconsciously—may still be engaging in magical thinking or seeing ourselves as omnipotent. When someone we know commits suicide, the child in us may feel that our hostility killed that person because we sometimes harbored hostile feelings toward him or her.

But hating people doesn't kill them. Our angry, hateful feelings and wishes in themselves cannot cause the physical death or suicide of another, with one important exception: if you severely or continually maltreated someone, and then that person committed suicide, some of your guilt may be appropriate. If not, some of the guilt you are experiencing may fall into the category of childhood omnipotent guilt.

Exercise: Identifying Your Guilt

Consider the three kinds of guilt described above: "I should have known better" guilt, Catch-22 guilt, and childhood omnipotent guilt.

1. Refer back to the writing you did in the preceding "life history" exercise. Do any of the reasons that you or others feel to blame for the suicide fall into any of the categories of false guilt? If so, which ones?

2. For each of the reasons you felt guilty, but now can view in the light of one of the three types of false guilt, write a paragraph reinterpreting your behavior and guilt in those terms.

3. Now consider the remaining actions or inactions about which you feel entitled to feel guilty. For each action ask yourself the following questions:

   • What were your motivations at the time?

   • Did you wish or desire the suicide or death of your friend or relative, or were you ignorant of your friend's emotional state or vulnerability to suicide?

- If you hadn't acted as you did, what is the probability that your loved one might have committed suicide at some other time?

Coping with the Effects on Your Life

The suicide of a loved one has been found to bring profound changes in the life-style, identity, health, and life goals of suicide survivors. You may assess some of these changes as positive, others as negative. Some of the changes you may want to retain; you may wish others did not exist. However, the first step toward any kind of change is to identify the specific ways the suicide has changed you and your life.

Exercise: Assessing the Impact of the Suicide

To the best of your ability, in your journal, answer the following questions as completely as possible:

1. How has the suicide changed your attitude towards yourself in your various roles—within the family, with friends, in the community, and on the job? Which of these changes do you wish to retain? Which do you wish to alter?

2. How has the suicide affected your behavior at home, at work, or with friends and intimates? Which of these behaviors do you deem positive and wish to keep? Which do you dislike and wish to eliminate or reduce in frequency?

3. Did the suicide heighten your anxiety about the meaning of life or otherwise raise spiritual or existential questions for you? What questions did it raise? Have you discussed these questions with people you trust or whose opinions you respect? What has prevented you from reaching out to others?

4. What role did the suicide victim play in your life? What empty spots have been left due to his or her death? Did the victim have a special relationship with you that no one else can fill? Write down what was precious and unique about your relationship with the deceased.

5. Your loved one can never be replaced. However, there may be ways that some of the needs your loved one fulfilled in your life can be met, at least in part, by others. In your opinion, are there any ways others can help to fill some of the emptiness left by the death of your loved one? What internal or external obstacles would you face in reaching out to these people or trying to meet your needs? Would you be criticized by others for reaching? If so, by whom? Would you feel you were betraying the memory of your loved one or otherwise feel guilty if you were to begin to reach out to others?

6. Are there any ways in which your relationship with the suicide victim helped to compensate for deficiencies in other relationships or areas in your life? What lacks in your life has the suicide of your loved one highlighted? For example, if you were especially close to a sibling, did that closeness to your sibling help compensate for emotional distance or other problems between you and your parents or for other deficits in your life, such as the lack of a love relationship or a job you find meaningful?

7. Which of these unmet needs or unsatisfactory situations must you accept because they cannot be changed and which can be improved through constructive action on your part?

8. What is the meaning of the suicide of your loved one in your life? Are you seeing the suicide, for example, as validation of your incompetence as a parent or partner or friend? Do you view the suicide as further evidence that life is not worthwhile? Do you view the suicide as a confirmation of parts of yourself that you judge to be negative or undesirable?

9. Has the suicide resulted in any positive action or attitudes on your part? Has the death of your loved one prompted you to take more control over your life and to take your life goals, needs, and desires more seriously? Have you grown closer to other family members or people as a result? Or has the suicide put a wedge in your relationships with family, intimates, friends, co-workers, and others?

Acknowledging Your Anger

If the suicide changed your like in negative ways, you are entitled to feel angry at a variety of people, including the suicide victim.

> Joseph, for example, kicked the grave of his dead brother. "Why did you leave me?" he growled. "You were my only brother and my best friend too. Now I have to help mom and everybody get over losing you. I hate you! I hate you! Why didn't you stay alive, for me? I needed you. You know that. Yet still you did it. How could you do this to me?"

Suicide survivors often feel like Joseph, but unlike Joseph, they find it hard to acknowledge or accept their anger at the deceased—much less express it so openly and freely. Yet every time someone we love or need dies, it feels like an abandonment, even if that person died unwillingly. You may feel that the suicide victim you are grieving had a choice. They didn't have to kill themselves, you might think. But not you nor anyone else knows that for sure.

Perhaps he or she didn't have a choice. Not all suicides are preventable—even by the victim. Your loved one's depression may have been too great or his or her circumstances too oppressive. Most certainly he or she felt as if there were no other choice; otherwise the deceased would not have exercised the option of self-destruction.

Nevertheless you are entitled to feel abandoned and angry at the victim not only for leaving you, but for leaving you with a legacy of guilt and shame, as well as the loss. If you do not acknowledge the anger you have, some of the anger you have toward the deceased may be turned in on yourself and experienced as depression or depressive feelings. Or you may find yourself intensely angry at others whom you feel contributed to the death of your loved one: members of the family, associates, or health care providers.

Perhaps some of these people did emotionally or otherwise hurt the suicide victim, and maybe some of the health care providers were negligent or did not do their utmost for your loved one. Perhaps the therapist, priest, clergyman, spouse, sibling, or employer of your loved one did not comprehend the severity of his or her depression or desperation. Perhaps someone failed to insist on hospitalization or failed to inform you of how vulnerable your loved one was to suicide. It may well be that your anger toward others is justified and grounded in the reality of their actions or attitudes. However, it is also possible that some of the anger you feel toward others, or yourself, is anger towards the deceased, which you are displacing onto yourself or others.

Exercise: Therapeutic Letter Writing

To help define and delineate the various angers and other types of feelings you may be having, do the following exercise.

1. Write your deceased loved one a letter, or several letters. In writing these letters, you may discover levels of grief, confusion, regret, self-hatred, and anger you did not know existed. If so, it is strongly suggested that you seek the services of a qualified therapist or counselor.

2. If you feel that other people contributed to the suicide of your loved one, write cathartic letters to them as well. You may want to write to the deceased's parents, neighbors, friends, siblings, doctors, clergyperson, lovers, co-workers, or others.

These letters are not intended to be literary masterpieces, nor are they to be sent to the individuals. Their purpose is to help you comprehend the full range of your feelings toward all who were involved in the life and death of your loved one.

Additional Coping Suggestions

Grieving the loss of a loved one through suicide is a painfully long process. Yet without embarking on this grieving process, your own development in a variety of areas may be impeded. Any unresolved guilt and anger you have may prevent you from forming relationships, developing your vocational potential, or discovering your creativity.

It is critical at this time that you seek a supportive environment where you can share your feelings and not be judged. You also need to carefully monitor yourself for signs of depression, post-traumatic stress disorder, or health problems that may be related to the stress of the suicide. Rather than think about erasing the memories from your mind, think in terms of how you can cope with the memories and feelings day by day.

You may also want to participate in a suicide survivors support group. See Appendix B for suggestions on finding groups.

15

Natural Catastrophes

Guidelines for Using This Book

If you are a natural catastrophe survivor, carefully review the exercises on self-blame in Chapters 3 and 8 with an eye toward any irrational answers to the question Why me? Although it is illogical for you to assume that a tornado or hurricane or some other natural catastrophe occurred because of some character defect or behavior on your part, it is critical that you become aware of any hidden or lingering suspicions you may have that you were the cause.

In reading about anger in Chapter 8, do not hesitate to list the catastrophe as a source of your anger. Also include the individuals or agencies that you feel contributed to the devastating effects of the disaster or that failed to provide needed or promised assistance. Especially relevant for you will be Chapter 10 on empowerment.

PTSD and Natural Catastrophe Survivors

If you have experienced a storm, flood, fire, earthquake, or volcanic eruption that caused death and destruction, you too could develop partial or even full-blown PTSD, in addition to other stress symptoms. Developing these stress reactions is not inevitable, but if you do find yourself suffering long-term reactions to the trauma, you are not alone.

Studies from around the world, including the United States, South America, Southeast Asia, and Europe, indicate that people who have endured major onslaughts from the forces of nature can develop a host of stress reactions. The symptoms range from depression, anxiety, and psychosomatic complaints, to partial or full PTSD. Some individuals also develop phobias or compulsive rituals, which may serve symbolically as attempts to prevent the disaster from recurring (Green et al. 1990; Langley and Gasner 1991; Sorenson 1990a,b).

For example, earthquake survivors in Greece, Italy, and Ecuador have manifested depression, anxiety, problems eating and sleeping (including nightmares), and numerous physical complaints with no medical basis. Following the October 1989 Loma Prieta earthquake in Northern California, survivors reported similar symptoms. Emotional distress was especially high among those who were unmarried, were in poor health, or who already had major economic or other problems. In addition, nightmares and other PTSD symptoms were also noted in survivors of Hurricane Hugo.

Also after the California earthquake, some survivors—adults as well as children—insisted on sleeping in the open. Increases in domestic violence, sexual abuse, and family arguments were common as much as eight months after the quake (Sorenson 1990b).

Natural Catastrophes vs. Other Types of Trauma

It is commonly thought that, in general, survivors of natural catastrophes suffer less psychological devastation than survivors of traumas caused by human beings (such as war, crime, and domestic violence). There are two reasons for such thinking. The first is that natural catastrophes tend to be shorter in duration than man-made ones. A tornado may last less than 15 seconds, for example, whereas a war can last months or years.

The second reason given is that natural catastrophes do not involve human error, betrayal, or violence. Crime victims, for example, are violated not by the impersonal forces of nature, but by one or more of their fellow human beings. In the case of family violence, the trauma is not perpetrated by a stranger, but rather by one's own flesh and blood. Hence, it is argued, victims of these and other man-made disasters must deal with the issue of trust in their healing process. In contrast, survivors of natural catastrophes are presumed not to have to grapple with the issue of trust.

However, such reasoning does not take into account two significant aspects of natural disasters: the man-made elements involved in most natural disasters, and the impact of the recovery environment on the natural disaster survivor. Both the recovery environment and the recovery process usually are, in today's world, heavily influenced by human beings and governmental and other institutions. And, to make matters worse, both domestic violence and stranger crime can run rampant following a natural catastrophe.

Although we cannot control weather or geologic events, modern technology has made tremendous strides toward preventing or lessening much of the death and destruction that used to result from natural catastrophes, as well as in assisting survivors in the recovery process (Lindy 1985). However, warning systems, emergency services, and disaster-relief agencies still have limitations. In some cases, these limitations can be experienced as betrayal by survivors of the catastrophe.

In addition, warning systems and other parts of an infrastructure sometimes simply fail. For example, in April 1991, the failure of a tornado-warning siren in Andover, Kansas more than contributed to a dozen deaths (*Washington Post*, 30 April 1991). Similarly, the freeway collapse that caused numerous deaths during the Loma Prieta earthquake can be seen as a technological failure, although its cause was the earthquake.

Thus, survivors of natural catastrophes frequently direct much of their rage at those individuals or agencies perceived to be the cause of such failure, rather than at the impersonal forces of nature that are the underlying cause.

Common Reactions to Natural Catastrophes

Not only the victims of natural catastrophes, but police officials, firefighters, medical personnel, and others involved in rescue and relief efforts suffer from PTSD and other stress symptoms. The exposure to death and injury and the destruction of homes, public buildings, and sometimes entire communities and cities seems to affect all involved (McFarlane 1986, 1988).

Social workers Keith Langley and Linda Gasner (1991) compiled the following list of common adult reactions to earthquakes:

- Feelings of being personally victimized

- Frustration, intolerance, and irritability

- Emotional numbness

- Changes in appetite—inability to eat or overeating

- Impaired memory or difficulty in concentrating

- Nightmares and other sleeping problems

- Substance abuse for self-medicating purposes

- Feelings of being overwhelmed or easily fatigued

- Somatic complaints, including headaches and gastrointestinal problems

- Anxiety or fear that the "big quake is yet to happen"

- Insecurity in both inter- and intrapersonal relationships

- Anger toward city, county, emergency, and federal organizations

- Grief over loss of loved ones, property, possessions, or landmarks

- Intrusive recollections or flashbacks of the event

- Psychogenic amnesia regarding important details of the event or its aftermath
- Sense of foreshortened future
- Feelings of omnipotence
- Avoidance of discussing the event or its effect
- Denial that the earthquake had any emotional effect

Although it is not documented, it is likely that these symptoms also apply to survivors of other types of natural catastrophe. Other reactions are also possible.

How Long Do Symptoms Last?

It has been found that, in general, during natural disasters people react calmly and appropriately. Only a small percentage become hysterical or immobilized in other ways. However, after the acute crisis has subsided, many of those who reacted so rationally at the time develop symptoms that reveal their emotional reactions to the disaster (Horowitz 1985, Mitchell 1986).

As with other types of trauma, the duration of stress symptoms resulting from natural catastrophes varies from person to person and situation to situation. But studies indicate that PTSD and PTSD-like symptoms tend to decrease over time. For example, following Cyclone Tracy, reports of psychiatric and emotional distress gradually decreased over a period of 14 months following the cyclone. In the long term, however, survivors of the cyclone still tended to have more emotional problems than the general population (Green et al. 1990).

Similarly, a study of the survivors of the 1972 flood in Buffalo Creek, West Virginia showed that although 14 years later there had been major decreases in reported symptoms, one-fourth of the survivors sampled continued to suffer from full-blown PTSD. However, since not all of the survivors were available or willing to participate in the study, this figure may or may not accurately reflect the incidence of PTSD among the flood's survivors.

The Waxing and Waning of Symptoms

Among natural catastrophe survivors, as among survivors of other traumas, a pattern of waxing and waning of symptoms can occur. For example, you may have experienced some symptoms immediately after the crisis. Then symptoms diminished or disappeared for several months, only to reemerge two or three years later in response to a current crisis or loss, or perhaps for no readily apparent reason.

Yet there is a reason: survival. Mardi Horowitz (1985), who has studied reactions to disasters for many years, explains that "even in conditions of relative safety, pangs of fear may return, for the threat is recorded in memory and the human mind tends to review the threat to prepare for its possible repetition." In other words, you continue to experience fear, grief, anger, and other symptoms associated with the catastrophe, because subconsciously your mind is reviewing the disaster in case it happens again. You may or may not be thinking of the event or be near a trigger that reminds you of it, but the event is permanently recorded in your memory.

The Resurrection of Unresolved Emotional Issues

A traumatic encounter with a natural catastrophe can bring to the fore one or more unresolved emotional issues. Internal conflicts or conflicts with significant others that in the past you were willing or able to let slide may have come to the forefront of your mind.

Perhaps something occurred during the disaster that involved one of your issues. Suppose you always felt your mother cared more for one of your siblings than she did for you. During the natural disaster, you noticed that she called out that sibling's name before yours. Even though there may have been no special meaning to whose name your mother called out first—she simply called out the name of the child closest to her, for example—you might feel rejected by her. And that feeling could revive similar feelings if you had felt rejected by your mother in the past. In short, your interpretation of her actions is what matters.

A natural disaster can also bring to the fore negative feelings you have toward others. For example, if your property was destroyed and the property of someone you disliked was less damaged, your dislike of that individual might drastically increase. On the other hand, if the reverse were true, and your property was less damaged than that of someone you disliked, you might experience joy, guilt, or other feelings you will have to deal with.

Being in a natural catastrophe can also resurrect any childhood or other traumas that you had repressed or discounted. For example, during the Persian Gulf War, a number of returning veterans were traumatized not so much by their experience in the Middle East, but by the memories of childhood trauma that the war brought to the forefront of their minds.

Perhaps you were physically or sexually abused as a child, or had been the victim of a crime or other trauma before the natural catastrophe, but you somehow avoided dealing with the earlier trauma until the present one put you on overload, and now you have both of them to cope with. Richard's story is a case in point.

Richard lived in an area struck by Hurricane Hugo. He was not directly injured by the hurricane nor were his property losses significant. However, he did see the body of a woman who had died in the storm, which caused him to begin dreaming about his early childhood.

When Richard was four years old, his father beat Richard's mother to death. Richard witnessed both her death and earlier beatings and had been abused himself, but he had successfully blotted out those memories until the sight of the woman's mangled body brought them back.

The Effects of Secondary Traumas

Natural catastrophes occur over a shorter period of time than war, concentration camp, or family violence experiences. However, the physical recovery of a community from a natural disaster can take months, if not years. In the United States, citizens affected by natural disasters are often surprised by how long resumption of services and reconstruction can take.

Although not as obviously traumatic as loss of property, physical injury, and the injury or death of loved ones, disruption of services and destruction of the public infrastructure or neighborhoods also take their toll. Failure of communications systems and increased demands on the police may lead to looting and other crimes, which, of course, affect survivors of the initial disaster. Also, as mentioned earlier, domestic violence becomes more prevalent following disasters.

Individuals who depend on specialized medical services or medical technology for their physical well-being may suffer due to the overburdening of medical services caused by the disaster. Other "hidden" traumas often accompany natural catastrophes as well; for example, it is not unusual for people to die of heart attacks or other medical problems related to stress and shock. These deaths are not included in official statistics of disaster-related deaths; however, they can deeply affect family members and friends, who then have a personal death to cope with in addition to their other losses.

Individuals who are seriously injured by the catastrophe may endure not only their injuries but rejection by others. Research shows that mates sometimes reject an incapacitated or scarred spouse. Debilitated individuals may also suffer job loss (Frances and Perry 1983).

Exercise: Identifying Losses

In Chapter 9 you were asked to specify your losses. More specifically, you were asked to list the financial, emotional, social, vocational, and other losses you sustained as a result of the trauma and any secondary wounding experiences that followed. However, you may have failed to include losses pertaining to your community.

In natural disasters, entire communities rather than individuals are affected. As with your personal losses, your community's losses may be financial, emotional, social, and spiritual. These losses, and their impact on you, need to be included in your list.

You may, for example, have lost your entire community or a significant part of it. You may have had to move away or the community may have been so damaged that it was irrevocably changed. Following certain floods, tornadoes, and other disasters, the topography of the land changes so much that it is impractical to rebuild on the original site. In other instances, a governmental body decides to build a highway, bridge, or other public project, forever changing the looks and location of the community. If something similar happened in your community, then you lost all or a large part of your geographic and social frame of reference to the disaster.

Review the list of losses you made in Chapter 9, and add as many community-related losses as you can identify. As you review your list, consider the following questions:

1. Does your community still exist? If not, specify the many aspects of the tremendous losses you have experienced. If there were negative aspects of your community that you will not miss or grieve, you may want to specify those as well.

2. How did the disaster affect community morale? Did it bring the community closer together, or was your community torn apart by looting and other crimes or by competition for public assistance and relief?

3. How has your contact with rescue operations and emergency agencies affected your view of the government? Are you experiencing any loss of trust or faith as a result?

4. How did the natural disaster affect your spiritual or philosophical beliefs? For example, has anyone stated or implied that you were affected because of a moral inadequacy? How has such an interpretation affected your attitudes and self-esteem?

5. Have you included all your financial losses in your list? Have you taken into account any losses of community resources or the cost of reconstruction?

6. Have you or any of your family members suffered health or medical problems due to the disaster? How have these problems affected your family and social relationships?

Pursuing Compensation

If you suffered financial losses (including physical injury) as a result of the catastrophe, you may be eligible for government assistance. State disaster relief agencies manage local disasters. They offer both grants and loans for reconstruction, provided eligibility requirements are met. In some areas, crisis counseling is offered also. When a disaster is of such proportion that state funding and resources are unable to handle it, or when a disaster spans several states, the President may declare the blighted area to be a major disaster zone. In these instances, the Federal Emergency Management Administration (FEMA) offers financial and other assistance to natural disaster survivors in need. However, such help may not be immediately forthcoming or may not adequately compensate you for damages. If this happens, you may decide to pursue legal action or join with others in a class action suit.

In some cases private companies contribute to, or even cause, the damage. In this case, the company may provide compensation. If such companies fail to provide you with promised or justifiable compensation, then do not close your mind to the idea of a lawsuit against them. Joining together with others who have suffered as the result of negligence or incompetence can have positive results—both financially and emotionally.

For example, the flood that overran Buffalo Creek, West Virginia (mentioned earlier in the chapter) was in reality a dam collapse. Much of the populace justifiably blamed the flood on the dam's poor construction. A group of residents came together and filed a lawsuit against the coal company that had constructed the dam. (After they won their suit, which included compensation for "psychic impairment," the incidence of PTSD and other symptoms sharply declined.)

Of course, should you decide to pursue a lawsuit, you will need legal advice in addition to the support of fellow survivors. Refer to Appendix B under "Legal Assistance" and "Natural Catastrophes" for lists of resources.

16

Vehicular Accidents

Guidelines for Using This Book

Chapter 3, which deals with self-blame and survivor guilt, is especially relevant to you if someone died in the accident you were in, if others were more severely injured than yourself, or if you to some degree contributed to the accident.

Like other trauma survivors, you will need to identify those situations that trigger memories of the accident. However, unlike many other traumas, reminders of vehicular accidents are everywhere. Consequently, you will need to carefully read Chapter 5, which helps you identify and deal with triggers. You may need to pay special attention to the exercises in that chapter that teach deep breathing and other forms of relaxation in response to triggers. Recent research has shown that motor vehicle accident survivors show increased heart rate and blood pressure in response to imagined scenes of their accident (Blanchard et al. 1991).

Also carefully review Chapter 8. That chapter helps you identify the various sources of your anger and provides you with some means of expressing your anger nondestructively.

Vehicular Accidents as a "Necessary Evil"

Modern, technological society relies heavily on vehicles of all sorts, from cars, trucks, and buses to ships, airplanes, and trains. Without these vehicles, our society would literally come to a standstill.

Most of us are utterly reliant on vehicles to get to work, shop for necessities, and attend to medical, social, and recreational needs. This dependence on vehicles causes society at large to view vehicular accidents, particularly car accidents, as a necessary evil—an inevitable cost of living in a highly technological society. However, this view fails to take into account the cruel realities that face survivors of car, airplane, and other vehicular accidents.

If you are a vehicular accident survivor—especially if the accident involved injury to yourself or the death or injury of others—it's unlikely that you view your experience as a necessary evil. For you, the sophisticated machines that are supposed to improve the quality of life may be associated with terrifying memories, immense physical or psychological pain, debilitating survivor guilt, and in some cases secondary wounding.

Although few psychiatric studies of vehicular accident survivors have been done, it is not unusual for these survivors to seek professional help down the line—even in cases where the accident did not cause serious injury (Goldberg and Gara 1990). One study conducted among survivors of a nonfatal aircraft accident and their families showed depression, anxiety, and PTSD symptoms not only among the survivors, but among their spouses and family members as well (Slagle et al. 1990).

The Psychological Aftermath of Vehicular Accidents—Acute Stress Reaction

A car, airplane, bus, boat, or train accident has the potential to change your life, especially if you were severely injured, if one of your loved ones was severely injured or killed, or if someone else died in the accident. Vehicular accidents can also create long-term problems if you hold yourself responsible, either in whole or in part, for the accident, regardless of whether your sense of guilt is grounded in reality.

Like other trauma survivors, as a vehicular accident survivor you are vulnerable to developing any number of *acute stress reactions* shortly after the accident. These include emotional numbing, denial, anger, fear, helplessness, depression, nausea, insomnia, hypersomnia (sleeping a great deal), loss of appetite, overeating, the startle response, and fatigue. Furthermore, severe accidents, like severe illnesses, can exacerbate any underlying conflicts you have either within yourself, with family members or friends, or on the job.

Immediate stress reactions involve several stages. The first stage, often called the shock stage, occurs while the accident is actually taking place and immediately afterward. Its symptoms include shock, physical or emotional numbing, and denial.

During the second stage, often called the recoil or impact stage, the shock and numbing lift. At this point, you begin to absorb the reality and full meaning of the trauma and to experience the feelings associated with the accident. These feelings include fear, anger, grief, resentment, dependency, powerlessness, desire for revenge, and perhaps shame and guilt.

You may experience troublesome mood swings, hypersensitivity to the reactions of other people and to noise, and mental confusion.

Physical symptoms not directly caused by the accident may also appear. These symptoms reflect stress put on the body and central nervous system by the psychological stress of realizing that you are vulnerable to injury or death. These symptoms include (but are not limited to) headaches, backaches, and other body pains; nausea and other gastrointestinal problems; and intense shaking. In addition, the trauma can intensify any medical, physical, or psychological problems that existed prior to the accident.

During the third stage, the attribution stage, you (and perhaps friends and family members) try to figure out what caused the accident. Blame may be pinned on yourself, on other parties involved, or both. You may even take responsibility for the accident, rather than acknowledge the important role chance has in determining when, where, and to whom an accident occurs.

The fourth stage is the resolution or recovery stage. During this stage, your emotional equilibrium returns, because to one degree or another, you have worked through the emotions pertaining to the accident and perhaps feel empowered by having taken measures to avoid being involved in future accidents.

Lack of resolution can lead to the development of phobias and fears, acute psychosomatic problems, and the intensification of any preexisting psychological problems. Under certain conditions, acute trauma reaction can develop into full-blown PTSD. In one recorded case, an individual began to develop PTSD symptoms from a life-threatening vehicular accident four years after it happened. The good news is that a combination of antidepressant medication and individual counseling helped him overcome his symptoms (Lim 1991).

Unlike those of PTSD, the symptoms of acute stress reaction do not last for more than a month. If the symptoms do persist, you need to evaluate yourself for PTSD using the questionnaires in Chapter 1 if you have not already done so.

The Shock Stage

Immediately following the accident you were probably in the shock and denial phase; you felt dazed or confused. Your disorientation and numbing may have been physical, mental, emotional, or all three. For example, you may have been injured, but experienced little or no physical pain. You may have been cold, but didn't think you needed a blanket or coat. You may have been bleeding, but were emotionally detached from your wounds, or you dismissed them as unimportant. Your denial and shock may have been so absolute that you were unable to believe that the accident had actually occurred, as Laura was.

When Laura's car was totaled in an accident, she looked at the crumpled bodywork in disbelief. "I felt as if I were watching a movie, that it wasn't real life," she said later. Then she glanced at her arm. One of the bones was sticking through the skin, yet she felt no physical pain, and instead of shrieking in horror, she felt detached. "Isn't that interesting," she remembered thinking, "I never knew bones were that color."

Laura's husband was also in the car. He remembered every detail of the accident: the color of the oncoming car, the face of the driver, the names of the police who arrived on the scene, and so on. Laura's memory was less vivid. She could recall the time of day and what she was thinking, but other memories were vague and confused. For example, she couldn't remember the exact sequence of events or how long it was before the rescue team and police arrived.

Like Laura, your memory of the accident may be crystal clear in some respects, but cloudy in others. If your memories of the event are partial or distorted, this may be due to the phenomenon of "tunnel vision," which frequently occurs during severe accidents. Tunnel vision, in this case, means that the survivor remembers vividly some aspects of the trauma, but not others—for example, the way crime victims may remember exact details about their attacker's weapon but be unable to identify his or her facial features, size, or clothing.

During the initial shock and denial stage, you probably experienced the adrenaline reactions common to people in life-threatening situations: the fight, flight, and freeze reactions. As explained in Chapter 2, in emergency situations, the adrenal glands function to produce extra adrenaline, which energizes you and mobilizes you for action. Alternatively, the adrenals may produce noradrenaline, which decreases your functioning. The freeze reaction in its extreme form is often called "going into shock." In that state you may lose consciousness or find yourself physically immobilized but aware of what is going on around you.

Both adrenaline and noradrenaline reactions are normal. Being cool, calm, and collected immediately following an accident is also normal. Also possible are near-death or out-of-body experiences. Such experiences usually occur to individuals who are close to dying, who have died but have been resuscitated, or who are undergoing an intense biological or psychological stress, such as occurs in a vehicular accident or criminal assault.

Such experiences are not signs of psychosis, brain damage, or mental illness. Although these experiences are not common, they occur more frequently than is usually thought. According to the International Association of Near-Death Studies (IANDS 1992), a 1991 Gallup poll indicated that approximately 13 million people in the United States had had a near-death experience.

During a near-death or out-of-body experience, you feel as if you have left your body and are in the sky or somewhere else removed from the immediate accident, and you view the immediate situation from a safe distance. You may even have a spiritual revelation or encounter. If you had an out-of-body experience, it may have brought you great peace. Alternatively, it might have created mental, emotional, or spiritual confusion. David and John, for example, had similar experiences, but were affected by them in different ways.

> David was in an airline crash in which his leg was severed. At one point during the accident he was near death and had a spiritual revelation that later enabled him to accept his amputation without undue bitterness or rage.
>
> John was in a serious car accident. While he was being tended to by a rescue worker, his heart stopped beating. Although he was quickly revived, during the moments he was dead he had an out-of-body experience in which he viewed the scene of the accident from somewhere in the air. During this experience he also had a spiritual encounter.
>
> This experience so challenged John's previous view of the world and himself that he separated from his wife and went into virtual seclusion to "get himself together." He also quit his job and refused to see his parents and other family members.
>
> John's life today is full of emotional agitation and spiritual questioning. Yet, prior to the accident, he had no previous emotional or substance abuse problems, and he enjoyed a stable job and a fulfilling marital relationship.

Exercise: Reexamining the Accident and Its Immediate Aftermath

Return to your journal entries that describe the accident and the secondary wounding experiences that followed. After rereading what you've written there, consider the following questions:

1. Are there any details you can add now to make the description more complete? If so, add them to your journal.

2. Are there details of the accident that you do not remember? List those events, smells, sights, and other aspects of the accident for which your memories seem to be missing.

As an aid to remembering, consider contacting any witnesses or reading newspaper accounts or police reports of the accident. If, however, you feel it would be too traumatic to remember, *do not* try to stimulate your memory in any way. There is no point to unearthing details you aren't ready to handle and which you may not need to handle in order to recover. Not every aspect of the trauma needs to be understood and emotionally felt for healing to progress. In some situations, traumatic memories are best left in repression. The best guide in this decision is your own gut reaction.

After you have made additions to your description of the accident, review your writing on any feelings of self-blame you have about the accident or being a victim. If you have not covered the following questions already, consider them carefully:

3. Prior to the accident, did you ever think you would be involved in an accident like the one you experienced?

4. How did you believe you would act if you were suddenly in a serious accident? Did your actual behavior match your expected behavior? How do you feel about any discrepancies between the way you anticipated feeling and acting and the way you actually felt and acted?

5. In assessing your reaction to the accident, are there any ways in which a surge of adrenaline might have influenced your behavior? Are there ways in which noradrenaline, or the numbing response, may have influenced your thoughts and behavior?

Also review your journal entries on secondary wounding, and think about these questions:

6. Did anyone criticize or negatively comment on how you behaved following the accident? Were you blamed for the accident, either wholly or in part?

7. To what extent did you agree with your critics? What evidence exists that the views of these critics and others are accurate?

8. If one of your children or someone you loved dearly or respected highly had been in your position during the accident, how would you feel if others criticized that person the way you were criticized? With which parts of the criticism would you concur and with which parts would you disagree?

The Recoil or Impact Stage

Following the shock and denial stage comes the impact stage. During this stage, all the feelings that were repressed during the initial shock phase begin to flood your awareness. These feelings can range from anxiety and anger to fear and grief to self-hatred, guilt, and shame. You can also vacillate from one extreme of the emotional spectrum to another within a single day, or even an hour. For example, one minute you may self-righteously declare revenge on the pilot or driver who caused the accident, and the next minute be consumed with guilt and remorse for not having saved the life of a fellow victim.

In the impact stage, your emotionality may confuse you, especially since your feelings keep changing, and in contradictory ways. Even more confusing is that at times you may feel nothing at all. This numb state, however, can be viewed as giving you a rest from the intensity of emotion experienced at other times.

In this stage fear may be one of your most dominant emotions. You may in part simply fear that the impact stage will never end. Is the heightened emotional stage going to persist and cause me ongoing emotional turmoil? you might wonder. How will I ever get on with the rest of my life if this continues?

If you are in this stage, you should keep in mind that it will end—if you allow it to run its course and don't try to interrupt it with some form of substance abuse or escapist activity. To divest yourself of these feelings, it is important for you to allow yourself to feel them as much as possible during the impact stage and not try to stifle them.

After the impact stage has run its course, you might still have recurring bouts of feelings associated with the trauma. However, as a result of the healing process, those feelings and other aspects of the trauma need not dominate your life.

Coping with Fears

You may also fear that the accident will repeat itself the next time you are in or near the kind of vehicle associated with your accident. In addition, for you as an accident survivor, some (or all) vehicles probably serve as a trigger not only for fear, but for all the other emotions associated with the trauma—helplessness and dependency, for example.

One way to control these fears is to change your life-style to minimize or alter your contact with the type of vehicle that triggers your fears (or with all vehicles). Doing so may make it difficult or impossible for you to get to work, go shopping, visit friends or relatives, and so on. The costs of this decision must be fully acknowledged and considered.

A fear of being involved in another accident is not unrealistic. But if you feel that every time you enter a vehicle you will surely be involved in an accident, this is not rational. Instead, this feeling stems from the trauma.

You can decide to take as many precautions as possible to avoid another accident. For example, you might decide never to drive in the rain or snow or to purchase an automobile with maximum safety features. Such actions can reduce, but not eliminate, the possibility of another accident. The exercise that follows will help you identify your specific fears and decide on a course of action to deal with them.

Exercise: Identifying and Countering Fears

In your journal, answer the following questions:

1. What were your fears during the accident? Be as specific as possible. Did you fear death, serious injury, disability, or the injury of a loved one? Were any financial fears involved?

2. Do you now fear vehicles? Which vehicles do you fear? Only certain kinds or all types? Would you now feel safe on an airplane, but not in a car, or vice versa? Is this fear generalized or is it specific to a certain situation? For example, do you fear being in any kind of car at any time under any conditions, or is your fear confined to certain circumstances, such as being in a small car during a snowstorm?

3. What other fears do you have stemming from the accident? Be as specific as possible.

4. In what ways can you reduce the risk of being in a vehicular accident again? Although there is no way to completely guarantee the absence of any further accidents, the more active measures you can take to increase your safety in a vehicle, the greater the chance that you will avoid future injury. For example, you may decide not to drive on Friday and Saturday nights or on certain holidays when people tend to drink more. You may make a commitment to always wear your seat belt or to buy a car with safety features.

5. Some people decide to restrict some of their activities to reduce the risk of being in a vehicular accident. This may or may not be the right decision for you. Or it may be a temporary decision, subject to change once you have begun to heal and feel safer in a vehicle again.

   If you have decided to avoid certain activities because they involve contact with vehicles, make a list of these activities. Then, for each activity, consider whether there are ways to continue to engage in the activity without having contact with the vehicle(s) you fear.

   For example, could some of these activities be conducted over the telephone or by mail? Could you arrange for certain meetings to be held at your home or at a location to which you could walk or take public transportation or reach by some other means you consider safe?

6. Is there an accident survivor group in your area? Such groups are somewhat rare, but they exist. Check with your local mental health agency or local hospital. Or you might consider starting one. See the section "Finding a Survivor Group" in Appendix A.

7. Do you have concerns about your physical health? If you were injured during the accident, no matter how much time has elapsed since the accident, do not hesitate to seek appropriate medical care for any physical problem.

Dealing with Anger

As an accident survivor, most likely you have plenty to be angry about. If you were in, for example, an airplane accident, you might be angry at the pilot, at those who failed to maintain the equipment, at the inadequacy of the rescue operations, or at other people or organizations that somehow failed to keep you safe or help you after you were injured.

For example, the pilot of the airplane that crashed in the summer of 1991, killing Senator John Heinz and six others, had only three hours of commercial experience and had had difficulties on a previous flight. In addition, the copilot of that flight had been on an assignment the entire previous night and hadn't had any rest before boarding the plane that crashed. Understandably, family members and friends of those killed in that crash were angry at the organization that permitted inexperienced and exhausted employees to assume responsibility for flying the aircraft (*Washington Post*, 4 July 1991).

If you were in an accident involving public transportation, you may feel enraged at who or whatever you feel is responsible for the accident on the administrative level. Perhaps you and other survivors have filed complaints about faulty management or equipment maintenance to a transportation agency, only to have your complaints dismissed as factitious or unimportant. Or perhaps you are angry at certain police actions or legal proceedings that you feel have failed to give you adequate retribution.

Your anger may also stem from the type of secondary wounding experience that sometimes occurs when the legal and police systems have not kept pace with the escalating number of vehicular accidents. In such instances, accident victims are not compensated for their injuries and may not even have the satisfaction of seeing their case fully or professionally investigated.

Exercise: Anger and the Costs of the Accident

Reread your journal entries on anger and spend some time writing about any additional angers you have since discovered toward either individuals involved in the accident; members of any rescue operation, police force, or the legal system; or any other individuals or institutions that added to your pain.

Much of your anger likely stems from bearing the costs of having been in an accident. The following questions will help you further identify any financial, emotional, medical, and social costs of the trauma. The more fully you understand the costs of the accident, the more of your anger you will be able to identify and ultimately manage effectively.

Answer the following questions in your journal:

1. How much did the accident cost you financially? Consider not only damage to your property but medical expenses, time lost from work,

and lost work or career opportunities due to time spent dealing with or recovering from the accident.

2. To what extent did the accident exacerbate any preexisting medical or psychological problems or family tensions?

3. What deprivations are you experiencing due to the restrictions you have imposed on your activities as a result of the accident? What pleasures, events, and activities are you sacrificing in order to feel safe?

4. What financial and emotional deprivations are you experiencing as a result of the physical and emotional aftermath of the accident?

5. What have been the emotional costs of the accident to your family and others in your life? How have these costs affected you?

The Attribution Stage

The attribution stage is sometimes called the stage of self-doubts or the "what-if" and "if-only" stage. During this stage, you will begin to question what you did during the incident and why. Thoughts such as If only I had ... and What if I hadn't ... ? are common.

Such thinking can be an attempt to evade the harsh fact that the accident was in all likelihood almost totally out of your control and that you were, regardless of your actions, an innocent victim.

Such intense self-questioning can also be an attempt to alter the stark realities of the accident and mitigate the losses involved. For example, Tom Williams (1987a) relates the story of a woman who lost a child in a car accident saying to herself, "If I hadn't been going down the road at that time, if I had not had him in the car, if only I had been on the road ten minutes earlier, the drunk driver wouldn't have hit me." Martin's case is a similar example of unrealistic self-blame.

> Martin, a businessman who must fly frequently as part of his job, has suffered anxiety attacks and insomnia before flying since the time he was on a plane that crash-landed, resulting in the deaths of half the passengers. He blames himself both for his symptoms and for not having been able to do more to help the other survivors.
>
> "I was scheduled to go on a later flight," he says, "but I got to the airport early, so I grabbed the earlier flight. If only I wasn't in such a hurry, I wouldn't have been a part of that horror. I feel terrible that I couldn't save the woman sitting next to me. There's not a day goes by that I don't see her face."
>
> In reality, however, the woman was already dead—and Martin knew she was dead—when he fled the burning airplane. Had he taken the time to disentangle her body from the seatbelt he might have died himself. Yet, like combat vets

who feel guilty for not saving comrades even when it would have been impossible, Martin still blames himself for not saving the woman's life.

Even when they sustain serious injuries themselves, survivors sometimes feel guilty that they were not injured as badly as others in the accident. Susan and Alice are a case in point.

> Susan's car was stopped at a red light when it was struck by a speeding car. As a result, Susan, an aerobics instructor, suffers from permanent nerve damage. For six months she was unable to work. Alice, a friend who was also in the car, suffered less serious injuries, but they affected her more because her body was not as strong as Susan's.
>
> Both women experienced depression, exhaustion, loss of appetite, difficulties concentrating and making decisions, and anger at the driver who hit them. They found themselves talking about the accident to anyone who would listen, while at the same time feeling ashamed that they needed to repeat the story so often. And even though Susan and Alice were clearly not at fault, and had both suffered, each of them experienced survivor guilt.
>
> Susan felt she should have been able to do something to avert the accident. In reality, however, there was nothing she could have done, since she was boxed in by other cars. She also feels guilty that her friend's body was not as strong as hers and so could not sustain the injuries as well. Alice, on the other hand, feels guilty that Susan's career has been negatively affected by the accident, even though she had nothing to do with causing the accident or her friend's injuries.

Martin's, Susan's, and Alice's survivor guilt, like the guilt and other forms of self-blame you might experience during this phase, serve an important function—up to a point. Like most human beings, you want the world to make sense and events to have a reason. It is easier for you to conclude that the reason for the accident or for the damage it caused was somehow your fault than to think that the accident was purely random.

Carried too far, however, or for too long, feelings of self-blame and survivor guilt become self-destructive and impede the healing process. The following exercise will aid you in examining these feelings.

Exercise: Reviewing Self-Blame

Review your journal entries on the self-blame you feel regarding the accident. Add to your journal any additional insights you may now have on how you blame yourself for the accident. Check out your thoughts with a therapist, caring friend, or other objective party to ascertain which of your self-blaming thoughts are rational and which are irrational.

For example, thinking that you caused an airplane crash because of some moral defect is not grounded in the reality of an equipment or personnel failure. On the other hand, thinking that you caused a car accident because your brakes failed and you had known for some time that they needed work may be grounded in reality.

Irrational self-blaming thoughts need to be countered with reality-based statements. Similarly, any true guilt needs to be understood in the full context of both your life and the accident. For example, you might not have attended to your brakes because of special life circumstances, such as being overloaded at work or trying to assist a family member who was ill. Although these circumstances do not excuse your lack of attention to the safety of your vehicle, they are mitigating factors that you need to take into account as you assess your guilt and innocence.

On the other hand, there may have been no compelling reason for your lack of attention to your car problem. In this situation, you are justified in blaming yourself, but only to the extent that the accident was caused by your negligence. In this situation, you need to ask yourself whether the accident might have occurred anyway, as well as examine what other factors contributed to the accident. Your faulty brakes may have been the sole cause, or they may have played only a partial role in the crash.

Acknowledging that your negligence or some other behavior on your part contributed to or caused the accident is extremely difficult. This degree of self-awareness is painful. But you are human and you make mistakes. Others have made the same or similar mistakes, but were fortunate in that their mistakes did not lead to a vehicular accident. You, however, were not so lucky. Take Bob's situation, for example.

> Every morning Bob would drop his two children off at school on his way to work. One morning he was running late, and making a left turn in heavy traffic he misjudged the speed of the oncoming automobiles. His car was hit and one of his children died.

Needless to say, Bob's self-blame and guilt are enormous. However, he did not desire or will this tragedy. Furthermore, his rush to make up lost time is a reflection of the pressures of living in modern society. Hurry and impatience are major contributors to car accidents.

The Resolution Stage

In the resolution stage, although memories and feelings about the accident do not disappear, they lose some of their power. This means you are less controlled by your fears, anger, self-blame, and the blame of others.

It is easier to reach the resolution stage if you did not contribute to the accident; if you have been adequately compensated for any damages incurred during the accident; and if the individuals or institutions wholly or partly responsible for the accident have acknowledged their role in the accident and at least attempted to make restitution to you and other victims.

Reaching the resolution stage is difficult if you have lost a loved one, suffer from major physical injuries, were in a major vehicular disaster, or played a role in causing the accident. Under such circumstances, the resolution stage consists of going on despite the memories, the pain, and the guilt. Reaching the resolution stage does not mean you will never feel anger, self-hatred, fear, or helplessness again. It simply means that you are determined to go on living, taking care of yourself, and giving back to the world, despite what occurred.

When Acute Stress Reaction Becomes PTSD

After an accident, you need to seek out emotional support from friends, family members, and others. If this is not sufficient, you may need to turn to a therapist for a while. Reaching out while you are having acute stress reactions may save you the development of more serious emotional and physical problems later.

If your reaction to the accident included many of the symptoms of acute stress reaction, not attending to them can cause them to develop into long-term phobias, psychosomatic problems, or full-blown PTSD. It is the consensus among both physicians and mental health professionals that since "PTSD may be chronic and difficult to treat if unrecognized, early intervention is desirable" (Blake 1986).

The vehicular accident you experienced may have caused irrevocable damage to your life in more than one way. However, your efforts at working through the trauma will yield greater peace of mind, increased control over the accident's negative effects, and increased personal power.

17

War and Combat

Guidelines for Using This Book

If you have lived with combat-related PTSD for many years and have not received help, or have received only partial or inadequate help, your PTSD may be expressed in the form of depression, addiction, or intense physical pain. Under these conditions, carefully assess yourself for depression and addiction as described in Chapter 2, and consider the possibility of seeing a psychiatrist for evaluation for medication to assist you in managing your PTSD symptoms and/or your depression or addiction. Your need for medication may be temporary, but medication could be essential in helping you get sufficiently free of the symptoms so that you can focus on examining your war experience and empowering yourself from it.

As you work through the exercises on self-blame in Chapter 3, you need to make careful distinctions between rational and irrational survivor guilt. Given that war is chaotic, there may have been traumatic episodes in which you contributed to an undesirable outcome. But these episodes must be considered in the context of war, where most choices are painful, and no matter what one does the costs are heavy. In many traumatic situations, but especially in war, there are often two or more conflicting sets of principles about what is right. Typically, it is impossible to choose one moral, patriotic, or life-preserving principle and not violate another.

If you were a soldier, you were trained to respond to stress and other problems with violence. Consequently, you may tend to respond aggressively in situations where outbursts of anger or rage are ill-advised, if not illegal. In addition, you may be expending a great deal of energy suppressing unresolved angers stemming from your war experience. As a result, your anger may be severely limiting your life-style and vocational and social opportunities. For these reasons, Chapter 8, on anger, will be especially critical for you.

Pay special attention also to Chapter 9, on grieving, since much of the anger of war veterans stems from unresolved grief. Some of your grief will stem from losing friends in combat, but do not forget to attend to other possible kinds of losses: your loss of innocence or loss of faith in the military, the government, or other institutions and beliefs.

If you used anger as a way to feel powerful, you will need to carefully complete the exercises in Chapter 10 on empowerment, so that you can find other ways of asserting your strengths.

War and Mental Health

In popular movies and books, war is often depicted as a glamorous adventure in which men test and prove their manhood. The reality of war is far more complex. War has its exhilarating moments, for some, but it is also ugly, brutal, and bloody. Both officers and soldiers can be incompetent, corrupt, or malicious. And the glamour of war is quickly eroded when a soldier feels betrayed by someone from his own side.

But war also produces acts of incredible courage and heroism, and can generate a camaraderie unmatched in civilian life. The number of men who have given their lives for the sake of their fellows is not known, but it is probably large. And although most of these men were never officially recognized as heroes, they are as heroic as any highly respected religious or political leader.

In short, war can bring out the best or the worst in human nature. It can also create a host of short- and long-term readjustment problems, only one of which is war-related PTSD. However, not all war veterans suffer from PTSD, and those who do vary in the degree to which the PTSD affects their personal and vocational lives. Research has shown that exposure to combat, to abusive violence, and to atrocities increases the risk for developing PTSD. The heavier and longer the combat, the greater the probability that the soldier will develop symptoms. Being a member of a minority group also increases the risk for developing PTSD.

PTSD is not restricted to combat veterans but has also been found among individuals who spent time in war zones where they experienced life-threatening situations or were surrounded by death. Medical personnel, transporters, body-bag counters, embalmers, administrative officers, and numerous civilians who lived or served in or near combat zones also have developed PTSD. During World War II, for example, "war neurosis" was found not only among combatants for whom the threat of death was ever present, but among soldiers in grave-registration units and in air corps emergency units (Futterman and Pumpian-Midlin 1951).

If you are a war veteran with PTSD, it cannot be overemphasized that having PTSD does not mean that you are "mentally ill," any more than the earthquake victim is mentally ill for exhibiting stress reactions due to his or her experiences. Two recent studies found that, whereas many veterans evidenced stress reactions to the war, they were, nevertheless, psychologically healthy. This phenomenon, the coexistence of stress reactions with healthy adjustment, has been found to be characteristic of survivors of other catastrophes as well (La Guardian et al. 1982, Frye and Stockton 1982).

PTSD and War Historically

The term *post-traumatic stress disorder* is most commonly associated with Vietnam veterans. Yet PTSD or PTSD-like symptoms have been experienced by soldiers throughout the ages. In fact, war-related PTSD has been documented by historians, dramatists, military officials, and others at least as far back as the ancient Greeks and Romans. War-related PTSD was noted in England and France during the Middle Ages, in the Civil War in this country, and in the first and second World Wars, the Korean War, and other wars of this century.

Shakespeare, in *Henry IV, Part I*, wrote about war-related PTSD, but, it was not until World War I that the psychological stress of war was first recognized by mental health professionals. At that time it was thought that exploding shells caused actual physiological damage, which led in turn to numerous psychological symptoms referred to as "shell shock." By the end of that war, the malady was called "war neurosis" (Glass 1969). Among American troops, PTSD-like symptoms caused the evacuation of some 10 percent of enlisted men (Grinker and Spiegel 1983, Goodwin).

In World War II, the psychiatric casualty rate was also high, despite elaborate psychological screening procedures intended to weed out those susceptible to mental collapse. After World War II, military experts concluded that the trauma of war was often enough to impair even the "strongest and toughest" of men (Grinker and Spiegel 1983, Goodwin).

Most World War I and II veterans who suffered from PTSD kept their problems to themselves or drowned them in alcohol. If it is not considered manly to admit inner turmoil today, it was even less so in the past. As a result, numerous World War II and Korean War veterans still suffer from nightmares and other symptoms of PTSD.

During the Korean War, the military provided immediate on-site help to afflicted servicemen. Such assistance reduced the percentage of evacuations for psychiatric reasons from 23 percent during World War II to 6 percent during the Korean conflict. And during the Vietnam War, in an attempt to further reduce the psychiatric-casualty rate, the one-year tour of duty was adopted. The military reasoned that if men were subject to combat for only one year, they would be less susceptible to psychological breakdown.

This reasoning proved false, however. It takes not years, months, weeks, or even hours to lay the foundation for PTSD: an individual can be traumatized in a couple of seconds.

However, "in-country" psychiatric casualty rates were low in Vietnam compared to previous wars, because the stress symptoms of combatants and other military personnel were frequently masked by alcohol or drugs. In addition, those who sought pastoral or professional counseling were usually reminded that they would be returning home within a year and were urged to resume their military duties as quickly as possible. Changes in military procedure also made it more difficult to obtain an early discharge from the service for psychiatric reasons during the Vietnam era than in previous wars. Thus the availability of alcohol and drugs combined with altered military procedures led to the suppression of many combat-related symptoms.

The symptoms emerged later, however, upon the soldiers' return home—sometimes immediately and sometimes years later. Some Vietnam veterans are experiencing their war-related reactions only now, more than 20 years after the end of the war.

The symptoms of PTSD in Vietnam veterans are almost identical to those suffered by World War II and Korean War veterans. And PTSD is not unique to U.S. veterans. The same symptoms have been found among Australian troops who served in Vietnam, and the psychiatric casualty rate is about the same.

Circumstances of War

Some veterans credit their military experience with helping them to mature and develop a sense of discipline and purpose. However, others feel that their war experiences impaired not only their physical health but their mental health as well. In addition to the threat to participants of being killed or maimed and the exposure to death in general, several other special factors contribute to the trauma of war.

- You were uprooted, dislocated, and disoriented due to leaving your family and community. If you were in a foreign war, you also experienced a change in culture. These changes made you more vulnerable to psychological fragmentation and psychological stress.

- Military training is itself a stressor. One of the goals of such training is to inculcate surrender to military authority, which entails some loss of the soldier's sense of individuality. Basic training also discourages intimacy and grief. In general, the military encourages the numbing of most emotions except one: anger. In the military, anger is not only permitted, it is encouraged.

- If you were in combat, you were subject to physical fatigue, extremes of temperature, inadequate meals, and other forms of physical stress. Such physiological stresses greatly compounded whatever psychological stresses you experienced. Few civilians can imagine, for example, the experience of carrying a 40-pound gear bag while wearing fatigues in temperatures well over 100 degrees. Yet the heat alone accounted for considerable stress during the recent Persian Gulf War as well as in Vietnam.

- Unlike survivors of other types of trauma, if you were a combat soldier, you were not only powerless but powerful. You could have been killed at any moment, but you could also kill almost at will. You were given weapons and permission to kill and act out your aggressions. This can create problems in civilian life since managing anger by violence is both unacceptable and punishable by law.

This last item has other repercussions as well, the first of which is what psychiatrist W. B. Gault (1971) calls "the natural ascendancy of the psychopath."

Psychopathology and war. War can generate a great deal of psychopathology in all involved, from the combatants to their officers to the civilians involved. However, there is a tendency for the least principled and most character-disordered individuals to come to dominate the formal and informal power structures of military units.

Because of the absence of law and order and other usual moral restraints, individuals who are sadistic, egomaniacal, or otherwise morally defective often have more opportunity for free rein in a war zone than they would in civilian society. Worse, they can easily become leaders, or at least exert considerable influence over others. The egoism, amorality, aggressiveness, and other qualities of psychopaths are not useful or generally valued in peacetime society. However, they can be extremely useful and valued in war conditions (Gault 1971, H. Glover 1985).

Whether a psychopathic individual exerts power formally or informally, reactions to him by individual soldiers can range anywhere from aversion to worship. And regardless of how a given soldier feels about such a leader, the leader's presence is stressful. If you were morally repelled by such a leader, for example, having to follow his orders or to respond to his pressures to commit or witness nonsanctioned wartime activities may have created a moral dilemma for you.

On the other hand, if you admired such a leader at the time, and saw him as the embodiment of military values and skills, now in peacetime and away from the stresses of war, you may have mixed feelings about his character, and about your own character for having admired him.

In addition, such leaders frequently verbally humiliate comrades or subordinates who fail to meet their expectations. If you despised such a leader during wartime, his comments may have angered you. If you admired him, however, his criticisms may have deeply shamed you.

Battle heat, blood lust, and the shadow. Another phenomenon that can have long-lasting effects on combat veterans is that of "battle heat" or "blood lust."

As explained in Chapter 2, the fear generated by being in combat can generate an intense flow of energy, caused by adrenaline secretions in response to the dangers of battle. This energy rush can be experienced as a form of exhilaration. It might seem contradictory that the basis for some of the physical energy necessary to fight stems from the fear born of a sense of powerlessness. However, the battle heat or blood lust generated in this way has served soldiers in combat throughout history. Yet it has a negative side as well.

According to the psychologist Carl Jung, every human being has a persona: the face or mask he or she presents to the world (Hall and Lindzey 1970). This persona consists of socially acceptable traits and behaviors. However, every human being also has a shadow, or darker side. Residing in this shadow are lust, greed, murderousness, and all the other socially unacceptable feelings and desires.

Most of us do not acknowledge—much less express or accept—our shadow. Although in literature, art, and entertainment the dark side of human beings is a staple, we are often highly offended if anyone suggests that we too have a darker side. And if and when we encounter this side, we tend to experience some degree of guilt and shame.

In combat, however, the shadow is not only acknowledged, but encouraged—if not glorified. Men are frequently rewarded for acting on aggressive or murderous feelings that would be socially unacceptable in civilian society. Hence, unlike noncombatants, combat veterans are not only forced to recognize their shadow but given the opportunity to let it loose.

The attendant guilt feelings (often experienced for many years) can be enormous. "I feel guilty that I killed," is a sentiment expressed by some veterans. Others say, "I don't feel guilty that I killed, because that was my job, but I feel guilty that I enjoyed killing." "It is not just what I saw," says another, "It is what I became."

Yet to kill and enjoy killing is exactly what is encouraged by the military. It can be a form of adaptation to wartime, as well as a result of the "adrenaline high" caused by the threat to life.

As a result, war can pose a spiritual or moral dilemma for many soldiers. Often they feel a conflict between the warrior, who has been trained to kill, and the human being, who learned that killing is morally wrong. Traditionally, society has forgiven warriors by justifying the killing. However, in instances where society does not provide such justification for killing, the moral pain of killing can be even more intense.

Until most recently, for example, the Vietnam veteran did not receive much societal justification or forgiveness for the killing he was required to do. But even in popular wars, such as World War II, an undetermined number of soldiers suffered from the moral pain of killing.

Everyone is different. Some can deal with killing and seeing killing; others cannot. In many instances the individuals who suffer the most moral pain in war are those with the highest moral standards or those who, for whatever reason, could not tolerate viewing or being part of any form of brutality.

Self-Blame

In addition to guilt feelings over the moral questions inevitably raised by war, there is also the self-blame that results from mistakes and misjudgments. War is fraught with chaos, and this chaos makes it almost inevitable that soldiers mistakenly kill others from their own side. Technological warfare has not diminished the probability of death from "friendly fire"—it may have even increased it. In the recent Persian Gulf War, for example, a significant number of American and English troops were killed by allies or their own people.

During combat, the chaos of war combined with the physical and emotional stresses can create numerous situations where even the most dedicated and skilled warrior can easily make a mistake. When that mistake results in the loss of friends or comrades, or in civilian casualties, the soldier's self-blame can be enormous. Some rage at themselves for mistakes they made during combat, others berate themselves for acts they perceive as cowardly or unnecessarily brutal.

Often such feelings are shoved aside, only to emerge years later, directly or indirectly. And without help, the guilt can last a lifetime. Some of the most common forms of indirect expression of self-blame are psychosomatic pains, addiction, and any of a host of self-destructive activities. Guilt-laden veterans also often suffer from chronic, but often disguised, low self-esteem. Post-traumatic stress disorder itself is a manifestation of unresolved war issues, including self-blame and survivor guilt.

Survivor Guilt and Self-Blame

Survivor guilt is so central to PTSD that it used to be considered one of the formal criteria for diagnosing the disorder. It was removed from the formal criteria, not because it isn't prevalent among trauma survivors, but because it was not seen as being essential to the numbing-reexperiencing cycle of PTSD. Yet, in my many years of work with traumatized veterans, I have yet to meet a veteran who, while grateful to be alive, is not also overflowing with guilt at having lived while others of his comrades died.

If you are a combat veteran, you can have survivor guilt even if you do not feel responsible in any way for the deaths of your fellow soldiers. However, your survivor guilt will be especially strong if you feel some act of cowardice, aggression, or incompetence on your part contributed to the death of one of your fellow combatants. According to veteran and psychologist Tom Williams (1987a), survivors of war need to learn that "it is okay to feel sad about someone's having died in a traumatic situation, but it is not rational or appropriate to feel total responsibility for that person's death. A war veteran, failing to comprehend that, will blame himself for the death of a friend, failing to realize that the enemy was the killer. The war should be blamed, not those who lived through it."

The exercise that follows will help you pinpoint and resolve any feelings of self-blame and guilt that you have.

Exercise: Reducing Self-Blame and Guilt Feelings

As difficult and painful as it may be, try to make a list of some of the actions or inactions about which you now, in peacetime, experience guilt or remorse or about which you have second thoughts. Then complete the following steps for each of those events:

1. Formulate as complete a picture of the situation as possible, taking into account

    • the physical condition of your body; for example, were you tired, hungry, or sick?

    • the temperature and terrain of the location.

    • the physical condition and morale of your comrades.

    • any significant events that preceded the event, for instance, a buddy's death, an atrocity having been committed, an officer getting fragged, an attack of friendly fire, combat boredom, lack of contact with family members, or a letter from home with upsetting news.

2. For each situation, indicate what you cannot remember, areas where your memory is incomplete or confused, and information you did not have at the time and perhaps still do not have. For example, during the combat situation, were you able to see how many enemy troops were against you or other important features of the situation, such as your own wounds or the wounds of a comrade? If the situation involved individuals in civilian clothing, was there a way to tell whether they were armed? What details of the situation might you have missed because you were preoccupied with the task at hand or with survival issues?

3. Given the circumstances you have described, what were your real choices? List the choices in as much detail as possible.

4. For each choice you listed in step 3, write down what you think might have happened as a result of following that particular course of action.

5. In retrospect, would any of the choices you listed in step 3 have been preferable to you than what you did at the time? If so, why?

6. If you feel you made the best choice possible and you are still blaming yourself for your choice, ask yourself why. Is your self-blame due to the feedback of your comrades, commanding officers, family members, friends, or others?

7. If you feel you didn't make the best choice and should have chosen differently, can you identify your reasons for choosing the way you did? This question is not meant to be accusatory but to help you search out the combat-related stresses that led you to make a decision about which today you suffer some guilt or moral confusion.

    For example, have you considered whether you were hungry, tired, or urged by others to make the choice you did? Were you seeking revenge for the death of a friend or some horror you had witnessed? Were you expressing rebellion against a particular authority or perhaps against the very war itself? Have you taken into account the adrenaline or noradrenaline responses of your body or the perceptual distortions inherent to trauma?

8. If you killed for the exhilaration of killing or feeling powerful, and you now have questions about your behavior, have you taken into account the fact that war creates the conditions that can lead men to enjoy killing?

9. How are you punishing yourself today for any of the actions or inactions you listed? Are your self-punishments serving to remedy the original situation? For example, assume that during combat you had to kill children because they were armed with grenades and about to blow up your unit. Are you punishing yourself now by hating yourself or making yourself a distant ungiving father to your own children? Is your self-punishment in any way assisting the dead children or their families? What are the real effects of your self-punishment?

10. Can you think of any constructive ways to handle the guilt you feel regarding your wartime behavior?

11. Have you considered talking over your guilty feelings and the incidents that provoked these feelings with counselors trained in combat trauma, with other veterans, or with a minister or other spiritual advisor you trust?

Anger and Grief

Like guilt, grief and anger are emotions that, left unresolved, can manifest themselves in PTSD. They can be even more difficult to cope with, however, in that they are often almost inextricably intertwined.

In military experiences, from basic training to combat, emotions such as fear and grief are considered signs of weakness. Anger, on the other hand, is not only tolerated, but encouraged. Hence anger can become the repository for all the feelings experienced during a military tour of duty.

Often anger is purely anger. But anger is often also a disguise or defense against grief, confusion, fear, and the sense of powerlessness. Your grief over the death of a buddy or others in your unit might have been expressed, for example, through rape, abuse, or revenge killings of enemy prisoners or civilians. Anger-motivated acts can also be a cover-up for anger at yourself for having made a mistake, for feeling cowardly, or for somehow not having lived up to your expectations of yourself as a soldier.

As anger can serve as a substitute for many different emotions, so there are many kinds of grief. Healing from war-related PTSD involves not only grieving the dead friends and others who died but grieving the death of parts of one's self. Those who are disabled must grieve the loss of one or more of their limbs or organs or the loss of their former abilities, physical health, and freedom from pain. Also to be grieved are loss of faith, either religious faith or belief in authority or institutions.

Even less tangible losses need to be acknowledged and dealt with. Ancient Greek legend provides a case in point.

> On the eve of the Trojan War, the Greek armies, under the leadership of King Agamemnon, were ready to set sail, but for weeks on end there was no wind. Finally Agamemnon traveled to Delphi to consult the oracle there. The oracle said that Agamemnon was being punished by the goddess Diana for his disrespect of her, and that to atone he would have to sacrifice his daughter, Iphigenia.
>
> Torn between his love for his daughter and his duty as a leader, Agamemnon eventually decided Iphigenia would have to die. He wept, then he killed her. After that, he never again wept, except once when the Greeks were losing the war. Otherwise he was so heartless that even his fellow warriors berated him for it.

In this story, Iphigenia symbolizes the "childlike" qualities of trust and innocence and the abilities to love, play, and enjoy life. The warrior, Agamemnon, was forced to kill this child of his (these emotions in himself) in order to go to war. Thus, the story of Agamemnon illustrates one of the most common psychological dilemmas encountered by warriors: the conflict between being a warrior and being a man. Ordinary men need to kill off their inner child so that they can become warriors. But in their civilian roles of husband, father, friend, the emotions of the inner child are very much needed.

The price Agamemnon paid for being a good warrior was the numbing of his emotions and the loss of his ability to love and bond with others. Many combat veterans with PTSD or other readjustment problems experience similar difficulties. They don't want to bond with another person because they don't want to lose that person as they lost others in war.

But only by allowing themselves to feel the pain of their losses can they regain the ability to bond with others. Reviving the buried emotions is the only way the qualities symbolized by Iphigenia can be reborn. Grief may be the hardest of these feelings to deal with.

Exercise: Distinguishing Grief and Anger

If you have served in the military, especially if you have participated in or seen combat, any unresolved grief and anger connected to your war experiences will be likely to contribute greatly to the persistence of your PTSD symptoms or other readjustment problems. However, because of the military environment and the nature of military training and war your grief and rage may be strongly interconnected.

To promote your healing, you need to separate your grief and other feelings from your anger. In Chapters 8 and 9 you were asked to identify sources of anger and specify your losses. At this point, review your journal entries under the categories of anger and loss, and answer the following questions:

1. Have you listed all your angers and losses? In your list of angers, did you include anger regarding your loss of innocence or loss of belief or principles? Did you list any loss of faith in the military as an institution, in certain military officers or practices, or in your country?

2. In what instances during combat or afterwards, was your anger or rage a cover-up for grief?

3. How did you deal with grief during your military experience? Did you ever deal with grief by acting on your anger?

4. How did others in your unit deal with their grief? Was their grief ever expressed through aggressive acts?

5. How have you dealt with your grief since your military experience? Have you used anger to cope with grief? If so, how?

6. How do you feel about how you dealt with your grief during combat? How do you feel about how you have dealt with it since then?

7. In your life today, are there instances when you express your unresolved grief and sadness from the war as anger or rage? What are those instances?

Exercise: Reviewing Triggers

Due to the magnitude of the horror you experienced during your war experience, the list of triggers you compiled in Chapter 5 takes on added significance. Wars of all sorts are going on nearly continuously in our world. Furthermore, war is a common theme for popular films and television programs. Therefore, you cannot help but be given frequent reminders of your war experiences.

Review the list of triggers you compiled in Chapter 5, and take some time to answer the following questions in your journal:

1. Toward which of these war-related reminders have you become immune? Toward which do you still react?

2. What measures have you taken to protect yourself from such triggers?

3. What is the price you pay for such protection?

4. Do you have any choice but to protect yourself this way? If you feel you have no choice but to avoid certain situations, do you have difficulty accepting this limitation? What would be required for you to accept this part of yourself?

Consider the fact that if you are a combat veteran, you have been trained to react with aggression and anger to provocation. A trigger in your environment today, even if it does not pose a threat, may be sufficient provocation to cause you to respond with anger and aggression. Equally likely is that you respond with a shutdown of emotion or with attempts to remove yourself physically or distance yourself emotionally from the individuals or situations that trigger you.

Because your potential for violence is greater than that of civilians, due to your training and military experiences, you need to take particularly good care of yourself in terms of managing trigger situations. This means there may be situations you need to avoid except under emergency conditions.

You may need to be especially watchful not only of situations that enrage you, but those that cause you intense pain and grief as well. Reacting with uncontrollable or unwanted aggression is painful, but equally painful is being shut down emotionally. Either way, you may feel you have failed in certain important relationships or on the job. This feeling of failure may be especially heightened if, in your case, part of your war trauma was feeling that you failed your unit, your commanding officer, or your own military standards.

Premature Death and Suicide

Studies indicate that combat veterans die younger than their contemporaries who did not see combat. This statement has been found to hold true not only for Vietnam veterans, but for World War II and Korean War veterans as well. Combat veterans die younger for a variety of reasons, including the following:

- Physiological strains of the war experience or the physical strain on the body caused by injuries incurred in combat

- Physiological strain, accidents, and other results of alcoholism, drug abuse, or other forms of addiction used to cope with readjustment problems

- Unresolved psychological stresses from the war that express themselves in forms of stress that damage the body

- Car accidents and other kinds of accidents that sometimes can be interpreted as suicidal or part-suicidal in motivation

At this point there is no firm data indicating whether or not combat veterans commit suicide more often than their peers. However, there are motivations for suicide among veterans that are not shared by most civilians.

Exercise: Examining Suicidal Thoughts and Feelings

If you struggle with suicidal feelings and thoughts, or if you have attempted suicide at some point, you need to carefully ask yourself why you want to die. Take some time to answer the following questions in your journal:

1. Do you feel your dying will bring back those you regret having killed? Or are your suicidal thoughts and wishes a form of atonement or repentance for other actions or inactions during your war experience about which you now feel great shame or guilt?

   For example, do you want to die as a form of self-punishment for being a coward at some point during your military experience? Or for having made a mistake that resulted in the death of a buddy or a civilian? For killing too much or not enough? For enjoying the killing or not enjoying the killing? For committing atrocities?

2. Do you really want to die, or do you just want to end the vicious hyperalert-numbing cycle of PTSD?

3. Is it death you seek, or an end to the feeling that you are constantly failing to meet expectations in areas of life that are important to you?

4. Do you seek to die in order to join your dead comrades? In your dreams, flashbacks, or thoughts, do your dead comrades call you to come to them?

5. Do you feel you abandoned your friends because you lived and they died? Even though you know the idea is irrational, do you believe that if you die, your dead war buddies will be given life?

6. Do you tend to become suicidal (and/or homicidal) at certain times of the year? Are these times of the year related to any of your war experiences? Mark these times on your calendar and share them with your family and friends or others who might be affected.

7. What can you do to take care of yourself (for example, to comfort yourself) during any fairly predictable times when you become suicidal?

If you frequently have suicidal thoughts, it may be a sign of clinical depression. Review Chapter 2 and its self-diagnostic questionnaire on depression. You should also get professional help. You owe yourself a consultation with a psychiatrist to assess whether or not you have a biochemical clinical depression as a result of prolonged or untreated PTSD or other war-related physical and psychological stresses.

Coping with Suicidal Thoughts

With the knowledge gained from having completed the preceding exercise (and from having determined in Chapters 1 and 2 whether you have PTSD and/or a biochemical depression), you now have some information with which to combat your suicidal thoughts. When the suicidal thoughts come, as they will tend to do when you are experiencing present-day stresses or when you are having an anniversary reaction or another trigger reaction, you can now talk to yourself as follows:

> I want to kill myself, but it's not that I really want to die. It is PTSD (or depression, or both) telling me to kill myself (or let myself be in an accident, or set myself up for dying). It's not my fault I was in a war and developed PTSD (or depression, or both). I was only trying to serve my country (or obeying my draft notice).
> I don't really want to die. I just want to be with my dead buddies (or bring back the people I killed, or for whatever reason you have identified). But killing myself won't achieve those goals. My dead buddies would want me to live and enjoy it. I can't bring back the dead, but maybe I can help the living in some way.
> Having suicidal thoughts doesn't mean I'm crazy. I have to expect to have them, as part of having been in war, and I have to battle them, the same way I did the enemy during combat, with any weapon I can find. A lot of times I wanted to just give up when I was in the military. But I didn't. I have to apply that same endurance now. I just have to hang on, endure, not act on my suicidal thoughts, just like I didn't act on certain feelings during those tough times in combat.

You also need to talk about your suicidal feelings with caring others, as well as with a qualified professional. Do not allow your suicidal thoughts and feelings to go unexpressed or unattended.

Beyond This Book

"War . . . is all hell," stated General Sherman, but the hell of war need not continue in your life today. You no longer need to consider those comrades who died in your war the "lucky ones." Through the healing process, you can acquire a greater understanding of how your war experiences affect your life in the present and find some constructive uses for those experiences.

But to do that you will need professional help, a support group of other veterans, or both to help you uncover and better understand your specific war experiences. As you confront your war experiences, your feelings will be intense. You will need as much help as you can get.

There are also many forms of assistance available besides individual and group talking-therapy, for example, biofeedback, hypnosis, body work, and PTSD-related medication. All these methods have helped countless veterans gain greater control over their symptoms and exert more mastery in their lives.

As with other forms of trauma, recovery from war-related PTSD does not mean a total disappearance of symptoms but rather a reduction in their frequency and intensity. Once the symptoms are under control, you will be able to enjoy a more satisfying life. And although you will think about the war, your war experiences need not paralyze you or be the focus of your life.

Part IV

Appendixes

A

Getting Help—
Survivor Groups and
Therapy Programs

Healing from trauma is something no one should have to go through alone. Indeed, in many cases doing so is almost impossible, and virtually any trauma survivor can benefit from the right kind of help. Notice, however, that I said "the right kind." The quality of a survivor group or therapy program—whether individual or group—must not only be good, it must also suit you as an individual.

Finding and evaluating therapists, treatment programs, and survivor groups is the subject of this appendix.

Finding a Therapist or Treatment Program

One of the most important tasks you will be faced with in helping yourself to heal is selecting the therapist or therapeutic program that will best meet your needs. This section is devoted to helping you decide which kind of counselor, program, or support group is right for you. Unfortunately, there are many therapists and programs that should be avoided. For example, in recent years PTSD—especially as it relates to rape and childhood sexual abuse survivors—has received considerable media attention. In consequence, some therapists and programs have simply jumped on the bandwagon. They may present themselves as able to offer help to trauma survivors even though the only training they have is a couple of workshops and, perhaps, some extremely limited experience.

In choosing a therapist or program, you have the right to shop around and ask questions. To do this you may need to overcome the passivity and low self-esteem that plague so many trauma survivors. But it is vital that you convince yourself that you deserve the therapist or program that is best suited to your needs.

There is a minimum set of criteria for effective PTSD therapy. Effective therapists and therapeutic programs (for you as a trauma survivor suffering from PTSD) must do the following:

- See the trauma as real and important in itself, apart from any preexisting psychological problems and any current social, family, or personal pressures

- View you as a survivor capable of being healed—not as a willing participant in the trauma or as a hopeless psychiatric case

- Educate you about the nature of trauma, PTSD, and secondary wounding experiences, about the specific factors in your particular category of trauma that may affect you, and about the nature of the healing process itself

- Either teach you coping skills, such as assertiveness, stress management, relaxation techniques, and anger management, or make appropriate referrals for you to receive such help

- Use medication and behavior-management techniques when appropriate, but not to the exclusion of examining your present and past with the goal of understanding what occurred and your feelings about those events

- Be aware of the effects of sex-role stereotyping, racism, and blame-the-victim attitudes on the healing process

Where to Begin

To begin the process of selecting a therapist or program, compile a list of names. Get recommendations from friends, doctors, other trauma survivors who have had positive experiences, and hospitals with specialized programs for trauma survivors.

The Anxiety Disorders Association of America maintains a listing of member therapists and self-help groups by area. Call 301-231-9350 anytime, to listen to a recording, or call between 9:00 a.m. and 5:00 p.m., Eastern time, Monday through Friday, to speak directly with an ADAA staff member.

Veterans Outreach Centers, or Vet Centers, specialize in the treatment of combat-related PTSD. However, Vet Centers' staff members are often familiar with private therapists and programs that serve survivors of other types of trauma. You may want to contact your local Vet Center for a referral. Check the telephone directory, or call your local Veterans Administration hospital or medical center, or any veterans service organization, for example, the American Legion.

Other potential sources of referrals are university health or counseling centers (if you are a student) and local mental health and social service agencies, which are usually run by either the city or county. If you contact one of these organizations, be sure to inquire if the therapists and programs listed are identified by specialty, such as trauma, addiction, eating disorders, and so on, and contact only those therapists whose specialty area(s) match your needs.

You can also check your phone directory or local library to see if there is a statewide association of psychologists, psychiatrists, or social workers. These might, for example, be listed as "Maryland Psychological Association" or "Psychological Association of Pennsylvania." Many of these statewide organizations list therapists by specialty.

If you are a victim of crime, the police may also have a useful referral list. Victims of sexual assault and/or domestic violence can also telephone local rape crisis hotlines, battered women's shelters, and local chapters of NOW (the National Organization for Women) for referrals. Other women's organizations may also have lists of qualified professionals. Your telephone directory, local library, or social services agency should be able to provide you with the phone numbers of these organizations.

The following organizations can provide child abuse survivors, including those with multiple personality disorder, referrals to qualified therapists:

American Professional Society on the Abuse of Children (APSAC), 407 S. Deerborne, Suite 1300, Chicago, IL 60605; 312-554-0166.

Childhelp USA, 1345 N. El Centro Ave., Hollywood, CA 90028; 800-422-4453, 213-465-4016.

VOICES in Action, P.O. Box 148309, Chicago, IL 60614; 312-327-1500 (for incest survivors).

Finally, the agencies and organizations listed under the various headings in Appendix B may be able to provide referrals.

The Screening Process

When you've come up with the names of at least four or five good prospects—ones whose specialties seem to fit your needs—call and interview each of them by phone. (If you are considering a program, you will interview a program representative or staff member.) Before going into the therapist's or program staff's qualifications, ask about fees, whether there are any openings, and whether the available time slots would be workable for you. Eliminate therapists and programs that are geographically inaccessible and those whose fees are prohibitive. When discussing fees, remember to ask about the possibility of a sliding scale, how payments are to be made, and what happens if you miss an appointment.

If the therapist or program meets your needs for these criteria, then inquire about training, experience, and focus. It may seem self-evident to you that a traumatic event such as the one you experienced would be seen as both important and real by any professional. Yet there are schools of thought in the mental health field that regard trauma as relatively minor compared to other problems.

Also, since coursework on trauma and resulting psychological problems is not required training even for licensed social workers, psychologists, and psychiatrists, it is critical that you inquire about the background of any potential therapist or the staff in any therapeutic program. Don't be afraid to ask how many workshops the therapist or staff members have attended or how many books they have read on PTSD and related subjects.

You can also ask how the therapist keeps up with the latest developments in the field of trauma today, and whether he or she has colleagues available for consultation who are experts in PTSD.

You needn't sound hostile, but don't avoid asking the hard questions for fear of offending, either. Remember, your mental and physical health are at stake. You might want to preface your questions by telling the therapist or counselor that you are faced with a bewildering array of alternatives now and you want to make the best choice for you. Consider asking such questions as the following (if you are considering a program, you would ask these questions in terms of the program's staff):

- How long have you been in practice?

- Are you a member of any professional organizations?

- How many trauma survivors have you seen in therapy?

- What is your background in the area of trauma?

- What, in your view, constitutes the healing process for a victim of trauma?

- What experience have you had in treating people suffering from depression/eating disorders/alcoholism? (Gear your questions to your particular problems.)

- How much and what kind of training have you had in these areas?

- What approaches would you take toward healing an eating disorder/alcoholism/suicidal behavior/depression? In the case of an eating disorder, would you work with a nutritionist or dietitian? In the case of clinical depression, do you have a psychiatrist with whom you consult on issues of medication?

- What would you do if I became suicidal?

- What is your view on self-help groups or other group therapy?

- (If you want family counseling as well, ask:) Do you also conduct family therapy? If not, do you work with a family counselor?

- What is your format for communicating with your clients? Under what circumstances would you contact your clients by mail? By phone?

- What limits do you impose on contact with clients? Do you accept phone calls outside of regularly scheduled sessions? Would you accept these calls at your office only or also at home? Is there a charge for time spent on phone calls?

When you have narrowed your list down to a final two or three therapists or programs, go to visit them. In the past, many therapists gave an initial consultation free of charge or at a reduced rate. Today most therapists charge the full fee for their time at the initial consultation. Despite the cost, it's essential that you meet with the therapist face to face before making your selection. (Programs should have a provision for a similar type of interview.)

After this initial interview, think about these questions: Does the therapist or counselor seem warm and supportive? Is he or she respectful toward you? Do you feel as if you could talk with this person about your inner feelings about the trauma?

Most importantly, what is your gut feeling about the therapist? Qualifications are important—and you should only be considering qualified therapists at this point—but the final decision may be a matter of finding the best emotional match for you. Pay attention to your feelings. If you have strong negative feelings toward a particular therapist after the first interview, it probably isn't a good match. If you are ambivalent, you might consider meeting with the therapist an additional time before making your decision.

Special note for women. Many psychologists—both men and women—call themselves "feminist" or "nonsexist"—but you need to decide for yourself if they actually are. Also keep in mind that just because a therapist is a woman does not automatically make her a nonsexist therapist.

You do not have to choose a woman therapist in order to find one who is unbiased. There are many male therapists who are committed to nonsexist treatment and provide excellent counseling. In general, though, it takes considerably more effort for a man to truly understand the influence of sex-role stereotyping on a woman than it does for a woman.

Evaluating the Course of Therapy

Once you've selected a therapist, you can start your therapy on a trial basis. Make a commitment to work with the therapist for a month, six weeks, or some other limited time period; then reassess your choice.

How do you seem to be faring? How effective has the therapist been in addressing your PTSD and secondary symptoms (such as alcoholism or depression)? What is the therapist's assessment of your progress and prospect for healing?

If the therapist you've selected turns out to have been a poor choice, use the knowledge you've gained to make a better one. The wrong therapist can do more harm than good. However, as you make your decision about whether to continue with the therapist, bear in mind that the course of therapy is not always smooth: backsliding, regression, and hostility on your part may all be part of healing. Stop seeing the therapist only if you believe that he or she is actually doing you harm—or if you feel that your prospects for progress with this individual are very slim.

A case in which you would definitely want to look for another therapist would be one in which the therapist blamed you for the trauma. You do not need more guilt, blame, or shame than you feel already. Even if you had nothing to do with causing the trauma, and could have done nothing to prevent it, on some level you probably feel guilty—such is the irrational nature of survivor guilt. If, as a result of the therapist's statements or nonverbal reactions, you continually leave the office feeling more debased, ashamed, and unsure of yourself than before, it is probably time to search for another therapist.

You should also question staying with a therapist who judges you to be "deficient" because he or she subscribes to one of the following myths:

- Having a good moral character and strong personality structure can make you resilient to trauma.

- You sought the trauma to gain attention, to meet your masochistic needs, or to fulfill some other neurotic need.

- The trauma plays a minor part in your problems compared to the mistakes you've made as a human being.

Since you are human, you probably have made mistakes in your life, even during the trauma and afterwards. You probably do have areas where you need to grow and inner conflicts you need to explore. Your therapist may want to help you better understand these mistakes and problem areas. However, this should be done in a manner that respects your dignity and good intentions. It is not only humiliating but in the long run self-defeating and ineffective for a therapist to try and change any of your problem areas through tactics of guilt and shame.

If You Are Referred to a Psychiatrist

If you have a clinical depression or your PTSD symptoms are severe, your therapist may refer you to a psychiatrist who can prescribe medication. If and when you go to a psychopharmacological psychiatrist, he or she will probably do a complete medical and psychiatric workup. You should be prepared to list your symptoms, their duration and frequency, and any other observations you have about your symptoms. In addition, you have the right to expect the psychiatrist to explain your diagnosis and the medication in detail. You might want to ask the doctor these questions:

- What is my psychiatric diagnosis?
- What are the various types of medications that have been found useful for this diagnosis?
- What are the potential benefits and the possible negative side effects of each of these medications?
- Are there any initial side effects that should disappear in time, such as nervousness or extreme fatigue? If so, how long should I wait for the initial symptoms to disappear before I call the office?
- Why is this particular medication being selected over another?
- How much research has been done on this particular medication and what is the probability that this medication will be helpful?
- How long does it typically take for this medication to have an effect?
- If I were to overdose on this medication, would I die?
- Should I give myself the daily medication or should somebody else have the responsibility of giving it to me?
- What if I forget to take the medication at the prescribed time? Should I take it later in the day or wait until the next day? If I skip a day, should I double the dosage the next day, or not?
- What should I do if I vomit the pill for some reason?
- Will this medication interact with other drugs, such as alcohol? If so, will the effect be harmful or possibly deadly?
- Will the drug be administered in ever-increasing doses?
- How will you determine if the dosage needs to be changed? Will blood tests be required? If so, how often?
- Do you have any literature on the medication that I can read?
- Can I become addicted to this medication?
- What will happen to me, physically and psychologically, if I suddenly stop the medication on my own? What if I don't tell any-

one I am stopping the medication, what are the signs others can see that will tell them that I have stopped? What should these others do to help me if I stop taking the medication?

- At what point can the medication be discontinued? Is there a point after which the body becomes immune to the effects of the medication so that it ceases to be effective?

- How long does it take for the effects of the drug to leave the body? How long after the drug is discontinued should any dietary or alcohol restraints be observed?

- If this medication does not work, what other medications might be available?

Medication needs constant monitoring. Before the right dosage is established, you may need to telephone the psychiatrist several times. You will also need to call if the negative side effects are problematic or seem to be causing more hardship than is warranted by the positive effects of the drug.

For example, if you are sluggish or extremely tired all the time, are unable to concentrate, or if you have physical symptoms such as bleeding, muscle tremors, seizures, dizzy spells, hyperventilation, dark or discolored urine, rashes, inability to urinate, constipation, loss of menstrual period, severe headaches, vomiting or nausea, loss of sex drive, or other physical difficulties, you should call the psychiatrist right away. Similarly, if you still feel suicidal, homicidal, or self-mutilating, or if you develop hallucinations, delusions, or begin to feel hyperactive or out of control, call the psychiatrist immediately. If your call is not returned promptly, call again. Do not let these side effects go unattended.

Finally, be wary of any psychiatrist who does not seem familiar with the medication, who seems to discount your concerns, or who does not return your phone calls regarding questions about the medication or problems with it. If contacting the psychiatrist is always a problem, consider changing psychiatrists. However, you might want to discuss your decision with your therapist or support group first.

Finding a Survivor Group

There is increased recognition today that trauma survivors can benefit greatly from participation in a survivor group. Groups for survivors of war, rape, and various forms of family abuse are becoming fairly common and thus easy to find. Survivors of crime, natural catastrophes, vehicular accidents, and other forms of trauma may have a harder time finding a group.

To search for a survivor group appropriate for you, consult the following resources:

- Your local library.

- Your local (county or city) mental health or social services department.

- Your local police department.

- Local hospitals.

- Local newspapers—survivor groups may be listed in the classified ads, in the community section, or in sections pertaining to family life and mental health.

You may also want to check with the local chapter of the **American Psychological Association**, the **American Psychiatric Association**, or the **National Association of Social Workers** to see if they can help you locate a survivor group. A therapist with expertise in trauma may also be able to refer you to such a group. In addition, the following support groups and referral services may be helpful:

AA World Service (Alcoholics Anonymous), P.O. Box 459 Grand Central Station, New York, NY 10163; 212-870-3400. Check local listings as well.

Al-Anon Family Group Headquarters and **Alateen** (both for the families of alcoholics), World Service Office, P.O. Box 862, Midtown Station, New York, NY 10018; 212-302-7240. Check local listings as well.

American Suicide Foundation, 1045 Park Ave., New York, NY 10028; 800-531-4477.

Group Project for Holocaust Survivors and Their Children, 345 East 80th Street, New York, NY 10021; 212-737-8524.

Incest Survivors Anonymous, P.O. Box 17245, Long Beach, CA 90807; 310-428-5599.

National Child Abuse Hotline, Childhelp USA; 800-4-A-CHILD.

National Coalition Against Domestic Violence, P.O. Box 18749, Denver, CO 80218; 800-799-7233, 303-839-1852.

National Organization for Victims Assistance (NOVA), 1757 Park Road NW, Washington, D.C. 20010; 202-232-6682.

National Self-Help Clearinghouse, 25 West 43rd St., Rm. 620, New York, NY 10036; 212-354-8525.

Ray of Hope (for suicide survivors), P.O. Box 2323, Iowa City, IA 52244; 319-377-9890.

Some survivor groups are led by professionals, others by survivors only. Some have a religious basis or are identified with a certain faith or denomination. Self-help survivor groups and church-led groups that do not employ professionals are usually either free or charge only what is necessary to meet expenses. Survivor groups that are led by professionals vary in price. Some offer a sliding scale; others do not.

If you are in a 12-step program such as Alcoholics Anonymous, Narcotics Anonymous, Overeaters Anonymous, Al-Anon, or Nar-A-Non, you might ask at your meetings whether anyone knows of a survivor group appropriate for you.

Also, if you have a physical or emotional problem related to the trauma—for example, if you lost a limb or developed some other physical or emotional problem such as depression—you might want to inquire (using any of the resources listed above) about survivor groups organized around your physical or emotional concerns, rather than the type of trauma you endured. For instance, if you developed an eating disorder as a result of your trauma, you may want to consider Overeaters Anonymous (OA) as well as professionally led groups. Similarly, if the trauma triggered, or worsened, a problem with alcohol or drugs, you may want to at least try some AA or NA (Narcotics Anonymous) meetings. It is usually suggested that you go to at least six meetings before you decide whether the program fits your needs.

If you don't have any luck in finding a group that fits your needs or experiences, you might consider starting one. You can start by contacting a therapist or clinic specializing in trauma work to see if there is interest in helping to organize and direct a survivors group.

Further Reading

The following publications offer further information that may be helpful in your search for help:

"If Sex Enters Into the Psychotherapy Relationship." Write to Order Department, American Psychological Association, 750 First St. NE; Washington, D.C. 20002; or call 202-336-5500.

A Woman's Guide to Psychotherapy, by Susan Stanford Friedman. Englewood Cliffs, NJ: Prentice-Hall, 1979.

"Seeking Professional Help: Finding the Right Therapist and the Right Treatment" in Back from the Brink: A Family Guide to Overcoming Traumatic Stress, by Don R. Catherall. NY: Bantam, 1992.

B

Resources

This appendix lists two types of resources: names and addresses or telephone numbers of agencies and organizations that may be able to provide assistance of various kinds; and titles of books, pamphlets, newsletters, audiotapes, and other materials that might be of use to you in understanding trauma and healing from it, and in controlling symptoms and secondary problems.

These resources are listed alphabetically by the following topics:

- Alcohol and drug abuse
- Battering
- Child abuse
- Crime
- Depression
- Eating disorders and compulsive behavior
- Legal assistance
- Natural catastrophes
- Rape and sexual assault
- Relaxation and symptom-management
- Suicide
- Vehicular accidents
- War and combat

The organizations and materials listed here are by no means all the resources available. In fact, this list is only a beginning. In some categories there are hundreds of articles and books available; in others, unfortunately, there is very little. I encourage you to look beyond this list on your own. Spend some time at your local library, and ask the librarian for assistance if you need it. Also talk to other survivors and helping professionals to see what resources they can recommend.

Alcohol and Drug Abuse

Agencies and Organizations

If you suffer from alcoholism or drug addiction, you will probably need to go to a detox center, where you will receive the medical care you need as you go through withdrawal. Do *not* attempt to detox by yourself; withdrawal can lead to medical emergencies. Furthermore, since withdrawal tends to create the symptoms of depression, the process can be so painful that you may be tempted immediately to begin using your drug again to ease the emotional distress. In some clinics, antidepressants are given to ease the transition.

After you have successfully withdrawn from your drug, you need treatment that not only help you abstain from your drug, but that offers insight into the reasons you needed it in the first place. Consider an inpatient or outpatient rehabilitation program that is specific to your drug. Some programs are free; others require insurance. Most programs include 12-step meetings such as Alcoholics Anonymous (AA), Narcotics Anonymous (NA), and Cocaine Anonymous, or will refer you to the local chapter of one of these organizations.

You can obtain the names of treatment centers from the phone book, from hospitals, and from city or county mental health or social service agencies. In addition to these local programs, there are specialized centers around the country. Names of these programs can be obtained from your doctor and/or therapist, from your local drug or alcohol-rehabilitation board or council, from a local hospital, or from 12-step meeting members.

If you have been addicted for many years, don't be surprised if you need to enroll in treatment programs more than once to complete your healing. Nationwide, multiple hospitalizations are the norm, not the exception. Also when you begin a program, be sure you receive a complete medical examination, as well as an evaluative interview for clinical depression. If you suffer from depression as well, your ability to stay clean and sober will be made that much more difficult.

Information about AA, Al-Anon, Adult Children of Alcoholics (ACOA), Cocaine Anonymous, NA, and Nar-Anon meetings can be obtained from your telephone directory or local library, or by calling the national offices of these organizations, listed below. See also the section "Finding a Survivor Group" in Appendix A.

Al-Anon: 800-356-9996

Alcoholics Anonymous World Service: 212-870-3400

Narcotics Anonymous: 818-773-9999

Books and Other Materials

Books, pamphlets, workbooks, and audio- and videocassettes on all issues related to alcoholism, drug addiction, and other forms of substance abuse are available through **Hazelden Educational Materials**, Box 176, Pleasant Valley Road, Center City, MN 55012. Call 800-328-9000 for a free catalog. Some of the best of these are listed below.

Addiction and Grace, by Gerald May. Center City, MN: Hazelden Educational Materials, 1988.

The Addictive Personality: Roots, Rituals, and Recovery, by Craig Nakken. Center City, MN: Hazelden Educational Materials, 1988.

Addictive Thinking: Why Do We Lie to Ourselves? Why Do Others Believe Us?, by Abraham J. Twerski. Center City, MN: Hazelden Educational Materials, 1990.

The Big Book and *The Twelve Traditions*. Available from Alcoholics Anonymous World Services, Box 459, Grand Central Station, New York, NY 10163.

From Chocolates to Morphine: Understanding Mind-Active Drugs, by Andrew Weil and Winifred Doren. New York: Houghton Mifflin, 1981.

I'll Quit Tomorrow, by Vernon E. Johnson. New York: Harper and Row, 1983.

Loving an Alcoholic, by Jack Mumey. New York: Bantam Books, 1988.

Marty Mann Answers Your Questions About Drinking and Alcoholism, edited by Marty Mann. New York: Holt, Rinehart and Winston, 1981.

Passages Through Recovery: An Action Plan for Preventing Relapse, by Terence Gorski. Center City, MN: Hazelden Educational Materials, 1989.

The Tranquilizing of America, by Richard Hughes and Robert Brewin. New York: Warner Books, 1979.

Under the Influence: Guide to the Myths and Realities of Alcoholism, by James R. Milam and K. Ketchan. New York: Bantam Books, 1981.

Battering

Agencies and Organizations

You can be directed to sources of help by courts, social service agencies, churches, battered women's shelters, or state chapters of the **National**

Coalition Against Domestic Violence. Call 303-839-1852, the national office of the coalition, for information about your state chapter, or check your local phone directory. The organization also maintains an information line: 800-799-7233.

You may also be able to get names and phone numbers of sources of assistance from your local police, local library, community crisis center, or mental health hotline.

It may be helpful for you to contact the **National Organization for Victim Assistance**, 1757 Park Road NW, Washington, D.C., 20010; 202-232-6682. This organization can provide crisis intervention, short-term counseling, medical and legal advice, and referrals to some 8,000 victim-assistance programs across the country, including battered women's programs and rape crisis centers.

You can also contact the **National Domestic Violence Hotline**, P.O. Box 7032, Huntington Woods, MI 48070; 800-779-7233.

If you are in the military or are being abused by someone in the military, you can contact a family advocacy officer or representative. There is one such person at every Army, Navy, Air Force, Marine Corps, and Coast Guard installation. Family advocacy officers can be contacted directly or through a family service or family support center. Abused spouses may also contact the chaplain, the medical department, the Staff Judge Advocate, a social worker, the nearest Woman's Advocacy office (when available), their spouse's commanding officer, or anyone in the chain of command.

More information about the military legal system and available resources for abused military spouses and children can be obtained from the **Center for Women Policy Studies**, 2000 P Street NW, Suite 508, Washington, D.C., 20036; 202-872-1770.

Also see the section "Ways Out" at the end of Chapter 13.

Books and Other Materials

Battered Wives, by Del Martin. San Francisco: Volcano Press, 1981.

The Battered Woman, by Lenore Walker. New York: Harper and Row, 1979.

Chain Chain Change: For Black Women Dealing with Physical and Emotional Abuse, by Evelyn White. Seattle: Seal Press, 1985.

Getting Free: A Handbook for Women in Abusive Relationships, by Ginny Ni-Carthy. Seattle: Seal Press, 1986.

Major Sola Que Mal Acompanada: Para La Mujer Golopeada/For the Latina in an Abusive Relationship, by Myrna M. Zambrano. Seattle: Seal Press, 1985.

Child Abuse

Agencies and Organizations

The **National Child Abuse Hotline** (800-442-4453), run by Childhelp USA, provides on-the-spot telephone counseling to any child being abused (physically or sexually) and offers immediate assistance, information, and referrals to anyone concerned about abused children, for example, neighbors, friends, school and other officials, and survivors of past abuse. Childhelp's address is 1345 N. El Centro Ave., Hollywood, CA 90028.

For information and free literature on child abuse, you can also contact the **National Council on Child Abuse and Female Violence**, 1155 Connecticut Ave. NW, Suite 400, Washington, D.C. 20036; 800-222-2000 or 202-429-6695.

VOICES in Action is a national network of male and female incest survivors, local groups, and contacts throughout the United States that offers free referrals to therapists, agencies, and self-help groups endorsed by survivors. (VOICES stands for Victims of Incest Can Emerge Survivors.) VOICES also maintains a listing of over 100 confidential groups in which survivors who have survived particular types of abuse can write to each other. In addition, the group publishes a newsletter, holds an annual meeting, and offers training for group leaders. Write to P.O. Box 148309, Chicago, IL 60614; or call 312-327-1500.

Also see the section "Ways Out" at the end of Chapter 13.

Books and Other Materials

Numerous books, pamphlets, and workbooks on recovering from physical and/or sexual abuse are available from **Hazelden Educational Materials**, Box 176, Pleasant Valley Road, Center City, MN 55012. Call 800-328-9000 for a free catalog.

Adult Children of Abusive Parents, by Steven Farmer. Los Angeles: Lowell House, 1989.

Adult Survivors of Child Sexual Abuse, by Christine Courtois. Available from Families International, 11700 West Lake Park Dr., Park Place, Milwaukee, WI, 53224.

Childhood Sexual Abuse: A Survivor's Guide for Men, by Suzanne Nice and Russell Forest. Center City, MN: Hazelden Educational Materials, 1990.

The Courage to Heal, by Ellen Bass and Laura Davis. New York: Harper and Row, 1988.

For Crying Out Loud. Available from Cambridge Women's Center, 46 Pleasant Street, Cambridge, MA 02139; (617) 354-8807. Although this newsletter is written by and for women with histories of sexual abuse, the information it contains is relevant and helpful for male survivors as well.

"Everything You Always Wanted to Know About Child Abuse and Neglect." Available from the National Center on Child Abuse and Neglect, Department of Health and Human Services, P.O. Box 1182, Washington, D.C. Also available from the same address is a listing of free and low-cost pamphlets on child abuse and neglect.

Free of the Shadows: Recovering From Sexual Violence, by Caren Adams and Jennifer Fay. Oakland, CA: New Harbinger Publications, 1989.

The Healing Way—Adult Recovery from Childhood Sexual Abuse, by Kristin Kunzman. Center City, MN: Hazelden Educational Materials, 1990.

The Newsletter. Available from VOICES in Action, P.O. Box 148309, Chicago, IL 60614; 312-327-1500. This newsletter for adult male and female incest survivors is provided as part of VOICES' annual $35.00 membership fee. It provides information, resources, book reviews, and writings by and for survivors. It is currently expanding to include more information on issues of male survivors.

The Other Side of the Family: A Book of Recovery from Abuse, Incest, and Neglect, by Ellen Ratner. Deerfield Beach, FL: Health Communications, 1990.

The Right to Innocence: Healing the Trauma of Sexual Abuse, by Beverly Engel. New York: Ivy, 1989.

Victims No Longer: Men Recovering from Incest and Other Sexual Abuse, by Mike Lew. New York: Nevramont Publishing Co., 1989.

When the Bough Breaks: A Helping Guide for Parents of Sexually Abused Children, by Aphrodite Matsakis. Oakland, CA: New Harbinger Publications, 1991.

Crime

Agencies and Organizations

Hopefully, your area has a victim-assistance center that can give you information about your legal rights and offer legal, financial, and psychological help. Usually these centers are listed under "Victim Assistance" in telephone directories. Addresses and phone numbers of these centers can probably also be obtained from the police, local social service agencies, your local legal aid society, or your local bar association. (If you were raped, see also the listings under "Rape and Sexual Assault" in this appendix.)

Many states provide financial assistance for certain types of crime victims. Each state varies in its qualifications and in the amount it offers for counseling, living expenses, medical help, funeral expenses for murder victims, rape evidence kits, legal fees, disability claims, and other kinds of assistance. Under certain circumstances, victims' families can obtain various types of help. This is most often the case for the families of murder victims.

If you were a victim of crime while working on the job, you may qualify for worker compensation. Inquire at your place of employment, your local office of the **Department of Social Services**, or your state worker compensation board or office. Your employer may also offer various forms of assistance.

If you have become disabled due to the crime, you may be able to apply for Social Security benefits through the **Social Security Administration**. You may also be able to deduct losses from theft from your federal income tax. Obtain publication 547 from the **Internal Revenue Service** (by calling 800-829-3676) for a full description of the circumstances under which you can take such a deduction.

Sometimes insurance companies raise premiums or refuse to cover victims of a theft. The **Federal Insurance Administration** has a policy that will cover your residence no matter how many times you have been victimized. It is not available in all states, however. Write to Federal Crime Insurance, P.O. Box 6301, Rockville, Maryland 29850, or call 800-638-8780.

You may also want to contact the **National Organization for Victims Assistance (NOVA)**, a private, nonprofit organization of victim and witness practitioners, criminal-justice professionals, researchers, former victims, and others who are advocates for victims. Write to NOVA, 1757 Park Road NW, Washington, D.C., 20010; or call 202-232-6682.

Books and Other Materials

The Crime Victim's Book, 2nd ed., by Morton Bard and Dawn Sangrey. Secaucus, NJ: Citadel Press, 1986. This book is one of the best resources available for crime victims and their families. It contains an excellent description of the psychology of crime victims and explains in simple language how victims can work effectively to claim their rights within government and legal bureaucracies. It also provides an outline of typical court procedures.

"Report to the Nation on Crime and Justice: The Data." Available from National Criminal Justice Reference Service, Box 6000, Dept. F, Rockville, MD 20850. Ask for publication NCJ 87068. This report provides general information about crime and the criminal justice system.

Victim Rights and Services: A Legislative Directory. Available from NOVA, 1757 Park Road NW, Washington, D.C., 20010; 202-232-6682. This publication gives an overview of the federal and state victim rights and services legislation and victim-compensation measures currently in effect.

Depression

Agencies and Organizations

As has been said repeatedly in this book, if you have a clinical depression, you need to consult a therapist or other mental health professional experienced in treating people who suffer from depression. See Appendix A for guidelines for finding such assistance.

Books and Other Materials

The Depression Workbook, by Mary Ellen Copeland. Oakland, CA: New Harbinger Publications, 1992.

Feeling Good: The New Mood Therapy, by David D. Burns. New York: Signet Books, 1980.

First Aid for Depression, by Louis Presnall. Center City, MN: Hazelden Educational Materials, 1985.

Here Comes the Sun, by Gail Rosellini and Mark Warden. Center City, MN: Hazelden Educational Materials, 1988.

Search for Serenity, by Louis Presnall. Center City, MN: Hazelden Educational Materials, 1973.

Eating Disorders and Compulsive Behavior

Agencies and Organizations

If you suffer from anorexia, bulimia, or compulsive overeating, you need to arrange a consultation with an eating disorders specialist, who can advise you whether you need an inpatient or an outpatient program. If your weight is dangerously high or low, or if your eating disorder is making it impossible for you to function or has caused medical complications, you may need hospitalization.

In the past, most inpatient and outpatient units specialized in anorexia or bulimia, but today more and more clinics are accepting individuals who struggle with compulsive overeating or obesity. Furthermore, an increasing number of insurance policies are paying for hospitalization for eating disorders.

Whether you need inpatient or outpatient help, your therapy should have a dual focus: symptom management (eliminating the destructive eating patterns and replacing them with constructive ones) and insight therapy. Follow the guidelines in Appendix A for finding a therapist or program. You might also consider attending **Overeater's Anonymous** meetings (listed in the phone directory) as well as being evaluated for depression.

Hospitalization is usually not advised for other forms of compulsive behavior, unless there are medical or life-threatening problems resulting from the compulsion. (In that case, the hospitalization would be for your medical problem, not the compulsion, per se.) For help in understanding and curbing your compulsive behavior, whether it surrounds gambling, spending, sexual activity, or other behaviors, you will need individual counseling with a counselor who specializes in addictions and compulsions (see the guidelines in Appendix A for finding such a person). You may also want to consider participation in **Gambler's Anonymous**, **Debtor's Anonymous**, **Sex Addicts Anonymous**, or **Sex and Love Addicts Anonymous**; consult your phone directory for listings.

Books and Other Materials

The Deadly Diet: Recovering from Anorexia & Bulimia, by Terence J. Sandbek. Oakland, CA: New Harbinger Publications, 1986.

Fat is a Family Affair: A Hope-filled Guide for Family and Friends of Eating Disorder Sufferers, by Judi Hollis. Center City, MN: Hazelden Educational Materials, 1990.

Feeding the Hungry Heart: The Experience of Compulsive Eating, by G. Roth. New York: Signet, 1982.

The Habit Control Workbook, by Nonie Birkedahl. Oakland, CA: New Harbinger Publications, 1990.

Judi Hollis's Collection for Recovering Overeaters, by Judi Hollis. Center City, MN: Hazelden Educational Materials, 1985.

Listen to the Hunger: Why We Overeat, by Elizabeth L. Center City, MN: Hazelden Educational Materials, 1987.

Showing Up for Life: A Recovering Overeater's Triumph Over Compulsion, by Heidi Waldrop. Center City, MN: Hazelden Educational Materials, 1990.

Sick and Tired of Being Fat: A Man's Struggle to Be Okay, by Eliot Alexander. Center City, MN: Hazelden Educational Materials, 1991.

When Once Is Not Enough: Help for Obsessive Compulsives, by Gail Steketee and Kerrin White. Oakland, CA: New Harbinger Publications, 1990.

Legal Assistance

Agencies and Organizations

If you need the assistance of an attorney but cannot afford the customary legal fees, you can search out sources of low-cost or even free legal aid. Many lawyers volunteer time doing *pro bono* work—work for which they don't charge. Contact the following sources and inquire about low-cost or free legal assistance for your particular legal problem: your local courthouse, state bar association, police department, local battered women's shelters and rape crisis centers, and your local legal aid society. The law school of a nearby university may also be able to refer you.

In the telephone directory, look in the white or yellow pages under "Legal Assistance," "Lawyer Referral Services," "Legal Aid," and "Legal Services Plans," for listings. You may also want to look in the yellow pages under "Attorneys" or "Lawyers," scanning the ads for lawyers who have sliding-scale payment plans, who offer a half-hour or hour of free consultation, or who specialize in your problem area. Then call a few of the numbers you find. If one lawyer can't help you, he or she may be able to refer you to someone who can.

Also, lawyers will sometimes work on a contingency basis, which means that if you win your case they get a percentage of any award or settlement you receive. But if you lose your case, you don't owe your attorney any fees.

Natural Catastrophes

Agencies and Organizations

Each state has its own disaster relief agency or office of emergency assistance. States vary in the types of compensation and services they offer. Contact your local agency for specific information about your state.

If the President of the United States declares a disaster area, the services of the **Federal Emergency Management Agency (FEMA)** become available. These services include some grants and loans, as well as crisis counseling. A local center is set up to provide assistance in disaster areas. To apply for assistance, call 800-462-9029. Also available is a publication entitled "Disaster Assistance Programs: A Guide to Federal Aid in Disasters," as well as other pamphlets that outline the types of aid available.

The **American Red Cross** also provides assistance for disaster victims. Contact your local chapter for further information.

Unfortunately, to date little has been written about stress reactions to natural disasters. General readings on PTSD should be helpful.

Rape and Sexual Assault

Agencies and Organizations

Contact your local rape crisis center for information and support. If your area does not have a rape crisis center, see if there is a battered women's shelter available. You might also call your local social services department for assistance.

Some rape crisis centers offer free or low-cost individual or group therapy; some do not. Most such centers have the names of qualified therapists. However, even if a therapist comes highly recommended, be sure to check out the therapist's credentials. As is discussed further in Appendix A, you should only work with a therapist who has expertise in the area of sexual assault and with whom you feel some emotional affinity and trust. The therapist's skills and experience are critically important in helping you to heal. However, equally important for your healing is that there be an emotional match between you and your counselor.

Also check victim-assistance centers and the other sources of assistance for victims listed above under "Crime." You may be able to receive financial help for counseling, medical problems, and any losses incurred as a result of the rape.

Books and Other Materials

The Depression Workbook, by Mary Ellen Copeland. Oakland, CA: New Harbinger Publications, 1992

Free of the Shadows: Recovering from Sexual Violence, by Jennifer Fay and Caren Adams. Oakland, CA: New Harbinger Publications, 1989.

If She Is Raped: A Book for Husbands, Fathers, and Male Friends, by Alan W. McEvoy and Jeff B. Brookings. Holmes Beach, FL: Learning Publications, Inc., 1984.

I Never Called It Rape, by R. Warshaw. New York: Harper and Row, 1988.

Recovering from Rape, by Linda E. Ledray. New York: Owl Books, Henry Holt and Company, 1986.

Victims No Longer: Men Recovering from Incest and Other Sexual Abuse, by Mike Lew. New York: Nevramont Publishing Co., 1988. This book, the first of its kind, explains the problem of male sexual victimization in layman's terms and provides first-person accounts as well as written exercises for male survivors.

Relaxation and Symptom-Management

Books and Other Materials

Anxiety and Phobia Workbook, 2nd ed. by Edmund J. Bourne. Oakland, CA: New Harbinger Publications, 1995.

Letting Go of Stress, by Emmett Miller (audiocassette). Available from Source, 945 Evelyn St., Menlo Park, CA 94025; 800-528-2737 or 415-328-7171 in California.

The Relaxation & Stress Reduction Workbook, 4th ed., by M. Davis, E.R. Eshelman, and M. McKay. Oakland, CA: New Harbinger Publications, 1995.

The Relaxation Response, by H. Benson. New York: Avon, 1975.

Relaxation Training Program, by Thomas Nudzynski (three-cassette set). Available from Guilford Publications, 72 Spring St., New York, NY 10012; 800-365-7006 or 212-431-9800 in New York.

Suicide

Agencies and Organizations

If someone close to you has committed suicide, you may benefit from participating in a grief-and-loss seminar, a bereavement group, or a special group for survivors of suicide. Many local hospitals, churches, and mental health agencies offer grief-and-loss seminars or groups. They may also be able to refer you to a grief counselor or a suicide survivor group in your area.

You can also inquire about survivor groups in your area from your local state or county mental health service agency, from your nearest suicide-crisis hotline, at local hospitals and churches, or from the following organizations:

The American Suicide Foundation, 1045 Park Ave., New York, N.Y. 10028; 800-531-4477. The American Suicide Foundation also offers referral service and lists of survivors groups sponsored by educational, religious, medical, and mental health institutions by state.

Ray of Hope, P.O. Box 2323, Iowa City, IA 52244; 319-337-9890. There are chapters in the Midwest and in New York, New Jersey, and other states. This organization offers a referral service and publications for suicide survivors.

Books and Other Resources

A Special Scar: The Experiences of People Bereaved by Suicide, by Allison Wertheimer. New York: Routledge, 1991.

After Suicide—A Ray of Hope, 2nd ed. by Eleanora Ross. Iowa City, IA: Lynn Publications, 1990. To order, contact Ray of Hope, P.O. Box 2323, Iowa City, IA 52244; 319-337-9890.

After Suicide—A Unique Grief Process, by Eleanora Ross. Iowa City, IA: Lynn Publications, 1987. To order, contact Ray of Hope, P.O. Box 2323, Iowa City, IA 52244; 319-337-9890.

Life after Suicide: A Survivor's Grief Experience, by Terence Barrett. Fargo, ND: Prairie House, 1989.

Please Listen to Me: Your Guide to Understanding Teenagers and Suicide, 2nd ed. by Marion Crook. Bellingham, WA: Self-Counsel Press, 1992.

Suicide and Bereavement, by Bruce L. Danto et al. Stratford, NH: Ayer Company Publishers, 1980.

Survivors of Suicide, by Rita Robinson. North Hollywood, CA: Newcastle Publishing, 1992.

Waking Up, Alive: The Descent, the Suicide Attempt, and the Return to Life, by Richard A. Heckler. New York: Grosset-Putnam Books, 1994.

Words I Never Thought to Speak: Stories of Life in the Wake of Suicide, by Victoria G. Alexander. New York: The Free Press, 1991.

Teenagers Talk About Suicide, by Marion Crook. Checktowaga, NY: University of Toronto Press, 1988.

Vehicular Accidents
Agencies and Organizations

You can contact your local Vet Center (see "War and Combat," below) to find the name of a therapist who is experienced in helping trauma survivors. Trauma-recovery clinics, rape crisis centers, and battered women's shelters may also be helpful in recommending specific counselors, and may have information about survivor groups. You might also want to telephone hospitals in search of a survivor group. As of this writing, however, survivor groups for accident survivors are rare. (See Appendix A for more information on finding therapists and survivor groups.)

Unfortunately, to date little has been written about stress reactions to vehicular accidents. General readings on PTSD should be helpful.

War and Combat
Agencies and Organizations

Veterans can seek assistance at their closest **Department of Veterans Affairs Medical Center** (VAMC). Most of these centers offer counseling

services for individual and family problems, as well as assistance or referral for alcohol and drug-related problems. VAMCs are increasingly becoming aware of PTSD, and some offer both in- and out-patient group
and individual therapy for veterans suffering from combat-related PTSD.
Application for inpatient units can be made through the psychiatry or
psychology services at your local VAMC, or through your local Vet Center.

Vet Centers may be listed in your telephone directory under "Vet
Centers" or as "Veterans Outreach Centers." Vet Centers are small counseling clinics aimed at providing therapy, social services, employment assistance, and other types of services to all Vietnam-era veterans and veterans who served in war zones in Grenada, Lebanon, Panama, the Persian
Gulf, and other conflict areas since the Vietnam War (and to their families).

The following veterans service organizations can also provide various forms of assistance:

Veterans of the Vietnam War, National Headquarters, 760 Jumper Rd.,
Wilkes-Barre, PA 18702; 717-825-7215.

Vietnam Veterans of America, 1224 M St. NW, Washington, D.C. 20005;
202-628-2700. Most states have local chapters.

American Legion, 1608 K Street NW, Washington, D.C. 20006; 202-861-
2700.

Department of Veteran's Affairs, 1811 R St. NW,, Washington, D.C. 20009;
202-265-6280.

Jewish War Veterans, 1811 R St. NW, Washington, D.C. 20009; 202-265-
6280.

Blinded Veteran's Association, 477 H St. NW, Washington, D.C. 20001;
202-371-8880.

Disabled American Veterans, 807 Maine Ave. SW, Washington, D.C.
20024; 202-554-3501.

Paralyzed Veterans of America, 801 18th St. NW, Washington, D.C. 20006;
202-872-1300.

Books and Other Materials

"Continuing Readjustment Problems Among Vietnam Veterans, The Etiology of Combat Related Post-Traumatic Stress Disorders," by Jim
Goodwin. Available from Disabled American Veterans, P.O. Box
14301, Cincinnati, Ohio, 45213.

Long Time Passing: Viet Nam: The Haunted Generation, by Myra MacPherson.
Garden City, NY: Doubleday and Colk, Inc., 1984.

The Ravens, by Christopher Robbins. New York: Crown Publishers, Inc.,
1987.

Recovering From the War: A Woman's Guide to Helping Your Vietnam Vet, Your Family, and Yourself, by P.H.C. Mason. New York: Penguin Books, 1990.

Soldier's Heart: Survivor's Views of Combat Trauma, edited by Sarah Hansel, Ann Steidle, Grace Zaczek, and Ron Zaczek. Luthersville, MD: Sidran Press, 1995.

The Trauma of War: Stress and Recovery in Vietnam Veterans, by S. Sonnenberg, A. Blank, and J. Talbott. Washington, D.C.: American Psychiatric Press, Inc., 1985.

Vietnam Wives: Women and Children Surviving Life with Veterans with PTSD, 2nd edition, by Aphrodite Matsakis. Lutherville, MD: Sidran Press, 1996.

References

Adler, Tina. 1990. "PTSD Linked to Stress Rather Than Character." *The APA Monitor* 21:3 (May).

Alcierno, Ronald, Michel Hersen, Vincent Van Hasselt, and Geoffrey Tremont. 1994. "Review of the Validation and Dissemination of Eye-Movement Desensitization and Reprocessing: A Scientific and Ethical Dilemma." Unpublished paper, Center for Psychological Studies, Nova Southeastern University, Fort Lauderdale, FL.

Alcoholics Anonymous. 1953. *Twelve Steps and Twelve Traditions*. New York: The AA Grapevine Inc. and Alcoholics Anonymous.

Alford, J. D., C. Mahone, and E. Fielstein. 1988. "Cognitive and Behavioral Sequelae of Combat: Conceptualization and Implication for Treatment." *Journal of Traumatic Stress* 1:4.

Allgeier, Elizabeth R., and Albert R. Allgeier. 1991. *Sexual Interactions*. Lexington, MA: Heath.

American Psychological Association. 1984. "APA Task Force on the Victims of Crime and Violence." Washington, D.C.: American Psychological Association.

Anixter, William. 1990. "Managing Difficult Cases: Anxiety Disorders, Alcoholism, and Substance Abuse." Paper presented at the Anxiety Disorders Association National Conference, March 1990, at Bethesda, MD.

Bard, Morton, and Dawn Sangrey. 1986. *The Crime Victim's Book.*, 2nd ed. New York: Brunner/Mazel.

Bass, Ellen, and Laura Davis. 1988. *The Courage to Heal*. New York: Harper and Row.

Beck, Aaron T. 1973. *The Diagnosis and Management of Depression.* Philadelphia: University of Pennsylvania Press.

Bentley, Steve. 1991. "A Short History of PTSD: From Thermopylae to Hue." *The Veteran,* January.

Bhatia, S., M. Khan, and A. Sharma. 1986. "Suicide Risk: Evaluation and Management." *American Family Physician* 34:3 (September).

Bigham, Denise, and Patricia Resick. 1990. "Victimization in a Chemically Dependent Population." Paper presented at the Society for Traumatic Stress National Convention, October 1990, at New Orleans.

Blake, J. D. 1986. "Treatment of Acute Posttraumatic Stress Disorder with Tricylic Antidepressants." *Southern Medical Journal* 79:2.

Blanchard, E. B., E. J. Hickling, and A. E. Taylor. 1991. "The Psychophysiology of Motor Vehicle Accident Related Posttraumatic Stress Disorder." *Biofeedback Self Regulation* 16:4 (December).

Blank, Arthur. 1985. "The Unconscious Flashback to the War in Vietnam Veterans: Clinical Mystery, Legal Defense, and Community Problem." In *The Trauma of War: Stress and Recovery in Vietnam Veterans,* edited by S. A. Sonnenberg, A. S. Blank, and J. A. Talbott. Washington, D.C.: American Psychiatric Press.

Bourne, Edmund J. 1990. *The Anxiety and Phobia Workbook.* Oakland, CA: New Harbinger Publications.

Brent, D. A., J. A. Perper, G. Moritz, L. Liotus, J. Schweers, and R. Canobbio. 1994. "Major Depression or Uncomplicated Bereavement? A Follow-up of Youth Exposed to Suicide." *Journal of the American Academy of Child and Adolescent Psychiatry* 33:2 (February).

Brent, D. A., J. Perper, G. Mortiz, C. Allman, L. Liotus, J. Schweers, C. Roth, L. Balach, and R. Canobbio. 1993a. "Bereavement or Depression? The Impact of the Loss of a Friend to Suicide." *Journal of the American Academy of Child and Adolescent Psychiatry* 32:6 (November).

Brent, D. A., J. A. Perper, G. Moritz, L. Liotus, J. Schweers, C. Roth, L. Balach, and C. Allman. 1993b. "Psychiatric Impact of the Loss of an Adolescent Sibling to Suicide." *Journal of Affective Disorders* 28:4 (August).

Brent, David A., Joshua A. Perper, Grace Mortiz, Laura Liotus, et. al. 1995. "Posttraumatic Stress Disorder in Peers of Adolescent Suicide Victims: Predisposing Factors and Phenomenology." *Journal of the American Academy of Child and Adolescent Psychiatry,* 34:2 (February).

Brown, Angela, and David Finkelhor. 1986. "Impact of Child Sexual Abuse: A Review of the Research." *Psychological Bulletin* 99:1.

Burns, David D. 1980. *Feeling Good: The New Mood Therapy.* New York: Signet Books.

Call, E., chair. 1995. "Efficacy of Eye Movement Desensitization and Reprocessing (EMDR) Treatment for Trauma Survivors as Measured by the Rorschach." Audiotape from The Treatment of Trauma: Advances and Challenges, the llth Annual Meeting of the International Society for Traumatic Stress Studies, Boston.

Carmen, Elaine. 1989. "Family Violence and the Victim-to-Patient Process." In *Family Violence: Emerging Issues of a National Crisis,* edited by Leah Dickstein and Carol Nadelson. Washington, D.C.: American Psychiatric Press.

Chambless, Dick, Dean Kilpatrick, and Bessel van der Kolk. 1990. "Symposium on Post-Traumatic Stress Disorder." Presented at the Anxiety Disorders Association of America Tenth National Conference, March 1990, at Bethesda, MD.

Condy, Sylvia, Donald Templer, Ric Brown, and Lelia Veaco. 1987. "Parameters of Sexual Contact of Boys with Women." *Archives of Sexual Behavior* 16:5.

Courtois, Christine. 1988. *Healing the Incest Wound: Adult Survivors in Therapy.* New York: W.W. Norton and Company.

Davis, M., E. R. Eshelman, and M. McKay. 1988. *The Relaxation & Stress Reduction Workbook,* 3rd ed. Oakland, CA: New Harbinger Publications.

Deepost, Robin, Allen B. Willett, Ronald D. Franks, Robert House, and Susan Back. 1981. "Childhood Exposure to Violence Among Victims & Perpetrators of Spouse Battering." *Victimology: An International Journal* 6:1-4.

Deschner, J. P. 1984. *The Hitting Habit: Anger Control for Battering Couples.* New York: MacMillan.

DSM-IV. 1994. Diagnostic and Statistical Manual of Mental Disorders, Washington, D.C.: American Psychiatric Association.

Dworkin, Andrea. 1978. "The Bruises That Don't Heal." *Mother Jones* (July).

Figley, Charles. 1995. "Systemic Traumatology: Family Therapy with Trauma Survivors." Presentation at Maryland Psychological Association, Rockville, MD, December 12.

Finkelhor, David. 1979. *Sexually Abused Children.* New York: Free Press.

Fortune, Marie. 1983. *Sexual Violence: The Unmentionable Sin.* New York: The Pilgrim Press.

Frances, Allen, and Samuel W. Perry III. 1983. "Burn Victims Face Impending Divorce, Potential Job Loss." *Hospital and Community Psychiatry* 34:6.

Friedman, Matthew J. 1991. "Biological Approaches to the Diagnosis and Treatment of PTSD." *Journal of Traumatic Stress* 4:1.

Frye, Stephen, and Rex Stockton. 1982. "Discriminant Analysis of PTSD Among a Group of Vietnam Veterans." *The American Journal of Psychiatry* 139:1.

Futterman, S., and E. Pumpian-Midlin. 1951. "Traumatic War Neuroses Five Years Later. *American Journal of Psychiatry* 108:6.

Gault, W. B. 1971. "Some Remarks on Slaughter." *American Journal of Psychiatry* 128:4 (October).

Glass, A. M. 1969. "Introduction." In *The Psychology and Physiology of Stress,* edited by P. G. Bourne. New York: Academic Press.

Glover, H. 1985. "Guilt and Aggression in Vietnam Veterans." *The American Journal of Social Psychiatry* 1, 15–18 (Winter).

Glover, J. 1988. "Four Syndromes of PTSD: Stressors and Conflicts of the Traumatized with Special Focus on the Vietnam Combat Vet." *Journal of Traumatic Stress*, 1:4.

Goldberg L., and M. A. Gara. 1990. "A Typology Of Psychiatric Reactions to Motor Vehicle Accidents. *Psychopathology* 23:1.

Goodwin, Jim. n.d. "Continuing Readjustment Problems Among Vietnam Veterans: The Etiology of Combat Related Post-Traumatic Stress Disorders." Cincinnati, Ohio: Disabled American Veterans National Headquarters.

Green, Bonnie. 1994. "Psychosocial Research in Traumatic Stress: An Update." *Journal of Traumatic Stress* 7:3.

Green, Bonnie L., Jacob Lindy, Mary Grace, Goldine Gleser, Anthony Leonard, Mindy Korol, and Carolyn Winget. 1990. "Buffalo Creek Survivors in the Second Decade: Stability of Stress Symptoms." *American Journal of Orthopsychiatry* 60:1.

Grinker, R. P., and J. P. Spiegel. 1983. *Men Under Stress.* New York: McGraw-Hill.

Grossman, J. A., D. C. Clark, D. Gross, L. Halstead, and J. Pennington. 1995. "Child Bereavement After Paternal Suicide," *Child Adolescent Psychiatric Nursing* 8:2 (April–June).

Haley, Sarah. 1984. "I Feel a Little Sad: The Application of Object Relations Theory to Hypnotherapy of Post-Trauntatic Stress Disorder in Vietnam Veterans." Paper presented at Society for Clinical and Experimental Hypnosis, October 1984, at San Antonio, TX.

Hall, Calvin S., and Gardner Lindzey. 1970. *Theories of Personality*. 2nd ed. New York: John Willey and Sons, Inc.

Harvey, M., chair. 1995. "Stories of Resiliency in Trauma Survivors." Audiotape from The Treatment of Trauma: Advances and Challenges, the llth Annual Meeting of the International Society for Traumatic Stress Studies, Boston.

Heckler, Richard A. 1994. *Waking Up, Alive: The Descent, the Suicide Attempt, and the Return to Life*. New York: Grosset-Putnam Books.

Hernian, Judith. 1992. *Trauma and Recovery: The Aftermath of Violence—From Domestic Abuse to Political Terror*. New York: Basic Books.

Herman, Judith. 1989. "Recognition and Treatment of Incestuous Families." In *Family Violence: Emerging Issues of a National Crisis*, edited by Leah Dickstein and Carol Nadelson. Washington, D.C.: American Psychiatric Press.

Horowitz, Mardi. 1985. "Disasters and Psychological Responses to Stress." *Psychiatric Annals* 15:3.

IANDS (International Association of Near-Death Studies, Inc.). 1992. "Encyclopedia Brittanica to Include Near-Death Experiences." *Vital Signs*, 1:1 (January-March).

Janoff Bulman, Ronnie, and Irene Frieze. 1983. "A Theoretical Perspective for Understanding Reactions to Victimization." *Journal of Social Issues* 39:2

Jelinek, J., and T. Williams. 1984. "PTSD and Substance Abuse in Vietnam Veterans: Treatment Problems, Strategies, and Recommendations." *Journal of Substance Abuse Treatment* 1, 87–97.

Katz, Bonnie L. 1986. "Effects of Familiarity with the Rapist on Post-rape Recovery." Paper presented at the American Psychological Association meeting, August 1986, at Washington, D.C.

Katz, Bonnie L., and Martha R. Burt. 1985. "Rape, Robbery, and Burglary: Responses to Actual and Feared Criminal Victimization with Special Focus on Women and the Elderly." *Victimology: An International Journal* 10:1–4.

Keane, T., J. M. Caddell, B. Martin, R. T. Zimering, and J. A. Fairbank. 1983. "Substance Abuse Among Vietnam Veterans with PTSD." *Bulletin of the Society of Psychologists in Addictive Behavior* 2, 117–122.

Kubany, Edward S. 1994. "A Cognitive Model of Guilt Typology in Combat-Related PTSD." *Journal of Traumatic Stress* 7:1.

Kubler-Ross, Elizabeth. 1981. *On Death and Dying*. New York: Alfred Knopf.

Kunzman, Kristin A. 1990a. *Healing from Childhood Sexual Abuse: A Recovering Woman's Guide*. Center City, MN: Hazelden Educational Materials.

Kunzman, Kristin A. 1990b. *The Healing Way: Adult Recovery from Childhood Sexual Abuse*. Center City, MN: Hazelden Educational Materials.

Lacoursiere, R. B., K. E. Godfrey, and L. M. Ruby. 1980. "Traumatic Neurosis in the Etiology of Alcoholism: Vietnam Combat and Other Trauma." *American Journal of Psychiatry* 137, 966–968.

La Guardian, R., et al. 1982. "Incidence of Delayed Stress among Vietnam Era Veterans: The Effects of Priming on Response Set." *American Journal of Orthopsychiatry* 42:3.

Langley, Keith, and Linda Gasner. 1991. "Normal Stress in Abnormal Times." *VA Practitioner* 8:5 (May).

Lee, N., John Richards, and James Mitchell. 1985. "Bulimia and Depression." *Journal of Affective Disorders* 9, 231–238.

Liberman, Harris, Judith Wurtman, and Beverly Chew. 1986. "Changes in Mood After Carbohydrate Consumption Among Obese Individuals." *American Journal of Clinical Nutrition* 44, 772–778.

Lim, L. C. 1991. "Delayed Emergence of Post-Traumatic Stress Disorder." *Singapore Medical Journal* 323:1 (February).

Lindy, Jacob. 1985. "The Trauma Membrane and Other Clinical Concepts Derived from Psychotherapeutic Work with Survivors of Natural Disasters." *Psychiatric Annals* 15:3 (March).

Madakasira, Sudhaker, and Kevin F. O'Brien. 1987. "Acute Post-Traumatic Stress Disorder in Victims of a Natural Disaster." *The Journal of Nervous and Mental Disease* 175, 286–292.

Malamuth, Neil. 1981. "Rape Proclivity Among Males." *Journal of Social Issues* 37:4.

Matsakis, Aphrodite. 1990. *Compulsive Eaters and Relationships*. New York: Ballantine Press.

Matsakis, Aphrodite. 1988. *Vietnam Wives: Women and Children Surviving Life with Veterans with PTSD*. Kensington, MD: Woodbine House.

McCarthy, Barry. 1986. "A Cognitive Behavioral Approach to Understanding and Treating Sexual Trauma." *Journal of Sex and Marital Therapy* 12:4 (Winter).

McFarlane, A. 1995. "The Black Hole of Trauma: The Indelible Past and the Uncertain Future." Audiotape from The Treatment of Trauma: Advances and Challenges, the 11th Annual Meeting of the International Society for Traumatic Stress Studies, Boston.

McFarlane, A. C. 1988. "The Longitudinal Course of Posttraumatic Morbidity, The Range of Outcomes and Their Predictors." *Journal of Nervous and Mental Disease* 176:1.

McFarlane, A. C. 1986. "Long Term Psychiatric Morbidity After a Natural Disaster: Implications for Disaster Planners and Emergency Services." *Medical Journal of Australia* 145:11–12 (December 1–15).

McKay, Matthew, Peter D. Rogers, and Judith McKay. 1989. *When Anger Hurts: Quieting the Storm Within*. Oakland, CA: New Harbinger Publications.

McKay, Matthew, and Patrick Fanning. 1987. *Self-Esteem: A Proven Program of Cognitive Techniques for Assessing, Improving, and Maintaining Your Self-Esteem*. Oakland, CA: New Harbinger Publications.

McKay, Matthew, Martha Davis, and Patrick Fanning. 1981. *Thoughts and Feelings: The Art of Cognitive Stress Intervention*. Oakland, CA: New Harbinger Publications.

Mitchell, Jeffery. 1986. "Critical Incident Stress Management." *Response*, September/October.

MMWR. 1995. "Suicide Among Children, Adolescents, and Young Adults—United States, 1980–1992." *Morbidity Mortality Weekly Report* 44:15 (April 21).

Morgan, C. A. III, C. Grillon, S. M. Southwick, L. M. Nagy, M. Davis, J. H. Krystal, and D. S. Charney. 1995. "Yohibine Facilitated Acoustic Startle in Combat Veterans with Post-Traumatic Stress Disorder." *Pharmacology* (Berlin) 117 (February).

Munroe, J., editor and chair. 1995. "Applied Psychopharmacology and PTSD: An Open Forum." Audiotape from The Treatment of Trauma: Advances and Challenges, the 11th Annual Meeting of the International Society for Traumatic Stress Studies, Boston.

NCCAN (National Center on Child Abuse and Neglect). 1983a. "Child Protection: A Guide for State Legislation." Washington D.C.: U.S. Department of Health and Human Services.

NCCAN. 1983b. "Everything You Always Wanted to Know About Child Abuse and Neglect." Washington, D.C.: U.S. Department of Health and Human Services.

New York Times. 12 June 1990. "A Key to PTSD Lies in Brain Chemistry, Scientists Find."

NIMH (National Institute of Mental Health). n.d. "The Mental Health Consequences of the San Ysidro McDonald's Massacre: A Community Study."

Ochberg, Frank M. 1988. "PTSD Therapy and Victims of Violence." In *Post-Traumatic Therapy and Victims of Violence,* edited by Frank M. Ochberg. New York: Brunner/Mazel.

Parsons, Erwin. 1985. "The Intercultural Setting: Encountering Black Vietnam Veterans." In *The Trauma of War: Stress and Recovery in Vietnam Veterans,* by S. A. Sonnenberg, A. S. Blank, and J. A. Talbott. Washington, D.C.: American Psychiatric Press.

Rappaport, Judith. 1994. "Sibling Suicide: Its Effects on the Wish for a Child and on the Maternal Transference/Countertransference Interaction." *Journal of Clinical Psychoanalysis* 3:2.

Richard, C. L., and J. G. Young. 1995. "Effect of Gun Control Legislation on Suicide." *American Journal of Psychiatry* 152:7 (July).

Rossi, Ernest Lawrence. 1986. *The Psychobiology of Body Healing.* New Concepts of Therapeutic Hypnosis. New York: W. W. Norton and Company.

Rovner, Sandy. 1991. "Depressing Facts." *The Washington Post,* Health Section. 17 December.

Russell, Diane. 1975. *The Politics of Rape: The Victim's Perspective.* New York: Stein and Day Publishers.

Scheppele, Kim Lane, and Pauline B. Bart. 1983. "Through Women's Eyes: Defining Danger in the Wake of Sexual Assault." *Journal of Social Issues* 39:2.

Schiffer, F., M. H. Teicher, and A. C. Papanicolaou. 1995. "Evoked Potential Evidence for Right Brain Activity During the Recall of Traumatic Memories." *Journal of Neuropsychiatry and Clinical Neuroscience* 7:2, (Spring).

Scott, Ronald L., and Laurie A. Tetreault. 1987. "Attitudes of Rapists and Other Violent Offenders Toward Women." *Journal of Social Psychology* 127:4.

Seligman, Martin. 1975. *Helplessness: On Depression Development and Death.* San Francisco: W. H. Freeman.

Seltzer, F. 1994. "Trends in Mortality from Violent Deaths: Suicide and Homicide, United States, 1960–1991." *Statistical Bulletin of the Metropolitan Insurance Company* 75:2 (April–June).

Shaffer, D., M. Gould, and R. C. Hicks. 1994. "Worsening Suicide Rate in Black Teenagers," *American Journal of Psychiatry* 151:12 (December).

Shapiro, Francine. 1989. "Eye Movement Desensitization: A New Treatment for Post-Traumatic Stress Disorder," *Journal of Behavior Therapy and Experimental Psychobiology* 20:3.

Slagle, D. A., M. Reichman, P. Rodenhauser, D. Knoedler, and C. L. Davis. 1990. "Community Psycholoical Effects Following a Non-fatal Aircraft Accident." *Aviation Space Environmental Medicine* 61:10 (October).

Slogan, G., and P. Leichner. 1986. "Is There a Relationship Between Sexual Abuse or Incest and Eating Disorders?" *Canadian Journal of Psychiatry* 31, 656–661.

Smith, B. J., A. M. Mitchell, A. A. Bruno, and R. E. Constantino. 1995. "Exploring Widows' Experiences After the Suicide of their Spouse." *Journal of Psychosocial Nursing Mental Health Services* 33:5 (May).

Sorenson, Gary. 1990a. "Counselors Aid Survivors." *Vet Center Voice* 11:7.

Sorenson, Gary. 1990b. "Tracking Natural Disaster." *Vet Center Voice* 11:6.

Southwick, S. M., J. H. Krystal, C. A. Morgan, D. Johnson, L. M. Nagy, A. Nicholaou, G. R. Heninger, and D. S. Charney. 1993. "Abnormal Noradrenergic Function in Post Traumatic Stress Disorder." *Archives of General Psychiatry* 50:4, (April).

Southwick, S. M., D. Bremner, J. H. Krystal, and D. S. Charney. 1994. "Psychobiologic Research in Post-Traumatic Stress Disorder." *Psychiatric Clinics of North America* 17:2, (June).

Staudacher, Carol. 1991. *Men and Grief: A Guide for Men Surviving the Death of a Loved One.* Oakland, CA: New Harbinger Publications.

Staudacher, Carol. 1987. *Beyond Grief: A Guide for Recovering from the Death of a Loved One.* Oakland, CA: New Harbinger Publications.

Taber, J. I., R. A. McCormick, and L. F. Ramirez. 1987. "The Prevalence and Impact of Major Life Stressors Among Pathological Gamblers." *The International Journal of Addictions* 22, 71–79.

Taylor, Shelley E., Joanne Wood, and Rosemary Lichtman. 1983. "It Could Be Worse: A Selective Evaluation as a Response to Victimization." *Journal of Social Issues* 39:2.

Terr, Lenore. 1991. "Childhood Traumas: An Outline and Overview." *American Journal of Psychiatry* 148, 10–20.

Tieger, Todd. 1981. "Self-rated Likelihood of Raping and the Social Perception of Rape." *Journal of Research in Personality* 15, 147–158.

UFCW (United Food and Commercial Workers Union). 1991. "Face to Face with Danger: UFCWs Local Unions Address: Robbery Prevention Safety." *Action: UFCW* 13:3 (May–June).

U.S. Bureau of the Census. 1995. *Statistical Abstract of the United States: 1995.* Washington, D.C.: U.S. Bureau of the Census.

U.S. Department of Justice, Bureau of Justice Statistics. 1988. "Report to the Nation on Crime and Justice," 2nd ed., NCJ-105506, March.

Valente, S. M., and J. M. Saunders. 1993. "Adolescent Grief After Suicide." *Crisis* 14:1.

van der Kolk, Bessel. 1990. "Symposium on PTSD." Presented at the Anxiety Disorders Association of America, Tenth National Conference, March 1990, at Bethesda, MD.

van der Kolk, Bessel. 1988a. "The Biological Response to Psychic Trauma." In *Post-Traumatic Therapy and Victims of Violence,* edited by Frank M. Ochberg. New York: Brunner/Mazel.

van der Kolk, Bessel. 1988b. "The Trauma Spectrum: The Interaction of Biological and Social Events in the Genesis of the Trauma Response." *Journal of Traumatic Stress* 1:3.

van der Kolk, B., and R. Fisler. 1995. "Dissociation and the Fragmentary Nature of Traumatic Memories: Overview and Exploratory Study." *Journal of Traumatic Stress* 8:4, (October).

Van der Walk, Jan. 1989–90. "The Aftermath of Suicide: A Review of Empirical Evidence," *Omega, Journal of Death and Dying* 20:2.

Veronen, Louis, and Dean G. Kilpatrick. 1983. "Stress Management for Rape Victims." In *Stress Reduction and Prevention,* edited by Donald Meichenbaum and Matat Jaremko. New York: Plenum Press.

Victoroff, Victor M. 1983. *The Suicidal Patient: Recognition, Intervention, Management.* Ordell, NJ: Medical Economics Books.

Wadden, Thomas A., Albert J. Stunkard, and Jordan W. Smoller. 1986. "Dieting and Depression: A Methodological Study." *Journal of Consulting and Clinical Psychology* 54:6.

Wade, Carol, and Sarah Cirese. 1991. *Human Sexuality.* San Diego, CA: Harcourt, Brace, Jovanovich.

Walker, Lenore. 1979. *The Battered Woman.* New York: Harper & Row.

Washington Post. 4 July 1991. "Pilot of Aircraft Inexperienced."

Washington Post. 17 June 1991. "Freed Rapist Reaccused."

Washington Post. 16 June 1991. "Profiles in Murder: The Art of Psychological Crime Is Evolving Into a Science."

Washington Post. 8 June 1991. "Panel's Report on Racism in N.Y. Courts Draws Praise."

Washington Post. 30 April 1991. "Tornado Siren Failed to Work, Officials in Hard-Hit Town Say."

Washington Post. 29 March 1991. "Kuwaiti Rape a Doubly Savage Crime."

Washington Post. 17 March 1991. "Why Won't Crime Stop?"

Washington Post. 15 March 1991. "Reported Sexual Assaults Increase Sharply in Area."

Washington Post. 10 January 1991. "Hit and Run: A Victim's Story—Sarah Pederson Lost a Leg and Has Not Found Justice."

Williams, S. L. 1990. "Models of Treatment." Paper presented at Anxiety Disorders Association of America, Tenth National Conference, March 1990, at Bethesda, MD.

Williams, Tom. ed. 1987a. *Post-Traumatic Stress Disorder: A Handbook for Clinicians.* Cincinnati, Ohio: Disabled American Veterans.

Williams, Tom. 1987b. "The Diagnosis and Treatment of Survivor Guilt." *In Post-Traumatic Stress Disorders: A Handbook for Clinicians,* edited by Tom Williams. Cincinnati, Ohio: Disabled American Veterans.

Wilson, Sandra, Robert Tinker, and Lee Becher. 1994. "Efficacy of Eye Movement Desensitization and Reprocessing (EMDR) Treatment for Trauma Victims," Presented at the Annual Meeting of the International Society for Traumatic Stress Studies, Chicago, November 8.

Wolfe, Barry, chair. 1989. "New Research." Audiotape of panel discussion, tape 405. Rockville, MD: Phobia Society of America.

Wolfe, Jessica. 1995. "Trauma, Traumatic Memory and Research: Where Do We Go From Here?" *Journal of Traumatic Stress* 8:4 (October).

Wolfgang, Martin, E. 1956. "Husband-Wife Homicides." *Journal of Social Therapy* 263–271 (May–June).

Wolfgang, Martin, E. 1969. "Who Kills Whom?" *Psychology Today* 3, 55–56, 72, 74.

Wurtman, Richard J., and Judith Wurtman. 1989. "Carbohydrates and Depression." *Scientific American* (January).

Young, Mitchell, and Cassandra Erikson. 1988. "Cultural Impediments to Recovery: PTSD in Contemporary America." *Journal of Traumatic Stress* 1:4.

Zweben, Jon. 1987. "Eating Disorders and Substance Abuse." *Journal of Psychoactive Drugs* 19:2.

Some Other
New Harbinger Titles

The End of-life Handbook, Item 5112 $15.95

The Mindfulness and Acceptance Workbook for Anxiety, Item 4993 $21.95

A Cancer Patient's Guide to Overcoming Depression and Anxiety, Item 5044 $19.95

Handbook of Clinical Psychopharmacology for Therapists, 5th edition, Item 5358 $55.95

Disarming the Narcissist, Item 5198 $14.95

The ABCs of Human Behavior, Item 5389 $49.95

Rage, Item 4627 $14.95

10 Simple Solutions to Chronic Pain, Item 4825 $12.95

The Estrogen-Depression Connection, Item 4832 $16.95

Helping Your Socially Vulnerable Child, Item 4580 $15.95

Life Planning for Adults with Developmental Disabilities, Item 4511 $19.95

Overcoming Fear of Heights, Item 4566 $14.95

Acceptance & Commitment Therapy for the Treatment of Post-Traumatic Stress Disorder & Trauma-Related Problems, Item 4726 $58.95

But I Didn't Mean That!, Item 4887 $14.95

Calming Your Anxious Mind, 2nd edition, Item 4870 $14.95

10 Simple Solutions for Building Self-Esteem, Item 4955 $12.95

The Dialectical Behavior Therapy Skills Workbook, Item 5136 $21.95

The Family Intervention Guide to Mental Illness, Item 5068 $17.95

Finding Life Beyond Trauma, Item 4979 $19.95

Five Good Minutes at Work, Item 4900 $14.95

It's So Hard to Love You, Item 4962 $14.95

Energy Tapping for Trauma, Item 5013 $17.95

Thoughts & Feelings, 3rd edition, Item 5105 $19.95

Transforming Depression, Item 4917 $12.95

Helping A Child with Nonverbal Learning Disorder, 2nd edition, Item 5266 $15.95

Leave Your Mind Behind, Item 5341 $14.95

Learning ACT, Item 4986 $44.95

ACT for Depression, Item 5099 $42.95

Integrative Treatment for Adult ADHD, Item 5211 $49.95

Freeing the Angry Mind, Item 4380 $14.95

Call **toll free, 1-800-748-6273,** or log on to our online bookstore at **www.newharbinger.com** to order. Have your Visa or Mastercard number ready. Or send a check for the titles you want to New Harbinger Publications, Inc., 5674 Shattuck Ave., Oakland, CA 94609. Include $4.50 for the first book and 75¢ for each additional book, to cover shipping and handling. (California residents please include appropriate sales tax.) Allow two to five weeks for delivery.

Prices subject to change without notice.